# HAVEL

Russian and East European Studies
Jonathan Harris, Editor

# HAVEL

## UNFINISHED
## REVOLUTION

DAVID GILBREATH BARTON

*University of Pittsburgh Press*

Published by the University of Pittsburgh Press, Pittsburgh, Pa., 15260
Copyright © 2020, University of Pittsburgh Press
All rights reserved
Manufactured in the United States of America
Printed on acid-free paper
10 9 8 7 6 5 4 3 2 1

Cataloging-in-Publication data is available from the Library of Congress

ISBN 13: 978-0-8229-4606-9
ISBN 10: 0-8229-4606-8

Cover photograph: Václav Havel in Cabo de Roca, Portugal, December
14, 1990. Photo © Tomki Němec.
Cover design: Alex Wolfe

*To Joli*

—

*And to the memory of my father,*
*Robert Clark Barton Jr.*
*(1930–2013)*

The totalitarian systems warn of something far more serious than Western rationalism is willing to admit. They are, most of all, a convex mirror of the inevitable consequences of rationalism, a grotesquely magnified image of its own deep tendencies, an extreme offshoot of its own development, and an ominous product of its own expansion. They are a deeply informative reflection of its own crisis. Totalitarian regimes are not merely dangerous neighbors and even less some kind of an avant-garde of world progress. Alas, just the opposite: they are the avant-garde of a global crisis of this civilization, first European, then Euro-American, and ultimately global. They are one of the possible futurological studies of the Western world.

—VÁCLAV HAVEL
"Politics and Conscience"

It would appear that the traditional parliamentary democracies can offer no fundamental opposition to the automatism of technological civilization and the industrial consumer society, for they, too, are being dragged helplessly along by it. People are manipulated in ways that are infinitely more subtle and refined than the brutal methods used in the post-totalitarian societies.

—VÁCLAV HAVEL
"The Power of the Powerless"

# CONTENTS

# CONTENTS

Map by Bill Nelson.

Map by Bill Nelson.

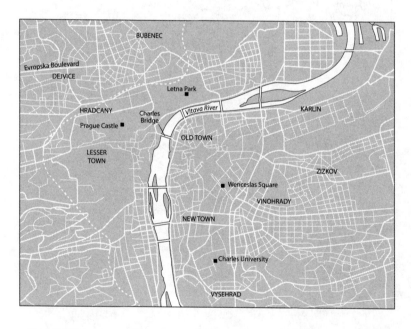

Map by Bill Nelson.

# A NOTE ON SPELLING, TRANSLATION, AND PLACE NAMES

MOST READERS OF THIS BOOK WILL HAVE only a passing knowledge of the Czech or Slovak languages. Although I have made use of Czech language sources, I have also used previous English language translations whenever possible. I have also tried to use English language place names wherever it seemed reasonable to do so. Thus I refer to the city as Prague, not *Praha*, and I refer to the area just east of the Charles Bridge as Old Town, not *Staré Město*. Consistency can be a hobgoblin, however, so I have not avoided using Czech place names when it seemed more appropriate.

In matters of translation, I have leaned toward a moderate position, rejecting word-for-word translations that don't capture the spirit or beauty of a phrase in English while also attempting to be somewhat faithful to the syntactical structure of the original Czech.

The name of the country in which Havel lived is a complicated affair, one governed by the fragile and complex relations between the Czech and Slovak peoples. From 1918 to 1938, the country was first called the Republic of Czechoslovakia and then, after 1920, the Czechoslovak Republic. In 1938 the term was hyphenated (Czecho-Slovak Republic), to emphasize the equal status of the two conjoined states. The hyphen was removed after World War II but then briefly returned in 1990, when the state officially became the "Czecho-Slovak Federative Republic" in Slovakia but the "Czechoslovak Federative Republic" in Bohemia and Moravia. Finally, the country peacefully dissolved in 1993, becoming two independent countries, the Czech Republic and Slovakia. I have preferred to refer to the government before World War II as the First Republic, which is a term sometimes used by Czechs.

# A GUIDE TO PRONUNCIATION

CZECH IS A SLAVIC LANGUAGE. The diacritical marks that make Czech so intimidating to English speakers were originally meant to adapt Czech to the Roman alphabet rather than the Cyrillic alphabet used in the Russian language. The most important of those marks is the *háček* (ˇ), which allows Czech to convey in a single letter what English conveys in two:

č       English "ch," as in charm
š       English "sh," as in shame
ž       approximated as "zh," as in measure
ř       the one sound unique to Czech, closely related to the Polish
           "Rz" or the Russian "zh," approximated in English to "r-zh"

The háček (ˇ) can also be applied to the letters "d," "t," and "l" to soften the sound, but the effect is slight and hardly discernable for English speakers. In addition, a diacritical mark (ʹ) or *kroužek* (°) can be added to lengthen a vowel slightly. Otherwise, the vowels are pronounced like this:

a       "ah," as in saw
e       "eh," as in mesh
i       "ih," as in fix

o     "oh," as in store
u     "oo," as in fool
y     "ih," as in flee

Most of the consonants in Czech are pronounced similarly to English, with the following exceptions:

c     English "ts," as in "its"
ch     considered one letter and pronounced as in the Scottish "loch"
j     English "y," as in yes

The stress in Czech words always lies in the first syllable. Thus Václav Havel is pronounced *VAH-tslav HA-vel*. Jan Patočka is pronounced *YAN PA-toch-KA*.

# PROLOGUE

ONE OF THE RESULTS OF WORLD WAR I, which destroyed so much of Old Europe, was the creation of a small liberal democracy in the northwest corner of what had been the Austro-Hungarian Empire. The new nation, originally known as the Czecho-Slovak State, was headed by an elderly professor of philosophy, Tomáš G. Masaryk, who had spent the war in Great Britain and the United States, among other places, lobbying for the creation of a new nation that would bring together the Czechs and Slovaks and the different ethnic groups who lived among them.

For a time, the new nation thrived. In the 1920s it boasted one of the most industrialized economies in Europe. During the 1930s, when much of Europe fell into one form of totalitarianism or another, the nation was known as a beacon of tolerance, a refuge for those fleeing the revolution of fascists, Nazis, and communists in nearby countries.[1]

The democracy of the First Republic was deeply bound, along with its first president, to the general ideas known as Masarykian humanism. As a philosophy professor, Masaryk had taught that democracy had a spiritual foundation, one based on the recognition that society existed for the individual. Nevertheless, Masaryk also understood democracy was a challenge, a tall order. It required an educated citizenry capable of participating in free and open discussion, which was only possible with a citizenry savvy enough to see through the language of demagogues.

The failure of any democracy is part mystery and part tragedy. Democracy is often unsatisfying, requiring a compromise between different factions. Everyone receives a voice, but no one gets everything they want. Moreover, the freedoms provided by a democracy are deeply unsettling, especially to those who fear their own freedom, those who prefer absolute authority to the hard work of forming a reasoned opinion. In the case of the First Republic, democracy failed the first time, in 1938, by the barrel of a gun. It then failed a second time, in 1948, at the ballot box.

This is the story of a man who tried to resurrect the spirit of democratic life. He was born into a time of chaos and absurdity, and he took it as his fate to carry a candle into the night. This is his story and the story of many others—the writers, artists, actors, and philosophers who took it upon themselves to remember a tradition that had failed so miserably it had almost been forgotten.

For many the primary image of Václav Havel comes from a happier time, perhaps November 22, 1989, day five of the Velvet Revolution. On that afternoon, a crowd of two hundred thousand demonstrators stood in the cobblestone boulevard that stretches a half mile from Můstek to the National Museum. Havel flashed a "V for Victory" sign from a balcony. As the shortest man addressing the crowd, Havel appeared anything but heroic. His hair was windblown, his mustache thin and wispy, giving him the appearance, as Timothy Garton Ash once said, "of nothing so much as a friendly walrus."[2]

Radim Palouš, a philosopher and longtime dissident, spoke first to the demonstrators, then Václav Malý, an underground priest. When Havel's turn came, he spoke while gazing downward, observing his feet. From any other speaker, the results would have been disastrous. For Havel, however, the slow, hesitant voice came across as authentic, even fresh. His posture seemed to reveal a shy, conflicted artist. Having listened to the triumphalism of communist functionaries for forty-one years, Havel's antiheroic nature seemed electrifying.[3]

Later, as president, Havel often talked about what the modern world could learn from dissidents. In dozens of speeches given across the globe, he also spoke about the "absurdity" of the "post-modern" world. Havel's great insight was that communism and capitalism shared more in common than we might care to admit. Leaders of both systems were obsessed with what could be measured, counted, and quantified. In the Leninist-Stalinist vision of the world, society is a rather simple machine whose levers can be manipulated by anyone who has undergone the right ideological education. In Havel's view, communism was simply a "convex mirror" that magnified the dehumanizing relationships we have with one another and with the mechanized world around us.[4]

As president, Havel was rarely interested in the machinery of politics as much as the politics of being. It was not just that he was an artist, or that he read Heidegger, or that his presidential speeches addressed philosophical ideas. For Havel, democracy had a spiritual and philosophical foundation. When he searched for political inspiration, he turned to absurdity, to art, and to rock 'n' roll. He held presidential meetings with Lou Reed and Keith Richards. Sometimes it seemed as if he trusted art more than politics.[5]

At crucial turning points in his adult life, Havel was given opportunities to leave Czechoslovakia, which meant not only freedom from the state but a chance to live in an open, democratic society. Each time he refused to emigrate. He was mysteriously bound to the totalitarianism society he lived in, and he dedicated much of his life to not only struggling against it but understanding what it stood for.

This is the story of what he discovered.

# PART ONE

## Where Darkness Is Born

October 1936–November 1970

Forget your perfect offering
There is a crack, a crack in everything
That's how the light gets in.

—LEONARD COHEN

# 1

## GROWING UP AND GROWING DOWN

BY NIGHTFALL, THE CROWDS GATHERED. In the central squares of the city, the mourners lit votive candles, whose small flames seemed like fragile witnesses under the darkened sky. Václav Havel, the conscience of the republic, had died that morning, December 18, 2011, two months after his seventy-fifth birthday. Many of the mourners stood at the foot of the statue of St. Wenceslas, the good king of ancient Bohemia, the *rex justus*, who was remembered by all as a medieval philosopher king.[1] There in front of St. Wenceslas, the crowd laid down wreaths and candles and placards painted with large red hearts. Many wept.

In the dark years, Havel had come to the statue of St. Wenceslas many times. As a dissident, he had laid many a wreath here and ended many a demonstration, usually paying homage to one of the martyrs of communism. He had been here at the time of magic, in 1989, when a half million people came to Wenceslas Square to demand an end to "communism."[2] And to hear Havel call for a free Czechoslovakia, for democratic elections, and for a return to Europe. The crowd of five hundred thousand demonstrators roared when Havel spoke.

"Havel to the castle," they chanted—which meant Havel for president. And sure enough, a few weeks later the thugs and dictators were chased from their positions of power, and Havel (dissident, ex-con, playwright) became a most unusual president. He was sometimes misunderstood and not always popular, but by the time of his death everyone understood he had already passed into legend.

Havel was full of enigmas. To one faction, he appeared childlike and innocent, even angelic; to another, shrewd, worldly, and calculating. At times, he appeared dry and pedantic, hopelessly rational. And yet even when reciting the long lists of dry facts that became a hallmark of his personal communication, his bent was always toward the unseen and unsaid, toward some dear principle or humanistic idea that he was willing to defend at all costs. He was, in short, an idealist, perhaps even a romantic, but he was an idealist embarrassed by his own idealism, as if this side of himself were best kept under wraps, like a dark mole one keeps hidden under a buttoned shirt.

References to light and to hearts were everywhere the week of Havel's death. Madeleine Albright, the former American secretary of state, told a crowd in Prague that Havel had been one of the true heroes of the twentieth century, a man who "injected light in places of deepest darkness." Nor was this simply a metaphor used by diplomats. In the funeral procession, as thousands followed a horse-drawn carriage that bore his corpse to Prague Castle, a simple midwife from Kladno, tears welling in her eyes, cried out that a great light had fallen from the sky.[3]

Those who had known Havel, or who had followed his private heroics or public turmoil through the strange and transformative decades of communism, could not help but wonder how Havel himself would have felt about the lavish state funeral and the requiem from Antonín Dvořák. In life, Havel was uncomfortable with praise, deeply so. And he had long preferred smoky bars and bouts of all-night drinking to official events. His humor was sardonic, dark. He often preferred to see the world from its underside, or through the broken mirror of what he called the absurd. As president, he was known for giving confessionals, for speaking about his metaphysical sense of guilt, his sense that others would be better in his place, or, as he put it in a speech he gave in Israel, that "the higher I am, the stronger my suspicion that there has been some mistake."[4] Many believed the funeral would have embarrassed him, or that he would have felt out of place or ambivalent about becoming the embodiment of official culture. As a child, he had longed for recognition, longed to be esteemed among the great, but the fantasy was at odds with suspicions of his own absurdity, the suspicion of his shortcomings and failings, the inner sense that he was somehow inferior and ridiculous.

As for music, some suspected he would have preferred rock 'n' roll to Dvořák, something along the lines of the Velvet Underground or the Rolling Stones. Havel loved the Velvet Underground. As far as Havel was concerned, Lou Reed sang like a prophet, his lyrics reveling in the nihilism of modern life. Reed's dark music had become something of an anthem for those who struggled against communism. When Havel coined the term "Velvet Revolution" to describe the political crisis of 1989, it was partly in tribute to Lou Reed's band. After the revolution, he asked Reed to join him while visiting the American White House, something of an embarrassment for President Bill Clinton, whose sex scandal was uncomfortably close to the illicit sex at the heart of much of Reed's music. Later, Havel insisted on making Reed a cultural ambassador. After giving Reed a personal tour of Prague, he presented him with a book of lyrics from the Velvet Underground that had circulated among dissidents. "If the police caught you with that, you went to jail," he told Reed, as if that explained how passionately dissidents clung to the music.[5]

I saw Havel only once. On a late summer's day toward the end of his life, I found myself standing in the backyard of his country house, at a spot where his garden disappears into a few scattered plum trees owned by his neighbor, an irascible man named Andrej Krob. Havel and Krob were hosting their annual "garden party," a tradition they began in the 1970s to stage music and plays that had been banned. Suffering from ill health, Havel walked about the party with great difficulty. Here and there he stopped to visit old friends, sharing chit-chat and snorts of *slivovice*, or homemade plum brandy, that he lugged about him in a heavy jug. Havel had lived long enough to achieve the recognition he craved as a child, but at the garden party he was painfully reticent. When he spoke, he seemed to mumble, looking down at his shoes with an occasional wry smile, as if he was uncomfortable with being at the center of attention, even while simultaneously enjoying it.

Any attempt to recount the life of Havel faces the same problem as attempting to balance a drop of mercury in the palm of a hand. As a subject, Havel refuses to remain still. Not only was he a man of many talents (poet, playwright, essayist, amateur philosopher, dissident, politician), but he remained in constant movement, leaping continuously between the contradictions of his personality. He possessed a profound need for order but pioneered a new movement in Czech theater that turned order upside down. He was a painfully courteous gentleman who despised disagreements, yet most of his life he found himself in conflict with the state. He inspired the nation through the power of language, but he spoke in a mumbling lisp, often doggedly plowing through hard facts.

At the heart of many of his contradictions was this oddity: He was a world-renowned playwright who hated to write. He often wrote with the help of pills and all-night bouts of wild energy, and he spent months, sometimes years, avoiding his plays as if they were infected by a dangerous virus. Writing was a way of ordering the world, of using his highly rational mind to impose meaning on the aching chaos around him, the senselessness, the brutality, the random absurdity of existence. And yet the medium he was drawn to—the only kind of theater he found he could appreciate—was the odd and relatively obscure branch of drama known as the theater of the absurd, a theater that fought to reveal the random, the senselessness of existence. He was a man of epic ambitions, a man with a deep need to put his stamp on the world, to impose on it some order of his own creation, and yet he was also suspicious of his ambition, suspicious of authority and control, suspicious of not just the twentieth century but the entire direction of the modern world—suspicious of our understandings of power, of the rational scientific attitude that had conquered the natural world and alienated us from it, of the industrialized mind that had mechanized the world and turned us into machines.

When Havel wrote, either his essays or his plays, it was almost always to express these themes. His plays were partly an act of exorcism, and the act of writing tormented him. His friends suspected that he became a dissident, and later a president, as a way to avoid finishing his plays.

For much of his life, Havel saw himself as an outsider, even an outcast. He was, of course. He was also the ultimate insider.

Born on October 5, 1936, in a posh, private hospital on Londýnská Street, Havel entered a world of privilege and luxury. As the first-born son of one of the most prominent and wealthy families in Prague, he was the constant subject of attention, what one writer has called "a pampered bourgeois child attended by a governess, relatives, [and] friends."[6] His paternal grandfather was one of the most important builders in Prague, while his mother's father had been ambassador to various countries. His own father was a well-to-do businessman, his uncle a film mogul, the most successful film executive in Central Europe.

Despite living in the lap of luxury, Havel always spoke of growing up on the "outside." He didn't mean that he had grown up outside high society, or its expectations, but the opposite: He had grown up *inside* the highest of social circles, which left him outside the life of everyone else.[7] He felt excluded from those beneath him, the world of servants and gardeners and working-class Prague: the world of the common man. For much of his life, he was haunted by this alienation, longing for the ranks of the common man, the person of the street. Their world—the world of physical work and simple pleasures—represented a kind of lost paradise, an earthy, lower-class world that was always just beyond his grasp.

While those around him reveled in the family success, Havel found his childhood oppressive. Perhaps he simply felt that he had not yet done anything to make himself worthy of the praise he received. He once commented on home movies that showed him paraded before a devoted family, a seemingly well-loved child who carried about him a secret sense of suffocation. "In those films," he said, "I am a small baby who is constantly the subject of everyone's attention, a pampered bourgeois child attended by governesses, relatives, friends, even the Mayor of Prague himself." The incessant attention, he said, left him with a deep sense of loneliness, a sense that the adoration he received was somehow misplaced. Such personal ambivalence seems common enough among Czechs, but for Havel the feelings of inferiority left him feeling "petrified and astonished," even overwhelmed by a personal sense of absurdity, as if he possessed "a fear of the world."[8]

Havel's earliest years were spent at 2000 Palacký Embankment, an elegant Art Nouveau, five-story building on the quay of the Vltava River near the heart of Prague. The Havel family occupied the third floor. In the middle of the penthouse stood an enormous central room with a chandelier and a large bay window that gave a panoramic view of the river and the old neighborhoods of Smíchov, Petřín, and Hradčany. To one side of the great room was a salon, and on the other side was the parental bedroom, which connected to a winter garden. Tucked away were other bedrooms and living quarters for a servant. The house had been built by Havel's paternal grandfather. The grandfather had been a stern, hardworking architect who made his first fortune paving the town square; his second fortune came from building the Lucerna Palace, an Art Nouveau masterpiece and perhaps the best-known private building in Prague, home to some of the city's most elegant shops and restaurants.[9]

Havel's father and uncle were the first generation of the family to grow up in exclusive circumstances. At the Lucerna Palace, the family-owned theater began showing the first moving pictures in the country in 1909. Business and entertainment went hand in glove, providing the children with a powerful connection to elite families in politics, art, and business.[10] Through the Lucerna, Havel's father would come to know Tomáš G. Masaryk (the first president of Czechoslovakia), Karel Čapek (the most important literary personality of the First Republic), and a wide circle of actors, artists, and government leaders.

By 1936, when the future playwright and president was born, the clan had become what Havel later called a "grand-bourgeois family."[11] The phrase suggests a family ethos. Grand-bourgeois refers not just to social status but to a certain style, a way of seeing the world, even to a series of understandings about the obligations of wealth. For Havel's father and grandfather, business was a complex social affair that was about much more than money. Success was measured by enterprise and by how well one lived up to responsibility.[12]

By the 1930s, however, the family's situation had become precarious. Havel's father and uncle were more influential than ever, but the Great Depression had forced them to borrow vast sums of money to keep their businesses afloat.[13] Havel's father still owned such establishments as the Barrandov Terraces (an enormous hillside restaurant with panoramic views of Prague), the Trilobite Bar (where an inner circle of guests could meet at night), and a pub at the Lucerna Palace. He also built a modern swimming stadium that held three thousand spectators. The stadium accumulated substantial debts, as did a garden city he built in the hills south of Prague, which was modeled after a neighborhood in San Francisco.[14] Meanwhile, Uncle Miloš expanded the Barrandov Film Studio at a time when people could no longer afford to go to the movies.

Perhaps the family fortune would have survived the Great Depression, but the coming war changed everything. In 1938 Adolf Hitler annexed the borderlands of Czechoslovakia, known as the Sudetenland. Hoping to avoid a worldwide conflict, France and Great Britain agreed to Hitler's expansion, signing a treaty known in Czechoslovakia as the Munich Betrayal. Rather than fight a war alone, the Czech government allowed Hitler to occupy the Sudetenland. A few months later, in March 1939, Hitler marched his armies across the rest of the nation, giving Germany control over one of the most advanced industrial economies of Europe.[15] Havel was three years old.

According to some, the conquest of Czechoslovakia gave Hitler the industrial backing to prepare for a world war. It also brought about thousands of arrests, especially among intellectuals and Jews. Most Czechs, however, learned to hide their patriotism and any hatred they felt toward Germany.[16] Havel's uncle adjusted to the war by continuing to manage his film empire under German bureaucrats, as well as taking over management of the family restaurants, which became hangouts for senior officers in the German army. At the insistence of Havel's mother, the family moved out of Prague to their secluded family estate, near the village of Žďárec. The estate was known as Havlov (or Havel's Place), and it seemed to provide some distance from the dangers of wartime Prague.

At Havlov, the family lived in a vine-covered mountain lodge with ten guest rooms, tennis courts, and a swimming pool. A one-lane road led through the woods to a small village, where Havel and his brother, Ivan, attended the three-room schoolhouse.[17] On the surface, life could still seem carefree. A chauffer, a maid, and two families of caretakers kept life comfortable. Guests arrived from Prague, including writers, actors, and the future Wimbledon champion, Jaroslav Drobný, who knocked around the tennis court with a young Václav Havel.

In such a secluded refuge, it was almost possible to forget that the family had lost their country, becoming (like all Czechs) foreigners in their own land.

Steeped in the humanism of Old Europe, Havel's father appears to have been a kind man who saw himself as a faithful caretaker of the family tradition. On his desk he kept a paperweight that he had inscribed with the phrase "tolerance and love." The paperweight described the father well enough. Business was a civic activity, requiring a keen intellect, but business hardly defined his life. Václav M. Havel (for three generations, the male children all shared the same first name) reveled in all manner of interests, including what he called the "high culture of freemasonry."[18] His library was full of books on literature, history, and philosophy. He was also attracted to spiritualism, an area of interest he inherited from his own father, who had once taken an active role in séances.

The young Havel and his father seemed to share a genuine fondness for each other, although the relationship was occasionally strained by issues of class, wealth, and status. When Havel later described his father as "a wonderful kind man, despite being a capitalist and a bourgeois,"[19] he was acknowledging how capitalists were perceived by others: men centered on their own, selfish interest, oblivious of the needs of others. Havel's father was no such man, but he was (like most fathers of Central Europe in that era) somewhat aloof and distant. He welcomed all sorts of discussions about history and ideas, but he rarely, if ever, discussed his private life or feelings. Such topics weren't exactly forbidden, but they weren't acceptable, either.[20]

Thanks to the rich foods at Havlov, the young Havel was a plump, clumsy child. He had difficulty, he later said, "jumping across a creek or turning a summersault." This, along with his social status, left him estranged from children in the village. Those at the village school naturally resented his privileged life. They took their revenge in all manner of ways, excluding him from games and activities or taunting him with verbal abuse. By Havel's own account, he felt ridiculed and mistrusted. Even more, the world around him seemed a problematic place.[21]

Books were one refuge. Havel read prodigiously from his father's library, poring over philosophy and Czech history. By the time he was five, he had read the entire Bible. By the time he was ten, he had read the Czech histories of František Palacký; the work of Ferdinand Peroutka, a legendary Prague journalist; as well as most of J. L. Fischer, an anti-Marxist philosopher. He not only read these books but talked to many of the authors when they came to visit his father.

Of the books Havel read in his father's library, two authors were of particular importance to the young boy: Walt Whitman, the American poet, and Josef Šafařík, a Moravian philosopher. For Šafařík, the modern, scientific outlook, with its emphasis on objective reasoning, revealed a dangerous tendency to distance ourselves from the natural world, thus "jeopardizing the foundations of existence."[22] Whether the ideas of Šafařík resonated with his own alienation, or whether Havel projected those ideas back into his childhood after reading Šafařík's work, the essays proved foundational. Havel would become linked with many philosophers over the years, but it was Šafařík who influenced him the most.[23] Šafařík's work explained Havel's own personal sense of alienation, the way in which his childhood seemed absurd. Alienation was an essential part of the modern condition, Šafařík suggested, and alienation was related to the way we had fallen out of grace with the natural world.

Later, as an adult, Havel would go on to explore the works of Martin Heidegger and Jan Patočka (the Czech Socrates). Heidegger and Patočka wrote a great deal about what had been lost in modernity—about the ways in which the Western tradition has alienated us from Being. Havel got the ideas first, however, from reading Šafařík and Whitman. Havel's own experience had convinced him, as he later put it, that we all inhabit a difficult existential situation: Like a newborn child, we live in a state of separation. It was as if birth itself were a metaphor for the way in which each individual intuited a larger Being that we can only dimly perceive. Having "fallen out of Being," we therefore always reach out toward it, longing for a more complete experience, a sense of our secret and mysterious relation to the cosmos.[24]

By the end of the war, even Havlov wasn't safe. In the spring of 1945, German troops took up a position in Žďárec, the village beneath the Havel mansion. Both the Germans and the village were bombed by allied planes. In a short essay written for school in the last few days of the war, the young Havel reported on scenes of destruction. On the morning of May 9, "Žďárec was bombed because German troops who had not surrendered were still there. After the air raid many residents of Žďárec came to our house to seek shelter. In the afternoon, we experienced a stampede of German troops near us and shooting at them. They left behind a lot of ammunition, wagons, cannon, horses" after fleeing west. Some of the artillery shells landed in the fields next to the house. Havel wrote, "We children were afraid (and I think the grown-ups were as well). At that moment I wanted to be in Australia and little Ivan [Havel's younger brother] poo-ed himself."[25]

For Czechs, the war seemed to rip open the cultural fabric, revealing a variety of terrors. The nation had been betrayed, and had been unable (or unwilling) to stand up to the German army. Even at a young age, Havel understood that the order for the Czech army not to resist the German invasion had been an act of compassion, an attempt on the part of national leaders to avoid a slaughter.[26] And yet many Czechs, especially the young, had been deeply shamed, even traumatized, by the refusal to fight, leading to a generational crisis that was later chronicled by Havel's literary friend and publisher, Josef Škvorecký, in his postwar novel, *The Cowards.*

On May 5, 1945, the Red Army broke through the German defenses in Dresden, crossing the Ore Mountains into Czechoslovakia. At the same time, the American Ninth Army advanced to Plzeň, just sixty miles from Prague. In the capital, Czech citizens stormed the radio station and Gestapo headquarters. After pleas for help were broadcast over the radio station, more than a thousand barricades were erected in the streets of Prague. Uncle Miloš joined the barricades on the morning of May 6, as the German army began a bloody, street-to-street fight to regain the city.[27] Two days later the German High Command announced their unconditional surrender, ending the war in Europe.

Like all of the Havels, Uncle Miloš had been a lifelong patriot. Joining the barricades was an act of physical courage, but it was also a shrewd attempt to prove he was no Nazi sympathizer, a charge that emerged because of his close work with Germans during the war. Trying to save his company, which had produced up to eighty feature films a year during the 1930s, he had negotiated to continue making Czech movies in exchange for filming Nazi propaganda. The Germans tolerated the compromise since all revenue from his company went into the Reich budget, helping the war effort.[28]

Miloš later said that negotiating with German bureaucrats took nerves of steel, since the Nazis could throw him into a concentration camp at any time. After the war, Miloš argued he had remained in his position to protect hundreds of individuals who worked for him. He was, he said, part of the "resistance." He had placed his life in danger for the sake of not only the employees but in order to produce films such as *Babička*, which brought traditional Czech culture to the big screen. Few believed that was the whole truth. In the aftermath of the war, he was condemned by the Board of Employees of the Czech film industry and ostracized from the business of making movies. He was also called before a special public tribunal, which in 1948 exonerated him of collaboration with the Nazis.[29]

Whatever others said, the young Havel admired his uncle deeply. Miloš was a brilliant, charismatic dandy, a chain-smoking tycoon who calculated the economics of a film deal by writing out numbers in the air with cigarette smoke.[30] Some of the affection that Havel felt toward his uncle may have had to do with similarities in their personalities. Both were artistic visionaries, eccentrics in a family of businessmen. Both also shared the same lisp. The young Havel admired his uncle's bohemian side, as well as his love of luxury. Much later, when he bought a Mercedes Benz in the early 1970s, despite being an out-of-work playwright, surely part of the appeal was his remembrance that his uncle had been among the first to drive a Mercedes in Prague in the 1930s.

Not everyone in the family was keen on Miloš. Havel's mother, Božena, disapproved of his homosexuality, a taboo subject in the household. Miloš was something of a playboy who kept a private apartment at the Lucerna Palace for his trysts. Keeping up the family interest in spiritualism, he also lent out the apartment for occultists who needed a place for meetings. Božena tolerated his upper-class boyfriends (and his interest in the occult) but not his taste in working-class men, such as waiters from the family restaurant. Showing up with such men at family gatherings made it difficult for Božena to pretend that these were simply friends.[31]

The financial situation of the family continued to erode after the end of the war. In all, Havel's father and uncle owed as much as thirty million crowns, more than half the capital of a midsize Czech bank.[32] Despite their precarious situation, in 1947 the Havels sent their eldest son to the finest boarding school in the country, the Academy of King George. The idea (conceived by Dr. Jahoda while serving time in the Dachau concentration camp) was to create an English-style boarding school to educate an elite group of postwar leaders. The school depended on wealthy patrons, like the Havels, but a large percentage of the students were war orphans who attended for free.[33]

One of Havel's roommates at the school was Miloš Forman, the future filmmaker. Forman later emigrated to the United States, eventually making such classics as *One Flew over the Cuckoo's Nest*, *Amadeus*, and *Hair*. Like many at the school, he was a war orphan. His mother died in Auschwitz, and his father was killed in Buchenwald. Forman admired Havel's background, with its hints of a high society that Forman knew only from the newspapers. After hearing Havel mention Café Mánes, on the banks of the Vltava River, Forman, who was several years older, ditched school, hitchhiking into Prague to feast on salami salad and hard-boiled eggs while sitting next to a lady in a fur coat, an experience he never forgot.[34]

When Havel entered the Academy of King George, he was still an awkward child of ten. His nickname at school was Chrobák, which was a type of slow-moving beetle. He was hopeless in school sports, but his pluck seems to have won him a number of admirers. In one incident, Havel and Forman were with a group of kids who were waiting to ride a bicycle. Each child was supposed to make a loop out the front gate and turn back, a distance of less than a hundred yards. When Havel's turn came, he wobbled out the gate and kept going, while the kids cheered that Chrobák had escaped. The professor on duty ran back to campus, returning with leather gloves, goggles, and a motorcycle, catching up to Havel halfway to the next village. It turned out Havel had never ridden a bicycle before. Not knowing how to stop or turn around, he simply kept peddling as fast as he could.[35]

Not long after the bicycle incident, the democratic government in Czechoslovakia collapsed as a result of pressure by the Communist Party, which had been strengthened in the 1946 elections. Havel learned the news while returning from a field trip with classmates, including Forman. They were sitting in a train station when the communist leader (he also served as prime minister of a coalition government), Klement Gottwald, suddenly came over the loudspeaker, announcing that he had just been given permission to form a communist government.[36] Life changed quickly after that. The following year, Miloš Forman was expelled from school for urinating on the son of a communist leader. In his defense, Forman pointed out that the young boy possessed a staggering and unmitigated ignorance, and that the school had only passed him along in order to gain favor with the Communist Party.[37] Nevertheless, the headmaster expelled Forman from school. He also told Forman he was concerned for his safety. One of the teachers, Professor Masák, had accused Forman of expressing counterrevolutionary intentions by disrespecting the son of a communist functionary. "Let me give you some personal advise," the headmaster told Forman. "Get lost from here and leave no tracks."[38] Forman left for Prague that same day, leaving no forwarding address.

Soon after Forman fled the boarding school, Havel and his brother, Ivan, were expelled for political reasons. Then the state, now controlled by the Communist Party, denied them entrance to a public gymnasium, the equivalent of an American high school. The Havels belonged to the old ruling class, the bourgeoisie. The children of such families no longer needed an education. Their old social positions had been liquidated, and the state would generously provide them with a new role: manual labor.

Having grown up as one of the privileged children of Prague, Havel now found himself on an entirely new stage. As a youngster, Havel had resented his privileged life. Now he experienced the situation in reverse: In the new classless society, everyone was equal, but some citizens were less equal than others. Whereas Havel had once been afforded every advantage, deserved or not, now a totalitarian state made him an outcast of a different kind, unable to attend school or hold a professional job.

The irony didn't escape him. The communist takeover was like a modern fairy tale, one expressing the inner reality of the twentieth century, with all of its alienation and absurdity. The state had become a collective expression of hope and despair, but it was also the result of a vast number of private choices, the consequence of individuals who had abandoned their own moral responsibility in exchange for the unbending ideology of the Communist Party. The faithful believed that the Communist Party alone possessed the truth. The Communist Party demanded complete loyalty, and in return the members believed that its doctrines were based on an infallible science and a thorough, if mechanical, understanding of the world.

Havel was never in danger of joining the Communist Party, but he understood the internal totalitarian state all too well. Since the earliest days of his childhood, he had always possessed "an amplified tendency to see the absurd dimensions of the world." And like many who had joined the party, he had experienced the terrifying and chilling alienation that descended, like a plague, on everyone during the postwar years, making the world seem as if it lacked logic or meaning or sense.[39] Years later, as a young playwright, he even delighted in writing speeches for the various functionaries he inserted into his plays, speeches in which, as he put it, nonsense and pure lies are "defended with crystal-clear logic." Or speeches in which everything personal and individual had been replaced by clichés, and by a mechanization of language that seemed to remove all traces of humanity.[40] Havel had a special talent for writing such dialogue. In those speeches, he recognized himself, and human nature, and he recognized the fatal desire to simplify the world, the desire to eliminate all mystery from our vision of life.

The allure of Marxism-Leninism was that it provided a simple and total picture of history, politics, and culture. Everything was knowable, everything was material, and everything was the result of a material cause.[41] Havel would spend the rest of his life fighting this idea. And fighting a totalitarian idea meant searching for a different vision of the world.

# 2

## UNDER A CRUEL STAR

THIRTEEN DAYS AFTER THE COMMUNIST COUP D'ÉTAT, Foreign Minister Jan Masaryk was found dead in a courtyard of Prague Castle, having apparently fallen from his ministry apartment high above the cobblestones. An investigation showed his room had been ransacked. The bathroom revealed signs of a struggle. Deep gouges showed in wall, as if someone had dug in their nails while fighting for their life. Nevertheless, the Ministry of the Interior declared his death a suicide, implying he had jumped from his bathroom window.[1] As the son of the first democratically elected president of Czecho-slovakia, Masaryk was perhaps the only man capable of uniting a resistance against the Communist Party. He was also the only liberal who still held a position in the government. With his death, any hope to resurrect the First Republic came to an end. Over the next few years, a reign of terror fell across the nation. One hundred and eighty citizens were executed for crimes against the state. Farms were collec-tivized, businesses confiscated. Tens of thousands were imprisoned, others sent to reeducation camps. Industrialists were forced into manual labor, and the factories were managed by appointees of the ministry.

Compared to many, the Havel family had it easy. Havel's father spent three months in a one-room cell with half a dozen roommates, accused of withholding information about his brother. One of his cellmates was beaten so badly during interrogation that he died three days later.[2] Havel's uncle, Miloš, served a two-year prison sentence after being caught crossing the border into Austria. He had been attempting to flee to Israel, where he hoped to establish a new film empire.

Perhaps Miloš Havel wanted out of the country because the communists had accused him of collaborating with the Nazis, charges he had already beaten in 1947. He could hardly expect a fair trial. It's also true that Miloš didn't relish the prospect of becoming a common laborer. Actress Adina Mandlová, a close friend, described him as "every inch a gentleman. He knew how to enjoy his life and had a grande lifestyle—making him unique among Czechs of that time. And I think that for this very reason—because he had outgrown our provincial conditions so much—he made other people envious."[3]

After spending two years in prison, Miloš returned to the family home during the Christmas holidays of 1951. At the time, the Havels were vacationing in the Krkonoše Mountains, and the apartment was occupied by Havel's maternal grandparents, who told Miloš that he was no longer welcome. His presence, they apparently told him, could only bring unwanted attention from the authorities.[4] In some accounts, Miloš was later confronted by Havel's mother, who reportedly told him: "We've had enough troubles because of you."[5]

Before leaving the country, Miloš did manage to see his nephews one last time, showing up for a weekend visit at Havlov, which wouldn't be confiscated by the state for a few more years. Somewhat destitute, Miloš was living with a waiter thirty years his junior in a small flat on Sokolská Street, but he gave each of his nephews, Václav and Ivan, a five-hundred-crown note, at the time a significant amount of money. Everyone understood the gesture was a secret goodbye. A few weeks later, Havel heard on Radio Free Europe that his uncle had safely escaped to Vienna and from there to the Federal Republic of Germany.[6]

As for Havel's parents, they somehow avoided deportation into the countryside under a sinister law known as Program B. Program B was the government's plan to relocate elite families far away from Prague, where they would be assigned manual labor.[7] The Havels managed to remain in Prague, but the state confiscated the family apartment building on the embankment of the Vltava River. The immediate result was that they were evicted from the penthouse where the family had been living for forty-seven years. Rather than leave the building, they moved upstairs to a small, three-room apartment that they shared with Havel's maternal grandparents, the Vavrečkas, the same people who had turned away Miloš Havel. To make ends meet, Havel's mother sold off the family jewelry.[8]

The new situation affected everyone. Unable to finish high school, Havel took a job as an apprentice carpenter. His mother worried that bouts of dizziness made carpentry dangerous, and she found him work as a technician in a laboratory. His brother, Ivan, became an apprentice in precision mechanics.[9] The family businesses (including the film studios, cinemas, and family restaurants) were gradually nationalized, and Havel's father was given a job helping a state-appointed administrator transfer everything to the government. Although the father had lost everything, he continued to visit his old restaurant, the Lucerna, often bringing his children with him to dine. Writing thirty years later, Havel remembered the atmosphere of those trips. "For years," he wrote, "we would go to the Lucerna for lunch every Sunday, and the administrator would sit with us. His relationship to our family was almost intimate and conspiratorial. Former employees would prepare special dishes for us, wink at us, and serve us enormous portions. It was a pure example of class reconciliation, within the firm of course."[10]

For the Havel family, life had once seemed like a broad boulevard, full of endless choices, each one better than the next. Now life had become a narrow and dangerous alleyway. The young Havel struggled to reconcile himself to his new station in society.

According to a number of accounts, Havel's mother felt haunted, even tormented, by how things ended with her brother-in-law, Miloš. Božena came from an ambitious family that was almost as highly regarded as the Havels. During the First Republic, her father had been an ambassador to several countries and a manager at the Baťa factory in Zlín, which was one of the largest shoe manufacturers in the world. Still, Božena married above her position in life, and she felt it keenly. Many concluded that this was the clue to her personality, as if she was gripped by an unceasing pressure to measure up. Much of her objection to Miloš was that of a woman who never grew accustomed to high society and who resented both the attention he brought and the fact that, in the eyes of others, his behavior was odd and disgraceful, a black mark that might mar the reputation of the family.[11]

Božena also had a nervous streak. As a friend noted, she "hated all discordance and anxiously avoided any embarrassment or faux pas. Her nervous system couldn't handle these."[12] As a young woman, Božena had also been something of a snob, keenly aware of the divisions of class and upbringing. Her snobbery didn't come from a small heart. Rules seemed to keep the world at bay, and they helped her keep track of where she fit in the social order, which was at the top.

When it came to her children, Božena could be fierce. She prized education, and as an Anglophile she dreamed of her children earning advanced degrees at Oxford, preferably in medicine. It's sometimes assumed that she wasn't a good nurturer, or that she was responsible for Havel's lifelong ambivalence toward women. Perhaps that was true, but at times she could be an attentive mother, at least for a woman of her stature. While a governess handled the daily life of her children, she personally gave them frequent lessons in music and art and taught them the alphabet. Nevertheless, the young Havel was both attracted to and repelled by his mother. Much of his adolescence was spent in minor rebellion. Božena wanted him at home, learning the family traditions, but Havel was drawn to all manner of escapes. Increasingly, he was drawn to café life, where he could hang out with literary friends and escape the dizzying heights of his mother's ambitions and of all the expectations placed on a gentleman's son. From those expectations, Havel recoiled like a man who had come face-to-face with an apparition. For a time, he even came to doubt the entire tradition he came from—not just his place in a "grande bourgeois family" but the entire spiritual and humanistic atmosphere of the First Republic that his family embodied.[13]

As a child, Havel's earliest ambitions had been to become a business mogul. Just after the war, when he was perhaps eleven, he drew up plans for an industrial empire he fantasized about building, probably with the help of his maternal grandfather, who was a manager of Baťa shoes. The industry (he called it Dobrovka, which can be translated as "Goodtown") would employ ninety thousand workers, with offices all over the world. Havel then drew a picture of himself sitting on a golden throne, admired by an adoring crowd.[14] That was his mother's ambition seeping through. It would remain with him all his life, just as he would develop a rebellion against that ambition, a desire to climb down from the stratosphere of all that she wished to orchestrate.

By the time he was sixteen, Havel's imagination shifted to the grittier reality of poetry, literature, and filmmaking. The ambition was still towering. Havel had dreams of greatness, but now the greatness placed him in the realm of his flamboyant uncle, the film producer his mother couldn't tolerate. Using his family connections, Havel began stoking his literary interests by meeting many of the most prominent writers in the country, asking for advice and direction. In the early 1950s, when he was still in his middle teens, he sent a handful of his early poems to Pavel Holátko, a minor Czech poet. Later, he contacted one of the great national poets, Jaroslav Seifert, who later won the Nobel Prize. Havel's father helped arrange an audience, and after meeting Seifert the teenager sent the great man a few poems. Seifert's response has been lost, but he must have offered sobering criticism. In a return letter, Havel agreed that his own poems were "too talkative." It was a beginner's mistake, Havel admitted, since poetry should "express much by telling less."[15] Then he drew up the courage to invite Seifert to join him and his friend, Miloš Forman, to see a film together at the theater. Havel was just eighteen. He and Seifert continued to correspond, and the two developed a lifelong friendship that lasted until the poet's death almost thirty years later.

Havel was still a shy, alienated young man, but he was also, ironically, a confident and precocious intellectual when he put his mind to it. Some have speculated that Havel's insecurity developed later in life, a point of view that simplifies both the man and the teenager. The truth is that Havel's insecurity and self-confidence were two sides of the same coin. The bolder he appeared to others, the more he felt haunted by self-doubt, as he remarked on a number of occasions. Even as a teenager, Havel longed for some great achievement, even if he didn't yet know what it would be. At the same time, he feared that others saw him as a fool. He was both brash and reticent, often at the same time. Letters to friends during his teenage years reveal a cocksure adolescent who could be arrogant, boorish, and something of an intellectual bully. The confidence behind his oracular pronouncements was paper thin.

Another writer whom Havel stalked in his adolescence was Vladimír Holan, a communist poet who came to despise communism. By the time Havel sent him a note in April 1954, Holan was a national treasure, much prized for dark poems that dripped with the sadness of life. Holan's work covered such metaphysical themes as life, death, and the relationship of humans to God. Havel's first trip to Holan's house was later recalled by Miloš Forman, who joined Havel for the excursion with a sense of trepidation, since Holan was rumored to be a recluse who hadn't left his home in years. The shaman-poet received the two youths in a dark room with closed shutters. A single lamp threw long shadows on the walls. When the two teenagers asked shyly if he would read his works, Holan seemed flattered, reciting from memory "intricate, tough-minded deeply spiritual verses without any theatricality or bombast, and with a great power of suggestion."[16] After that, Havel came to visit Holan about once a month, always bringing a bottle of wine. The two got drunk together on a number of occasions, including Holan's fiftieth birthday, when Havel was just nineteen. Holan had what Havel called an "odd, almost demonic personality," and his advice to the young upstart was that a poet, like a sorcerer, had a duty to absorb the fate of everyone he meets. Poetry was a way of living, a way of turning suffering into art, with an emphasis on suffering.[17] The visits continued until Havel could no longer stomach Holan's dark side, which included a nasty anti-Semitic streak.

During these visits, Havel was learning about his extraordinary gift to connect with other people, to win them over. It's true that he used family connections to get an audience with Holan and Seifert and Holátko, but it also took a certain amount of gumption for a shy teenager to hold his own with the premier literary figures in the country. Part of his gumption still contained a touch of arrogance and ambition, the desire to prove himself, but all of the older men responded to the young Havel with friendship and enthusiasm, seeing beyond the awkwardness in the teenager. They may have also seen something in the young man that he was not able to see in himself.

Havel was not only learning about himself in these meetings; he was also learning about the deeper nature of poetry. His first poems had been amateur efforts, written out of a sense of triumphant optimism. Holan and Seifert helped him see that poetry was related to something different, to the dark mysteriousness of human existence.

In those same years, Havel also met a great number of aspiring poets of his own age, such as Jan Zábrana, who introduced Havel to what could be described as the underground of Czech literary society, consisting of authors who were unpublishable under the communist regime. Slowly, Havel was being initiated into a strange new culture, one that was utterly unlike the privileged world of his childhood. The literary underworld existed in secret opposition to the times, forming what Havel would later call "the second culture," meaning a culture that existed, more or less secretly, with a set of values antithetical to the totalitarian system. The second culture was hidden, secretive, almost nonexistent, but within its shadowy confines art, music, and literature thrived while simultaneously being officially prohibited.

The literary outlaws that Havel met in those years included Jiří Kolář and members of the so-called Group 42, a circle of poets who had been active during World War II. For the young Havel, Group 42 represented "the last living achievement of Czech poetry, perhaps of Czech art."[18] Kolář served as a kind of underground university professor, preaching modernism and the importance of poetic truth. He himself was both a painter and poet who used collage to create wild visual experiments. Kolář had a tremendous affinity for young artists, for anything new and experimental. He also saw art in moral terms, handing down artistic injunctions as if giving a sermon, telling Havel and his friends to "make it new," to fill their work with intellectual and moral courage. With Kolář's help, Havel was beginning to perceive art in an entirely new way. Art was not simply play, created for its own sake. Art was primarily a moral enterprise, an attempt to care for the burdens of the world, and a way of shaping the culture. Eventually, this became central to Havel's own self-understanding, leading him to believe that the role of the artist was to attend to the hidden spirit of society, the deep fantasies and images that seemed to animate the entire social milieu. Havel later said that the plays and essays he wrote "would be unimaginable without [Kolář's] initial lesson in a writer's responsibility."[19]

Havel's intimate circle of literary friends called themselves the Thirty-Sixers, a name that referred to the fact that most of them were born in 1936. They formed what Havel called "an intellectual circle," holding symposiums, self-publishing a typewritten magazine, and convening their own version of a writer's congress, held at Havlov, the family retreat, in the summer of 1954. Other symposiums were held at Havel's home in Prague in the year before and after the summer congress, with his mother serving food, or at the family's weekend retreat, with Havel serving as master of ceremonies. The group had no real purpose beyond allowing a bunch of overachieving adolescents a chance to discuss important issues of the day, and in self-publishing five issues of a journal called Dialogues 36.[20] Letters from those years, however, reveal that they were fascinated with the hidden literary world that existed underneath the façade of communist society.

Most of the Thirty-Sixers were political outcasts, so-called class enemies who had been forced out of school. In addition to discovering the Group 42, they read Franz Kafka and Jindřich Chalupecký (a member of an artistic movement deeply influenced by cubism, futurism, and surrealism). Havel arranged a meeting with Chalupecký in the early 1950s, most likely with a few other members of the Thirty-Sixers. After the visit, Havel struck up a correspondence, sending the poet letters, postcards, and holiday greetings. In January 1956 he mailed the poet a self-bound book of juvenilia he had put together under the title *Silent Beasts*, which dealt with the problems of a seventeen-year-old man. This was his second book of poetry (by which he meant a book of juvenilia he manufactured at home), and Havel told Chalupecký that he was sure he was a poet. He felt it with his whole being.[21]

Kafka might have been dead, but that hardly limited his influence. Havel had come across his name in a German book by Max Brod. Soon he was reading not only Kafka but Eugene Ionesco and Samuel Beckett, all writers who had been removed from libraries and bookstores. Here, at last, was literature that spoke to his own soul, presenting the world as if seen from beneath the vantage point of reason. The strange fantasies of Kafka revealed the hidden logic of situations, giving Havel a sense of how he had always intuitively understood the world.[22] More than twenty years later, in a letter from prison, Havel was perhaps thinking of his first encounter with reading Kafka when he wrote that he had always "harbored a feeling . . . that I somehow understand Kafka better than others, not because I can claim a deeper intellectual insight into his work, but because of an intensely personal and existential understanding of experience that borders on spiritual kinship."[23] If Kafka didn't exist, he said, he would have written the works himself.[24]

The philosophical debates among the Thirty-Sixers were fierce, and the discussions spilled over into letters. In a typical exchange from 1952 (when Havel was fifteen going on sixteen), Havel and Radim Kopecký fought over the meaning of dialectical materialism, trying to understand "the source of our mistakes," by which they meant the mess of Central Europe and the empty outlook of modern philosophy, which no longer seemed to have anything to offer.[25] At a "symposium" that they organized at Havel's house, the topics included the difference between the social and technical sciences (Havel wanted to link those two domains of thought) and the importance of a "pan-European philosophy."[26] Religion and spirituality were common themes as well, and a spirited fight broke out because Havel objected to the word "God." He said he had no idea what was meant by the word, and he suggested substituting the phrase "the reason of the world," which his friends found ridiculous.[27] Havel saw God in a platonic sense, as "the All and the Absolute," which he had put together from reading Rousseau and Whitman. From Havel's point of view, the absolute existed not as a someone, the God of the Old Testament, but as the timeless and the immaterial.[28]

Many of the discussions with the Thirty-Sixers were understandably naive, tinged with the kind of curious perspective that belongs to adolescence. Among his friends, Havel developed the idea of what he called "humanistic optimism," which he regarded as something like Marxism with a smile. What the world needed, he told his friends, was a "dialectic" between Marxism and capitalism that would provide free expression while also controlling the selfish instincts of the capitalists. Such a society was being born, Havel told his friends, in the United States. Perhaps, as some have suggested, Havel picked up the idea from reading American authors from the left, such as John Steinbeck, but it was also a part of the family tradition to project an enormous amount of idealism onto the West. While it had been natural for many Czechs after World War II to identify with the Slavic culture of Eastern Europe, the Havels looked to America.

The letters and debates of the Thirty-Sixers reveal a quarrelsome young man who could be overbearing, dogmatic, and opinionated. Havel was clearly struggling with asserting himself in a hostile world, trying to find a place for his large ambitions in a society that was busy tearing down the humanistic ideals that he had been taught to value. If Havel had yet to find the humility that would later mark his personality, it was perhaps because humility often comes from achievement, and from the peace of mind that one has earned a measure of success.

Many of the Thirty-Sixers, at least those who lived in Prague, met each Saturday morning at the Slavia Café, a clean, well-lit place with large, plate-glass windows facing the National Theater and side windows overlooking the river. Fixed with grand old chairs and leather sofas, and thick with smoke, at night the café filled with actors, musicians, and singers. During the daytime, it was the closest thing in Prague to a literary scene. The group organized itself in concentric circles of importance, with Havel and Miloš Forman at the center.[29]

Although not everyone at the Slavia Café was anti-communist, most of them suffered horribly under the regime. Both of Radim Kopecký's parents were serving time in prison. Another friend, Petr Stránský, descended from lower nobility; his grandfather had been the speaker of parliament in the First Republic. Under the communists, however, his father had been sent to a reeducation camp, and both of his brothers were in prison, one having been sentenced to work in the uranium mines.

Stránský remembers visiting the Havel household to have tea with the family. While sitting at the table, he became aware that the purpose of the visit was for Havel to show off his new friend, as if asking for his mother's approval. Although Mrs. Havel was outwardly polite to the young man, "her voice was very cold and the message for Václav was something like, 'though your friend, you shouldn't establish a more tight relationship with him.'"[30] Apparently, the Stránskýs had even more difficulties with the state than the Havels, and Božena didn't want any more trouble for her son.

Others also met Božena's disapproval. As one of the few young women who joined the Thirty-Sixers, Viola Fischerová came under intense scrutiny. She was a brilliant poet who later emigrated and worked for Radio Free Europe, but what Havel's mother saw was a young woman from a lower social class. Worried that a romance might blossom, Havel's mother asked her son to cut off the friendship. Havel refused. He took Viola on excursions all across the city, such as to Žofín island, where they drank beer and loafed about the public swimming pool. On one of those trips, they ran into an elderly gentleman, who was clearly a throwback to the bourgeoisie of the First Republic. "You're Václav Havel," the gentleman told him. "I know because I knew your uncle, Miloš, who would have had no time for this riff-raff here." He was pointing to the men of working-class Prague who were busy enjoying a summer day at the pool.[31]

Havel's mother did approve of Jiří Paukert, an aspiring poet who seemed more mature and elegant than her son. Ironically, Paukert was a homosexual who later developed a crush on Ivan, Havel's brother, during the summer of 1954, when the Thirty-Sixers all spent a week at Havlov.[32] The entire situation appears to have been handled gracefully by everyone, including Havel's mother, who may have been atoning for the lack of understanding she had previously shown her brother-in-law, Miloš.

As the nephew of a flamboyant gay man, Havel knew something about Paukert's predicament. Havel encouraged him to come out of the closet and also introduced his friend to Waldemar Sent, an older gay poet. Though still a teenager, Havel had developed significant connections in the literary underground. Eventually, Paukert, after changing his name to Jiří Kuběna, became one of the most celebrated homoerotic poets in Czech literature.

In the 1950s, however, Paukert was given to a dark, cynical view of the world. Probably a result of his impossible situation, he dwelled on suicidal fantasies. Havel encouraged him in letters to push such dark thoughts out of his head.[33] Paukert's pessimism was partly based on the conviction that everyone lived a life of selfishness, if one could only look deeply enough into their motivations. Havel believed—or wanted to believe—just the opposite. He told Paukert that deep within the human soul, everyone possessed goodness and love.[34]

Despite their differences, the two youths became intense friends, exchanging long, philosophical letters in which they attempted to refine their views on art and culture. Although Havel's letters are quarrelsome, full of adolescent attempts to assert himself, a sea change was taking place. Havel was knee-deep in Walt Whitman, whose celebration of passion and creative energy was so at odds with Havel's personal need for order and control. Paukert encouraged Havel to find a more emotional voice. Paukert himself was a deeply lyrical poet. His poems were filled with allusions to the classical world, but unlike Havel he was not writing about facts or things as much as his own inner feelings. When Havel asked him for criticism, Paukert told Havel that his poems were "ridiculous and naïve and self-confident." Havel's work was too "photographic," too rational. He needed to learn to see "the inner space" of things.[35]

The advice stung but also goaded him forward. Havel slowly began to regard Paukert as a mentor, telling him in October 1953 that he had become his teacher in the art of poetry. With the help of Paukert, Havel decided he was going to dedicate his life to art, which meant, he said, opening the mind to every impulse of the world around him— not just the contemplation of such beautiful things as "the moon and the river, but also the ordinary rain, working in a factory, taking a tram to work." Art came out of life, Havel realized, which meant that life needed careful tending for the sake of the poetry it would inspire. In a letter to his friend, Havel described the world as a giant churn, and it was important, he said, to live in such a way that the "INNER LIFE" was agitated into art.[36]

One of Paukert's lessons to Havel was that the true artist had little control over his muse. Poems weren't didactic tools but mysteries, he told Havel, and the poet's job was to record verses that he himself could never fully understand, an idea that Havel would return to many times.[37] If Havel had originally been guilty of didactic poetry, now he turned to exploring something deeper. Like poets whose works were "covered in blood and fed through love," he strived for a more exuberant style, wanting (he said) to create poems that thundered like a company of soldiers, marching off to die.[38]

By the following year, Havel had made some progress. He was now writing what he called "total poetry," which attempted to describe both "the deep inner reality" of the poet and the "objective outside reality" of daily things. The thought may not seem original, but Havel experienced it as revolutionary, as a chance to create a new harmony between subject and object, himself and the world. In his walks around town (he was now moonlighting as a tour guide in Prague), he began, he told friends, to see the entire city in a new light, as series of images presenting themselves for investigation.[39]

When Havel turned twenty in 1956, the first cracks in the totalitarian system appeared, sparked perhaps by the anti-communist revolt in Hungary. In Czechoslovakia, students demanded the right to read Western books, and a number of writers gave courageous speeches at the Second Congress of the Writer's Union, an organization that played a key role in policing literature. Havel was one of the youths who had been invited to attend the writer's congress. In typical fashion, he disliked the entire scene, with its whiff of official culture. On the opening morning of the congress, someone from the podium asked if anyone had anything to say. Havel, still a neophyte and a virtual unknown in the mainstream, rose to give extensive remarks on the suppression of literature and the hypocrisy of reformers who wanted to "take a new look at old mistakes" without really daring to look at what was happening.[40] His audacity seems to have shaped the entire congress, so that the rest of the event was marked mostly by those who condemned or criticized him, or, occasionally, by those who applauded the youngster for speaking up.

Havel later remembered the late 1950s as a time of "the first widespread collapse of illusions, and the first efforts to reconstruct [the communist illusion] in a more or less 'renewed' or 'reformist' shape."[41] As far as how the period of Stalinization affected him, he had survived physically unharmed. He had even managed to earn a high school diploma by enrolling in a special night school. But it was not yet clear how he might earn a living under communism, or whether he would ever be allowed to publish his poetry. As an aspiring artist, he focused on training his vision, seeing into the existential realm of society, which he increasingly saw as morally and spiritually bankrupt.

In one way or another, the young Havel circled the question of what had happened to his country. Through his poetry, Paukert had helped Havel discover something authentic and vital, an inner experience of being that was both responsible for his poetic vision and extremely problematic, since it existed apart from the official ideology of the state. In some way that Havel was attempting to articulate, Being resisted dogmatism and totalitarian rule. Years later, when he was able to fully develop his ideas in a mature way, Havel put it this way: "We live in an age in which there is a general turning away from Being: our civilization, founded on a grand upsurge of science and technology . . . transforms man its proud creator into a slave of his consumer needs."[42] Society, Havel thought, had lost touch with the essence of things. As a consequence, we were also losing faith in the goodness of the world.

Havel believed in optimism. By optimism, however, he didn't mean the childish illusion that everything would turn out well. In his own experience, things did not. Optimism was something far more mysterious. Havel had never trusted ideology, not even as a teenager. Ideology seemed to warp individuals, turning them into fanatics. He suspected that fanatics had no real faith at all. It was their lack of optimism that forced them to cling to a utopian vision with such desperation, knowing they would be left with nothing if their vision collapsed.[43]

# 3

## SMOKEY ROADS AND MUDDY PATHS

JUST SHORT OF HIS TWENTY-FIRST BIRTHDAY, HAVEL arrived
at an army base for his compulsory two-year service, his pants fas-
tidiously tucked into drill boots.[1] The Fifteenth Motorized Artillery
Division, stationed near České Budějovice, assigned Havel to harmless routines, including digging ditches and then refilling them with
dirt, typical assignments given to "class enemies." He served as an
anti-tank infantryman in a unit of sappers, or combat engineers, a
common assignment for men of his background because of the expected high casualty rates for those whose job was to advance to the
front lines to dig ditches, clear minefields, and conduct various defensive operations. His first year, Havel carried a bazooka, but after the
first year the company commander demoted him for insolence—and,
perhaps, for having been the son of an industrialist.[2]

Havel hated military life. He especially disliked the physical
drudgery and the lack of contact with Olga, whom he saw now only
irregularly, when she came for Sunday visits or when Havel was allowed to return to Prague. He spent most of his Christmas vacation
with her in 1958, creating what Havel called a surge of "resentment"
from his mother, who was never a fan of Olga.[3]

Havel's relationship with his mother had been particularly rocky at the time he entered the service, a common subject of letters and postcards to his good friend Jiří Paukert. Havel told Paukert that he had faced a constant barrage of disapproving lectures for being "a flop," which led him to think of his life as something of a family embarrassment. As he told Paukert, "admittedly I have somehow failed at a certain stage of my life, but first of all there is no need to throw it in my face thirty times a day, and second, I do not accept that I have lost my life. This is ridiculous."[4]

Presumably, Havel's mother was concerned about his future, or lack thereof, and the growing seriousness of his relationship with Olga. His mother was a sternly ambitious woman, accustomed to the privileges of upper-class life. It's unclear the exact nature of their disagreements at this time, but Havel still dreamed of following his uncle into film, which meant gaining entry into the film academy in Prague, which his mother saw as a political impossibility.

Once in the army, Havel hit on the idea almost immediately of forming a theater troupe with one of the other fellows in his unit, Karel Brynda, who later ended up a theater director in Ostrava. In many ways, this was nothing but a lark, a way of escaping his military duties, but Havel had also begun to take the theater seriously, to read the playwrights who would influence him most deeply: Eugene Ionesco, Samuel Beckett, and Arthur Miller. After Havel had been in the army only a few months, his childhood friend Petr Stránský, who was also in the military, stumbled across Havel and Brynda in the town square of České Budějovice, where they were sitting in a café and discussing how to stage a production of N. Richard Nash's *The Rainmaker*.[5]

Havel and Brynda never did stage *The Rainmaker*, but they did put together an amateur production of Pavel Kohout's *September Nights*, a play that had been a favorite among the communists (and thus a more pragmatic choice). The play was successful enough that the following year, the two men decided to write their own play, *Life Ahead*. While the play was written in the "socialist realist" vein, it also offered what Havel later called a "daringly critical" view of military life. Surprisingly, the play was something of a hit with soldiers.

After a winning notice at the Army Youth Creativity Contest, it was advanced to the national contest at Mariánské Lázně. Before the play could be staged, however, a group of senior officers intervened, having discovered Havel's class origins. A tribunal was held and Havel's play was condemned as anti-army, since it failed to exalt the role of Communist Party officials.[6] Havel would later make light of these plays, which are clearly amateur works, but they appear to have given him a taste of the theater.[7]

On his return to civilian life, at the end of 1959, Havel faced the same old problem of what to do with his life. His political profile made it difficult to find work. Somewhat out of the blue, however, Havel received an offer to join the ABC Theater as a stagehand for the 1959 season. The offer came from Jan Werich, a bighearted actor who had once started the legendary Liberated Theater, a group that had thrilled audiences in the 1920s and 1930s with something akin to American vaudeville. Werich had been an associate of Havel's uncle, Miloš. He also knew Havel's father, who almost certainly approached Werich, enquiring if he might hire his son as a favor. If so, the two would have met in secret, which would explain why no record of the meeting exists.[8] Such sensitive business would have been too dangerous to trust to a letter.

As it turned out, the authorities didn't seem to care whether Havel got the job. A stagehand, after all, is little more than an artist with a penchant for carpentry. For Havel, however, the new job carried potential. His first love may have been poetry, but by 1959 he believed he would never amount to anything in that field. He also believed he didn't have the sensibility to become a professional philosopher—another potential career choice—and he couldn't envision being allowed to work in a university. Theater gave him a meaningful profession. Even as a lowly stagehand, he could indulge his whims in literature and philosophy. Further, Havel was by nature a dabbler. He loved to try his hand at everything, and the theater gave him an opportunity to do just that.[9]

By the time Havel arrived at the ABC Theater, Werich was at the end of a long, distinguished career. His fame reached back to the

First Republic, in the days before the outbreak of World War II. The Liberated Theater, which he started with Jiří Voskovec, had specialized in making fun of the Nazis. After the Germans invaded in 1938, Werich and Voskovec fled to the United States. Returning after the war, Werich became one of the most beloved of entertainers, the king of improvisation, and a film star as well. Eventually, Werich would destroy his reputation by collaborating with the regime, going so far in the late 1970s as signing a petition to denounce Charter 77, the human rights organization later cofounded by Havel. When he died in 1980, he was a bitter and broken man.[10]

In 1959, however, Werich was still an icon, a man full of exuberance and goodwill. Havel thought he seemed to be "the embodiment of love for the world and everything good in it." Night after night, Havel was able to witness the special atmosphere that Werich created around him. Each performance seemed to be "a living and unrepeatable social event, transcending in far-reaching ways what seem[ed], at first sight, to be its significance." Working in Werich's theater was a revelation to Havel, a refuge from a troubled world. Suddenly, Havel saw that the stage could be more than just a sum of its parts or "a factory for the production of plays." Theater, Havel began to realize, was utterly unlike the industrial conception of society that was constantly articulated in newspapers and the speeches of communist functionaries. Existing on a different plane of human endeavor, theater had the potential to be "an area of freedom, an instrument of human liberation."[11]

The 1959 season was Werich's last year at the ABC Theater. Knowing that he was witnessing the end of an era, Havel watched every show, memorizing scenes by heart, especially the stand-ups, known as *forbíny*. Despite hearing Werich give the same lines every night, Havel laughed at every show, electrified by the way Werich helped the audience participate in the great comedy of life.[12]

Before joining the ABC Theater, Havel had tried his hand at two amateur plays. The experience at the ABC Theater was altogether more profound. With Werich at the helm, something mysterious was happening. The theater, Havel realized, was a place of meaning. A place where the audience and the stage could come together in some secret understanding of the world, helping to embody (and to reflect upon) the spirit of the times.[13]

Despite Havel's enthusiasm for the ABC Theater, he and Werich had misgivings about each other. From Havel's point of view, Werich had a tendency to place his career ahead of his conscience. Werich probably felt the young upstart carried more than a whiff of the rebel.

After writing a series of articles for small theater magazines (including a piece on the ABC Theater, which Werich praised just as he was about to step on stage one evening), Havel was offered a new position for the 1960 season, this one with a marginal troupe known as the Theater on the Balustrade. It was a stagehand job again, but the creative director, Ivan Vyskočil (who was impressed with Havel's articles on the theater), promised him a chance to moonlight on the creative side. Havel jumped at the chance. While working at the ABC, he had used his nights to write his own play, *An Evening with the Family*. Now he immersed himself in the idea of becoming a playwright, despite (or perhaps because) the physical act of writing distressed him. His writing process, he later said, was largely a matter of stumbling in the dark and succumbing to despair.[14]

The Balustrade was a far cry from what Havel called "stone theaters." Those were the large theaters of official culture that had become identified with government ideology. From 1948, when the communists shut down most theaters, until 1958, the stone theaters were one of the few games in town, Werich's theater and the Theater on the Balustrade being two exceptions. The government monitored theater tightly, thinking of the stage (much as Lenin did) as a kind of machine for controlling society. Theater, like film and literature, was expected to tell people how to live.

Perhaps for this reason, Havel had little interest in the stone theaters. Aside from the occasional classic (Shakespeare, for instance, or sometimes Chekhov), they mostly showed social satires that revealed human frailty from the Marxist point of view. Havel hated that kind of theater. Too often it seemed like simple propaganda. At best, such theater simply depicted life as we know it, usually a somewhat glamorized version of life. Havel thought the fatal flaw in such theater was that it ignored the existential situations of its characters, simplifying the complexity of experience.[15]

Havel's characterization of mainstream theater was not altogether fair, nor were the large official theaters as monolithic as Havel pretended. While it is true that the Communist Party saw theater through the lens of social engineering (as the Soviet politburo put it in the 1930s, all art should mix realism with Marxist content), playwrights often found ways to resist. The extraordinary director Alfréd Radok, for instance, worked steadily through the 1950s, staging plays that are still known for their sense of irony and metaphor.[16] Havel even had a chance to work with Radok on a few occasions, serving as an apprentice and assistant director.

Nevertheless, the big theaters never caught Havel's fancy. Even the ABC Theater (with its emphasis on gags and improvisation) failed to hold Havel's attention. But the small, experimental theaters excited him tremendously. These theaters had a touch of what he called "obscurity," and part of the appeal of the Balustrade was that it felt "suspect," suggesting that it was a far cry removed from official culture. The interior of the Balustrade was reminiscent of a cheap nightclub, with performances taking place in a former warehouse, the stage at one end of the narrow hall and an enormous wood-burning stove at the other, belching smoke into the audience. People who didn't have tickets stood outside, watching through the windows on an upstairs balcony.[17] Havel found the "decay" and "degeneration" thrilling.

In its first few years, the theater used amateur actors and shared the building with a pantomime troupe. Havel did just about everything imaginable, working not only as a stagehand but building sets, doctoring scripts, selling tickets, and managing financial records. In 1961, Havel's second year, Vyskočil (the creative director) asked Havel to write one of five skits for a short one-man play called *Hitchhiking*. It wasn't really a play so much as a series of scenes satirizing the new Czech fascination with automobiles. Nevertheless, Havel's skit (he called it "Metamorphosis," tipping his hat to Kafka) received a great deal of praise, both among theater critics and members of the audience.[18]

At the time, the theater of the absurd was still quite new. Absurdism referred to works that had flowered at the end of the 1950s, especially the plays of Samuel Beckett, Eugene Ionesco, and Edward Albee. Kafka was one influence. Another was Albert Camus, whose existentialism described a modern world without meaning or familiarity. Humanity, Camus wrote, lives in exile. The divorce between man and his life "truly constitutes the feeling of absurdity."[19]

Looking back on his early years, Havel would later call absurd theater "the most significant theatrical phenomenon of the twentieth century." He defined the theater of the absurd as an attempt to describe "humanity in a state of 'crisis,' as it were. That is, it shows man having lost his fundamental certainty, the experience of the absolute, his relationship to eternity, the sensation of meaning—in other words, having lost the ground underneath his feet."[20] Plays in the theater of the absurd tended to depict characters as puppets, or to chronicle the meaninglessness of existence. Unlike the literature promoted by communists, the plays didn't teach anything or tell the audience how to live. Scenes were often clownish, irreverent, or full of nihilism and disintegration. But such theater was also essentially mythic, attempting to make the audience aware of man's precarious position in the universe.[21]

As creative director, Ivan Vyskočil encouraged this kind of theater, and he couldn't have found a better disciple than Havel. Havel seemed almost perfectly made for the theater of the absurd, and in truth it was the only kind of genre that interested him. His profound, almost obsessive need for order was simply the flip side of nihilism. The theater of the absurd focused on chaos and meaninglessness, but the deeper purpose was altogether different. By depicting a meaningless world, the theater of the absurd seemed to create a counterposition in the audience. They emerged from such shows seeing meaning everywhere.[22]

By the 1961 season, Havel was already working nights on a full-length play: *The Memorandum.* The play came to him in violent fits, and he rewrote each scene "a hundred times." The family had turned a small room behind the kitchen into an office of sorts, and Havel took to writing all night, often pecking at the typewriter until dawn.

He sustained himself with amphetamines (his drug of choice was phenmetrazine, a mild version of speed), which he liked to refer to as vitamin F.²³ Vitamin F helped him stay up all night, and it stimulated his creative juices.

Havel continued using the pills for the next twenty years, and he would occasionally become desperate when his supplies ran low. In 1974 he begged his close friend Pavel Kohout, a fellow playwright, to send him some supplies immediately. He needed the pills to finish writing *Mountain Hotel*. In order to keep Kohout from becoming alarmed by his request, Havel joked that there was no danger of him becoming an addict, although he might well become an alcoholic, he added, if he didn't get the pills, since his day job at a local brewery required him to drink beer every day, and his coworkers felt slighted if he didn't go to the pub after the shift.

Sly references to vitamin F occur in letters to close friends throughout the 1960s and 1970s. In the mid-1980s, a reference slips into his play *Largo Desolato*, one of his most autobiographical works. In that play, a dissident intellectual and writer named Leopold Nettles finds himself dependent on pills, alcohol, and his own past. As he falls deeper into depression (taking more and more "vitamins"), he realizes that everyone, including both the police and his dissident friends, expect him to continue his dissident activities. Leopold is powerless to upset their expectations, falling deeper into depression and paranoia. Havel knew a great deal about pills and depression by the time he wrote that play. He worried that one or the other might destroy him.

In the early 1960s, two old friends joined Havel at the Balustrade. The first was Petr Stránský, a tall, lanky lad whose family had been embroiled in political trouble, leading him to get kicked out of architectural school for political reasons. Stránský remained at the Balustrade from 1960 to 1964, when poverty forced him to find more lucrative work. He later emigrated to Switzerland, losing touch with Havel for twenty years. In 1989, however, Stránský telephoned his old friend after reading news reports about the growing protests that ended in the Velvet Revolution. After learning that Havel and his group of advisors were exhausted, sleeping only four hours a night, he immediately mailed a box of supplies: five kilos of sweaters, winter clothes, chocolates, and multivitamins. A few weeks later, when Havel was appointed president, Stránský called Paris to order Havel a copy of the *International Herald Tribune*. "Every president has to have a copy of the newspaper on his desk in the morning," he explained.[24]

Another familiar face at the Balustrade was Olga Šplíchalová, the woman Havel would marry in 1964. Olga was a street-smart blonde from Žižkov, the roughest neighborhood of Prague, and the daughter of a horse butcher. Havel had dated her on and off in the late 1950s, when she was still an aspiring actress who haunted the Slavia Café.

In many ways, Olga was a conventionally attractive woman, although her right hand had been disfigured from an industrial accident that cost her two fingers, a wound she often kept hidden with a bandana or handkerchief. Olga didn't have much formal schooling, having never made it past high school, nor was she as well read as Havel or his friends. What she lacked in sophistication, however, she made up for with a fierce tongue. Where Havel was shy and painfully courteous, Olga was brusque, even rude. Her straight-talking, working-class style left Havel spellbound, opening a window to a world he had never known.

Olga wasn't originally attracted to Havel, finding him something of an awkward young man when they first met, sometime around 1956. Havel pursued her with intellectual conversation and poems, like this one, after talking to her at the Slavia Café:

> Half a day has passed since we last spoke.
> You Žižkov daughter, me still untested
> haunter of writerly cafes. Us two,
> Somewhere on the edge of spring.[25]

The two dated on and off for several years, but the relationship heated up considerably when Olga became an usher at the Balustrade, the two of them spending endless hours trying to keep the little theater on its feet. At such a small theater, everyone became dependent on everyone else. Olga often helped Havel put up sets, and Havel would help her collect tickets. After closing down the theater at night, they hung around with the rest of the crew, drinking wine in the foyer or joining friends in one of the many nearby cafés.

Havel's mother strongly disapproved of the affair. Olga came from the wrong type of family and from the wrong part of town. She had little education, few manners, and fewer prospects. While Olga bragged that she was "as cruel as the scourge of God" (a reference apparently to Olga's prized ability to speak the unvarnished truth), Havel's mother found her common, even rude. Even worse, from his mother's perspective, Olga encouraged Havel to give up his dreams of getting into the arts academy.

In 1964, the same year that Havel wrote his smash hit *The Garden Party*, Olga proposed marriage. Havel agreed, and they held a secret ceremony at City Hall, with no family present and only Libor Fábor and Jan Grossman attending as witnesses. The arrangement may have been a way to avoid an awkward situation, since his mother would have felt forced, through a kind of social hypocrisy, to attend a wedding of which she didn't approve.[26] Conversely, it's also possible Havel couldn't bear to face his mother with an open rebellion. Not only did he keep the impending marriage a secret, but he didn't tell his family about it until five days later, finally writing a letter to his father from Karlovy Vary, where he was on his honeymoon.

Havel appears somewhat sheepish in the letter to his father, trying to explain his decision while acknowledging his mother's objections. While the letter never mentions love, Havel says the two have an "understanding" of each other. Although he recognized that Olga would never become "a professor at Harvard," he insisted that she possessed a natural intelligence. More importantly, Olga had a primal feeling for life, Havel wrote, an earthiness that he himself lacked.[27] That may have been the most important point, from Havel's point of view. In Olga, he had found someone who could compensate for the common touch that had always been missing in his own family. Her soul, as he wrote in a poem after he first met her, "was a suburb full / of smoky roads, muddy paths / walls, cemeteries and telegraph poles."[28]

After the honeymoon, Havel and Olga moved into Havel's bedroom in the family flat. Havel's mother was disappointed but tried to make the best of things by keeping a polite, if unenthusiastic, distance from her new daughter-in-law. Luckily, Olga didn't know how to cook and didn't want to learn, which kept her out of the kitchen. She and Havel were rarely at home anyway, since they spent almost all their time at the Balustrade, coming back to the embankment just long enough to sleep and catch breakfast, which in Olga's case meant a cup of coffee and a few cigarettes.

Žižkov, where Olga grew up, really was the roughest place in Prague, a neighborhood of factory workers and state shops. Jaroslav Seifert, the national poet, had once described the neighborhood as a sad, romantic place, the edge where Prague seemed to turn into a rough village, the city streets ending up in fields. The apartments were small and utilitarian, and everyone in the neighborhood was equally poor. Every corner in the neighborhood sported a pub, with some of them opening as early as 6 a.m.

Olga's father appears to have been a kind, gentle man, but he left home when Olga was six. Her mother worked in a factory during the day and, like almost everyone in Žižkov, was a staunch communist, having joined the Communist Party after World War II, later keeping an altar in the small apartment with photographs of Joseph Stalin and Klement Gottwald, the first communist president of Czechoslovakia. Olga herself despised communists, whom she regarded as "cheats" and "criminals," and the two fought fiercely over politics, sometimes not talking for days. In the 1950s Olga threw her mother's altar to communism out of the apartment window onto the street below. Tit for tat, Olga's mother threw Olga's clothes out the same window. Sometime later, her mother became an anti-communist herself, apparently becoming disgusted by the stupidities of the party.[29]

After trying her hand at acting, Olga gave writing a whirl, attempting a television script on Jane Austen's *Pride and Prejudice*. She loved literature, particularly American literature (Ernest Hemingway and

William Faulkner being favorites), but she was no writer. Realizing she had no talent in writing or acting, she was content to work as an usher. Part of her attraction toward Havel may have been that she recognized in him the talent and intellect she didn't herself possess. As for Havel, Olga represented a break from his mother. Years later, writing Olga a letter from prison, Havel explained that before meeting her he had felt trapped by his social background. With typical introspection, he wrote that "not only was our marriage ... an act, among other things, signifying my definitive emancipation from dependence on my mother and through her the social milieu of my family, but when we began to 'go out' together ... it marked the moment when I (perhaps) got over my 'fat boy' stereotype. Such things may be superficial, but they symbolize far more."[30]

In later years, many of Havel's friends would remark that Olga often behaved like a mother to Havel, becoming the woman who shielded Havel from the world and nourished his art. Like Havel, she placed his writing above everything else, chasing away anyone who might disturb the quiet Havel needed. Meanwhile, Havel always confessed to her whenever he misbehaved, often in the form of sexual infidelities. Havel's strange creations—first his plays and then his dissident politics—seemed to take the place of the children they would never have.

As a lab assistant, stagehand, and soldier, Havel had the sense of being thrown into a somewhat cold world. He was one of the multitude, one of the many tiny helpless ants, as he put it.[31] The Balustrade gave him a profession. And in the 1962 season, his profession got a boost when a new creative director came on board and offered him a position as assistant dramaturge.

The new creative director was Jan Grossman, a tall, charismatic man who had already made a name for himself as one of the best theater critics in the country, as well as a translator, editor, and cofounder of the newspaper *Mladá Fronta*. Havel had been reading Grossman's authoritative articles on the theater for years, and he must have been thrilled on Grossman's first day, when the director jumped up on the stage with a bit of flair. "I promise you," Grossman told the group, "that I will do everything in my power to use this small stage as a field for big and provocative questions."[32] Grossman had a sense of greatness about him, and the Balustrade was immediately transformed.

The first creative director, Ivan Vyskočil, had been a chaotic if somewhat brilliant leader who pushed theater to the extreme. On stage, he experimented with psychodrama, with bringing the audience on stage, with various theories of anti-theater and "the denial of theater," all of them attempts to break down the expectations of the audience. But Vyskočil was also a disorganized eccentric who came up with brilliant ideas one day and dropped them the next. Once, he announced that "tomorrow we're going to try out whatever comes into our minds" but didn't show up the next day for rehearsal.[33] The troupe, including Havel, finally forced him to leave.

Grossman brought discipline and direction. He replaced the previous emphasis on improvisation with a classical format in which a playwright wrote a play and then worked with the creative director and dramaturge. He also used his personal prestige to invite outside directors to the Balustrade. He also began working intimately with Havel, directing a popular play with him (*The Best Rock Years of Mrs. Hermanová*) that toured across the country after making a splash at the Balustrade.[34]

Besides being something of a theatrical genius, Grossman also had an uncanny ability to hoodwink authorities. One of his gifts was the ability to build into plays underlining meanings and allusions that were difficult for censors to detect. One of his ideas (which he called the "Little White Dog Theory") was that every play should have something convenient for a censor to strike out, thus keeping their attention away from the vital organs of his project. The theory came from a portrait artist who made it a habit to paint a little white dog into all of his oil paintings, thereby allowing his clients the satisfaction of knowing what was wrong. "The painting is fine," his clients would tell him, "but I don't see why that white dog should be in it at all. Could we have it removed?"[35]

Havel learned a lot about theater from Grossman, but he developed his own ideas as well. Havel felt that the magic of theater was that it was never finished and never perfect. Each show unfolded in front of the audience in its own unique way, which meant the audience witnessed every night the birth of something new. The palpable excitement behind a play, Havel thought, had to do with this sense of adventure and with the relationship that developed between the audience and the actors. Going to a play wasn't a trivial event, but something like a modern ritual, one based on the distance between the actor and the role he played, and on the audience and their distance from the action on the stage. At its best, theater could be something like an ancient mystery, one that threw members of the audience into the heart of the human riddle. Seeing an actor strut on the stage, the audience reflected on their own role and identity, their own "hour on the stage," and what was being lived through them. Theater, Havel argued, was an existential event.[36]

Curiously, Havel didn't read plays himself, not often, and he didn't enjoy going to the theater. He was bored by theory. His interest was almost exclusively in the theater of the absurd. This kind of theater was not merely entertainment but a kind of social phenomenon. It tried to represent the spirit of the times, revealing the hidden themes and dilemmas of a culture. Anyone who saw a play by Samuel Beckett was changed forever by the play, or so it seemed to Havel. Theater helped shape the culture by helping the culture see itself. In Havel's language, it not only affected the spirit of the times but also made a permanent mark on the "more mysterious chambers" of Being. Once performed, such a play became a part of the memory of a culture.[37]

In another time and place, Havel's ideas on theater might have seemed esoteric, obscure, or marginal. In communist Czechoslovakia, however, his ideas were contagious. For Havel, the purpose of modern art, as well as modern theater, was to address the state of crisis in the world. Theater left a mark in the great, collective memory of Being, and no one could predict what the outcome might be on society as a whole.

Havel's first big hit was *The Garden Party*, a full-length play that the Balustrade produced for the 1964 season. The idea for the play came from Ivan Vyskočil back in 1961. At the time, Havel was talking up another play he was writing, *The Memorandum*, but Vyskočil thought it would never make it through the censors. While the two drank wine together after a performance, Vyskočil suggested Havel work on a new idea. Vyskočil rattled off something about a young man who tries to build a career through networking, or about a man "who loses his way, comes home, and doesn't recognize himself." Vyskočil always had a million ideas. He rarely turned them into plays, but the ideas were endless, and Havel took up the challenge of turning this idea into a full-length play.[38]

By the time Havel had finished a draft, Vyskočil had long since been replaced by Jan Grossman. Sometime in either the spring or summer of 1963, the two men went to the Krkonoše Mountains for either two or three weeks, in order to work on revisions. Fueled by vitamin F, Havel stayed up nights rewriting scenes and handing off the pages in the morning to Grossman, who would offer new suggestions. Officially, Grossman was the dramaturge (a position that is more common in European theaters than in the United States), but every page bore his influence. What had started out as a light comedy became far more quirky and original. Grossman helped Havel find his voice.

By the time Havel finished *The Garden Party*, the play had no plot and no conflict. The action followed Hugo Pludek as he discovered his uncanny ability to adapt to the world of bureaucracy. The real subject of the play was the spectacle of language. Much of *The Garden Party* is almost impossible to understand. Characters mostly speak in prefabricated clichés, often repeating them over and over again without any real sense, using language that lacks any connection to the world it is supposed to represent.[39]

Fortunately, the first audiences didn't mind that they couldn't understand the play on any rational level. They found the clichés and doublespeak hilarious. News cut through Prague that the Balustrade had created something dangerous and new. Rumors around town described it as something "very important and special like the Americans flying to the moon," and the 140-seat theater sold out for the entire season.[40] Those who could get their hands on tickets came to the theater again and again, some as many as a dozen times. Young people memorized the most absurd lines, delivering them at pubs to roars of approval. There was a sense, especially among intellectuals, that one couldn't miss the play, a sense that it captured, in a few hours on stage, the very essence of the times. One of the most delightful aspects of the play was its savage assault on the language of the regime, with its endless doublespeak and empty abstractions. In many ways, language itself was the antagonist in the play.

One who managed to get tickets was Jan Patočka, the great philosopher who would later become known as the Czech Socrates. He attended the play with his son-in-law, Jan Sokol, who would (after the fall of communism) become both a minister of education and a member of parliament. Patočka thought the play was about the decay of language, a topic he found explosive, verging on the taboo. He and others took *The Garden Party* as a bit of philosophy, and the play became a vital part of discussions among artists, intellectuals, and writers.[41] In short, *The Garden Party* became exactly the kind of play that communist censors were supposed to liquidate.

Success brought its own problems. According to an old Bohemian proverb, if a Czech buys a goat, his neighbors don't long for a goat of their own; they merely wish for the neighbor's goat to die. Since the Battle of White Mountain in 1620, which marked the beginning of the end of Czech nobility, an egalitarian streak has run through Czech culture.[42] According to the unwritten rules of society, no one was supposed to rise too high or stick their neck out too far. Like his Uncle Miloš, Havel was beginning to do both. And his international success over the next three years turned him into someone who had risen too high.

In 1965 *The Memorandum* became Havel's second hit. He also published his first book, a collection that contained two plays and an eclectic mixture of essays and typographical poems. Havel's rising fame caught the interest of a television station in Germany, which wanted to make a documentary, and of Lincoln Center in New York, which wanted to stage one of his plays. And then there was Martin Esslin, who came to Prague for the theater festival in 1965 to see what all the fuss was about.[43]

Esslin was a theater critic, one of the most influential in Europe. He worked for the BBC and coined the term "theater of the absurd" around 1960 in order to connect the work of a new breed of playwrights, such as Beckett, Albee, and Ionesco. After seeing *The Memorandum*, Esslin added a sketch on Havel when he revised his book on the theater of the absurd, saying that Havel was one of the most important playwrights in Eastern Europe. Havel's plays reminded him of the work of Franz Kafka, he wrote. Both authors wrote out of a sense of despair, exploring the idea that life has lost its meaning. Like Kafka, Havel's plays explored "human anguish . . . that was both dreamlike and concrete, fantastic and real."[44]

In 1965 the state security police (StB) started to take notice of Havel's rising fame. The Balustrade was becoming popular among foreigners, which seemed suspicious. Havel had taken to attending parties at the American embassy, where he was treated like a star. Finally, it was reported that Havel had been present at an after-performance party in which someone made a joke at the expense of the Communist Party.[45]

All of this brought Havel to the attention of Captain Karel Odvarka, who suggested in August 1965 that Havel be cultivated as an informer. The recommendation was apparently related to another entry in the StB files, one noting that Havel had personal contact with an espionage agent at the American embassy who was known by the code name "the professor." Perhaps Captain Odvarka thought Havel could be blackmailed with information about "the professor," or perhaps his only desire was to use Havel as an important asset in their campaign to uncover "the professor." Either way, Havel was given an official registration number in the StB files (24486). Two agents contacted him at his family home under the pretext of discussing a flyer, or placard, that Havel had put up that was not sufficiently flattering to the Communist Party.

According to StB files, Havel welcomed the agents warmly and even appears to have invited them to stay for tea. The agents mistook Havel's extreme politeness as a sign of encouragement. In their official notes, they wrote that Havel seemed excited by their visit. In a bit of intellectual irony, he even told them that their visit would be "good for his literary enterprises." StB agents typically had nothing more than an elementary school education, and they clearly didn't catch his hidden meaning. Encouraged by his friendliness, they stated in their report that Havel "seems to be a good fit to become an agent type."

For the next three months, the agency attempted to recruit Havel before coming to the conclusion that he was hostile to their cause. In November Captain Odvarka typed up a report admitting that Havel was unlikely to be an informant. He was involved in "unfriendly actions" against the Communist Party and very likely an "agent of imperial espionage." Odvarka then proposed an intensive campaign to monitor and read Havel's mail, tap his telephone, and install secret listening devices in his home. In addition, Odvarka proposed assigning a civilian to gain Havel's confidence and inform on his activities.

Thus began a long and complicated game of cat and mouse. The StB pretended it wasn't spying on Havel, and Havel pretended he didn't care. Among friends, Havel took the position that he was free to do anything that wasn't illegal under Czech law, and he didn't plan on making any secret of his activities. Sometimes he said things that most Czechs would never speak out loud. At a gallery event for Jiří Kuběna, for instance, he told the crowd that he purposely blurted things into the phone because he knew it was being recorded.

Other times, Havel took a different tactic. At an evening event in the mid-1960s, someone asked him if he was a Marxist. Suspecting the conversation was being recorded by the secret police (which it was), Havel answered that the entire question was ridiculous. Terms such as "Marxist" and "communist," he said, had become so vague and abstract that they had lost any meaning. The last statement was typical of Havel's feeling that it was easy to confuse agents from the StB.

He used a similar tactic early in 1965 when he was called into the offices of the Central Committee of the Communist Party, whose attention he had attracted by personally gathering 275 signatures in support of a small magazine known as *Tvář*, which had become the target of the regime. The petition enraged authorities, who demanded he stop collecting signatures. Havel responded that if he stopped collecting signatures, it would prove that his actions were unfriendly to the Communist Party. Then he added (perhaps for the listening devices that recorded the conversation) that "this entire conflict is coming to a crisis. That's why it's very important for us to be united and tactical."[46]

Havel's statement was clearly calculated to suggest that he wanted to help save communism from itself. That's hardly what he meant, of course. He believed that communism was beyond repair, and he longed for the day when it might collapse.

# 4

## THE AUGUST SURPRISE

AFTER TWENTY YEARS OF COMMUNISM, PRAGUE WAS a city of broken elevators and run-down trains. Stores lacked basics, like toilet paper and potatoes, and factories made second-rate consumer products that no one wanted to buy. Nevertheless, an uncanny optimism filled the air. Long-haired youths played rock 'n' roll, copying musical styles they heard over Voice of America and Radio Free Europe, which had an audience of four million Czech listeners, or a third of the country.[1] A new generation of film directors, led by Miloš Forman (Havel's old friend from boarding school), created a striking new style of film known as New Wave, using black humor and long, unscripted dialogues with amateur actors to poke fun at just about any kind of authority.[2]

As for Havel, he was now an international star. *The Garden Party* was shown in more than twenty theaters in Switzerland, West Germany, Austria, France, Italy, and Belgium. *The Memorandum* had been even more successful, making Havel the best-known Czech playwright since Karel Čapek of the First Republic. As Havel's fame grew, so did the suspicion of the regime. The state security police monitored him through the use of listening devices and informers.

Havel's files from the secret police reveal one such informer, a bumbler code-named Umělec—or "Artist"—tagged along with Havel and Grossman to a bar known as Viola. He ended up too drunk to remember what they talked about, or even how he got home.[3]

The harassment began in earnest in 1966, just before Havel was to leave for a trip to London and New York City. In a search of the Havel family apartment, the StB discovered part of a lecture Havel planned on giving at the Penn Club in New York City, as well as a proposal he had written up for reorganizing the writer's union along more democratic lines. As a result, agents interrogated Havel for forty-eight hours straight.[4] They also made sure Havel and Jan Grossman couldn't get exit permits to leave the country, confiscating their passports.[5]

The following year, the state writer's union asked Havel to travel to the Soviet Union and Switzerland, where he would see a premiere of one of his plays. The state police again denied him permission to travel, explaining that no one could leave the country if they were being prosecuted. To Havel's knowledge, he wasn't being prosecuted, nor would the state police explain what they meant by the statement. As Havel wrote his friend, Jiří Kuběna, the whole situation reminded him of Josef K., the character in Franz Kafka's novel *The Trial* who is persecuted for unnamed and mysterious crimes that neither he nor the reader can understand.[6]

Despite being harassed by the regime, Havel managed to finish both a correspondence course at the Dramatic Faculty of the Performing Arts (DAMU) and *The Increased Difficulty of Concentration*, his third full-length play.[7] On the personal front, Havel was feeling the need to make changes. After three years of marriage, Václav and Olga still slept in the cramped family flat. The fifth-floor apartment was becoming what Havel called "a schlock joint," a makeshift collection of living spaces whose former grandeur, such as the high, stately ceilings and elegant woodwork, had fallen into seedy disrepair. For Havel, such a combination of magnificence and decay had become all too common in the homes of those "who used to be but are no longer rich after 20 years of socialism."[8]

It didn't help that Olga felt unwelcome in the apartment. She was still the brash outsider, a working-class girl who could never live up to the expectations of Havel's elegant, strong-willed mother. Olga kept the peace by holding her tongue and avoiding the apartment as much as possible. After rising for a late breakfast—usually a strong Turkish coffee and a few cigarettes—she and Havel rode a tram from the quay to a stop near the Balustrade, which was in Old Town. They worked all day at the theater and then on show nights they drank wine late into the night in the theater foyer, chatting with friends and patrons. By the time they walked home in the semidarkness, everyone else had long gone to sleep.⁹

In February 1967 a theater friend, Andrej Krob, gave the couple a short reprieve from their living situation, arranging for them to stay in a state-owned chateau near Prague for two weeks. Officially, the purpose of the vacation was for Havel to finish his latest play. Both Havel and Olga were urban creatures, used to carousing the pubs, bodegas, and literary cafés of Prague. The chateau offered a different scene. Built in the thirteenth century as a Gothic fortress and rebuilt later as a Renaissance palace, the building was surrounded by extensive gardens, wooded parks, and ponds: a sort of rural paradise. For a young couple who had never lived alone, the privacy felt intoxicating.¹⁰ The chateau reminded Olga why she had latched her wagon onto Havel's star; for Havel, it brought back memories of his childhood, and just how much his family had lost.

Working at a desk in the chateau's library, Havel spent two weeks rewriting *The Increased Difficulty of Concentration*. As he later told an interviewer, he focused on cutting his play into thirty-three sections, obsessively reshuffling the action until it seemed disjointed and meaningless. As usual, Havel wanted to disturb the audience, making them feel, as a critic later wrote, "the absence of any real human motivations, needs and feelings."¹¹ The dark absurdity in the play was meant as a reminder of what it felt like to live under communism.

Later, when Havel spoke to Andrej Krob about the erotic pleasures of sharing a chateau with Olga, Krob encouraged Havel to buy his own weekend house. Krob had a place in mind, a run-down farm-house for sale in Hrádeček, a remote mountain village where Krob's own family had owned a house since the 1940s. The Hrádeček farm-house was no chateau, but it offered privacy and the thrill of escaping into the woods.

The Havels weren't the only couple longing for the countryside. Thousands of families were building small garden houses, or *chatas*, or renovating old farmhouses. Such weekend cabins were simple, usually no more than a single downstairs room and an upstairs loft for sleeping. In many ways, simplicity was the point. Weekends at the chata, characterized by gardening and mushroom hunting, provided relief from the strains of daily life.[12]

The cabin at Hrádeček, however, was nothing like the garden houses that were in vogue. Unlike these suburban cabins, easily reached by train or bus, Hrádeček lay on the edge of the Krkonoše Mountains. The only other cabin in sight was a rough-hewn shack belonging to Krob. Civilization in the form of Mladé Buky, an isolated ski town, lay five miles down a narrow road.

The Havels had been searching for their own Prague apartment for three years. Houses and cars could be purchased by signing up to a waiting list, and given Havel's political profile they could expect to spend several more years waiting. The farmhouse at Hrádeček gave them a shortcut, as well as a weekend escape that would give them both freedom and privacy, the sort of space that any young couple yearns to have. And at 24,000 crowns (less than one thousand American dollars), it was also astonishingly cheap.

After purchasing the property in 1967, the couple threw themselves into renovating the small farmhouse one room at a time, starting with the kitchen. Libor Fábor, one of the most gifted set designers in the country, helped add a courtyard and convert an old granary into a modern guesthouse. The room smelled of livestock.[13]

Although the Havels continued to live with his parents, weekends were spent at Hrádeček. Reveling in their newfound freedom, they invited scores of friends and colleagues from the theater to join them. Guests arrived with the Bee Gees blaring from the car stereo and drank late into the night. During the morning, guests lazed in the orchard, discussing art and politics, or took long walks in the woods. The highlight of the day was usually the evening dinner, in which everyone gathered in the renovated den. Havel did most of the cooking, experimenting with outlandish dishes such as Devil's Goulash, whose main ingredient seemed to be horseradish. After dinner, there was another round of wine drinking and ironic repartee.[14]

Whether consciously or unconsciously, Olga and Václav had recreated many of the touches of Havel's childhood, making Hrádeček a rustic throwback to the family estate at Havlov. Hrádeček may have had a postmodern feel, but it also offered a taste of what life had been like in the First Republic.

By 1967 Czech theaters were some of the best in Europe. Any artistic awakening is ultimately a mystery, but what was happening in Prague seemed unfathomable, especially given the difficulty of working under a totalitarian regime. To investigate the phenomenon, *The New Yorker* sent a legendary theater critic from London, Kenneth Tynan, to report on the Czech miracle. Tynan came back impressed, writing that "Prague has a strong claim to be regarded as the theatre capital of Europe."[15]

At the time, Prague boasted nineteen professional theaters, all of them subsidized by the city or state, which meant that the best tickets in the best theaters cost little more than a dollar. More importantly, many of the new theaters—the so-called small theaters—had suddenly become an outlet for protests, even if those protests had to be cast in symbolic or allegorical language. The better plays in those small theaters, Tynan wrote, were either "bulletins of unease" or "parables conceived by and addressed to honestly troubled people." The best of the small theaters was the Balustrade, with Havel its undisputed star.

Tynan was an iconoclast who loved controversy. He had been the first person to say the word "fuck" on British television, leading a critic of BBC to suggest he should be reprimanded by having his bottom spanked. Tynan immediately recognized Havel as a kindred spirit. Despite his apparent shyness, Havel had a deep, almost obsessive need to bring together interesting people, especially if drinking was involved. Havel not only agreed to squire him around the city in the Renault he'd bought from royalties from *The Garden Party*, but he also introduced Tynan to directors, actors, playwrights, and the Slavia Café. Tynan responded to the kindness by making Havel one of the centerpieces of his *New Yorker* article, calling him "a dapper, utterly assured man of thirty" who "exudes moral integrity and resilience." Tynan thought of Havel as a "dandy in the classic rather than the romantic mode," and he had no doubt of his theatrical genius.

By late summer of 1967, Havel put aside revisions on *The Increased Difficulty of Concentration* to prepare for the fourth congress of the writer's union. The communists had empowered the writer's union to police writers. From its shabby, run-down building at 11 Národní Street, with its ill-fitting front door and cracked linoleum floors, officials determined who did and didn't receive book contracts and literary prizes. Ironically, such power made the writer's union one of the few organizations that could (and did) challenge the state. As a result, the regime anticipated each congress with unease, approaching writers with a mixture of threats and bribes. As a noncommunist, Havel was something of a wild card, and in 1967 he aligned himself with a gang of conspirators who wanted to use the writer's congress to discuss reform.[16]

Preparing for the 1967 congress, Havel began holding meetings with reform communists who held a certain amount of power in the organization, including Milan Kundera, who would later become the most famous anti-communist writer in Europe; Ludvík Vaculík, a hardheaded eccentric who would soon be kicked out of the Communist Party; and Pavel Kohout, a fellow playwright who, like Kundera, had written Stalinist poetry in his youth. All of them used their talks at the congress to openly condemn the repression of literature. They also expressed their concern that although writers were officially encouraged to write about the themes of modern life, few did so out of fear that anything perceived as negative would threaten their careers. Kohout read from a letter written by the Soviet dissident Alexandr

Solzhenitsyn, calling on the end to literary censorship, and Vaculík blistered both the writer's union and the head of the Communist Party, causing several people in the audience to look about the room, fearing police might arrest him on the spot.[17]

No one was arrested, but Jiří Hendrych, the chief ideologist of the Communist Party (and thus one of the most powerful men in the country), stormed out of the meeting, vowing to exact his revenge. A few weeks later, the president of the country denounced the delegates in an angry speech. "We certainly cannot tolerate accusations that in past years we have been passing through a 'second dark age,' as was indicated by some delegates to the fourth Congress of Czechoslovak writers," he said. "These people have attacked the policy of the party, the country's domestic and foreign policy, they have been asserting coexistence with bourgeois ideology and they have failed to recognize the class struggle."[18] A few months later, Vaculík and Kohout were kicked out of the Communist Party. Kundera would be kicked out a few years later.

If nothing else, the congress of the writer's union showed that the state could no longer control its critics. Within months, the Central Committee of the Communist Party deposed the general secretary of the Communist Party, replacing him with Alexander Dubček, a reformer who nevertheless still believed in the central role of the Communist Party. Dubček had been educated in the Soviet Union, but he was also a pragmatist who believed the party had become overrun by dogma. Less than a month after taking over, he legalized freedom of association and promoted intellectuals to important governmental positions. Then he threw his support behind reforming the economy.[19]

The goal of reform under Dubček was sometimes difficult to understand. There was a great deal of talk about tolerance and creating, in the words of Dubček's action program, "socialism with a human face." By the spring of 1968, with the fruit blossoms covering Petřín Hill, newspapers ran daily accounts of the misdeeds of the previous regime. Censorship was abolished except in cases of military or state secrets.[20]

With the gates of freedom opened, it was unclear what might happen next. The chairman of the writer's union, Professor Eduard Goldstucker, spoke openly about protecting civil liberties. Others talked about national sovereignty, or about becoming an independent partner of the Soviet Union. Newspaper articles compared Dubček's rise to the Battle of White Mountain in 1620, or to the founding of modern Czechoslovakia as a democratic state in 1918.[21] In thousands of daily interactions, Czechs and Slovaks began speaking of their past, and in April, in front of a graying bookstore on Příkopy Street, someone posted a small photograph of T. G. Masaryk, the president of the First Republic. "Thank God!" one elderly woman said as she looked at the photograph. "I had lost hope that I would ever see him again."[22]

Havel felt strangely ambivalent about the springtime euphoria. Even the most liberal communists, such as Dubček, still believed in the "special role" of the Communist Party, which appeared suspiciously close to a political monopoly. Their ideas had been shaped by living inside the machine. Havel doubted any of them were independent enough to see beyond their Marxist point of view. But he also found the promise of change difficult to resist. If he squinted just right, it seemed possible to believe this was the one opportunity, the moment when transformation was possible. By late March he joined 150 prominent writers and intellectuals in an open letter supporting reform and calling for further democratization. Later, in a weekly newspaper, *Literární Noviny*, he published an essay calling for a noncommunist opposition party and thus "a public, legal contest for power."[23]

Although Havel remained pessimistic about the ability of the communists to change, he enjoyed taking part in the energy that was unleashed by the Prague Spring, what he later called "binges," or parties where the drinking and music lasted all night long. One of milder parties was a political gala held for prominent writers at a palace on Neruda Street, its terraces overlooking the cobblestone streets of Malá Strana. Among the luminaries at the party were Jiří Hájek (the foreign minister), Josef Smrkovský (one of the brains behind the reform movement), and Alexander Dubček (the First Secretary of the Communist Party). Flushed from high-dollar cognac, Havel cornered

Dubček on the terrace and lit into one subject after another. He told Dubček to rid himself of illusions about the Kremlin, then explained how to avoid an invasion.[24] Much to Havel's surprise, Dubček listened intently, demonstrating the skills that excited the entire country. He actually seemed to care. And he listened to the entire harangue.

One of the advantages of the Prague Spring was that the government lifted travel restrictions. In late April Václav and Olga flew to New York City, where Havel had been invited to see a premiere of one of his plays. During the transatlantic flight, Havel swilled whiskey and reworked a speech for the Circle of Independent Writers. Later, after being chauffeured from Kennedy Airport to the East Village, he arrived at the Public Theater in bell-bottoms and a turtleneck sweater. There he found Joe Papp, who was putting on a dress rehearsal, staging the play exactly as Havel had imagined it when writing the script.[25]

The next day, Papp introduced Havel to the seedier side of New York, escorting him two blocks east of Lafayette to St. Marks Place, an East Village alley-can of cafés, record stores, and head shops. The streets were swarming with users and long-haired hippies who came for the cheap fifth-floor walk-ups and the smoke-ins held on Tompkins Square. Havel loved it all. He knew Czech intellectuals who saw hippies as the end of Western civilization, but that wasn't his view. Although he was too strict with himself to incorporate much of the hippie lifestyle, he identified with their longing, which he understood as the desire for "a free and colorful and poetic world without violence."[26]

After spending a few days in a hotel, the Havels moved into a spare bedroom of Jiří Voskovec, a legendary Prague actor who had once been the partner of Jan Werich, the man who gave Havel his first job in the theater. Still later that week, Havel hooked up with Miloš Forman, who happened to be in New York City to raise money for the Czech film industry. Forman took Havel back to the East Village to watch the hippies and to roam the cafés and music stores, their conversation moving between Czechoslovakia and the United States. It was there in St. Marks Place that Havel bought rock posters to decorate Hrádeček, and it was there that he bought his first vinyl recording of Lou Reed and the Velvet Underground. In many ways, Havel was still a straight-laced son of a rich industrialist, but Reed's music, however strange, opened up something Havel couldn't understand. On the surface, the music celebrated sexuality, excess, and the drug culture, but Havel was drawn to the music's nihilism, which seemed joyful. The lyrics had little to do with Havel's life, except that (like those that Reed sang about) he, too, had lived between the margins of society.

Havel's respect for the hippies only intensified a few days later when peace demonstrations swept the city. On the morning of April 27, Havel, Miloš Forman, and Klaus Juncker (his literary agent from Germany) walked in a light rain to Washington Square where members of leftist youth groups staged a civil rights rally. By afternoon, the weather cleared and Havel joined eighty-seven thousand people in Central Park to denounce racism and the war in Vietnam. Sitting on the sodden ground, still wet from the morning rain, he watched Coretta Scott King walk to the platform to give a keynote address. She was speaking in the place of her husband, who had been assassinated twenty-three days earlier. After King spoke, Havel joined the parade down Fifth Avenue, singing throaty choruses of "We Shall Overcome." Throughout the entire experience, he kept thinking that the desire for freedom and justice in his own country seemed to be the same social movement that he found on the streets of New York City. There was a solidarity between the two groups, Havel thought. Witnessing the American rallies suggested what might be possible in Prague.

On May 6 Havel drove to Long Island with a mid-level administrator from Radio Free Europe, whose code name was Walter. They discussed a project Havel had been contemplating, which would involve him interviewing people who had emigrated from Czechoslovakia, asking them under what circumstances they would return. A few days later, he met with the administrator again, this time at the Overseas Press Club on West 45th Street. The meetings weren't dangerous, not physically, but there were certainly hardline elements within the country that would regard such a meeting as treasonous, as evidence that Havel was working with "counterrevolutionary forces." There is no sign that he was followed, however, or that anyone ever learned of these visits.

As part of Havel's project, he wanted to interview people who worked at Radio Free Europe, presumably because it was an easy place to find émigrés from Czechoslovakia. He planned on turning the interviews into a book. Exiles fascinated him, Havel said. He didn't see how democratic reforms could be discussed without first addressing the problem of exiles, "since many people are in exile simply because they tried to do something for democracy some years before the communists thought of it."[27]

Walter liked the idea. In a two-page memo stamped "strictly confidential," he recommended to his immediate supervisor that staff members at Radio Free Europe be allowed to speak with Havel. But he also voiced reservations, saying that Havel "appears to be relatively inexperienced politically and could get himself (and others, including Radio Free Europe) into trouble if there is a serious retrogression in Czechoslovakia." In two other memos, dated May 10 and May 13, he also voiced concern that Havel's questions might reveal the identity of employees, or the fact that they worked at Radio Free Europe, which had been accused of all kinds of crimes by the regime. Although Havel struck Walter as being "extremely honest, courageous, intelligent, and frank," he also thought Havel was probably naive and inexperienced. When Walter had asked him about the military exercises the Soviet Union was conducting along the Czechoslovak border, Havel said there was nothing to worry about. He dismissed any suggestion that there could be a reversal back to "old-fashioned communism." Now that Czechs had tasted freedom, there was no turning back, he said.

When the conversation turned to the Communist Party, Havel showed a spark of contempt. None of them could be trusted, not even Dubček, he said. When Walter asked if Havel could discuss his experiences in the United States with anyone in the Communist

Party, Havel laughed. "You don't understand their mentality," he said. "Their mind is deformed."[28]

After returning to Czechoslovakia, the Havels spent the rest of the summer at their weekend house in the Krkonoše Mountains, enjoying one of the happiest times of their lives. Some months earlier Havel had informed the Balustrade that he wouldn't be returning for the fall season. The long summer at the Hrádeček allowed him to imagine a different kind of life, enjoying the freedom of living in a house in the woods, playing their vinyl records of Lou Reed at whatever hour they wished, something unimaginable at the family flat in Prague, what with parents and neighbors to consider.

Although Havel loved Hrádeček, he also craved intellectual conversation. The solution was a steady stream of guests. Two of the most frequent guests that summer were Věra Linhartová, a poet who later immigrated to France, and Jan Tříska, a small-framed, wiry actor who was sometimes referred to as the Czech Marlon Brando. Tříska was Havel's closest friend during the summer of 1968. The two shared a whimsical sense of humor, and they kept up a long-running gag based on the discovery that both of their eccentric fathers had owned thermometers using the Réaumur scale, where water boils at 80 degrees. They told others that they were forming an international organization to resurrect the reputation of René Réaumur and spun elaborate jokes on the theme, Havel telling friends, "Celsius was Swedish. Fahrenheit was a German, born in Poland. And our Réaumur was French, so there's no reason to suspect that he was the victim of an extreme nationalist plot."[29]

Despite reforms, the government was still run by what Havel called "normal party bureaucrats with the right pseudo-education." Worse, the reformers seemed to be surprised by their popularity, or even to be unnerved by it. As Havel put it, those who had begun the reforms of the Prague Spring both sympathized with and feared the rising expectations in society. They supported the liberalization of society, yet they also feared it, knowing it potentially threatened the position of the Communist Party and their own ability to hold on to power. In short, they wanted reform, but only within the limits of their limited imaginations.[30]

Given this atmosphere, the discussions at Hrádeček revolved around whether the Soviet Union would invade. Everyone tried to analyze what might happen from tidbits of information they picked up from the newspaper, television, and radio, including the latest troop movements along the border.[31]

On August 21, 1968, Václav and Olga woke to unseasonably cool weather. After sending off the latest round of houseguests (a group of "wild and prominent writers" who swilled wine late into the night), the Havels joined Tříska for a trip to Liberec, a beautiful, historic city near the East German border.[32] The drive took two hours, as they wound their way through a dozen villages and towns in Havel's stylish Renault.

After arriving in Liberec in late afternoon, Tříska and the Havels joined friends for dinner and a few drinks at an art gallery near the town square. In 1968 having "a few drinks" took all night long. The small group danced and listened to Western records, including the Beatles and Tom Jones, while slowly getting drunk.[33] The drinking and dancing hardly skipped a beat by 4 a.m. when Hana Seifertová, the director of the gallery, received a telephone call from a panicked friend. The country had just been invaded, the friend said. A foreign army was already on the main plaza in Liberec.

What happened next is a blur, and later everyone remembered the events differently. At one point, someone turned on a radio, searching for news. At another point, someone opened a window, which revealed the mysterious and unmistakable rumble of tanks. Sometime later, Jan Tříska and the Havels climbed onto the roof of the gallery. In the blue-black light of dawn, they saw military helicopters and airplanes and columns of troops. The streets were filling with the residents of Liberec, many of them crying. By the time Tříska and the Havels reached the street, they, too, were weeping.[34]

From a rational point of view, or at least from the point of view of self-preservation, it would have made sense to return to the gallery.

No one even thought about that option. This was a time for action, for defiance, a moment to throw caution to the wind. His face still wet from tears, full of anger and resentment, Havel hurried with Olga and Tříska to the town square. From the accounts of those who were there, there was little conversation—and even less internal chatter. Everyone was simply in shock.

While the Havels marched to the main plaza, the country plunged into chaos. At Prague's Ruzyně International Airport, Soviet cargo planes landed every ninety seconds, unloading light tanks, armored vehicles, and troops. Elsewhere, twelve Russian mechanized divisions (along with a smattering of troops from Poland, East Germany, Hungary, and Bulgaria) wheeled their way up streets and highways and across open fields. News of the invasion reached Dubček shortly before midnight, while he was meeting with an eleven-member council, known as the presidium, in the presidential palace. He took the news badly, crying in front of his men. "I have devoted my entire life to cooperation with the Soviet Union, and they have done this to me!" he told them. Then the liberal members of the group sent a short declaration to Radio Prague that criticized the invasion as a violation of international law but also announced that the army and the People's Militias had been ordered not to defend the country.[35]

Meanwhile, in Liberec Havel watched an angry mob gather on the town square, bombarding tanks with bottles and bricks. Young men climbed aboard the military vehicles, forcing Soviet soldiers to disappear behind locked hatches. The army had been told to spill as little blood as possible, emboldening the crowd even more until a Soviet officer sprayed a machine gun across the plaza. Six people were killed and forty-seven wounded.

Sometime that morning, Havel and Tříska heard that Liberec Radio was organizing a clandestine broadcast from a private house on Alšova Street, a little more than a mile from the city center. The location allowed them to connect to a nearby transmitting tower without much danger of being shut down. Havel immediately went to the house and threw himself into activity, gathering information and writing news bulletins, leaflets, and commentaries. That afternoon, someone put him on the radio. By this time, he and Tříska were "running on adrenaline, with just little snippets of intellect present." Havel told listeners to "search for new ideas about how to fight! Organize yourselves, ensure contact between each other, establish action cells and coordinate your activity."[36]

Over the next few days, Havel watched a spell fall over the country. Hundreds of thousands of citizens protested in the streets, and the resistance grew. On the Thursday after the invasion, more than twelve hundred delegates of a Special Party Congress gathered secretly in a factory near Prague, where they voted overwhelmingly to call for a national strike. In Liberec, a gang of about a hundred Czech hippies removed all the street signs from town in order to confuse foreign troops, reminding Havel of the youth he had watched in New York City. They wore the same long hair, the same clothes, and even listened to the same songs. The thought suggested that Czechs were participating in the same cultural revolution that was sweeping Paris and the United States, which was itself something of a miracle given the recent tragedy of Czech history. As he later wrote in a letter to a friend, "It may be the only week since 1938 [when Germany invaded] when the whole nation was really united, when all were courageous, everybody spoke the truth, when people were very kind to each other, when the smartest ones became natural leaders."[37]

Havel wrote at least five speeches for the radio that week, fueled by vitamin F he had commandeered from the hospital. He also served, rather ironically, as an advisor to several communist functionaries, who gave him an office in the town hall. For a brief time, it appeared there might be some measure of hope. After all, worldwide outrage might make occupation seem too costly to the Soviets.[38]

Olga was less optimistic. On the first day of the resistance, she helped scrounge food from plundered stores, bringing treats to the radio studio. She soon returned to Hrádeček, however. As a clear-eyed realist, she saw no sense in fighting the inevitable victory of brute force. She tried to suggest as much to her husband, but he couldn't sit still long enough to listen. As the days passed, he realized his need to keep moving had been a desperate attempt to avoid thinking about what had occurred. As he wrote in a letter, he feared being "engulfed" by one of his depressions and avoided being alone for even a moment.[39]

Within a few days, however, Havel realized Olga was right. On Monday, speaking through radio static, Havel told listeners he was one of the "few Czech writers who can still use a free transmitter in this country." He went on to say that since writers such as himself were at the forefront of democratic reform, it was reasonable to assume they would soon face persecution by the occupying powers.[40] And on Tuesday evening, Havel joined the mayor of Liberec to listen to a televised broadcast that was to be given by the president, Alexander Dubček. Since the invasion, Dubček had been held in captivity near Moscow, but he had recently been released after secretly agreeing to dismantle the reforms of the Prague Spring. On television, he now appeared to be a changed man. His face was ashen, deep bags showed under his eyes, and he seemed to be on the verge of a breakdown. At 6:30 p.m., everyone turned on their televisions to see Dubček speak to the nation. "Dear listeners," he said, struggling to speak, "I ask you to forgive me if every now and then there is a pause in this largely improvised speech and impromptu appearance. I think you know why it is." He thanked the public for its support and paid tribute to the many brave acts of the previous week. Then, his voice breaking, he said that the country might be forced to take "some temporary measures" to limit reform. If citizens would submit to "the normalization" of life, he said, he would negotiate the removal of Soviet troops.[41] After listening to the address, Havel didn't say a word. No one spoke. They all just got up and left in silence.[42]

There are conflicting memories of when and how the Liberec adventure ended. In one account, given by Tříska, Olga finally put her foot down, sternly telling the two men they were fighting a lost cause. No one cared about their resistance, she told them. Whatever the circumstances, it was time to return to Hrádeček, where Havel retreated to his study.[43]

If he ever wanted to lead a so-called normal life, a life with some measure of personal freedom, it was time to leave his country. At least forty thousand Czechs or Slovaks had driven across the frontier since the invasion. Border guards had been turning a blind eye to those who lacked passports or exit visas, winking or shaking the hands of those who were leaving, even wishing them luck.[44]

Rolling an onion skin into his typewriter, Havel wrote a quick letter to Měda Mládek, an American patron of the arts who had left Czechoslovakia in 1946. Would she help him find money to travel to the United States, perhaps through the Ford Foundation? Naturally, he was reluctant to leave his country, he wrote, but getting out of harm's way seemed the most reasonable thing to do.[45]

# 5

## A CURTAIN OF IRON

THE IRON-GRAY SKIES WERE DARK AND REPROACHFUL. In
Prague, a drizzle fell for the first ten days of October 1968. One hundred and sixty kilometers to the north, the hills at Hrádeček turned
orange, and the mountains filled with snow.[1]

For the first time since returning home from the army, Václav
Havel didn't have a job. He also felt the need to move on, to try something new. His foreign royalties freed him from the necessity of earning a regular paycheck. Freed from the drudgery of the workweek, his
mind was full of endless possibilities.

Despite his optimism in what he might accomplish, however,
Havel was suffering from one of his many bouts of writer's block. Released from the daily complications of the theater, which Havel had
carried like a heavy weight, he felt listless, lost, as if he didn't know
where he was going or why he wanted to get there. He got almost no
writing done that fall, spending his days at Hrádeček reading—and
corresponding with Jan Tříska, who kept him abreast of the latest
depressing news from Prague.[2]

At the heart of Havel's malaise was a series of fateful questions.
The most important was whether to flee the country. But bound to

that central question were all sorts of tangled knots that were impossible to unravel, questions regarding not only his deepest desires but also the personal and literary dangers of trying to escape the gravity of home and country.

In the period leading up to the invasion, Havel had been personally attacked as an anti-socialist in the Soviet newspapers. He had also been among the first to publicly call for a return to democracy.[3] Hence there was good reason to believe he might be arrested at any time. The more he and Olga discussed the situation, however, the more Havel felt reluctant to flee the country. For one, he was terribly sensitive about his lack of talent in foreign languages, which he regarded as a deep embarrassment. He wondered whether he could ever learn English well enough to write professionally in that language, or to have the sort of complex intellectual discussion that came so easily to him in Czech. Even more worrisome was the possibility of never again hearing his mother tongue. Even if he chose to continue writing in Czech as an expatriate, Havel wondered whether he would be able to maintain the special atmosphere he relied on for his creativity, the books and daily interactions and scores of friendships that nourished him.

Then there was the ghost of his uncle, Miloš, who had emigrated to West Germany in 1952. For a time, Miloš had appeared successful, sending packages of exotic Western goods, including knee socks and blue jeans, but Miloš had never been able to recreate the financial success he had known in Czechoslovakia. In Prague, he had relied on surrounding himself with dozens of family friends who could implement his wild and brilliant ideas. He had never been able to create that atmosphere abroad. In West Germany, he started an upscale restaurant and produced several films, but each project he started sank into failure. When he died in February 1968, he was a lonely and broken man.[4] Václav Havel worried that his fate might resemble that of his uncle's.

Havel also struggled with the ethics of his personal situation, including the question of whether he had a right to leave the country. While still a teenager in the 1950s, he had published an article in a youth magazine in which he argued that an artist was required by his craft to rise above the petty and mundane concerns of everyday life. "It is impossible," he had suggested, "to write about great causes without living for those great causes, to be a great poet without being a great human being." In other words, great art was forged from the difficulty of growing down into the roots of life.[5] Would such an artist flee the country—or would he fight to save it, even against long odds?

By his own estimation, Havel was oversensitive, neurotic, and prone to panic. He found arguments and disagreements thoroughly unpleasant. He often longed for nothing more than peace and tranquility, and yet at the same time he had spent much of his life in constant conflict with the state.[6] Now he was caught between two forces, each pushing him in opposing directions. If he emigrated, he would presumably find the tranquility that he longed for. If he remained, he could expect nothing but a great deal of suffering.

When Měda Mládek received Havel's plea for help, which he had sent soon after witnessing the Soviet occupation of Liberec, she immediately translated his letter into English and delivered it to her friend McNeil Lowry. The director of the arts for the Ford Foundation, Lowry had long wanted to bring Czech and Slovak writers to the United States on fellowships. In 1968 he had asked Mládek to nominate a few worthy candidates.[7] The Soviet invasion accelerated those plans, since many of those writers were now in personal danger. For the first few weeks after the invasion, all telephone service to Prague was shut down, so Lowry sent a West German colleague to Czechoslovakia to locate four artists, including Havel. The idea was to pass along assurances of help. Anyone in serious danger would be driven immediately to West Germany.[8] Havel was never located, but the Ford Foundation did learn that, contrary to rumor, he had refused to join the wave of some two hundred thousand people who had fled the country.

Unable to reach Havel by telephone or messenger, the Ford Foundation sent a letter by post, letting Havel know the Ford Foundation would cover his living expenses for a year if he wished to come to the

United States. It was exactly the sort of offer Havel had asked Mládek to arrange. By the time he received the news, however, he had second thoughts. Perhaps it was simply cold feet, or perhaps his life had momentarily clarified. He immediately typed up an eight-page response, expressing thanks but explaining that his plans had changed. He now thought it would be better to remain in Czechoslovakia for a few more months. First of all, he wrote, "not everything is definitely lost as yet, and it would probably not be correct—just at a time when things are still in a flux—to abandon [the country] and so to weaken in fact, as well as psychologically—the crowd." He also worried that going abroad might allow the state to revoke his citizenship or encourage authorities to place him on trial in his absence.[9]

Havel's letter contains a number of fascinating passages in which he wrestled with whether to flee. From a moral point of view, however, he felt he should be willing to stand behind the consequences of his actions, including all of the public statements from the past few years about the failures of the socialist system. He also felt that remaining in the country had a sort of "social-moral meaning." If every artist and intellectual abandoned the country, the nation would "succumb to moral decay and opportunism." Ordinary Czechs would surely resent the fact that well-known intellectuals, who had called out for change, had simply scampered away at the first sign of hardship. Havel had opportunities in foreign countries that weren't available to ordinary Czechs, and it didn't seem right to leave them behind when he had been among those who helped create the crisis. Conversely, Havel also understood there was a limit to what he was willing to face. For instance, he wanted the chance to immigrate if he faced immediate arrest. His solution was to ask Mrs. Mládek if she could arrange an open invitation, one that he could use in case he had "to leave hurriedly" or if his presence no longer felt urgent. Havel assured Mládek that he still looked forward to the possibility of returning to the United States. Should the Ford Foundation be able to provide an open-ended invitation, he believed he and Olga could leave sometime in the spring.[10]

The Ford Foundation responded immediately, offering an open-ended invitation that would also pay for everything imaginable, including books, theater tickets, and field trips to ten American cities.[11] On paper, the trip would begin on a date of Havel's choosing and last eight months. In reality, however, the proposal opened the door (or even the likelihood from the perspective of the Ford Foundation) for the Havels to immigrate permanently to the United States, just as many others were doing.

In January 1969 Havel wrote to thank Lowry for the fellowship. The chance to live in the United States, Havel said, "was the fulfillment of an old desire of mine."[12] Regarding when he would leave, Havel was cagier than ever. A few weeks earlier, he had said that he would travel in the spring; now he mentioned leaving in the fall. His ambivalence was partly about how his choice would affect others, including the many friends he would be leaving behind. So many people he knew were swinging back and forth between optimism and despair, he wrote, that he thought his departure might be read as a sign that all was lost.

As a result of his ambivalence, Havel began making a series of double plans. While arranging to leave the country, he also simultaneously made contingencies for remaining at home. One concern, should he remain in Czechoslovakia, was protecting his foreign royalties. Just ten days before the government restricted the rights of citizens to travel abroad, Havel drove to West Germany, where attorneys drew up a one-page contract giving his English-language translator, Věra Blackwell, power of attorney over both contractual and editorial matters relating to his entire literary life, thus making sure that literary negotiations over his work could continue no matter what happened to him personally. Blackwell's new powers included the right "to receive, hold, and disperse any and all royalties." Havel notarized the document at a cost of seventy-two deutsche marks and drove back to Prague.[13]

Blackwell had emigrated from Czechoslovakia shortly after the communists seized power, first working for Radio Free Europe and then eventually settling in London, where she married an Englishman. She wasn't a writer or professional translator, nor was it common for a translator to work from their native tongue into a second language. Literary translations almost always worked the other way around, meaning that Blackwell was more suited to translate from English into Czech rather than the reverse. All that mattered in 1969, however, was that Blackwell was a great and loyal friend, as well as a champion of his plays. By giving her the complete rights to everything, Havel prepared himself for the worst.

Although Havel was much better known abroad, Milan Kundera was arguably the most important writer inside the country. He had written three books of poetry, two successful plays, and a best-selling novel. As a member of the Communist Party, he also held a prize teaching position at the film academy, where he had taught Miloš Forman, one of Havel's oldest friends.[14]

As a youth, Kundera had been a true believer, writing that the communists would create "an idyll of justice for all." His poetry glorified communism, one verse declaring that "Stalin's land / is the well of our strength."[15] By 1968, however, Kundera found his past embarrassing. Like many Czechs, he remained in the Communist Party out of cynicism, understanding that his career depended on the benevolence of the party. Privately, he rejected not only communism but all forms of idealism. He even turned his back on poetry. He didn't trust its lyrical language, which he believed had fostered his own naivete. Instead, he focused on writing ironic novels with an extraordinary sense of detachment.[16]

Whereas Havel had thrown himself into the resistance of the Soviet invasion, Kundera urged everyone to face the situation calmly. In the leading literary journal, he argued that citizens should stop protesting in the streets and trust their leaders, such as Alexander Dubček, to act in their best interest. Perhaps the Soviet invasion had been unfortunate, but it wasn't yet a catastrophe, Kundera wrote. No one, for instance, had yet been arrested for his or her ideas. Further, the reforms of the past year had shown "what limitless democratic possibilities" could be born from the socialist project. In fact, there was every hope that the military occupation might burnish the spirit of the historic achievements of the past few years of communist rule.

In short, Kundera advised caution, moderation, and patience. Czechs were an antiheroic people, known for their sobriety, and the best course of action, he wrote, was to avoid any hint of extreme action.[17]

Although Havel was typically polite to a fault, he also had a tendency, as he once put it, to fall into a black rage once every "seven to ten years." The tantrums were usually triggered by small (even petty) events that took on a life and significance of their own.[18] Such was Kundera's article, which exhausted his patience. Kundera seemed to blame artists and the press for expressing their ideas. Even worse, Kundera suggested that a group of muddled politicians could be trusted to defend civil liberties.

Havel immediately arranged to publish a blistering attack of Kundera in the next issue of *Tvář*, the small literary journal he had defended in 1965. In his rebuttal, Havel questioned Kundera's courage and honesty, suggesting that Kundera represented the tendency among communists (even communists interested in reform) to ignore reality, preferring instead to wallow in "all kinds of illusions and every form of self-deception."[19]

From Havel's point of view, Kundera was asking citizens to put aside their concerns. As to the idea that some of the reforms of the past year would have to be sacrificed in order to negotiate the withdrawal of foreign armies, he wrote that "freedom and legality are the first preconditions of a normally and soundly functioning social organism." No one could negotiate away the rule of law, or the right to speak one's mind.[20] Kundera soon responded with his own blistering rebuttal, which he published in *Listy*. Havel had publicly accused him of cowardliness; now Kundera accused Havel of "moralistic exhibitionism," asking citizens to take actions that would be both meaningless and dangerous. Havel, he wrote, wanted citizens to go on resisting the inevitable because he was a "narcissist." He longed for a lost cause, something that would allow him to "fully express the righteousness of his character in all of the glory of defeat."[21]

In many ways, the public dispute was little more than a squabble between literary giants, a chance to let off steam. On a deeper level, however, these points of view represented two approaches to living under an oppressive system. How should one behave while watching the dissolution of basic rights and liberties? Kundera saw resistance as little more than vanity, an attempt to display one's moral superiority. Havel believed in speaking truth to power, regardless of its futility. Standing up for oneself might be painful, but he suggested it strengthened one's moral focus, nourishing the unseen roots of the culture. Not everyone could afford such beliefs, but Havel was fortunate in that he had no children to protect. He also had a steady income from foreign royalties that provided him a measure of independence.

The squabble between Kundera and Havel soon grew into a Prague legend. Both men nursed the grievance for another decade, and Kundera went so far as to insert their feud into his next novel, using a character based on Havel to emphasize his point that actively resisting the Soviets was futile. By the time Kundera wrote that novel, he had been expelled from the Communist Party. He had also emigrated to France, where he wrote *The Unbearable Lightness of Being*, the great classic of resistance. In that novel, the narrator tells the reader that "anyone who thinks that the Communist regimes of Central Europe are exclusively the work of criminals is overlooking a basic truth: the criminal regimes were made not by criminals but by enthusiasts convinced that they had discovered the only road to paradise."

It was a great line. No one could match Kundera's bitter insights into the communist mentality, not least because he himself had once believed in its angelic vision while refusing to notice the diabolic crimes committed in its name. As Kundera put it in reflection, communism was "an idyllic house of glass with the Gulag put to one side."[22]

By the end of 1968, it was clear that the invasion of Czechoslovakia had been a political catastrophe for the Soviet Union. Soviet leaders had been led to believe that hardline elements in Czechoslovakia would seize control of the government and endorse the invasion. Instead, they faced animosity at every turn even while forcing its will on Czechoslovak political leaders.[23]

Meanwhile, some members of the Czech government continued to pretend that the invasion of their country was no more than a temporary setback to the Prague Spring. Alexander Dubček, for instance, refused to accept the legitimacy of the invasion. He still spoke in public of the need for reform, of creating "socialism with a human face." It was a dangerous game. Out of necessity, Dubček agreed to many Soviet demands, while he tried to soften their affect in daily governance. In this way, he tried to maneuver between outright defiance and surrender.[24] And for many months, it seemed like such a course might actually be possible.

Temperatures during the Christmas season of 1968 hovered just below freezing. Light snow dusted the streets, and the sky carried the gray tarnish of a city that receives less than fifty hours of sunshine in a typical January.[25] A few weeks after New Year's Day, Havel rode the tram across the river to the Malá Strana, or Little Town, the quarter known for its seventeenth-century palaces and cobblestone streets. From the stop on Little Town Square, it was just a few blocks uphill to the American embassy. In better years, Havel had been a guest of the ambassador.

Waiting to apply for a travel visa, Havel ran into Josef Škvorecký, a writer who had been in and out of trouble since the 1950s, when his second novel, *The End of the Nylon Age*, had been condemned by authorities. He and his wife, the actress Zdena Salivarová, told Havel they were in the process of moving to Canada, where Škvorecký had been offered a teaching position at the University of Toronto. First they planned to fly to New York City. When Havel told them about his Ford Foundation fellowship, the two were overjoyed, suggesting they all fly together to the Big Apple.

According to Škvorecký's account of the conversation, Havel appeared to consider the matter for a few moments, as if nothing would please him more than to fly with them to New York. Such an idea appealed to Havel's social nature, his need to rub elbows with other artists. When Škvorecký told him they were leaving the next morning, Havel replied that he couldn't join them. "Too soon," he said. "I think

I'll wait at least until the first anniversary of the invasion. It should be—interesting."²⁶

Once again, Havel was pulled in multiple directions. One chamber of the heart wanted to emigrate; another wanted to suffer in Czech-land. A few days later, Havel wrote McNeal Lowry at the Ford Foundation, informing him he definitely couldn't come to the United States in the spring. "The situation in this country is still open, matters are in motion, and I feel I ought to stay here for some time yet," he wrote. He begged for his contract to be rewritten to begin in June. By June, however, he had changed his mind once again, and he asked Lowry if he could wait to come to the United States in September.²⁷

The "situation" that Havel alluded to was the loss of civil liberties. In a speech given in January, a powerful member of the Central Committee, Gustav Husák, announced that it was time to "strengthen internal discipline." Husák also warned citizens not to attend "private meetings in apartments" in which the Communist Party was criticized. A few days after the speech, the government officially reinstated censorship. Editors were given guidelines explaining what could and could not be published. Larger newspapers once again received censors who examined everything, even crossword puzzles, for suggestive language or hidden irony.

Havel found the new rules disturbing enough to call a press conference, along with his friend Jan Němec, one of the few talented filmmakers who refused to leave the country. The two men read a written statement denouncing Mr. Husák. They also showed reporters a telegram they sent to the nation's president, Ludvík Svoboda, warning him that Husák's words reminded them "in a striking way of the style of those politicians who brought police terror to our state." The new laws, Havel and Němec predicted, would lead to "police interrogations and shadowing and arresting people."²⁸ Havel never got a reply from the letter to Svoboda, but a few weeks later he did find a new listening device in his Prague apartment, one obviously placed there by the secret police.

The pressure in the country continued to build throughout the winter and spring. On Wenceslas Square, a young man named Jan

Palach doused himself with gasoline, set himself on fire, and ran screaming through the streets. He left a letter protesting censorship and the Soviet occupation. A few weeks later, tens of thousands of Prague citizens rioted in the streets when the Czechoslovakian ice hockey team won two matches against the Soviet Union. To the hard-liners these were not merely signs of discontent but a signal that deep anti-communist feelings continued to fester. On April 14, 1969, the pro-Soviet faction finally took action, installing Gustav Husák as First Secretary of the Communist Party. Husák immediately announced that he would "normalize" the country. The first step, Husák announced, would be to cleanse the Communist Party of "opportunists."[29] Eventually, he would expel half a million individuals from the Communist Party.

Once again the state became a machine of totalitarian control. Its sole objective would be to intimidate the population into accepting a new set of rules.[30]

The Havels planned on traveling to Vienna in early September 1969, where Havel would be presented with the Austrian state prize in literature. After a brief vacation, they would board a Pan Am flight to New York City on September 12. As the departure approached, Havel's activities became riskier—so risky, in fact, that they seemed designed to throw a monkey wrench into his ability to leave the country.

In August he sent a long, private letter to Alexander Dubček, the former First Secretary of the Communist Party. In the letter (which was surely read by the secret police) Havel urged Dubček to refuse to renounce his own reforms. Refusing such self-criticism, Havel wrote, would surely lead Dubček to be expelled from the Communist Party, but it would also "strike a blow against the policies" of the current leadership. Havel asked Dubček to "speak the truth" and to reject "everything that stands that truth on its head." Naturally, such defiance would have little effect on the immediate situation. It might even be used as an excuse for further repression. Nevertheless, Havel wrote, it would represent a moral victory, perhaps even leading people to "realize that it is always possible to preserve one's ideals and one's backbone; that one can stand up to lies; that there are values worth struggling for; that there are still trustworthy leaders."[31]

About the same time that Havel sent a letter to Dubček, he also signed (along with nine other individuals) a manifesto known as the Ten Points Petition, which condemned the Soviet invasion and the loss of civil liberties. The document had been drafted by Luděk Pachman, a chess champion, and revised by Ludvík Vaculík, who had delivered one of the fiery speeches at the Writer's Union in 1967.

On the first anniversary of the Soviet invasion, the manifesto was delivered to parliament as well as to the Central Committee of the Communist Party. The document was presented as a petition to the government, protected under Article 29 of the constitution. Among the petition's many items was a list of illegal activities conducted by the state and a call for free and open elections, demands that would almost certainly bring immediate retaliation, endangering Havel's ability to leave the country.[32] And, sure enough, on the Saturday morning after delivering the petition to parliament, Václav and Olga were awakened at daylight by what Havel described as "two very important gentlemen" from the secret police who were banging on the cottage door at Hrádeček. They immediately confiscated the Havels' passports and exit visas and left without explanation.

Havel pretended to be shocked by the entire episode. He immediately drove to Prague, visiting several police officers, none of whom would provide an explanation for why his passport had been confiscated. On Monday afternoon, he telegraphed the Ford Foundation, writing: "I CANNOT COMME LETTER FOLLOWS."[33] Havel then typed up a follow-up letter, using the English he had been studying all summer. Somewhat defensively, he claimed that he really did have every intention of flying to New York City on September 12. He wrote, "You already probably know the cause, why I couldn't come to the USA—the passports were taken away not only from me but also my wife. I am extremely sorry being again the source of new complications for you but you surely understand very well that it is not my fault."[34]

Naturally, Havel didn't mention that he had provoked authorities and all but forced authorities to prevent him from leaving the country, nor did he explain that on some deep level he simply couldn't leave and that he felt a sense of guilt toward all of those who had worked so hard to help him.

Later that week, Havel also sent an explanation to Věra Blackwell, his translator. Havel told Blackwell that he wasn't "especially heartbroken" about the incident with the passports. He had become used to "such rogueries," he said, and he hinted that he had suspected the state might prevent him from leaving the country. Once again, he avoided explaining that he himself had provoked the authorities and that, in truth, he was terrified of leaving Czechoslovakia and never being allowed to return. Instead, he pretended to hold out hope that he might eventually be allowed to travel to the United States, knowing full well that this was now the remotest of possibilities.

Whether or not Havel had secretly wished to remain in Czechoslovakia, the new situation electrified him. By October he was cooking again (his favorite screwball recipe was horseradish with apples and vinegar). More importantly, he was writing like mad, his writer's block having vanished with his passport. By mid-November he had finished the first third of a new play, *The Conspirators*, a speed record for Havel.[35] Then in November Havel decided to drive into Prague to settle his long-term situation. While visiting the state agency, known as DILIA, that served as the literary agent for all writers in the country, he was told by his official representative, a fellow by the name of Kalaš, that the state had directed him to obstruct any negotiations for producing Havel's plays in foreign countries, an obvious attempt to cut off Havel's financial independence.

It was probably on that same trip to Prague that Havel was "very, very, very interrogated" by a gentleman from the StB. After his release, he learned that the prosecutor's office was preparing to charge all ten signatories of the Ten Points Petition with treason.[36] He also learned that the state was gathering thousands of pages in its case against Havel, most of it drawn from Havel's own writings and communications. None of this could have come as much of a surprise, but nevertheless the experience (as well as the dawning realization that he could spend a great deal of time in prison) sucked the air from his lungs. He went from feeling energized to feeling isolated and depressed.[37]

On November 21, 1969, Havel sat down at the manual typewriter in the Prague apartment to write Věra Blackwell, who was becoming one of his most vital links to the outside world. Although Havel had just learned that the Lincoln Center had invited him to attend the premiere of his play, *The Increased Difficulty of Concentration*, in New York City on December 4, there was no chance he could attend, he said. As he told Blackwell, "I will not be able to free myself, just as you are not able to free yourself to go to Prague. We have between us a sterling Iron Curtain."[38]

# 6

## INTO THE WOODS

THE FARMHOUSE AT HRÁDEČEK WAS DRAFTY and cold, but the Havels remained there like hermits through the first snows of what would be the coldest winter in more than one hundred years. They finally retreated to the well-insulated family apartment in Prague in time for the Christmas holidays.[1] They stayed in the city for less than two months before returning to the farmhouse. By the time Havel wrote Věra Blackwell, on February 22, 1970, one of their cats had wandered off in the frozen woods, never to return. Three weeks later, the snowdrifts were two meters deep.[2]

Olga loved living in the country. She also loved being the master of her own house. Although Havel's father had eventually warmed up to her, her relationship with Havel's mother was still cold and distant. As for Havel, he felt that the isolation at Hrádeček calmed his nerves. He now felt lost when visiting Prague. For one thing, he had no job, no place to be. But it was more than that: The grand city, with its medieval streets and Renaissance palaces, seemed oppressive. Havel felt the political situation had made his literary friends neurotic. He no longer looked forward to the social life in Prague, to the gatherings and little parties and late nights at the Slavia Café. Instead, he worried constantly about who he should and shouldn't visit, and whether being seen with a friend might get them into trouble with authorities. Even inviting someone over to the apartment was fraught with unpleasant complications. Havel felt it put others in an impossible situation, since declining might make it appear that they were afraid of the state. With his highly developed sense of courtesy, Havel worried it was rude to even ask.[3]

By 1970, the basic outlines of the future could be seen. The state had closed the border, travel had been restricted, and the shelves at the grocery store began to empty. Once the borders closed, the only toothpaste Havel could find was made in Czechoslovakia. He found this infuriating, since (as he wrote to his translator in London) Czech brands were "idiotic." They didn't "foam" when he brushed his teeth. Now that few of his friends were able to travel abroad, he had to write to foreigners, begging them to mail him toothpaste from a "capitalistic province."[4]

As for the arts, technically everyone was free to work. No book had been banned or removed from the libraries (although that would come soon enough). Writers were free to write what they wished to say, but in the brave new world only those graced by the regime would find a publisher or a theater who would dare to produce their play.

The entire cultural atmosphere was like a house without any light. In order to find anything, one had to grope about in the darkness or simply take a wild guess in order to find a wall or a doorknob, or to navigate down a corridor. There were no longer any laws or rules except what the Communist Party chose to enforce.

The chaotic situation made Havel's life seem strangely doubled. Was Havel destitute or fabulously wealthy? Was he shackled or free? It all depended on how he looked at the situation, and how he looked at the situation changed every week. For the moment, Havel was wealthy, at least by Czech standards. A single $1,200 royalty advance from the Lincoln Center, received in 1970 for the *Increased Difficulty of Concentration*, was equivalent to a full year's salary in Czechoslovakia.[5] At the same time, there was almost no chance he would find a meaningful job should his foreign royalties be cut off. (As Havel put it, the only job he would be allowed to work would be a job that he wouldn't want). And while Havel enjoyed far more personal freedom than most people, this was simply because he had no position and no job for the state to take away. The state could throw him in prison, however. In his upcoming court case, there was little chance he would have a fair trial.

The plays rarely came to him without a painful birth. Havel wrote slowly and with great difficulty, often giving in to despair or recriminating himself for not writing more quickly or having more ideas or more talent. Havel tended to piece together his plays as if they were a strange geometric puzzle. He often became obsessed with repeating elements from scene to scene, putting words or slogans of one character in the mouth of another or replaying entire conversations, as if the characters on the stage were broken records. He used such devices to create an aura of absurdity, evoking a world that, as he put it, felt frighteningly "schematic, almost machinelike." He thought of this as an attempt to unveil the fantasies underneath the communist ideology, but he was working out his own obsessions as well.[6]

Writing *The Conspirators* that long, snowy winter of 1969–1970, Havel fell back on all of the writing tricks that had served him in the past. He experimented with writing quickly, slowly, either spontaneously or by exact schedule, by hand and by typewriter, by day and night. At the center of his writing process was what he called "a thinking theme," basically a web of connections that made up the heart of the play. The "thinking theme" might be abstract or philosophical, but in order to be effective it had to be deeply personal. It had to reach deep into his life, evoking the personal questions and problems that he kept picking at, like an old scab.

The "thinking theme" on Havel's mind that winter revolved around human identity. He began to imagine identity as deeply haunted and fragile, prone to leaving us feeling as if we had lost ourselves and our inner world. One of the issues, he thought, was that our experience of the world is often betrayed, or subverted, by ideas that are imposed on us by others, by the intellect, or by an ideological position.[7] By human identity, Havel wasn't referring to an identity crisis as much as to the disintegration of man's oneness with himself and the loss of a meaningful order to the world. It was easy enough to see this estrangement among the communists he knew. Many of them lacked any understanding of how ideology cut them off from an authentic experience of the world. But Havel was also thinking of himself, becoming increasingly aware of what he lacked in his own life.

The difficult part of playwriting, at least for Havel, was embodying his thinking theme into a concrete story.[8] By March, however, he had worked out a plot. The play would be about five politicians who attempt to protect a weak democratic government that (much like the Dubček regime) had recently freed itself from a dictatorship. After growing rumors about a coup, the politicians become conspiratorial and paranoid, eventually seizing dictatorial power and double-crossing each other in order to save the democracy. Ironically, the rumors that bedevil them are about themselves. Becoming frightened of their own shadow, they destroyed a democracy in order to save it. The plot showed how individuals could be trapped by their own logic, and how politicians seemed to stand for one thing (like reform) but could then stand for the opposite (the return to totalitarian rule).

Havel was trying to capture the sort of absurdity that had been unfolding before his eyes for the past two years. What captivated him, however, was the sense that his play was a metaphor for modern life. As he wrote in a commentary to the play, the plot was meant to suggest the ways in which all of us are "enmeshed in the same ghoulish mental machinery" that crushes authentic life—the way in which we all tend to betray ourselves, saying A and doing B, all the while convinced of the righteousness of our actions.[9]

Sometime in February Havel chain-smoked his way through a rewrite and turned the play over to Olga, who often served as his first audience. He read her the play out loud, a trick he had learned in the theater. Hearing the words, he would become aware of where the play seemed to contain tension, humor, and intelligence, and where it was boring, dry, without teeth, or simply confusing. Olga wouldn't have to say anything, and, as if picking something out of the air, he would suddenly understand how to solve problems that had bedeviled him for weeks.

A few days later, he wrote to Věra Blackwell, saying he felt good about the early draft. The play, he wrote, "is against everybody and everything," and he believed it might reach a wide audience in England. In March he drove to Prague to read his draft to a gathering of writers in the living room of Ivan Klíma, where the play was well received.[10] Mailing the manuscript to Blackwell was out of the question, since the secret police were riffling through his correspondence. Instead, he asked a friend, who had been given a visa to travel abroad, to smuggle his manuscript into England.

Unfortunately, *The Conspirators* would prove to be a great failure. The idea for the play might have been workable, but Havel was writing in a vacuum. Perhaps that forced him to push too hard, to force the play, to overwrite it. The end result, he later concluded, was "a chicken that had been in the oven too long," leaving it all dried out. Sometimes, he regretted writing the play at all. Certainly, he regretted the fact that the play was later published in English in an early draft, one he felt was unsuitable for publication.[11]

While Havel worked on his play, the state developed a legal case against him and the nine other authors of the Ten Points petition. Unlike the show trials of the 1950s, the regime had no need to forge documents. The chief prosecutor gathered more than two thousand pages of Havel's own writings and communications as part of its effort to prove that Havel had been plotting to undermine the government. Havel's own point of view, of course, was that he had been exercising his legal right of petition.[12]

Feeling professionally and emotionally vulnerable, in May 1970 Havel reached out to his German literary agent, Klaus Juncker. After losing contact during the Soviet invasion, Juncker had been desperately trying to get a message to Havel through DILIA, the state bureaucracy that represented all writers and playwrights. Representatives at DILIA told Juncker they had never heard of a writer named Havel, which was the sort of lie that bureaucrats had learned to tell exceedingly well. Juncker eventually reached Havel through a German cultural attaché, who (in at least one account) arranged for Havel to hand off a stencil copy of *The Conspirators* in the men's room of a Prague restaurant.[13]

When Juncker came to visit Havel in May, the two of them sat down at the Ministry of Culture with DILIA agents for what Havel called a "strange and depressing meeting." First, Havel was told that his translator, Věra Blackwell, had been accused of espionage. Havel was forbidden from working with her in the future. Then the agent at DILIA threatened Klaus Juncker, suggesting he might face similar investigations if he continued to represent Havel. It was an obvious attempt to intimidate both Juncker and his German publishing house, Rowolt Verlag. To Junker's credit, however, he refused to be intimidated.[14]

To Havel, the whole situation felt bizarre, as if he had been dropped into some kind of ancient Czech folktale. By law, DILIA received an outrageous portion of Havel's foreign royalties in exchange for representing his legal rights, and they were using their position to sabotage his work.[15] Obviously, the agency was being pressured, probably from somewhere quite high in the Communist Party, as part of a campaign to teach Havel to shut his mouth.

A few weeks later, Havel learned that his trial, originally scheduled for June, had been postponed until the fall. But that was hardly welcome news, as the noose seemed to be tightening. Lengthening the legal process was part of the punishment, a way of making his future seem uncertain or of providing a general feeling that he was slowly being swallowed into some obscure region of the system. Meanwhile, he was attacked in both the newspapers and on television, accused of sending anti-governmental information to Pavel Tigrid, perhaps the most prominent anti-communist exile then living.[16] Tigrid had fled to West Germany in 1948 in order to avoid arrest, eventually settling in France. He had once been head of Radio Free Europe, earning him the hatred of the government. After the Soviet invasion, the government convicted him, in absentia, for crimes against the state.

As the first beautiful breath of summer warmed the hills around Hrádeček, Havel put aside revisions to *The Conspirators*. By June 1970 the Havels had retreated into a very different kind of life. Olga had taken charge of the garden and the orchard, and Havel increasingly felt himself drawn to spending time in the woods, with his books, and with their cats (the older of them was named after the Czech writer Ludvík Vaculík). He had decided to work full time on renovating the farmhouse in order to turn it into a year-round cottage.

Perhaps the idea came from Pavel Kohout, a communist playwright whose vigorous extroversion complemented Václav's shy, inward personality. Despite their different political orientations, the two men had always enjoyed each other's company, and over the winter Havel had gone to stay with Kohout and his wife, Jelena Masinová, at their weekend house in Sázava. While visiting, he helped the couple with a renovation, working in sweaters and winter gloves during the day and drinking plenty of beer at night. In pictures from that week, Havel looks relaxed, as if manual labor freed up his own insecurities.

The idea behind renovating Havel's own cottage was to enlarge the place, providing more guest rooms, as well as to make the house livable throughout the year. The most important part of the renovation, at least from the Havels' point of view, was adding hot and cold running water, but as the plans expanded they added a large common room (for entertaining guests from the city), a pantry, a stylish, modern bathroom, and an electrical heating system.[17] The project swallowed up the whole summer, the two of them enjoying the pleasant feeling of watching the house take a new shape.

Finding the right building supplies in a communist-run economy was always a challenge. Like most Czechs, the Havels relied on friends (and friends of friends) to find materials, much of it through the flourishing black market. Havel bought the bricks and wooden planks through the foreign currency stores. He had to transport the materials himself, filling his little Renault with cinder blocks, bags of cement, and fixtures for the house, just about everything he was able to scrounge up.[18] By the end of summer, they had turned the farmhouse into a country retreat, one that would be envied by others.

Then, after renovating the farmhouse, they embarked on renovating the dilapidated family apartment in Prague. When that was done, he bought a dark red Mercedes 230, which he was able to drive home the same day due to his ability to shop at the special foreign currency stores that existed for those who earned their money abroad.

All of the reconstruction left Havel psychologically tired, but he was intent on creating some kind of foundation for the upcoming years. His whole life, he told Blackwell, he had been "living in some kind of schlock joint, usually divided apartments of people who used to be but are no longer rich after 20 years of socialism." He was desperate to make a new beginning, even if it was costing a fortune.

The complete renovation of two houses was a financial drain, especially for a playwright who might never be able to work again. As he put it in a letter, he had "never spent so much money as I have in this time when [the government] is preparing a trial against me, and in this time when I have stopped receiving an income. But in the end it is explainable: In more favorable times one is earning money. In less favorable times, one is spending the money one has earned."[19]

After the expenses, he had enough money to last him no more than a year, but it all seemed worth it. He was afraid that if he waited, he would no longer have the money or the will to get the renovations done.

Havel paid for the renovations with foreign royalties, which had been sent to him in deutsch marks, pounds, and dollars. By law, he was required to turn the hard currency over to the state. In exchange, he was given Bony, little certificates that could be spent in foreign currency stores, called Tuzex.[20] Bony weren't as valuable as hard currency, but on the black market they were worth five crowns apiece, chiefly because Bony could be used to buy Western goods (e.g., French perfume, Marlboro cigarettes, Barbie Dolls, blue jeans, and Western electronics) that could not be purchased otherwise. Entering a Tuzex store was like crossing the Iron Curtain. The shops were filled with the sweet smell of tobacco, glossy magazines, and the fantasy of a consumer paradise that was unavailable to most Czech citizens. Hustlers and black marketers waited outside the stores to exchange money.[21]

In the late 1960s, the government gave Havel at least ninety thousand Tuzex certificates. On the black market, those certificates were worth ten times the yearly salary of the average Czech worker. The stores were normally used to reward party leaders and their families, who were given large stacks of Tuzex certificates to reward their loyalty. But there was an irony related to the foreign currency stores as well: Dutiful citizens often found it difficult or impossible to get into the stores, since they had no access to hard currency. Because of his Western contracts, Havel got to shop with the party bosses.

After the Soviet invasion, isolation was a simple fact of life. For most Czechs that meant hiding not only opinions but basic facts about one's life. Those publicly opposed to normalization faced isolation. The government cut them off from their profession and from opportunities, and made sure their children suffered as well. Anyone who associated with them faced similar pressure. The end result was political and economic blackmail in which very few people had to be sent to prison and large sections of society were coerced into behavior they found distasteful. As long as most people pretended not to notice the small humiliations of everyday life, the system worked fine.

Like others who spoke out against the occupation, the Havels quickly became outsiders. Only a few friends visited them at Hrádeček, and they focused on becoming part of the village, trying to lead ordinary lives. Havel suffered the most. He missed the daily interactions of the theater, and the little meetings over coffee, and the pressure of knowing someone was waiting for a play. In order to ward off another round of depression and apathy, he threw himself into a regimen. He slept late, but in the afternoon he listened to Voice of America and read more than ever; at night, he wrote until well past midnight.[22]

At some level, the forced isolation must have affected his marriage. The Havels were used to spending great swaths of time together, but at Hrádeček there was no escape from each other. Havel had always felt a deep need for social interaction that had been easy to satisfy in Prague. And he had a long history of trysts with other women, affairs that dated back before their marriage. As he had written to his father while on his honeymoon, all his infidelities had only confirmed how meaningless sexual matters were when compared to companionship.[23]

Olga was never pleased with the infidelities, but they were part of their marriage and part of the times in which they lived. Havel's father had maintained a mistress, and most of the men Havel knew in the theater (and a good number of the women, too) strayed beyond the marriage bonds on a regular basis. Sexuality was one of the few areas of life unregulated by the government. The erotic life, especially that of artists, took on an unusual importance, often substituting for the lack of freedom they felt elsewhere.

Havel rarely hid his infidelities from Olga. He tended to tell her everything and then ask for absolution, as if he needed her approval even in this area of his life.[24] Some, including Olga's Czech biographer, have seen this as proof that Olga served as a kind of mother figure to whom Havel could confess whenever he was naughty.[25] The actual truth is probably closer to Havel's own observation that he was attracted to Olga's working-class background, to her sober and unsentimental perspectives and the fact that she could be "somewhat mouthy and obnoxious." She was someone who compensated for what Havel thought of as his own "mental instability," someone who could "offer sober criticism" of his own wild ideas and provide support for his adventures. Perhaps the relationship was not so much a son to his mother as an artist to the world. As Havel put it, Olga represented his "endless search for a firm point, for certainty, for an absolute horizon."[26]

Unlike Havel, Olga didn't torture herself with how life would turn out, or even with questions of meaning. Her earthiness cut through such issues, seeing them as irrelevant or flighty, since life would sort everything out on its own terms. Havel had a tendency to retreat into his intellect or to escape into his art. Olga represented reality.

Havel was struggling with reality that year, struggling with all of the questions of what to do with his life—and with whether he had made the right choice in remaining in Czechoslovakia. In many ways, the first act of his life was over. The glory and success he had dreamed of as a child had all come rather easily, arriving with all the improbability of a meteor falling from the sky. Now at thirty-two years old, he entered into a dark night of unknowing. He had chosen his fate himself, or at least its basic outlines. He had even somewhat knowingly chosen to remain in Czechoslovakia, or at least chosen to remain behind until it was too late to leave. But knowing that he had accepted this fate didn't keep him from feeling pangs of doubt and regret.[27] He had let go of what his old nemesis, Milan Kundera, called "the unbearable lightness of Being." In return he had discovered the heavy gravity of life. And sometimes the weight seemed too much to bear.

# PART TWO

## The Many Underworlds
## of Normalized Life

Fall 1970–August 1979

Isn't it the moment of most profound doubt that gives birth to new certainties? Perhaps hopelessness is the very soil that nourishes human hope; perhaps one could never find sense in life without first experiencing its absurdity.

—VÁCLAV HAVEL

# 7

## VZDOR

WHEN IVAN KLÍMA RETURNED TO PRAGUE with his wife after working for a year as a visiting professor at the University of Michigan, the shaggy-haired writer gathered a small band of friends to read one another's work. At one early meeting, Havel read an early draft of his play *The Conspirators*; at another, he read an early draft of *Beggar's Opera*. Klíma lived on the second floor of an old villa on the southern edge of Prague, a stone's throw from the forest, and the meetings became an event, a bright, sunny garden in a world of frightening shadows. Soon, Klíma's living room couldn't hold all the guests.[1]

Returning to Prague had been excruciating for Klíma. While he was teaching in the United States, the communists revoked the passport that allowed him to remain abroad. That left Klíma with the choice of immigrating to the United States, which meant he might never see his family again, or returning to Czechoslovakia, where he might face persecution. As he wrote to the president of Bucknell University, in Pennsylvania: "To my sorrow my fate is not only in my own hands and my position is not the easiest in my country."[2]

Home, roots, language, family: To many Czechs, these things were more important than career. For a man who had devoted his life to literature, no choice seemed possible except returning to his home-land. Back in Prague, he found himself unpublishable. To support himself, he took a job as a hospital orderly, then as a street sweeper. He retained his sanity by hunting mushrooms in the forest by his house.

Klíma was no stranger to hardship. He witnessed the death of the First Republic and spent much of World War II living in the Terezín concentration camp, despite the fact that his family had converted to Christianity. In Terezín, more than 90 percent of the population either died of disease or were shipped to even more deadly camps in the East, such as Auschwitz. Klíma's survival was a minor miracle, one that left him with a profound sense of survivor's guilt.

The concentration camp proved to be a breeding ground for radi-cal politics of all kinds, especially communism. Klíma's father became a devout Marxist while they lived in Terezín, no doubt influenced by reports of the Red Army advancing toward the concentration camp, which he documented on maps he kept hidden in the barracks. His son, who would later befriend Havel, also became a communist, al-though it's not clear as to why. Even in his memoirs, Klíma admits he knew little about the politics of the Communist Party. In many ways, he was just following the spirit of the times, and the spirit of the times said that liberal democracy had failed and that it would be replaced by a grand utopia.

Years later, reflecting on the mistakes of his youth, Klíma wrote that the communist ideology satisfied "the need of people, especially the young, to rebel against a societal order they did not create them-selves, and did not consider their own."[3] Communism, he wrote, had given youth a sense of religious zeal. Marxism provided a simple sys-tem of ideas that could explain anything as long as one gave up the freedom of thinking for oneself.

As a postwar student at Charles University in Prague, Klíma was appalled by the purge of professors, and by the simpleminded way in which foreign literature was attacked by communists as degener-ate, but he nevertheless joined the Communist Youth League, read *The Communist Manifesto,* and practiced calling everyone in the movement "comrade." He was rewarded by being treated as a rock star. The Communist Party, through the Writer's Union, provided money, resources, and publishing opportunities. As Stalin had said, writers were the engineers of human souls, and Klíma became one of the most important Marxist writers of the era, first as an editor working for one of the leading newspapers in the country, where state censors received galley proofs of everything he wrote. In some ways, the process resembled the give-and-take one finds in any newsroom, except that the job of the censors wasn't to improve Klíma's writing but to standardize it, making every sentence conform to the position of the party. Censors rarely gave an explanation for why they spiked an article or made a change, preferring (as Klíma later said) to issue vague statements that the party had other priorities.[4]

Klíma first began harboring doubts about communism in the 1950s, when his father, Vilém, was imprisoned as part of the political infighting of that era that ended in the show trials and the hanging of the former general secretary of the Communist Party, Rudolf Slánský. Klíma remained a member of the Communist Party, but he also realized that the movement, while pursuing lofty goals, was prone to "baseness, lies, intrigues, or even villainy."[5] He remained officially in the party until 1967, when he and Havel (along with Milan Kundera, Pavel Kohout, and Ludvík Vaculík) criticized the censorship of artists at the Fourth Congress of the Writer's Union. The Central Committee immediately formed a disciplinary committee to look into the rebellion. Klíma, along with Vaculík and Kohout, were expelled from the party (as well as denied the right to speak at the hearing where the expulsion took place).

Klíma later recalled that he experienced the loss of his party membership with a sense of relief. He hardly worried about the cost of his rebellion, or so he remembered later. He was thirty-six years old, and he felt it was high time to choose his own path, one not dictated by doctrine or ideology—or by the fear of what authorities might say.[6]

In 1970, newly returned from the United States, Klíma began his monthly salon in order to recreate the experience of parties at the University of Michigan, where "everyone ate, chatted, listened to the latest records of Iron Butterfly, Joan Baez, Bob Dylan, and Cream, and maybe even smoked some pot." He was still full of "the energy and optimism" of living in the United States, and he wanted to create something that would lighten the literary mood in Prague, where everyone was still in shock or depressed from the Soviet invasion. The most important part of the evening would be having one of his friends—they were all banned writers—read a work in progress, which meant a work that could never be published, not in Czechoslovakia.[7] Carbon copies of the manuscripts were provided to everyone attending, a way of circulating the material.

The secret police got wind of his little enterprise within months of its founding. Using a hidden camera, the police recorded video of everyone who attended Klíma's salon, the footage of which was then played on state-run television, along with commentary that suggested the group was plotting to overthrow the government. Soon after the report aired, Klíma and a number of leading participants, including Havel, agreed that the salon was too dangerous to continue. At the last meeting in December 1970, everyone submitted humorous sketches based on a random word that had been plucked from the dictionary by the writer Karol Sidon, one of the few members who had not yet been banned.[8] The word he had put his finger on was *hromobiti*, and they all met to read humorous sketches whose central plot involved a thunderstorm.

By the time the literary salon came to an end, most of the important writers in Prague had been officially ghettoized. As Havel remembered later, the literary atmosphere was the picture of gloom. "The public knew us [writers] well," Havel said, "and were aware of us and sympathized with us, but at the same time they were careful not to have anything to do with us as it seemed too dangerous." With no contact with the public and little contact with one another, many of the writers retreated to their living rooms to write about their experiences, knowing that their work might never be published in their own country.[9]

Havel was one of the few writers in the country who had an international name, and he hoped to smuggle his manuscripts abroad, where there might still be a market for his plays. Even that scenario was fraught with literary dangers. It was difficult to know what to write and whether dedication and calling weren't, in fact, leading into an endless pit of despair. Still more difficult was the nagging question of moral responsibility to country and culture. Was it best to simply keep one's head down, avoiding the attention of the state? Or was there some form of positive action, of opposition and resistance, that made sense?

It would take years to find an answer.

Originally, liberals in Czechoslovakia used the term "normalization" to mean a return to the democratic reforms of the Prague Spring, including freedom of expression. But hard-line communists used the same term. For them, "normalization" meant giving absolute authority to the state. In their mind, returning to "normal" meant returning to the model of the Soviet Union, returning to a system built upon the titanic power of the party and its unquestioned supremacy.[10]

By the end 1971, it was clear which side had won. Just about everyone who didn't support the Soviet invasion was kicked out of the Communist Party. Those who held government posts were forced to renounce the Prague Spring or find a new job. Meanwhile, thousands of intellectuals were purged from universities, labs, and research centers. In order to compromise every employee in the country, the party added in 1971 a new item on the extensive questionnaire that was kept on every worker, asking if the Soviet invasion had been an occupation or "a brotherly attempt to stop counter-revolution in socialist Czechoslovakia."[11] There was only one right answer.

Although the party enjoyed unquestioned dominion over official society, in many respects its support was thinner than ever. Power was exerted by way of threats and the selected repression of a few individuals. Zdeněk Mlynář, who had been a member of the Central Committee during the Prague Spring, argued that normalization represented a new and more advanced form of tyranny in which the ideal was not to punish individuals but to compromise the entire society. In this new climate, the majority of citizens chose to support the

Communist Party in public while making jokes behind closed doors. Such a system of control—Havel would later call it a "post-totalitarian" system—worked by scuttling the moral compass of the entire society.

As a child, Havel had been raised by parents committed to humanistic democracy, to the belief that every citizen was responsible for fostering a civil society. Nothing was more central to the First Republic or to its first president, Tomáš G. Masaryk, who believed that democracy was rooted in philosophical and spiritual ideals. Havel had always believed that communism had "warped the minds" of party officials so that they could no longer perceive the ideals of liberal society. After the Soviet invasion, however, the situation got considerably worse. The few intelligent, self-reflective individuals who remained in high office found their position untenable. The retreat of good people from public life meant that influential positions now became occupied, Havel said, "by notorious careerists, opportunists, charlatans, and men of dubious record; in short, by typical collaborators, men, that is, with a special gift for persuading themselves at every turn that their dirty work is a way of rescuing something, or, at least, of preventing still worse men from stepping into their shoes." From Havel's point of view, the entire cultural situation was a catastrophe and a crisis in human identity.[12]

In the fall of 1972, as the forests were turning yellow and orange, Olga and Václav Havel drove to Prague to move into a newly built apartment in the Dejvice district, on the northeastern outskirts.[13] They had been on a waiting list for housing for twelve years, looking for an apartment in the city they could call their own. The apartment was three blocks from Evropská Boulevard, which ran long and straight from Prague Six to the airport. In the other direction, trams scooted back through the hills and across the Vltava River to the center of the city.

The new apartment came at an opportune time. Havel's brother and his wife were returning to Prague, to the old family apartment on the embankment that they would share with Havel and Ivan's father (his mother died in 1970). Ivan and his wife had been living in California, where Ivan finished his Ph.D. in computer science at the University of California at Berkeley, having been given permission to attend in 1969, just before the borders closed. While in California, Ivan socialized with Czech émigrés who seemed to live a life of contradiction, having won their personal freedom while losing their connection to home, country, and family. Like Ivan Klíma, and many other intellectuals who remained in Prague, Ivan couldn't imagine such a life.[14]

After returning to Prague, Ivan attempted to return to his old job as a computer scientist at the Institute of Information Theory and Automation, where he had been on official leave to pursue his doctorate. The director, perhaps surprised that Ivan would return to Czechoslovakia, told him on his first day back that it was impossible to work at the institute, given his brother's notoriety. Eventually, however, he did find a job at the Czech Academy of Sciences, which regarded his knowledge in computers as indispensable. Ivan's work involved pure science, and such work was relatively free from the scrutiny faced by professionals who worked in university or government positions, although they were still required to file a report any time they encountered a foreigner. Ivan managed to hold on to his job at the Academy of Sciences for seven years, until the secret police pressured the Academy of Sciences into firing him for being the brother of a dissident.[15]

Václav and Olga never considered returning to Prague full time, but they did spend considerable time and money creating a cozy nest at U dejvického rybníčku 4, in the Dejvice district, where they stayed on their many forays into the city. As at Hrádeček, Havel obsessed over every detail of the decorating, managing it as if it were one of the plays he could no longer produce. He covered the walls with expensive modern art, including the erotic photography of Jan Saudek, whose surrealistic and highly sexualized nudes upset some visitors. And he commissioned an architect to hand-design avant-garde furniture, which gave the apartment a clean, hypermodern sensibility that some found impersonal.[16]

As Havel himself realized, his obsession with interior decorating (which he would later lampoon in a one-act play) was a form of escapism, a way to avoid facing the uncertainty of life. Focusing on the material parameters of his apartment gave a feeling of control, while also making it easier to ignore the outside world.

The Havels remained in Prague during the fall and winter of 1972, draining their bank account with a dizzying number of renovations, which provided relief from the fact that Havel found it impossible to work on a new play. The city felt cold and distant, and he found little comfort with his literary friends, who were either frustrated by working conditions or, if they had already lost their jobs, "nervous and neurotic" from the fact that they no longer had an outlet for their creative talents. As he wrote to Věra Blackwell, the Prague of his childhood now felt "oppressive."[17]

As soon as the spring snows melted, the Havels returned to Hrádeček, where Havel grew out his hair, in the shaggy fashion of the 1970s, and added a thin wispy mustache, giving him the look of a bohemian writer. One of the friends who visited them often that spring and summer was Pavel Landovský, a gregarious actor who had once worked at the Theater on the Balustrade. Landovský and Havel were something of an odd couple, Landovský playing the motorcycle-riding tomcat who drank hard and chased women. Olga had always regarded Landovský as a rogue, perhaps because he had a habit of "kidnapping" Havel to go out drinking late into the night. When Landovský was around, booze and women were plentiful.

Despite their differences, the two men seemed to complement each other. A series of photographs from the time shows them sitting together in an unnamed pub, Havel wrapped in a scarf and coat, his shoulders bent. His eyes are downcast, his gestures introverted. Across the table, Landovský is rolling his eyes, jabbing a forceful finger high into the air.[18] Landovský was the carefree, outgoing man that Havel wanted to be, and Havel was the sober intellectual whose respect Landovský craved. The two became intimate friends throughout much of the 1970s, until Landovský emigrated to Austria, but the friendship was often tested by Landovský's taste for wild pranks. On one occasion, he and Jan Němec, a film director, kidnapped Havel's Mercedes for several days, forcing Havel to track them down in a Prague pub, where the meeting devolved into shouting and mutual insults.[19] On another occasion, Havel lent Landovský his car only to find out that Landovský, presumably drunk, drove it into a tree. No one was injured and the Mercedes was unharmed except for a dent in the front fender. The police used the accident to suspend Landovský's driver's license, as well as Havel's, even though he hadn't been in the car at the time of the accident. As Havel told Věra Blackwell, the state was finding new ways to expand their "political and existential persecution."[20]

One of the most important tests of normalization came in 1972, when the playwright Pavel Kohout prepared a rough draft of a petition requesting that the government release "political prisoners" for the Christmas holidays. Havel and Kohout had been close friends since the 1967 Congress for the Union of Writers, where they had given blistering speeches against the establishment. Since then, they had formed a mutual admiration club. Kohout asked Havel to edit his petition and gather signatures, which was sure to catch the attention of the state.

The petition itself was neither long nor complicated. It simply noted that the signers, while differing widely on many social matters, agreed "that magnanimity regarding political prisoners cannot in any way threaten the authority and capacity of the state's power."[21] It's unclear how many political prisoners were in the prison system, but the number had been growing since the Soviet invasion. Although Havel had not been jailed for signing the Ten Points Petition in 1969, several others had, including chess grandmaster Luděk Pachman, who had been charged with sedition. Tortured in prison, he attempted suicide on Christmas Eve 1969. Another group of political prisoners belonged to a radical communist group led by Petr Uhl. Forty-seven members of his organization were imprisoned after publishing a manifesto criticizing normalization.[22]

Havel and Kohout began gathering signatures shortly before the

Christmas holidays of 1972; they were joined by Ivan Klíma, who had formed the first underground literary salon, and Ludvík Vaculík. The group split into two pairs, with Havel and Kohout visiting some writers and Klíma and Vaculík visiting others. They met immediate resistance from better-known writers who seemed embarrassed by their unwillingness to sign. Some argued that the petition would only annoy the government, or worse, that Havel and Kohout "were trying to drag down those who still had their heads above water into their own abyss by misusing their charity."[23]

After the four men had gathered thirty-four signatures, Vaculík was picked up by the secret police. From the paranoid point of view of the state, the petition was an international conspiracy, an attempt to undermine socialism, possibly involving International PEN, an organization for writers that had recently formed a committee to support banned writers in Eastern Europe.[24]

One of the first to be brought in for questioning was Ivan Klíma. Two interrogators sat him down in a small, third-floor room of the state security headquarters on Bartolomějská Street, asking him endless questions about who had approached him with the petition. When Klíma refused to reveal any information, the room grew heated until the agents made a number of veiled threats. After a barrage of questions about his activities, his foreign income, and his support of the "criminals" he wanted to release from prison, the conversation turned back again to the matter at hand. One of the interrogators, named Nezval, began shouting: "Now, for the last time, tell us who came to see you with this piece of paper. Was it Vaculík? Havel? [Alexander] Kliment?" Klíma refused to answer, and the interrogator took a different tactic.

"What were you talking with Kliment about yesterday?" he asked. "You think we don't know you were at his place?" Klíma told them he didn't remember. "What don't you remember?" the interrogator asked. Klíma said nothing. The conversation went on in this vein for a considerable length of time, probably for several hours, and ended with an offer to allow Klíma to reveal everything he knew anonymously in order to save face with his friends. Klíma refused, which earned him a rebuke from one of the interrogators, who lied to him and said they had already interrogated Havel, who had provided them with all the information they needed. His friends, the interrogator said, would be laughing at him for holding out for so long.[25] Havel hadn't given up any information, of course, but such techniques could be effective at times, causing an individual in interrogation to reveal more than he or she wished.

Kohout's petition was later borrowed by Milan Kundera for literary purposes. In *The Unbearable Lightness of Being*, Kundera presents a slightly stooped dissident, evidently based on Havel, who is collecting signatures from "the most important Czech intellectuals, the ones who still mean something." One of the conceits in the novel is that the petition is an act of exhibitionism, an attempt by desperate men to prove they still mattered. Or worse, to emotionally blackmail others into signing a petition so that they, too, will be in just as much trouble with the regime. One of the main characters in the novel, Tomáš, is incensed at being asked to sign the petition, since it puts him in the awkward position of either appearing cowardly or facing persecution.[26]

Havel never cared for Kundera's novel, and believed that Kundera was trapped by his own cynicism. Far from being meaningless, Havel thought such petitions helped the culture imagine what was possible. In a totalitarian society, no action could have immediate results, but taking a moral stand was designed to encourage the growth of something new in the "hidden sphere" of society. Unlike Kundera, Havel also thought such petitions forced the Communist Party to back off on its prosecutions since it now had to consider the prospect of future protests. "I don't want to do Kundera an injustice," Havel later said, when asked about their differing points of view. Havel went on: "Naturally there may be a little of what Kundera is ridiculing in every petition and perhaps in every signature. That is why I can't hold his ridicule against him, especially since it was in a novel. What I hold against him is something else: that he does not see, or willfully refuses to see, the other side of all those things, those aspects that are less obvious, more hidden, but more hopeful as well. I mean the indirect and long-term significance that these things can or may have."[27] What was the long-term significance of a petition? Havel thought people were learning to stand up for the rule of law.

After closing down his literary salon in 1972, Ivan Klíma and his colleague Ludvík Vaculík visited a sympathetic lawyer who advised them that under law it remained legal to distribute copies of a literary work, as long as no financial profit was involved. In other words, writers had the right to distribute a manuscript, as long as they weren't publishing it, selling it, or making a profit of any kind. Dozens or even hundreds of such manuscripts could be handed out, as long as the literary work remained aloof from any business enterprise.

The idea of creating an underground publishing system clearly appealed to both men, especially Vaculík, who was an iconoclast and eccentric, long known for his principled stands against the regime. Like Klíma, Vaculík was extremely close to Havel during those years, having taken to calling him "Mr. Václav" in the Old European manner of calling a gentleman by his first name. With his legal advice in hand, Vaculík made copies of his own novel, *The Guinea Pigs*, which he distributed among friends under the suggestive name of Padlock Press (Edice Petlice). Next, he published Havel's play *The Beggar's Opera*, and then a novel by Pavel Kohout and the verses of Jaroslav Seifert, the great Czech poet who would later win a Nobel Prize in literature. Under Vaculík's influence, home publishing became something of a new art form, providing "banned" writers with a small but erudite audience.

In the early 1970s, there was no name for what Vaculík was doing. Officially, Padlock Press was neither a business nor a publisher, since it claimed (somewhat dubiously) to be distributing manuscripts among friends as private entertainment, much as one might send a letter. Some began referring to Vaculík's products as "unofficial literature," or even as "unbooks." Vaculík himself used the term *samizdat*, a Russian word meaning "self-published." The term had first been coined in the 1940s by a Russian poet who was referring to a typewritten, bound copy of his own poems that he circulated with fellow poets. A few such manuscripts had been distributed in Czechoslovakia in the 1950s, but Vaculík now turned samizdat into a cultural movement. By 1989 his "company" had published more than four hundred titles in fiction and poetry.

In the early days of Padlock Press, the manuscripts were typed by Vaculík's mistress, Zdena. By using carbon paper, she could create eight books at once on thin onionskin typing paper, the final few carbons being so light they were difficult to read. Final corrections were then made directly on each manuscript. If more than eight copies of an edition were needed, the entire book was typed a second or third time, and each book was passed person-to-person, eventually reaching scores or hundreds of readers.

Originally, samizdat books were "published" in a three-ring binder. In later years, after the operations got more sophisticated, the loose-leaf pages were secretly sent to a state-run bindery for finishing, and each copy was signed by the author, making it appear like a personal copy.[28] To further satisfy legal requirements, Vaculík included a statement on the title page that "further copying of this manuscript is forbidden." Vaculík loved a good joke. In Czech, the statement formed the acronym VZDOR, a Czech word meaning "resistance."[29]

Overseeing Padlock Press was exhausting. Vaculík often had to handle editing and proofreading himself, as well as production, distribution, and subscriptions, meaning he had to personally collect cash from everyone who ordered a publication so that he could keep the whole operation going. Distribution was a complex and tricky affair. No one in the underground post knew more than two links in the distribution system, meaning that they only knew the person who handed them a samizdat book and the person they gave the book to.[30]

Despite his many provocations, the state refused to prosecute Vaculík for running Padlock Press, calculating that imprisoning a world-famous writer might cause more problems than it would solve. Instead, the secret police undertook a campaign of harassment, interrogating Vaculík on hundreds of occasions and bugging his apartment for years on end. He and his wife learned to avoid any conversations in their home that they didn't want to be overheard by the state, instead communicating on slate board that could be immediately erased. When they did use paper to write longer notes to each other, they immediately tore them up and flushed them down the toilet.[31]

The overall impact of such samizdat operations is hard to overstate. When the Eastern European scholar H. Gordon Skilling traveled to Czechoslovakia in 1975, he wrote that the nation had become a Soviet province, with Czech and Slovak culture on the verge of being lost forever.[32] That never happened, in part because of the spread of samizdat, which expanded significantly in 1975 when Havel decided to create his own samizdat brand, Expedition Edition (Edice Expedice). Whereas Vaculík had focused mostly on publishing Czech literature, Havel expanded his offerings to include philosophy, poetry, scholarly works, and translations of works from Western countries. After Havel was jailed in 1978, Havel's wife, Olga, and his brother, Ivan, took over the operation until they were detained themselves in 1981. In all, Expedition Edition published 232 titles, all of them books that were unofficially banned in Czechoslovakia.[33]

Although Havel once appeared to entertain illusions that he might make a separate peace with the regime by living at Hrádeček, such fantasies were dispelled in the early 1970s when the Ministry of Finance began targeting his only source of income. In a new law aimed at dissidents, writers such as Havel were no longer allowed to keep the money they earned from Western publishers. Instead, writers who were designated as "anti-socialist" were required to exchange their hard currency for Tuzex crowns at one-fifth of the rate of other writers. In addition, they were forced to "donate" another 40 percent of their foreign income to a literary fund, meaning that more than 90 percent of their writing income was being confiscated by the state.[34]

Unfortunately for Havel, the new rules came at a time when his foreign audience was disappearing. Since the time of the Soviet occupation, Havel had worked on two plays (as well as on an idea for a comic book), all of them going nowhere. The most promising prospect had been *The Conspirators*, which Havel sent to Věra Blackwell in 1971, asking her to make a translation to present to National Theater in London. The director of the theater, Kenneth Tynan, had practically begged Havel for the play, sending him an advance before he had seen it. After reading *The Conspirators*, however, Tynan's enthusiasm cooled. He didn't know what to make of the play, nor did he think it would work in England.[35] There were other problems as well, including the legal question of whether it was even possible, given Havel's legal troubles with the state, to purchase the production rights, or whether the Czechoslovakian government would make an incident if the play were produced abroad. The most difficult issue, however, was that *The Conspirators* didn't feel like a play that had been written by a banned writer. As a provocateur, Tynan wanted a dissident play, a play that would stand up to the tyranny of the communist system, while Havel had written an avant-garde exploration of paranoia. And given his long, often excruciating writing process, he had done so while missing repeated deadlines over more than a year. Czechoslovakia no longer seemed topical.[36]

In the end, the deal fell apart, and *The Conspirators* premiered much later in a German theater before disappearing quietly into oblivion.[37] Upon some reflection, Havel admitted he wasn't surprised, telling Blackwell that the play suffered from "not going through the fire" of creative collaboration that he had enjoyed while working at the Balustrade. But even though the play had its flaws, he couldn't face working on it anymore. It would be better to kill the play than to go back through the revision process. He had been working on the play too long, he said. If there were still problems, they were probably in the very foundations of the story.[38]

By the time Havel gave up on *The Conspirators*, he was working on another play, *Mountain Hotel*, which he wrote and rewrote over the next five years. Havel thought of *Mountain Hotel* as an "existential Dada" gag.[39] As he wrote the play, he removed all of the traditional features of storytelling, such as plot, continuity, and fixed characters. The result, in Havel's mind, was "a nostalgic and vaguely unsettling poem about a world with no firm center, no fixed identity, no past and no future, with no coherence or order." He wrote the play as a kind of experiment, he said, and he told others that it didn't really matter whether the play was staged.[40] That wasn't exactly true. Havel worried about the play endlessly, telling friends (such as the director Alfréd Radok) that he wasn't sure he could pull it off.[41] He didn't.

Writing directly for foreign audiences proved to be a psychological minefield. Plays are public by nature, and Havel had gained his first success in the theater by connecting directly with the feelings and live undercurrents of the audience at the Balustrade, men and women he knew through daily interaction in the streets of Prague. How do you write for a foreign audience you've never met? Havel seemed to be stumped. He could never quite get to the obvious conclusion that he should just keep writing plays as he always had, for the same Czech audience, since that's what had led to his initial success abroad. Havel felt lost at sea.

The distance and language barriers didn't help matters, nor that the government had cut Havel's telephone lines and regularly interrupted his mail. In moments of paranoia, it even seemed to him that foreign producers were afraid of angering the Czech government. On November 1, 1971, for instance, Havel wrote to Blackwell that "it bewilders me a little that my foreign partners in Hamburg and London are more afraid of the regime here than I am, and I'm the one who lives here and is even indicted." He wondered if Tynan was distancing himself because he feared becoming involved in some kind of intrigue. "Perhaps he's even become afraid of us?" Havel wrote.[42]

The lack of foreign cooperation was infuriating. By the spring of 1972, Havel hadn't held a job in four years. His money was running out. In England, there were rumors that he was battered by depression, having fallen victim to drugs and alcohol. The reality was much more nuanced. He was reading a great deal and writing occasionally. Sometimes he gardened with Olga or worked in the orchard. Emotionally, however, he began to guard himself once again, much as he had after the Soviet invasion, avoiding any kind of emotion, he wrote, that was "so big it could quickly change into depression."[43]

# 8

## AN OPEN LETTER

IN THE OUTER DISTRICTS, SOCIALIST-ERA HOUSING projects loomed over long, wide boulevards, but getting into central Prague meant crawling through a maze of narrow streets and neighborhoods. In order to relieve the congestion, in 1974 the city opened up an underground metro system built by Soviet engineers. From his apartment in the Dejvice district, Havel could now walk to Lenin Station in fifteen minutes and travel under earth and stone to anywhere in the city for just ten cents.[1]

At the same time that Soviet engineers were constructing the underground metro, a different set of underground networks were being formed in living rooms and kitchens throughout Prague. Some of these groups were devoted to literature or theater, others to music, and still others to professors who, having been banned from the universities, began lecturing in their homes in the style of an underground university. In Prague alone, there were at least forty such underground networks, all of them existing in the shadowland between illegal activity and action that was technically legal but extremely frowned upon by the state. None of the groups were talking to each other. Everyone lived in a state of paranoia.[2]

Beginning in the early 1970s, Havel launched his own version of living-room culture, inviting a group of banned writers to Hrádeček for what he called, somewhat ironically, a "writer's congress," a reference to the meetings that had been organized by the writer's unions for those whose work was supported by the state. Havel continued hosting his underground congress each year for more than a decade. Those in attendance were the usual suspects, many of them writers who had attended Ivan Klíma's literary salon. Many, like Klíma, were former communists who had all taken part in pushing for the reforms of the Prague Spring.[3] The chief players were Klíma, Pavel Kohout, Ludvík Vaculík, and Karel Kosík, a philosopher who wrote a book that explored the mistakes and frauds committed by Marxists.[4]

In addition to meeting with ex-communists, Havel gathered a second group, this one consisting of strident anti-communists. These were literary types he had met during the Prague Spring at the Circle of Independent Writers: Zdeněk Urbánek, Jiří Gruša, Josef Topol, and others.[5] Taken together, the two groups represented a sizable number of the best writers in the country. All of them visited Hrádeček regularly and merged, at least into Havel's mind, into one group, perhaps partly because they all shared the common problem of how to make a living as banned writers.

Kohout and Klíma attempted to solve the problem by publishing translations of their books in Switzerland. Others took to literary odd jobs, such as translating foreign literature into Czech, usually working under a pseudonym or the name of a sympathetic friend. Vaculík, for instance, often took anonymous work that was paid in cash by editors, ensuring the transaction could never be tracked down. It wasn't enough money to provide a real income, and he often had to resort to the kindness of strangers, such as dentists and plumbers, who showed solidarity by refusing to let him pay his bills, giving him a wink to let him know that they sympathized with his cause.[6] Klíma had similar experiences. Despite being an enemy of the state, he drew a disability pension concocted by a friendly doctor.[7]

Kohout was the most colorful figure of the group and Havel's closest literary friend in the early 1970s. The two couldn't have been more unalike. A brilliant and braggadocio playwright with a cocksure personality, Kohout had once been the most famous communist writer in the country. Kohout's great ambition had been to become the poet of the 1948 revolution, something like a Czech version of the American journalist John Reed, who chronicled the Russian Revolution. On the eve of the 1948 coup d'état, he had practically lived in the communist headquarters, which was hidden behind sandbags and machine guns on Old Town Square. Later, schoolchildren were forced to memorize his poems praising Stalin and the Communist Party. "With one hand I write verse, in the other I hold my gun," went one of his famous lines from the 1940s.

Kohout's private doubts about communism surfaced early. Like most Czechs, he saw a number of profound injustices, including a girlfriend who was prevented from finishing high school because of her class background. Later, when he served as a cultural attaché in Moscow, he saw the horrors of the Soviet system firsthand and had a personal scare when the Soviets accused him of spying. By the late 1950s, Kohout suffered crying fits at night, convinced that his personal guilt and "idiotic innocence" had helped destroy his country. The communist revolution, he was convinced, had been run by charlatans.[8]

Despite their differences, Havel relished Kohout's company and his flair for drama. Havel was also warming up to Kohout's martial discipline, his love of battle. By the early 1970s, Kohout was telling his fellow writers that totalitarianism was a gift. Literature, Kohout argued, was the "only thing that does well in oppression." They were lucky. In Western countries, writers had to search for problems, while Czech writers had something to write about.[9] Kohout was also a devil at challenging his colleagues to begin new work, to try new styles, to keep their noses to the grindstone. He once dared Havel to write a play about a man who, like Havel, had a minor speech impediment, and Havel responded within a few weeks with a short, outrageous parody of himself and a psychiatrist.[10] A similar autobiographical impulse led Havel to write a short, one-act play titled *Audience*, which was originally written as entertainment for his friends. The first colleague to read the play was Kohout, who immediately recognized it as a work of genius. He was so charmed by the central character, Vaněk, that Kohout later inserted the same character into two plays of his own.[11] Havel was delighted with the experiment, and at least two other Czech playwrights wrote plays about Vaněk, who also made an appearance in Tom Stoppard's play *Rock 'n' Roll*.

The unusual friendship between Kohout and Havel was part of the extraordinary atmosphere being created at Hrádeček, part of a trans-political solidarity between classes and ideologies. Kohout, for instance, had once eagerly participated in helping to confiscate the property of "the bourgeois," including that of the rich and beautiful medical student he fell in love with in the 1948 revolution. As he recounted in a memoir, he had wooed her, on the night they first made love, by telling her she was "a typical daughter of a class which is incapable of creating anything of real value, which only knows how to make money. Can you wonder that we hate you so much?" In typical Kohout fashion, he vowed to marry the woman the next morning, saying to himself, "She'll make a man out of me. And I'll make a communist out of her."[12]

Whatever their previous history, the writers gathering at Hrádeček were becoming a small but vibrant community that was trying to understand, on a deep level, what had happened to each of them and to the country. Reflecting later on their meetings, Kohout said the group had learned to understand one another without surrendering their own personal convictions or individuality, discovering, beneath the history of the past, what they all held in common.[13]

One of the things the group was discovering at Hrádeček was that their old political differences no longer mattered. Like his Uncle Miloš, Havel was rediscovering that he was at his most creative in the company of others. He enjoyed the spark and catalytic energy from opposing points of view. With his deeply intuitive sense of order, he had a knack for seeing how each perspective could be woven into a cohesive whole, even when each of the participants violently disagreed. Just about everyone marveled at his ability to find a middle ground, his ability to articulate the differences between points of view. He was, in short, a man who was not only open to ideas but who was thrilled at seeing them discussed and reconciled.

Sometime in 1974 Kohout tried out his own experiment in writing a play to amuse his friends at the annual Hrádeček writer's conference. The conceit of the play was that Havel, Klíma, Vaculík, himself, and a few others had taken up arms against the state.[14] Kohout set the action in a "perfectly hidden foxhole" that seemed to resemble Havel's Prague apartment, and the play itself is also full of inside jokes about the affairs, foibles, and peccadillos of everyone involved. Havel speaks in ridiculously obscure paradoxes and tries to hide one of his many affairs; Vaculík constantly hawks his samizdat material; Klíma worries over having no time to write his short stories; and Kohout struts about the apartment with an itch to put a machine gun in his hand. Together, they develop a plan to blow up a railroad. The plan is brilliant but hopelessly disorganized, lacking military discipline. As Kohout shouts at one point, "This is not a conspiracy, it's a mess."[15]

Aside from the sexual innuendos,[16] part of the fun in Kohout's play is the military fantasy, the idea of writers and intellectuals at war. There is a long history in the Czech lands of writers who served as the conscience of the nation, not least František Palacký, the nineteenth-century writer who helped plant the idea of Czech independence from the Austria-Hungarian empire with *History of the Czech Nation*, and, of course, the first president of Czechoslovakia, Tomáš G. Masaryk, had been a university professor who had written eight books of serious philosophy. For Kohout, it was entirely logical to think of writers as *like* partisans, or guerilla fighters, just as Havel always saw his role as a playwright as essentially political, as helping the culture understand itself.

While it was true that Czechoslovakia had no "underground" in a classical sense, Havel and Kohout saw themselves as creating a metaphorical underground that would fight the war of ideas. By 1974, Kohout and Havel had taken to speaking in code when they thought they might be overheard by listening devices. On several occasions, Havel sent Kohout notes under a fake name, an obvious attempt to throw off anyone rifling through Kohout's mail.[17] Such intrigue came naturally to Kohout, who had been active in the 1948 revolution. He served as a tutor of sorts to Havel while constantly complaining, in typical Kohout fashion, that Havel remained as leaky as a broken coffee cup when it came to clandestine activities.

The letters from the 1970s give us a sense of the game they played, the ways in which they lightheartedly prepared for confrontation with the state. In one early letter, Kohout jokingly told Havel to eat his letter as soon as he finished reading it.[18] In another letter, Kohout described being interrogated for twelve hours in response to granting an interview with a foreign journalist. During the interrogation, Kohout reported, he refused to speak to the secret police. From his point of view, answering a question meant admitting that the secret police had the legal right to interrogate him. Rather than respond to questions, he lectured the police over the way they were defiling the Czech constitution. Kohout's tactic infuriated the agents so much that one of them got muddled and called him "Mr. Havel."[19]

How to face interrogations was a topic of interest to both men. Havel replied to Kohout that his own practice for the past fifteen years had been to create a dialogue with police, answering their questions as reasonably as possible. He was now rethinking his approach, however, and he decided that in future interrogations he would refuse to discuss anything except politics, the law, and constitutional rights.

The stakes were high for both men. In 1973, the secret police burned down the Kohout weekend house, apparently to send him a warning. Kohout wrote to Havel the same day, advising Havel to immediately get fire insurance for his own house at Hrádeček.[20] Havel received the news of the fire well ahead of Kohout's letter, by way of state radio. As soon as he heard about the fire, he and Olga opened a bottle of vodka, to toast Kohout and to mourn the loss of his weekend paradise.

By the early 1970s, seemingly invisible networks of opposition were emerging in many areas of society. The American embassy, in a confidential cable, estimated that this opposition to the country included at least four thousand former communists. In an analysis of the situation, the embassy said that "the opposition, accepting the passive character of many Czechoslovak citizens and the overwhelming military and police apparatus backing the government, realizes that no 'Vietnam or Ireland' will be possible here. Still, Czechs admire intellectuals who are brave enough and clever enough to seize the moment and speak out. The regime is like pig iron, so strong and yet so fragile."[21]

Two of the most important leaders of the reform communists were Zdeněk Mlynář and Jiří Hájek, former political leaders of the Prague Spring. Mlynář had been a stalwart communist since 1946, working his way up through the ranks. In April 1968, with the help of Alexander Dubček, he became a member of the presidium, a handful of individuals who oversaw the Central Committee of the Communist Party. Like many others in the party, he originally saw Marx, Engels, and Lenin as infallible guides to organizing both society and his personal life. When he was expelled from the party two years later, after the Soviet invasion, he was a changed man. The expulsion, he later wrote, liberated him from the straitjacket of communist ideology. Mlynář still considered himself a socialist, but he believed passionately in democratic reform.[22]

Like Mlynář, Jiří Hájek was an intellectual who spent a lifetime working for the cause of socialism, ideas he had picked up while living in a Nazi concentration camp during World War II. In the 1950s and early 1960s, he worked as a professor, ambassador to Great Britain, minister of education, and a member of the Central Committee before becoming a foreign minister during the Prague Spring. His chief interest as foreign minister had been developing a closer relationship with Western Europe, which earned him the enmity of the Soviet Union. During the 1968 invasion, which found him vacationing in the former Yugoslavia, he flew immediately to New York, pleading for help before the United Nations. As a result, he became both a national hero and a pariah who lived under constant police surveillance for the next twenty years.

After Hájek's expulsion from the Communist Party in 1969, he remained in contact with other former communists, as well as former students who used their background in international intelligence to pass him confidential reports on the inner workings of the government. One of his private sleuths was Miroslav Pohlreich, a former protégé who had been with Hájek at the United Nations and was now passing Hájek top-secret intelligence reports on dissidents through a third party who visited Hájek's house on a weekly basis.[23]

Few people would eventually have a more influential role in developing an effective dissident movement than Jiří Hájek. He had the name, the gravitas, and the connections among world leaders. He was also intimately familiar with the Conference on Security and Cooperation in Europe, which had been meeting since 1972 to build an international agreement, later known as the Helsinki Accords, to ease the tensions of the Cold War. Hájek became among the first to recognize that those accords could be the basis for a human rights movement, one that would be protected by international treaties being negotiated by the Czechoslovakian government.

Havel and Jiří Hájek hardly knew each other before 1976, moving in different social circles. That was about to change, however, and the consequences would be profound.

In late February 1974, Havel woke up at 4:30 a.m. and drove Merda, his Mercedes, ten kilometers down an icy road piled high with snow. In the village of Trutnov, he parked his car several blocks from the brewery, part of his intricate plan to arouse as little excitement as possible. Havel had been looking for a job for the past half year, and the brewery was the only employer willing to hire him.

After punching a time card at 6 a.m., Havel's routine was to change into overalls and a work coat, then head out to whatever odd jobs were handed his way, cleaning rust from old pipes, dragging junk from place to place, clearing debris. He worked until half past four and returned home from the brewery hungry and exhausted. The first month on the job he ruptured a hernia, which tortured him all day, leaving him feeling sick and nauseated much of the time.[24]

The hours at the brewery were long, at least for a man used to working at a desk, and he was often cold and wet for hours at a time. The hard work may have been good for his spirits, however. After spending the past four years without any daily employment, Havel felt relieved to have a regular schedule. He told friends that it "was quite calming" to know that he could handle the physical demands of manual labor.[25]

To his surprise, Havel discovered that the workers at the brewery accepted him easily. He even felt he shared a secret bond with them, a mutual sense that they were all outcasts.[26] The brewery was an employer of last resort, a harbor for anyone who couldn't find work elsewhere, full of drunks, desperadoes, gypsies, and enemies of the state.[27] Many drank beer all day at work. After work, they went to the pub to get smashed.

Although Havel told friends he took the job because of money woes, that was only half true. Havel worked at the brewery for almost a year at seventeen hundred crowns a month for a grand total of just under twenty thousand Czech crowns, or less than a thousand American dollars. In the past three years, he had spent at least ten times that much, if not quite a bit more, on renovations at Hrádeček and the family apartment in Prague and purchasing his Mercedes. The foreign royalties from just one play would cover a decade of backbreaking work at the brewery, meaning it would have been far more efficient to spend his time writing for the foreign theater.

It would probably be closer to the truth to say that Havel needed a change in his daily routine. He seems to have believed that holding down a full-time job would somehow, magically, make him more productive, forcing him to manage his time more effectively, especially if he could lay his hands on some pep pills. With this in mind, Havel wrote to Kohout asking him if he knew where to find "vitamin F." Feeling somewhat defensive, Havel also wrote Kohout that taking the job at the brewery wasn't a result of masochism or "a provocation for attention." Instead, he wrote that it was an "attempt to refresh my relationship with reality."[28]

Havel put the situation in different terms when he wrote to Alfréd Radock, the director who had recently emigrated to Sweden. Havel told Radock that his life had become unbearable. Not only was Havel losing hope that "the situation in the country had some reason or sense," but he found it impossible to write. For one thing, the idea of completing a play for a theater in a foreign country filled him with panic. He had tried his hand on a number of ideas, but in the end the work ended up "as dead as a cold fish."[29]

Havel's correspondence with Radock is a fascinating glimpse into Havel's internal state of mind in the early 1970s, revealing a man who had grown dissatisfied with life and bored with himself. "I am the kind of social type who can't stand to stay for years in the background, even if it is in relative luxury," he wrote Radock. He felt that he was beginning to boil over with a kind of self-directed rage, a sense that this "relatively calm life of retirement is nothing more than one big laziness." In moments of introspection, he accused himself of frittering away his time when he should have been reading piles of books and learning a foreign language.[30]

Havel later recalled the early 1970s as "bland, boring, and bleak," a time of "moribund silence" in which his own life seemed like "a single, shapeless fog."[31] Working at the brewery did serve to shake up his personal world. Working among the dispossessed gave Havel a whole new, fascinating universe to study. He threw himself into learning how the brewery organized itself, how the barrels were manufactured, and how the beer was made. After two months, the director promoted him to the warehouse, where Havel's job was to roll beer barrels into the fermentation cellar. Havel beamed at his new position in life. He joked to Kohout in a letter that he now occupied "a position of national importance," an ironic reference to the value of beer in Czech society.[32]

Unfortunately, working at the brewery also created a new confrontation with the state. Shortly after Havel received the new job, officials in the regional Communist Party headquarters asked the brewmaster to keep a close eye on his activities. In order to simplify his life, the brewmaster asked Havel to write reports on himself in exchange for a cozy job, presumably working at a desk, an offer Havel declined.[33]

Nothing could have been more absurd in his own mind than being asked to inform on himself.

In 1974 Havel had little knowledge of the "unofficial" music scene except for a few "wild . . . and distorted stories" about a group that called themselves "the underground," outcasts who imitated the hippie movement in the United States. If the movement had a leader, it was Ivan Jirous, the musical director of a psychedelic band known as the Plastic People of the Universe, a reference to Frank Zappa and the Velvet Underground. The teenagers in the band were so influenced by Zappa that they sang his songs in English. The government had revoked the band's professional license to play music in 1970, making it illegal for them to perform in public.[34]

Jirous imagined the musical underground as a spiritual space. As an academic, he had studied the American counterculture, and he saw his role as akin to the one Andy Warhol played for the Velvet Underground.[35] Just as Warhol raised the profile of the Velvet Underground in New York City, Jirous championed the Plastic People of the Universe in lectures around Czechoslovakia, where he described rock 'n' roll as a serious form of social protest.[36]

By 1974 underground concerts were taking place almost every weekend, events known as "going to the mountains." The concerts, often in the backyards of village homes or in cottages in the woods, served as pilgrimage sites. There were no flyers or advertisements, and the exact location of these concerts were disclosed no more than a day in advance. Invitations were passed by word of mouth.[37]

What did the audience come to hear? The lyrics were subversive, rebellious, vulgar, and antiestablishment, celebrating raw emotion over technique. When one of the band members, Vratislav Brabenec, played dead drunk, Jirous bragged that "you could clearly see that he was drunk through and through, that the music was emerging, independently of his condition, directly from the inside."[38]

Sometime after Havel stopped working at the brewery, one of the members of the Plastic People of the Universe sent an envoy to meet with Havel. The envoy was Franta Smejkal, an old friend, and when he showed up unannounced with a bottle of cognac, Havel was sitting alone at his writing table at Hrádeček during a February snowstorm. The two ended up drinking cognac all night long, discussing the old days in Prague. At some point, Franta told Havel what was happening in the music underground. Drunk on brandy, Franta told Havel that he should get together with Ivan Jirous and "brainstorm" ways to collaborate.[39]

A month later, Havel met Jirous and a number of other long-haired musicians in a Prague apartment. As Havel remembered it, the meeting did not start off well. Jirous and the others saw him "as a member of the official, and officially tolerated, opposition—in other words, a member of the establishment." Further, as Jirous told Havel as soon as they were introduced, he suspected that Havel was a paid police informant.[40]

Havel was no doubt guarded himself, fed by accounts that the musicians were vulgar oddballs, but he had also decided that it was vital for the different undergrounds to begin working together, not least because the groups were often afraid and suspicious of one another. After he explained the idea to Jirous, the two retired to a basement apartment to talk. To illustrate the philosophy of the music underground, Jirous read poetry and played music by the Plastic People of the Universe and another rock band while "long hair people" came and went. For Havel, the experience seemed magical. He felt as if he had stumbled across something profoundly authentic, an expression of life among people who had been battered "by the misery of the world." As he later put it, he had a revelation that "regardless of how many vulgar words these people used or how long their hair was, truth was on their side." Beneath the facade, he also sensed what he called "a special purity, a shame, and a vulnerability" in their music, a "longing for salvation" that attempted to give hope to those who had been most excluded from the system.[41]

Already late for a party at the house of Pavel Kohout, Havel telephoned that he couldn't come. He and Jirous went straight to a pub, where they talked until morning. Thus began an unusual partnership. The music underground, formed by Czech hippies, had been united with a gentlemen's son. For Havel, the relationship was personally liberating. He was growing downward into the belly of something that had always been just out of his reach. More importantly, the musicians would provide a cause he had been unable to find on his own.

For generations, the Havel family had believed not only in the humanistic democracy that had flourished in the First Republic but in the Masonic ideal of citizenship. The early 1970s shook Havel's faith in these ideals. Havel wasn't exactly paralyzed in those years, but his steps had been slow, exceedingly deliberate, even constipated. Those were the years in which he constantly reworked his failed play, *Mountain Hotel*, rewriting it again and again over five years until the characters were drained of their life and vitality. His nerves were frayed, his emotions overcooked, and his health deteriorated. He spoke of being tired, unfocused, unable to concentrate, and he suffered from reoccurring bouts of hemorrhoids.

By the spring of 1975, however, Havel felt a sea change in himself. He had become, he later said, tired of passively waiting for the situation to change, tired of playing the victim, and "tired of being tired." Energized with his collaborations with dozens of other writers, artists, intellectuals, and musicians who shared a similar fate, Havel was determined to shake things up by writing an open letter of complaint to Dr. Gustáv Husák, the First Secretary of the Communist Party.

Such "open letters" already had a literary history in Czechoslovakia. Only a few years before, the historian Milan Hůbl had sent a similar letter to Husák, describing the feeling of hopelessness that had settled over the country. And Alexander Dubček, who was in internal exile in Slovakia, had written two open letters to federal parliament documenting abuses of power. Dubček's second letter, written in February 1975, was particularly strident, accusing the government of being "inconsistent with the tenants of Marxism-Leninism." Any true communist, he had suggested, would work to dismantle the regime.[42]

The idea for Havel's own letter probably emerged from discussions he had been holding with Pavel Kohout, Ivan Klíma, and Ludvík Vaculík. They all agreed, at least in principle, that it was time to take some form of decisive action. During February and March, Havel informed his friends of his detailed plans to publish and publicize an open letter that would describe the creeping fear, apathy, and humiliation felt by Czechs and Slovaks. His colleagues agreed to run a parallel campaign to publicize the same accusations. After Havel provided his letter to Husák to the press, Pavel Kohout wrote a letter to Arthur Miller and Heinrich Böll (the American and German writers, respectively), describing the repression of literary life in Czechoslovakia. About the same time, Ludvík Vaculík wrote a similar letter to Kurt Waldheim, secretary general of the United Nations, and Karel Kosík wrote to Jean-Paul Sartre, the well-known French philosopher. In England, Věra Blackwell, Havel's translator, put pressure on the BBC to provide news coverage. The attention provided by the press was unwanted by the government, as it was involved in international negotiations, eventually to become known as the Helsinki Accords, designed to improve relations between the communist bloc and the West.[43]

Havel and his fellow conspirators seemed to have few concrete objectives beyond forcing the regime to play defense. For one thing, they didn't know whether the regime would ignore their letters or throw them all in jail. In a sense, their campaign wasn't political at all, not in the tactical sense. Havel simply felt that he could no longer keep silent. Having been "poisoned by the boredom and passivity" of the early 1970s, Havel felt the need to regain his balance and self-confidence. Writing the letter, he later said, helped him "stand up straight again." He could no longer be accused, by either his conscience or anyone else, "of just looking on in silence at the miserable state of affairs." As a result, he could breathe more easily because he had "stopped waiting for the world to improve and exercised my right to intervene in that world, or at least to express my opinion about it."[44]

A photograph from the era shows him sitting at Hrádeček in an armchair between the television and the turntable. He's smoking a cigarette while editing a typed copy of the letter, pencil in hand. His expression is pensive, tentative, worried, as if he hadn't yet gotten the words right (and knowing Havel, he feared he never would). Aside from his concerns about language ("I wondered if I didn't just summarize things that were notoriously familiar to everyone and if in some ways I didn't distort reality"), Havel fretted endlessly about how to distribute the letter to the samizdat underground and how to get it into the hands of the foreign press. Suspecting his house might be searched at any moment, for weeks he kept the initial drafts hidden in the forest around his house, where he sometimes stashed manuscripts in the hollow trunk of a tree.

On April 8 Havel drove to Prague to hand off the letter to Pavel Landovský, who had secret access through a friend to a photocopy machine at the National Academy of Sciences. The two of them had a scare that evening, the night before they planned to release the letter, when they ran into a high-ranking official from the secret police in a Prague restaurant. Nothing came of the event, but Havel felt relief when he was able to get copies of his letter in the mail—and even more so when he heard it read by the BBC and Voice of America.[45]

The state responded first with silence. Havel's original letter, which ran to ten thousand words, was returned from Prague Castle unopened. Within a few weeks, however, the state security police had searched the homes of Havel and most of his closest friends.[46] At Vaculík's house, the police carried away books, notes, and a draft of a novel he had been working on for several years. Kosík had his philosophical notes confiscated.

Given the circumstances, Havel steeled himself for prison. With his usual thoroughness, he prepared a small overnight kit, including a toothbrush, toothpaste, soap, books, a T-shirt, paper, and laxatives. Leaving the house became a rare occurrence. In order to protect friends, Havel placed himself in a private quarantine. Knowing that his mail would be closely monitored, he wrote no one and sent word that no one should write or visit.[47]

Havel began his open letter to Dr. Husák by depicting two layers, or realities, within Czech culture. On the level of everyday appearances, "normalization" had been a clear success. The state had eliminated dissent, the newspapers were free of criticism, and almost no one dared to criticize the government. In a word, the regime had "consolidated" power.

Taken on another level, however, Havel argued that normalization was less than a total success. Quite the contrary. By the standards of "private human experience," the new policies had not only done little to advance "the moral and spiritual revival of society" but had actually plunged the nation into a spiritual crisis, one all the more severe because communism was supposedly built upon the ideal of creating a just society.[48] Over the ten pages of his letter, Havel thus painted the picture of an utterly schizophrenic society whose surface tranquility was based on little more than fear and suppression. No citizen, Havel wrote, could challenge the power of the state, forcing everyone to live "a perpetual charade." Consolidating power had required the regime to tolerate and actively encourage duplicity, insincerity, and self-interest. When pressuring hundreds of thousands of individuals to sign statements of self-criticisms, managers and party bosses admonished individuals to look out for themselves. What did it matter if individuals signed statements that were offensive, or untrue, or violated their deepest values? Was that really so important? Was it worth jeopardizing one's position, or the ability to live a comfortable life? Such were the arguments effectively delivered in tens of thousands of interrogations and interviews. They proved highly effective, and, Havel suggested, they contributed to the moral disintegration of the entire culture. From this point of view, Havel suggested the entire totalitarian system gained its authority by creating a chasm between the public face of the individual and the interior world that individuals learned to keep mute, hidden, and disguised. A whole society had been taught indifference to such things as truth, justice, and the abuse of power. Normalization, Havel wrote, had caused "a paralysis of the spirit, a deadening of the heart and a devastation of life." Meanwhile, selfishness and careerism were at new heights.

Havel concluded his public letter to President Husák with the following statement. "For the time being," Havel wrote, you have chosen to promote what is most convenient for you but most dangerous for the society: outward prosperity at the cost of inner decay, and your own power at the cost of our own moral decline.

But you have the ability to improve the situation if only in a limited way. As a citizen of this country, I am publicly calling on you and all the other leaders of the present regime to consider the issue I have brought to your attention and live up to your responsibility.[49]

It is difficult to gauge the impact of Havel's letter. Before that date, for instance, the term "dissident" had hardly been used in the Czech language for the simple matter that no such phenomena existed. Within the following year, the foreign press was meeting "dissidents" for interviews. Havel's letter didn't create the dissident community, but it did suggest that open criticism was possible. It became a symbol of resistance, not only in Czechoslovakia but also Poland, where it was read by members of the Solidarity movement.[50]

Not long after finishing his letter, Havel's self-imposed quarantine was broken by Jiří Lederer, who visited Hrádeček to interview him as part of a samizdat collection of conversations on the state of Czech society. Havel clearly expected to be handed a prison sentence at any moment. He spoke of the "small, everyday pleasures" that he took comfort in, despite what was happening in the country: the small gatherings of friends at Hrádeček, the happiness he felt when the weather turned unusually beautiful or when he discovered his roses had survived a hard frost. Those small moments, Havel suggested, were also a form of dissidence.[51]

Havel had begun playing a long game, one measured in decades. The rules of the game were determined by the asymmetric power of the totalitarian state, a force so formidable that it made no sense to oppose it directly. In Havel's mind, his letter wasn't based on a contest for power. Rather than oppose the regime directly, at the level of official culture, he was beginning to imagine a different scenario. The monolithic power of the communist system depended on order, manipulation, and the complete dominion over the entire culture.

Resistance, he was beginning to understand, was as simple as what he would latter call "living in truth."[52]

When Havel suspended his self-imposed quarantine in early June, he was so swamped with visitors that he had almost no time to write. In a note to Věra Blackwell, he reported that the response to his open letter had exceeded all expectations, with "hundreds of copies" circulating through the samizdat underground, "strengthening" the resolve of the country to take action against the government. He begged for news of how the letter had been received abroad, admitting that the reception of his letter was far more important to him than the reception of his plays.[53]

Few guests were more welcomed that summer than those attending the yearly "writer's conference" in June.[54] For a bit of amusement, Havel dashed together a one-act play about Vaněk. When the play was read in the garden where Havel had just planted carpet grass and where one could see across the wooden fence to Krob's house, it was an immediate hit, perhaps partly because it was one sustained, inside joke, providing a slice of what life had become under normalization. The play was almost purely autobiographical. Havel didn't even bother to disentangle Vaněk from himself as author, which was part of the fun.[55]

*Audience* never became Havel's favorite play, but it became his most popular. After it was circulated in samizdat, young people memorized lines, reciting little bits and pieces in pub conversation. What began as a bit of private entertainment ended up as Havel's most spectacular success. Like Havel, its main character was an unlikely hero, a shy, obliging intellectual who faced the indignities of the world with impeccable manners and a stumbling, nervous restraint. Like Havel, Vaněk also quietly refused to do anything that disagreed with his conscience, making him the sort of antihero that was just right for the times.[56]

Another one of Havel's plays was getting attention that summer. In the early 1970s, Jaroslav Vostrý, the creative director of the Činoherní Klub, had asked Havel to write an adaptation of *Beggar's Opera*, an eighteenth-century play written by John Gay. Since nothing with Havel's name on it could get past the censors, Vostrý devised a plan to translate Havel's adaptation into a foreign language and then have it mailed back to his theater from abroad, making it appear as if it had been written by a foreign author. By the time Havel had finished the play, however, Vostrý had given up on the idea, concluding that the true author of the play was bound to be discovered. Havel sent copies abroad to both Věra Blackwell in England and Klaus Juncker in Germany, but no one could make a sell.

Sometime during 1973 Havel's neighbor, Andrey Krob, came across the manuscript. Not only was Krob taken with the play, but he told Havel that he wanted to create an amateur troupe that would perform it for a private audience. Havel seems to have harbored a number of doubts, including the hard fact that Krob had no experience directing plays. Krob won him over a year later, however, when he invited Havel to watch the troupe rehearse in Krob's kitchen, a group consisting mostly of former stagehands and lighting technicians who had been kicked out of the theater.

Havel was delighted. The amateur actors, who would become known as Theater on a String, lacked professional training, but their amateur enthusiasm had its own charm. In addition, Krob, who had worked as a technical director for the Theater on the Balustrade, seemed to have a knack for working with amateurs, helping the actors seem fresh, unrehearsed, and earthy. Havel not only gave his blessing to the project but typed out a twelve-page letter in which he critiqued the performance.

Havel's theater notes were always somewhat sharp, at least in the sense that he strived, like any world-class playwright, to provide a bare and honest assessment of a performance. The first two pages complimented Krob and the amateur actors, and the last ten pages explained what they had done wrong.[57] As Krob later told the story, Havel eviscerated their efforts, which were unquestionably the work of amateurs.

In truth, the notes were hardly as harsh as Krob pretended. In places, Havel's praise was quite high. "Nobody does it like amateurs do," Havel wrote. "Which means that they don't imitate theatrical mannerisms. Everyone is simply himself/herself, without desperate attempts at making theater with a capital T." Havel also added that

> no matter whether you finish [the production] or not and what the outcome might be, I consider it all to be wonderful. It is wonderful that you all stick together, that you search for something, and that you have time and energy for an activity which will not bring you any profit. In today's material world, this seems to me very precious, very meaningful, and I admire that very much. I think that the group of people you have put together is a very fine bunch, and I was fascinated by the atmosphere of your rehearsals; the collaborative spirit made me nostalgic because it reminds me so much of our beginnings at the Balustrade. I think this is the only way to do theater which makes sense. More exactly, this is the only theater which attracts me and which I enjoy.

Much of the rest of the letter provided Havel's detailed suggestions on their performance.

John Gay's original opera, written in 1728, was set among whores and thieves who fought over the spoils of power. Havel's adaptation cut the music but kept the dystopian storyline, emphasizing, as one of the jailors says, that "of all animals of Prey, man is the sociable one." In the absurdist world of Havel's play, betrayal becomes erotic and predators yearn for the approval of their victims.[58] Once again, Havel was using the theater to open up an interesting line of fantasy about the connection between idealism and the darker impulses of human nature. In Czechoslovakia, the communists had always possessed a profound need to believe in their own righteous cause, just as the Soviet Union had described their invasion of Czechoslovakia as an act of brotherly love. The need to save humankind had been inexplicably bound to their violence and cruelty.

Much of Havel's advice to Krob involved blocking, acting, and the intricate details of what made each scene work. To Havel's mind, the most central element in the play was its artificial, even pretentious dialogue—which is to say, as Havel put it, "that thieves and tarts speak like psychologists and sociologists," giving the play a certain amount of ironic tension.

For Krob, the letter was a gold mine, something akin to a graduate school textbook on stage direction. Soon he began a second round of rehearsals, which took place at the Reduta Jazz Club in Prague, under the eccentric theory that it was best to conduct secret business in the least expected of places. Other rehearsals took place at the Theater on the Balustrade. Krob told the new artistic director at the theater that his group was working on Christmas carols.[59]

On November 1, 1975, the Theater on the String staged its first and only performance of Havel's play in a suburb north of Prague known as Horní Počernice. The suburb had a dance hall and pub that was well known to members of the underground literary community, who used it as a depot for samizdat publications, leading some to refer to it as "Václav Havel's Underground Library."

Although no tickets were sold and the event was closed to the public, some three hundred friends, writers, actors, and intellectuals showed up for the performance, many of them aware they were witnessing history. Photographs from the evening show a crowd sitting in closely spaced folding chairs, everyone full of tense excitement.[60] Havel's brother and father were in the audience, and so was Jan Grossman, Havel's old partner at the Balustrade. Jan Tříska was there as well, and so were Ivan Klíma, Pavel Kohout, and Ludvík Vaculík. Havel later called it his proudest moment as a playwright. Up until the closing curtain, he had secretly believed that the StB might burst in on the play in the middle of the performance, or arrest everyone as they left the room.[61]

While the idea of unofficial theater had been around from at least the early 1970s, no one had yet explored it on this scale, involving a famous international author. A year later, Vlasta Chramostová would stage the first of her famous living room theaters in her house, a reading of the poet Jaroslav Seifert and then an adaptation of Shakespeare's *Macbeth* written by Kohout. These performances played over and over again to small groups of friends and acquaintances who could fit into the living room, thirty or so people watching a performance, usually with police cars on the streets to record who was attending.[62]

There was nothing technically illegal about Chramostová's performances nor the staging of Havel's play, but the stakes were substantial. In order to prepare those who wanted to attend, Havel insisted that each person read his letter to Husák before arriving. As Tříska later recalled, "Everyone knew the play was risky. Even attending the play was a risk."[63]

A week after *Beggar's Opera* had been performed, Radio Free Europe and *Der Spiegel* (the West German newspaper) both carried the news, and everyone involved in creating the play was interviewed by the secret police. Krob, the director, was interrogated for twelve hours, after which he was removed from his position at the Theater on the Balustrade. Jan Grossman, who merely sat in the audience, had his passport revoked, and Tříska was fired from his acting job at the National Theater. He would remain in the country for another fourteen months. After hearing of Havel's arrest on January 6, 1977, he and his wife planned "very, very carefully, step by step" how to escape the country, and then quietly slipped away one day without sharing his plans with either his own parents or with Havel, since "you didn't talk about those things, because you didn't want friends and families to carry the weight of knowing."[64]

In addition to punishing those who attended the *Beggar's Opera,* state bureaucrats canceled plays across the city and announced that they were tightening controls in every theater in Prague. Naturally, the state blamed Havel for the new rules. Punishment worked best when it was collective. If the communists were unhappy with you, they punished your children and your grandchildren. If you had no children or grandchildren, they punished your friends.

# 9

## THE SOLIDARITY OF THE SHAKEN

WHEN HAVEL HEARD IN THE SPRING OF 1976 that band members of the Plastic People of the Universe had been arrested, he drove to Prague immediately. He knew "that something had to be done," and it was obviously up to him to do it. Few others would be willing to speak up, since most people thought of underground musicians as "layabouts, hooligans, alcoholics, and drug addicts." Havel's role, as he saw it, would be to "stir up some interest" in the case, organizing a public defense.[1]

The first step was to meet with Jiří Němec, a psychologist who had close connections with the music underground. Originally, Němec and the band didn't want anything to do with Havel, since they worried that politicizing their case might make the regime dig in their heels. When they finally gave Havel the okay to come to their defense, he jumped in with his typical gusto, organizing a petition, arranging multiple interviews with Reuters and Radio Free Europe, and sending out letters of protest to all the important foreign embassies in the country. The result was a classic confrontation between a handful of long-haired musicians and the unquestioned authority of the state.[2]

Havel also had other business to attend to that spring. In July, his brother, Ivan, received an exit visa to attend a two-week scientific symposium in London. Havel used him to carry a series of messages outside the country, one to his translator Věra Blackwell and another to be sent to Josef Škvorecký, who had inquired into publishing Havel's plays from Canada. In order to prevent any interception by the secret police, Ivan committed the messages to memory.

Ivan's first communication with Škvorecký was presumably by telephone, but he followed up immediately with a letter from London on July 9, writing that "the situation in our country is quite nasty. People are poisoned. There are a few light experiences but overall the situation is dark and passive."[3] He also informed the publisher that Havel preferred for his plays to be published in Czech and that Havel was concerned it might prove difficult to smuggle the manuscript out of the country. Even more difficult would be the problem of sending editorial changes back and forth across the Iron Curtain. Finally, Ivan also laid out the complicated legal situation, including the fact that the rights for everything published outside Czechoslovakia belonged to Klaus Junker, Havel's German agent. The situation provided Havel with protection from the state, but it also meant that Havel could no longer directly sell his own work.

Škvorecký replied seven days later from Toronto with a dense, three-page note that was so detailed that Ivan struggled to commit it to memory before returning to Prague. The upshot was that Škvorecký agreed to publish all of the plays Havel had written since the invasion. He already had samizdat copies of *Beggar's Opera* (given to him by Věra Blackwell) and *Audience*. The book would be printed in Czech, primarily for émigrés, and sold for five dollars. Havel would receive royalties of 5 percent of the first thousand copies and then 10 percent after the first two thousand copies were sold.[4]

The terms of agreement weren't ideal, but 68 Publishers was a shoestring operation run from Toronto with the help of Škvorecký's wife and a few part-time employees. The operation rarely made much, but they were developing a loyal following from tens of thousands of émigrés from across Europe and North America. Most of the books, many of them written by banned authors in Czechoslovakia, would have never seen the light of day without their help.

Škvorecký had once been the boy wonder of Czech letters. At age twenty-four, he had written the great Czech postwar novel *The Cowards*, which described the liberation of Czechoslovakia at the end of World War II. For political reasons, the book went unpublished for ten years. When it was finally released in the late 1950s, the book ignited a firestorm, leading to a purge of the arts and the firings of everyone who encouraged its publication. Among other things, the book depicts the emergence of a heroic idealism, especially among those who leaned toward the Communist Party, by those who felt guilty about their cowardice and inaction during the German occupation. As many commentators have noted, the book was attacked precisely because it hit so close to the truth.[5]

Havel and Škvorecký had known each other since the early 1960s, enjoying a distant friendship. In the coming years, their collaboration would prove to be a vital lifeline for Havel, although one complicated by the fact that their communications were fraught with difficulties. Many letters to Havel never arrived in his mailbox, presumably stolen by the secret police, and his telephone was tapped, making communication dangerous. Outgoing letters could be disguised or mailed from other towns, but Havel was never certain if they would arrive in Canada safely. For important matters, Havel relied on what he called "dissident" mail, which involved passing along a letter to a tourist or diplomat who then smuggled a letter or package to Western Europe before putting it into the mail. A typical example was a package that Havel sent by dissident mail in the summer of 1976, including two plays that Škvorecký had not yet seen. The package arrived in Canada three months later, having been smuggled from Hrádeček to Prague to Vienna, where it was then posted to Toronto.[6]

Throughout the late summer and fall, Havel and Škvorecký exchanged a whole string of letters, many of them arriving late or not at all, or crossing in the mail. In the end, Havel suggested a simple title, *Hry 1970–1976 (Plays 1970–1976)*. He also constantly fretted about the quality of the work, feeling particularly unsure about his one-act plays, since he had written them simply to read to friends at Hrádeček. He also worried that *Mountain Hotel* "wasn't very readable" and that *The Conspirators* had been destroyed by his constant rewrites. His thrill at being published was, he admitted, complicated by what he called "my questions and insecurities as an author."[7]

After receiving what they thought were the final manuscripts, 68 Publishers worked quickly, immediately setting the plays into typeset and ordering cover art. Given the difficulty of communication, Havel never had a chance to see the final galleys. When he finally saw the book after it was published, he discovered that Škvorecký had used an early draft of *The Conspirators* that didn't include extensive revisions that Havel thought he had sent. The discovery must have been a terrible blow—even an existential crisis—but in January Havel sent Škvorecký a gracious postcard in which he wished him "a lot of happiness and success in the new year." He went on: "True one mistake occurred, but that's not your fault. *The Conspirators* is not published in its final version. It's my mistake. . . . It's too late to do anything. It's good that I am complaining about this play in the afterwards, at least the readers will take this play with reservations. (I didn't want to write you this in the first place, but I feel that you should know it.)"[8]

While Havel was scrambling to communicate with Škvorecký about his book, the state continued with the prosecution of the Plastic People of the Universe. In the first trial, which took place on July 5 and 6 of 1976, three members of the music underground were convicted with disturbing the peace for organizing a lecture in which Ivan Jirous discussed underground music, followed by a short concert by Karel Soukup and Svatopluk Karásek. During the trial, the state produced five witnesses and twenty-eight depositions objecting to the vulgar language found in the songs and to what the judge later called the "socially dangerous ideology of the underground movement." Karel Havelka received thirty months in jail for organizing the lecture, Miroslav Skalický received eighteen months for designing the invitation, and František Stárek received eight months for handing out invitations.[9]

For Havel, the convictions represented a new and dangerous evolution in the tyranny of the state. There had been many unfair trials since the era of normalization, but those trials mostly involved opposition members who had voluntarily entered the arena of politics. Havel put it this way: "The objects of this attack were not the veterans of old political battles; they had no political past, or any well-defined political positions. . . . A judicial attack against them, especially one that went unnoticed, could become a precedent for something truly evil: the regime could well start locking up everyone who thought independently, even if he did so only in private."[10]

Havel's description of the event was, perhaps, slightly exaggerated, as many of those in the music underground were, after all, rebels who ridiculed the official culture of communism in their music. His outrage, however, was sincere, perhaps because he saw the youths as innocent versions of himself. Just as they wanted to be free to write their own music, Havel wanted to be left alone to write his plays. Or, to be more accurate, a part of him wanted to be left alone to write his plays while another part of his soul craved the distractions of running an opposition to the regime.[11]

Working with Jiří Němec, Havel began orchestrating a campaign to get the state to back down from a second trial of four additional musicians that was planned for September. When the state refused to back down, Havel wrote a short, seven-paragraph letter to Heinrich Böll, the German novelist who in 1972 had called Czechoslovakia a "cultural cemetery." "We are turning to you," Havel wrote Böll, "because our own voice has remained unheard; no one has reacted either to the private appeals to the President of the Republic, nor to the proclamation which some of us sent in this matter, first to the Czechoslovak communications media and later for publication abroad." Six others signed the letter, including Jaroslav Seifert and Jan Patočka, the philosopher who would soon help Havel cofound a human rights organization.[12]

Böll had won the Nobel Prize for literature in 1972, and he used his heavyweight status to scare up international coverage and the interest of other prominent writers, including Arthur Miller. Meanwhile,

Havel and Němec began a petition inside Czechoslovakia asking for the president of the country to intervene in the trial. Among former communist officials, he recruited Jiří Hájek and Zdeněk Mlynář, who collected sixty signatures.[13] Sixty signatures felt like an avalanche.

By the time of the second trial of the music underground, the Plastic People of the Universe had become an international cause. Under pressure to adhere to the Helsinki Accords on human rights, the trial judge allowed the proceedings to be open to the public. About 150 individuals attended the trial, including writers, actors, philosophers, intellectuals, former government ministers from the era of the Prague Spring, and hippies from the music underground. Those who attended the trial later recalled the event as mesmerizing. Until that moment, most of those who had opposed the regime had circulated in small, isolated underground groups that rarely interacted with each other. Former communists, for instance, had organized around Zdeněk Mlynář, but none of them had any experience with the music underground until the two groups began mingling in the hallways and staircases outside the courtroom, realizing they were unlikely allies.

The trial itself began with opening statements in which each of the four defendants pleaded not guilty. Jirous himself described his work as "urban folklore." He was not only band manager of the Plastic People of the Universe, he said, but an academic who studied underground music. He denied the songs could be described as culturally "subversive," suggesting the vulgarity in the lyrics was simply a criticism of consumer society. Pavel Zajíček, who was a member of the band DG 307, defended his own band by saying that its songs merely expressed his own private "interior life." He had never heard anyone suggest that his music had a "negative social impact."[14]

Mounting an exhaustive defense, the lawyers for the defendants called psychologists who testified that rock and psychedelic music was harmless and might even provide a sense of cathartic relief. Dana Němcová, a child psychologist, testified that the music was joyful and expressed concern for the young. The testimony was powerful enough that one of those observing the trial, Svatopluk Karásek, shouted out of the audience to say that "if Jirous was found guilty, he wanted to be found guilty too."[15]

During recesses, it was clear to Havel that an unusual type of community was developing. A new etiquette even developed right on the spot: no one bothered with the usual conventions and introductions required in Czech society when strangers typically meet. As Havel later remembered the encounters, the people in this new community "were not only more considerate, communicative, and trusting toward each other, [but] they were in a strange way democratic. A distinguished, elderly gentleman, a former member of the presidium of the Communist Party of Czechoslovakia spoke with long-haired youths he'd never seen in his life before, and they spoke uninhibitedly with him, though they had known him only from photographs. . . . Everyone seemed to feel that at a time when all the chips are down, there are only two things one can do: gamble everything or throw in the cards."[16]

On the second day of the trial, Havel left the courtroom during the lunch hour on Karmelitská Street and walked with a number of friends to the Malá Strana Café. He was lost in thoughts and impressions of what he had seen the previous day, unable to think of anything except the meaning of what had happened. In the café, he met an acquaintance, a young film director who had somehow managed to remain in his profession. When Havel told him he had just come from the trial, the acquaintance asked him whether it had to do with drugs. "No," Havel told him, trying to describe the whole essence of the trial, the miscarriage of justice, and the spontaneous coming together of various groups in order to protest the actions of the state. When Havel finished, his acquaintance quickly changed the subject, obviously wishing to avoid their conversation. Havel felt an immediate sense of revulsion, a feeling that his old professional colleague "belonged to a world that I no longer wish to have anything to do with"—the world, as Havel put it, "of cunning shits."[17]

It was no surprise to anyone that all four defendants were found guilty, with prison sentences from eight to eighteen months. In his ruling, the judge concluded that the musicians were guilty of disrespecting society and exhibiting a dangerous contempt for "moral laws." Havel pronounced himself disgusted with the result, which he regarded as a farce.

At the same time, however, he admitted that "at a deeper level," the events were exhilarating. As he explained, "This was perhaps because of the very awareness that we were participants in a unique illumination of the world." He felt inspired not only by members of the music underground but by the crowd who had come to support them. By the trial's end, Havel felt that "much of the wariness and caution that marks my behavior seemed petty to me. I felt an increased revulsion toward all forms of guile, all attempts at painlessly worming one's way out of vital dilemmas. Suddenly, I discovered in myself more determination in one direction, and more independence in another. Suddenly I felt disgusted with a whole world, in which—as I realized then—I still have one foot: the world of emergency exits."[18]

Havel wasn't the only one to feel inspired. Němec also felt that something important had been galvanized at the trial, something that shouldn't be allowed to dissipate. Kohout felt the same way, suggesting that resistance shown at the trail could be harnessed into a larger movement. And the former communist officials, represented by Jiří Hájek and Zdeněk Mlynář, were already imagining a diverse opposition that would build a human rights movement around the Helsinki Accords, which had been under negotiations since August 1974 as a way of reducing Cold War tensions between NATO and the Warsaw Pact. The final agreement, signed by the United States, Canada, and all European countries except Albania, called for respecting the rights of sovereignty of all nations. Section seven of the agreement required each nation to respect the human rights of its citizens, and to provide them freedom of thought and religion, terms that had been insisted upon by the United States.

The meetings to create a common oppositional movement began a few days later on the opposite side of Charles Square from the courthouse in the sprawling, book-lined apartment of Václav Benda and his wife, Kamila. Benda was in his early twenties, a former philosophy student who went to work in boiler rooms after being forced out of the university. His flat had the advantage that it wasn't yet being observed by the secret police. The preliminary meetings included Havel, Němec, Kohout, and Zdeněk Mlynář, the former communist minister. Together they discussed the problems of creating a broad-based opposition group that would include different subcultures—Catholic, communist, anti-communist—each group having little reason to trust the others. One of the difficulties in creating such a group was that as soon as it became operational, the government would try to shut it down. Meetings would soon become all but impossible.

After a few preliminary discussions, the group had two serious meetings in December that were based on the simple premise that they didn't want to just put together another petition, or even a manifesto, but create an organization that would challenge the government whenever it violated the rule of law. Everyone agreed the organization would have to be pluralistic and permanent. It would not and could not be a formal organization, which would place it under state regulations, but a "citizens' initiative," open to anyone who wished to participate, and a spokesperson would be given authority to speak for the entire group.

At about this time, Miloš Rejchrt, a prominent religious leader, happened to meet the legendary Jiří Hájek on a tram. It was Hájek who had pleaded before the United Nations in 1968 to condemn the Soviet invasion. After the two struck up a conversation on the tram, Hájek told him, somewhat mysteriously, to watch for an initiative that would make the government accountable to new international standards in human rights. Such was the way news spread, and the next week, Rejchrt was approached, just before the Christmas holidays, by a member of the organization for his support, which he immediately gave.[19]

The text of the initial document was straightforward. It pointed out that citizens of Czechoslovakia enjoyed a number of human rights and freedoms found both in the registry of national laws and under the Helsinki Accords, but that such rights existed "on paper alone." The founding document of Charter 77 went on to point out that freedom of expression, guaranteed in Article 19 of Czech law, was "purely illusory." Tens of thousands of professionals had been prevented from working in their profession because they held views at odds with the government. Hundreds of thousands of other citizens lived in fear of being punished for their political opinions. The document went on to document the lack of religious freedom and basic civil rights. Charter 77, it declared, was being created "to promote the general public interest." It would not suggest any positive reform or change, or promote any form of government, but would exist in order to create dialogue with the state, particularly in regards to any violations of human rights.

At one early meeting, Peter Uhl, a former political prisoner in the early 1970s, proposed that the organization should have three spokespersons, who would express the pluralism of the charter. From the outset, it was clear that Jiří Hájek, the former foreign minister during the Prague Spring, should be one. He had the foreign contacts and international experience to give the organization stature. Uhl suggested Havel as the second spokesperson, since Havel had himself become a symbol of the pluralism the charter was supposed to represent. Almost alone among the participants, Havel seemed comfortable with all of the paradoxes and tensions of everyone present. The choice of the third spokesperson caused more controversy, but it was generally agreed that it should be someone from the religious or academic community, someone of considerable gravitas. Some suggested Václav Černý, a former professor at Charles University. Others, such as Václav Havel, leaned toward the legendary philosopher Jan Patočka, who was already thought of in some circles as the Czech Socrates.

By the time of Charter 77, Patočka had already lived a long and rich life, gaining a reputation among his colleagues as the most important Czech philosopher of the twentieth century (and perhaps since Jan Amos Komenský, also known as Cominius, who died in 1670). Patočka was a large, stern man, deeply serious, but he also possessed a joyful vitality. Havel held him in awe, having participated in several unofficial seminars that Patočka had given at the Theater on the Balustrade in the 1960s to help actors understand the philosophical background of the theater of the absurd. As Havel remembered, "These unofficial seminars pulled us into the world of philosophizing in the true, original sense of the word: no classroom boredom, but rather the inspired, vital search for the significance of things and the illumination of oneself, one's own situation in the world." He later remembered Patočka as an inconspicuous, dignified man whose "every word" touched him with "a more profound and more truthful expression" than he could find in any book.[20]

As a youth, Patočka had finished his Ph.D. in philosophy at Charles University in Prague in 1932, after which he went to study with the two most important philosophical figures in Europe, Edmund Husserl, the father of phenomenology, and Martin Heidegger, the legendary author of *Being and Time*. Patočka spent the rest of his life reconciling the ideas of the two men. One of his driving interests was working out Husserl's idea of the crisis in European civilization, which both Heidegger and Patočka believed was rooted in a misguided rationalism, including the Enlightenment's tendency to see the exact sciences as the exclusive representative of reality. The result of this tendency was a materialistic view of the world that left no room for spiritual and humanistic ideas. Husserl himself had called for a renewal of a deeper form of reason, one that would lead us back to the roots of the ancient world, and Patočka spent his life trying to fulfill the dream, trying to root it in Socrates' idea of the care of the soul.[21]

Patočka's career as a philosopher had been continually uprooted, first by the Nazis in the 1930s and then by the communists in 1948, both of whom banned him from teaching in the university. He worked instead in a variety of low-level jobs as a cleric and librarian. Twenty years later, the reforms of the Prague Spring allowed him to return to his university position, briefly, until he was forced out again during the government crackdown in the early 1970s.

Those who had been fortunate to take his classes during the Prague Spring described him as an unbelievably charismatic professor. His two-hour lectures, which he delivered from a single slip of paper, were standing room only and attended by other professors and docents. During the Stalinist era, the university had been a graveyard of the intellect, and Patočka represented something that few of them had seen in person. He was not only a good raconteur, retelling stories or anecdotes, but the arguments in his lectures were subtle, sophisticated, full of complications that were far more complex than anything the students had encountered in a generation. By all accounts he had a remarkable gift for formulating ideas, speaking with the precision of the written word, and he seemed to have an enormous store of knowledge. Students didn't always understand what he said, but they regarded him as a visionary. After the lectures, many of them gathered regularly to try to compare notes, and in several of his classes groups of students attempted to duplicate exact transcripts of his impromptu talks.[22]

After 1972, when Patočka was forced to leave the university under the pretense that he was too old to teach, students continued to gather at his house to hear him lecture. Since it was difficult for one person to take enough notes to fully reconstruct his discussions, this eventually evolved into a working group that met twice a week to read the major works of Heidegger and Husserl. In 1974 another group met under Patočka to study the history of philosophy, beginning with Socrates' idea of the care of the soul.

It is, perhaps, difficult to capture the importance of Patočka's underground lectures, but no one who attended the meetings ever forgot the experience. As Ivan Chvatík, who studied under Patočka, later recalled: "It was obvious from his talks that here was a man who really thinks, who doesn't just memorize his lectures from something he read in a book. At the time, this was both unusual and exciting."[23] In the Plato and Europe lectures, for instance, Patočka attempted to provide an overall theory of the development of modern European civilization and its ills. For Patočka, the only salvation for Europe lay in a renewal of the spirit of individual conscience.

The decisive event in Patočka's later life may have come in 1973, when he was allowed by the state to travel to a philosophical congress in Varna, Bulgaria. There he gave a paper on Heidegger and the dangers of technology. He was prevented from finishing his speech, presumably because the topic was considered dangerous from the point of view of the Communist Party. His paper was also omitted from the conference proceedings. Upon returning home to Czechoslovakia, Patočka had the fantasy impression that his former professor, Edmund Husserl, was watching him in judgment.[24] He immediately recalled a line from one of Husserl's essays that "the dead are looking over our shoulders." Patočka had long meditated on that line and had taken it to mean that the living have an ethical responsibility to the dead, to carrying on their traditions, and to seeing our own actions in the light of eternity. The pang of conscience became a source of reflection for the next three years.[25]

Out of those nominated for spokespersons of Charter 77, only Jiří Hájek accepted without reservations.[26] Havel reluctantly agreed, thinking he would appear ungrateful not to accept after he had asked so many others to join the group.[27] Jan Patočka had the most reservations of all. Although Patočka despised the communist worldview, he had spent most of his long life trying to avoid direct confrontation with the regime. His approach to living under communism was essentially conservative, a strategy that Havel regarded as something like trench warfare, trying "to hold out as long as he could without compromise" while also avoiding any statements "that might have put an end to his work."[28]

The decisive factor in joining Charter 77 may have been Patočka's own ideas about the nature of sacrifice. In 1973 he had suggested that self-sacrifice had the potential to save both society and the individual from a world where Being itself was in danger. Sacrifice was the reminder that not everything fits into a "technical calculation," and that, for those willing to make a sacrifice, some values form a higher absolute. From Patočka's point of view, one sacrifices something lower to a higher level of Being, suggesting that there are principles and values that are more important to us than our own life. For Patočka, all of this exposed the flaw in the "technological view of the world" that characterized the communist state.

Similarly, in his lectures in the 1970s Patočka had spoken of what he called "the solidarity of the shaken," which referred to a particular bond between people who have been deeply shocked by the big and small disturbances of life, allowing them to change their perspective on the world. The solidarity of the shaken referred to those who had come to see the nature of life and death and who had been freed from their alienation from life. And how did they free themselves from alienation? By agreeing to sacrifice themselves for the greater good.

By December 1976 Patočka had come to believe that a version of the "solidarity of the shaken" was being created in the dissident community. Sometime around Christmas 1976, he agreed to become a spokesperson, with the condition that he had the blessing of Václav Černý, who Patočka felt had a better claim to the position. Havel took it upon himself to visit Černý and explain the whole situation, including why he thought Patočka would be more effective in the position, having no previous history in attacking or antagonizing the Communist Party. Patočka was also a widower with grown children, thus someone who would be somewhat free from political pressure.

The holidays were a particularly somber time for those who understood what was about to happen. Just before Christmas, Patočka was approached by his daughter, who sensed that he felt troubled over what would happen to him personally. The exact nature of their conversation was never recorded, but Patočka intimated to her that his remaining days would be troubled with darkness.[29]

# 10

## DEATH OF A PHILOSOPHER

THE PLAN WAS SIMPLE: IN EARLY JANUARY, the signature cards for Charter 77 would be organized and counted in Havel's apartment. A typed carbon copy of the charter would then be mailed to each of the 242 signatories of the original charter, and Havel would then deliver a copy to the federal assembly. Much like the "brilliant and primitive" plan in Kohout's play *Six and Sex*, this one contained a paradox. Their secret weapon would be the secrecy of hiding in plain sight.[1]

Although members of the charter had met regularly throughout the holidays, the secret police seemed to have little understanding of what they were up to until the night of January 5, when a Czech spy stationed in Paris discovered that *Le Monde* was preparing to print a human rights manifesto by Czech dissidents. In response, the secret police immediately posted teams in Prague, three men to a car, in front of the homes of the usual suspects. Late that night, they also sabotaged Havel's Mercedes, either cutting the brake lines or destroying the hydraulic clutch, depending on whose memory you accept, a vandalism that seems more akin to desperation than anything else.[2]

In the early morning hours of January 6, while the secret police were busy sabotaging his Mercedes, Havel was at the home of his good friend Zdeněk Urbánek, the mild-mannered literary critic and Shakespearean translator.[3] The two men were taking care of the last-minute details of addressing envelopes. Havel had a long history of staying up all night, either for drinking parties or bouts of writing, but on this night Urbánek sent Havel home just before dawn, fearing he was on the edge of exhaustion. The two agreed to meet again at 9 a.m., and Urbánek and his girlfriend, Markéta Hejná, finished preparing the envelopes.

Both men lived in the Dejvice neighborhood, no more than a ten-minute walk from each other. By 9 a.m., when Havel discovered the damage to his Mercedes, Ludvík Vaculík had stumbled by Havel's apartment, looking for gossip and a bit of fun, as well as a ride downtown to buy a pair of shoes. Whatever the motivation, Vaculík tagged along with Mr. Václav (as he liked to call him) as they stepped out on the narrow, snow-dusted street, trudging through the tree-lined neighborhood to Urbánek's house at 64 Střešovická Street.[4] At Urbánek's house, they helped seal a last batch of envelopes until Pavel Landovský showed up, warning everyone that he had spotted the secret police observing the house from a car. The mood was later described as giddy, even slightly hysterical, punctuated by short bouts of uncontrollable laughter, as if everyone, running on nervous energy and exhaustion, could hardly believe what they were about to do.[5]

Havel and Landovský had been planning to drive Havel's Mercedes across Prague that morning, placing no more than ten envelopes in each public mailbox they could find and then hand-delivering copies of the charter to parliament. Instead, they changed cars, loading the mail into the back seat of Landovský's Saab, along with Vaculík, who was still tagging along in order to buy a pair of shoes. Pulling onto the snow-lined street, they were tailed by two cars from the secret police. Beginning a high-speed chase, Landovský temporarily lost the tail when he cut sharply onto an icy side road, the two secret police cars fishtailing and then colliding into each other behind them. A few blocks later, two new Škoda's pulled up on either side, after which Landovský headed up the wrong way on a one-way street. Perhaps as many as ten to twelve police cars joined the chase before forcing them to a halt near Dejvická circle. At that point, according to Landovský's account, a group of

> about 20 guys rushed out [of the cars] to us. I just locked all the doors from inside, so they couldn't get to us so easily. I said to [Havel]: "See, now they'll pound away at the car, get a bit tired, and when they start pounding us, it won't hurt so much." And [Václav] replied with a memorable sentence: "What a way to start a struggle for human rights." The enraged cops outside had calmed down a bit and instead of pounding the car, they began slapping their secret police IDs against the window. [Havel] remarked: "Pavel, it looks like these gentlemen really are from the police," and because he was convinced that we weren't doing anything wrong, he unlocked the door next to me and suddenly all I saw were the soles of his shoes. They grabbed him and pulled him out like a roll of carpet, like a piece of pipe. All I saw were his shoes. I didn't open the door myself, on the contrary, I entwined my hands in the steering wheel, then suddenly I saw the soles of Vaculík's shoes, he was flying out along with the bags he held in his hands.[6]

Immediately after their arrest, the three men were taken to the headquarters of state security on Bartolomějská Street, where they were later joined by Urbánek. All four were released late that night and brought back again the next day at 6 a.m., joined by Jan Patočka and Jiří Hájek, the co-spokespersons of Charter 77, and virtually everyone who had read or signed the charter.

That night, after returning to his flat, Havel turned on the radio to find Voice of America discussing the charter, thanks to copies that Pavel Kohout snuck out of the country with the help of diplomats. Every night after that—the interrogations went on for weeks—members of the charter met afterward to compare notes on their different interrogations.[7] It was a grim, serious business, and it was exhilarating as hell.

According to a joke making its way around Prague in 1977, an optimist believes everything is already as bad as it can get, while a pessimist knows it will get worse. Those who signed Charter 77 were hardly optimistic about any immediate change. Signing the charter was not about change as much as a matter of self-respect, of refusing to be intimidated, of being willing to take a symbolic stand regardless of its immediate impact. Almost everyone understood that signing Charter 77 would make their own lives immediately worse.

The day after the secret police arrested Havel and Landovský, the presidium of the Central Committee of the Communist Party met to discuss the political fallout, deciding to prosecute those who signed Charter 77 for sedition. Charter 77 was declared an illegal organization, and the telephones of those who signed the charter were immediately tapped. Almost all of the individuals were fired from their jobs, and managers were told to keep the dismissal as secret as possible.[8]

Although fewer than 250 individuals signed the charter out of a population of almost ten million, the state regarded the document as a direct assault on its consolidation of power and on the appearance that the population fully supported the slogans and ideals of the Communist Party. In order to combat this impression, the state began a public relations campaign to discredit the charter. Just about every major factory, office, and school in Prague asked its workers to sign statements condemning Charter 77, and anti-charter signature sheets were handed out to be signed at the same time that wages were dispersed, just in case anyone misunderstood what was at stake.[9]

In the meantime, the state-run television programs and newspapers began a news campaign. An article in *Rudé Právo*, on January 12, 1977, said that the founders of Charter 77 were "bankrupt persons who, for whatever reasons of class and reactionary interests, of vanity or vainglory, of renegade-ism or notorious characterlessness, are ready to lend their names to the devil." The editorial in the same newspaper listed those involved as a "medley of human and political has-beens, including V. Havel, of a millionaire's family . . . J. Hájek, a bankrupt politician . . . and J. Patočka, a reactionary professor, who placed himself in the service of anti-communism."

Another article in *Rudé Právo* suggested that the members of the charter were controlled by "anti-communist and Zionist" elements from the West.[10] In addition, an internal bulletin directed party officials, when discussing Charter 77, to characterize the authors as misguided individuals who had forgotten that only communism could establish genuine human rights.[11]

The controversy reached both houses of parliament. In April the prosecutor general appeared in order to answer the allegations of human rights abuses laid out in the charter. His speech demonstrated the precarious position of the state, which depended on tens of thousands of unhappy bureaucrats continuing to publicly support the Communist Party. In his talk in front of the National Assembly, the prosecutor general declared that all of the rights and freedoms required by the Helsinki Accords and the socialist constitution were still guaranteed by the state. After his speech, the chairman of the Supreme Court rose to defend the state. It was simply a lie, he said, that anyone in the nation was being persecuted, either administratively or criminally, for personal beliefs.

The first few days of interrogations were held at the state security headquarters on Bartolomějská Street in the Old Town. After four days, Havel and friends were moved to Ruzyně prison, presumably because of the extra space. The interrogations were grim affairs that were occasionally punctuated by levity. In his account, Pavel Landovský said that shortly after his arrest he was escorted to a small room, where he was ordered to go through a pile of confiscated items, describing each one. Most of the evidence included copies of Charter 77, but when Landovský came across a cellophane envelope with aspirin inside, he tore it open, tossed the pills into his mouth, and yelled "I give my life for the fatherland!" According to Landovský, the police agents laughed.[12]

Despite the situation (and the cruelty involved), an odd sense of decorum prevailed. Interrogations often began with series of niceties, followed by an offer, usually from a young, sympathetic secretary, to bring a refreshment, perhaps Turkish coffee or a cup of tea. There were usually at least two interrogators in the room, and sooner or later they usually got around to the tactics of intimidation. Some interrogators, however, took a different strategy, pretending to be shocked when they heard about violations of rights that were chronicled by the dissidents, assuring whoever was being interrogated that the matter would be investigated immediately.[13] Instead of physical violence, interrogators preferred psychological warfare to get under the skin of dissidents. One of their favorite techniques was to release selective information or question the character of Havel, Hájek, or Patočka in an attempt to drive a wedge between different members of the charter.

After the first eighteen days of interrogation, Havel was formally charged with the crime of violating the laws of currency exchange. He was told of his formal arrest late on a Friday evening and then was escorted to a seven-by-twelve-foot cell he shared with a grocery store burglar. Shortly after Havel was imprisoned, Kohout was charged with distribution of foreign literature and Jiří Leerer was accused of communication with Radio Free Europe.[14] The criminal charges brought a swift international outcry. Arthur Miller said that the persecution of Charter 77 meant that "the Czech regime is simply demonstrating to anyone who may have doubts that it is prepared to cut out a black hole in the cultural map of Europe."[15]

For reasons that are still unclear, the regime declined to arrest Hájek and Patočka, the remaining spokespersons. Undergoing several interrogations each week, the two men released seven additional charter documents in the subsequent two months, documenting the human rights abuses of the new year and other illegal government practices, such as discriminating against students whose parents were out of favor with the Communist Party. The documents were typed with carbon copies, disseminated to members of Charter 77, and then smuggled to the West, where they could be read on Radio Free Europe.

In addition to producing these documents, Hájek and Patočka continued to collect additional signatures to the charter. Despite the campaign of intimidation, the membership had almost tripled, to 617 citizens by March 9, 1977.[16] The workload of collecting signatures, producing documents, and attending interrogations was unrelenting. Patočka, who was an elderly man, fell ill with influenza for most of the month of February but nevertheless continued to play the leading role in explaining the philosophical background of the new movement. Some of the members of Charter 77 had conceived of the charter as little more than a legalistic initiative, whose purpose was to draw attention to the problem of meeting the international obligations of the Helsinki Accords.[17] Patočka made sure that Charter 77 saw itself in broader terms. In an influential letter he wrote in early January, released and copied throughout underground society just a few days after the charter was released, he made the case that Charter 77 should be seen as the moral conscience of the nation. "No Society," Patočka wrote, "no matter how good its technological foundation, can function without a moral foundation, without conviction that has nothing to do with opportunism, circumstance and expected advantage. Morality, however, does not just exist to allow society to function, but simply to allow human beings to be human."[18]

Patočka further suggested that members of the charter should not see themselves as a political organization. The aim of Charter 77 was "the spontaneous and unbounded solidarity" of everyone who believed that society should be based on an ethical and moral foundation. When he was asked in interrogations about his treatise on the nature of Charter 77, he gave them a lecture on the history of ethics and told them that disseminating his philosophical meditation on Charter 77 had been important in order "to add to the charter an account of my personal conception of its deep moral meaning."[19]

By March, Patočka's health had deteriorated further, and he was suffering from exhaustion and a nasty case of bronchitis. He was also refusing to make allowances for his illness. When asked by well-wishers to hand over some of his more difficult duties to others, the elderly Patočka replied: "I'm a spokesperson and I can still walk."[20]

In early March, while having a conversation with Ludvík Vaculík from his sick bed, a foreign reporter showed up at his basement apartment to pass along a message that the Dutch foreign minister, who was in Prague on business, wanted to meet. Patočka immediately agreed, changing out of his green dressing gown and into a dark suit, tie, and white shirt. Vaculík warned the aged professor that he ought to remain in bed, but Patočka insisted on going.[21]

The meeting with the Dutch foreign minister, Max van der Stoel, sent the government into a fit of apoplexy. On March 3 Patočka was called in for a daylong interrogation at Ruzyně. Patočka complained about feeling ill and asked to go home. By all accounts the interrogators were worried about his health, too, but they lacked the authority to let him go.

By coincidence, Patočka and Havel were able to spend the noon break, between interrogations, together in the waiting room. The professor, tired as he was, gave an impromptu lecture to Havel on the meaning of life and death, an idea on his mind. Havel's relationship with Patočka had always been based in deference and a certain degree of shyness on Havel's part—a shyness, Havel later said, that was "a chronic obstacle in my relationships with people who I entertain too high a regard, and particularly those who had meant something important to me in the days of my initial awareness of myself." To some extent, Havel later admitted, he felt "uptight" around the old professor, even what he called a sense of personal shame in the face of all that knowledge and the fact that Havel himself "had done so little" while receiving "public attention" that felt undeserved. On this day, however, the shyness faded. Patočka had seemed increasingly human, and the shared burden of Charter 77 had driven them together in an extremely intimate way. And as they had gotten closer, Havel had felt awed by what he called "the moral greatness" of the philosopher's personality. Patočka had a way of discussing moral issues that helped Havel understand himself.

Havel later remembered this conversation fondly, all the more so, perhaps, because it was to be their last. As he remembered it:

> At any moment, they could have come for any one of us, but that did not bother the professor: in his impromptu seminar on the history of the idea of human immortality and on human responsibility, he weighed his words as carefully as if we had unlimited time before us. I not only asked him questions, I even submitted some of my own philosophical insights (something that would have been unthinkable earlier), and it seemed to me that the fact that I was not just a polite listener seemed to inspire him. Finally, he invited me to come and see him soon, because he would like to talk with me about it all the more thoroughly. Earlier I would have taken it as flattering and would have postponed any visit out of shyness, but at that moment I felt such a strong desire to talk with him about the basic matters of existence that I would have perhaps liked to invite myself for that very evening...[22]

After returning home late that night, Patočka apparently suffered from a heart attack and was rushed to the hospital. Over the next couple of days, he continued to work, reading and signing charter documents and finishing his most important text, in which he pointed out that Charter 77 could be expected to make things worse in the short term. Be that as it may, the risk was worth taking. He argued that "submissiveness never led to any improvement but only to a deterioration of the situation. The greater the fear and servility, the more daring those in power will become."[23]

He then fell unconscious and died on March 13, 1977.[24]

The death of Patočka appears to have haunted Havel a great deal. Although the two men had never been as close as some would later suggest, Havel had enormous respect for the old philosopher, even reverence. While in jail awaiting his trial, one of his favorite pastimes would be daydreaming about that trip to Patočka's apartment to finish their discussion on the nature of immortality. It was, Havel said, his "favorite escape from that depressive emptiness and hopeless inner solitude."

Havel never spoke of how he learned of Patočka's death. We can assume that his interrogators used the information against him (unlike Hájek and Patočka, he was being held indefinitely in prison). In all likelihood, they used the news to try to break him, not only to suggest that Charter 77 had been annihilated but that Havel himself was responsible for Patočka's death. After all, it was Havel who convinced Patočka to serve as a spokesperson. Sitting in prison, in what must have seemed a hopeless situation, it would be easy for an interrogator to make it seem as if the charter were nothing but an organization created for Havel's own vanity.

About six weeks after Patočka's death, Havel suffered from something akin to a psychological breakdown, or what he called a prison psychosis. Cryptically, he avoided discussing how he heard of the death or how it affected him, going only so far as to say that "when a person receives word there, in prison, of the death of someone close, it is many times harder—it's difficult to explain why, perhaps for many reasons, including the fact that there isn't anyone who could even remotely comprehend what it is that happened."[25]

Havel had little news of the charter from his prison cell. His interrogators claimed that the organization had collapsed. Psychologically unprepared for prison, the news caused Havel to spiral into what he later called a "strange and somewhat psychotic" state, in which he was haunted by peculiar dreams and troubling ideas. He had the overwhelming sense that he was living out the medieval story of Dr. Faustus, and that "in a very physical sense" he was being "tempted by the devil," unable to escape. Havel never provided more specific information about what led to these fantasies, but we know they were accompanied by a series of uncanny events, such as ordering his usual books from the prison library only to find that they mistakenly delivered Goethe's *Faust* and then *Doctor Faustus* by Thomas Mann.[26]

It does seem likely that Havel's personal identification with Faust might, in part, relate to his own personal ambition, the sense that (like Faust) he thought he could outsmart his opponents. He had played his little game, organizing a very small protest against the state, and now he was in their clutches. Prison taught him there was no escape, an idea he returned to a few years later in his essay "The Power and the Powerless," writing that the essence of totalitarianism is that it draws all people into its sphere of power, forcing them to become "agents of the system's general automatism." Thus, he wrote, the individual is ensnared like "Faust by Mephistopheles."[27]

On another level, Havel's feeling that he was Faust was clearly related to a devil's bargain that the secret police offered him sometime in May, after five months in prison. His interrogators suggested he might be released from prison to await a trial if Havel agreed to write a routine promise that he would no longer be involved in Charter 77. In Havel's version of the story, he says that he sensed a possible trap but proceeded anyway on the understanding that Charter 77 no longer existed, making any promise irrelevant. Moreover, his defense attorney (who was an informer secretly working with the police) told him that his family insisted that he sign.

In a fit of arrogance, Havel wrote out the request in highly abstract language that, read on one level, suggested he was resigning from his position as spokesperson of Charter 77. Havel later claimed this was little more than a ruse, a word game, since he clearly hadn't been serving as a spokesperson while in prison. He thought nothing more of the matter until he was informed by his interrogators that he would be released and that "political use" would be made of his signed statement, including a sentence in which Havel claimed that various statements of his had been "tendentiously interpreted by the foreign press and misused against Czechoslovakia."[28]

With a flash of intuition, Havel immediately understood his predicament. Not only would the letter be used against him, but it would appear that he had sold out the charter to save his own skin. And nothing he could do could stop the approaching catastrophe. No denial or correction on his part could erase the shame.[29]

By the time he was released on May 20, the Czechoslovak Press Agency had published the news that Havel had turned his back on the charter. Waiting for him outside the oversized, dark blue gates at Ruzyně, his old friend Pavel Landovský was visibly upset, an accusatory tone in his voice.

Already shaken, Havel tried to explain the situation. Then Havel gave a simple request. "Can you take me to Hájek's right away."[30]

Ruzyně prison lies at the end of Evropská Boulevard on the northeast end of the city, near the international airport. Getting to Hájek's house meant driving Landovský's battered white Saab back into Prague and then out to Zahradní Město, a "garden neighborhood" a few miles south of Vinohrady. The neighborhood was one of the early suburbs, built in the 1920s and 1930s, although by the 1970s the cozy garden houses had become surrounded by high-rise housing projects.

The neighborhood is still as green as its name implies, thick with parks and walking trails. Hájek himself was a jogger, a habit he picked up while a diplomat in London and later kept up as he rose through the ranks of the Communist Party. You would never know it from his demeanor, however. Hájek was an eagle-eyed intellect, a workaholic with a famously awkward body. His daily jog was perhaps something of a sweet release that allowed him to concentrate more thoughtfully on the work of the day.

As Hájek's son remembers that evening, Havel arrived straight from prison, looking "something like a broken man." Havel seemed to him a small, unimpressive man, full of self-doubt. It was Landovský who was the towering figure, full of courageous and humorous accounts of his own experiences in prison. The young Jan Hájek couldn't understand why Landovský permitted the company of "this pitiable person with him" or why his father held Havel in such high regard.[31]

Whatever Hájek told him that night, it clearly bucked him up. Havel had made one slip, in a moment of weakness, and vowed to himself to compensate for his mistake. The sense of "shame, inner humiliation, [and] reproach" stayed with him for months, years even, leaving him with the visceral feeling that he needed to make up for his mistake, even if it meant returning to prison to erase what he had done.[32]

With Patočka dead and Havel compromised, Hájek was the only spokesperson left. By most accounts, he provided the stable steely leadership at the helm of Charter 77 that allowed the organization to survive. Having lived through a concentration camp, the Stalinist purges, and his ouster from the government in 1968, he was not easily intimidated.

In addition to continuing to produce documents on human rights abuses, Hájek remained in constant contact with diplomats from across Western Europe, many of whom he knew personally. He also spoke regularly with foreign journalists, including an on-air interview for French radio in which Hájek reported that his driver's license had been revoked, his telephone had been cut off, and the secret police kept a detail parked in a car in front of his home.[33]

But although Hájek had provided strong leadership, it was not without controversy. He was, after all, a former communist official who still believed in "socialism with a human face," basically what had been attempted by the government in 1968. For the anti-communist faction of Charter 77, Hájek was unacceptable, and in the summer of 1977 the matter boiled over in a series of conflicts. Although the first three spokespersons had represented a variety of groups, Havel and Patočka were now out of the picture. Some dissidents didn't trust Hájek, and they resented his leadership style, with its acute sense of hierarchies.

There were substantive issues as well. A number of prominent members accused Hájek of confusing his own personal beliefs with those of the charter and of making statements based on his Marxist philosophy rather than on the principles of Charter 77. Another member accused him of being too eager to agree with the regime, perhaps as part of an agenda to get back into the good graces of the Communist Party,[34] an idea that carried more than a bit of paranoia.

Because the charter was so diverse, different groups and subgroups interpreted the mission of the charter in diverse ways. Some members considered themselves dissidents; others weren't interested in creating an opposition to the government.[35] Still others felt that the charter was becoming too legalistic, interested mostly in generating documents for the foreign press. In order to discuss these differences, about two hundred charter members met during 1977 to find common ground and decide whether the organization should be terminated.

Shortly afterward, Petr Uhl and Jaroslav Šabata crafted a samizdat statement known as "What's to be done about the charter?" They suggested that the charter should seek constructive dialogue with the state, establish itself as an opposition party, and work with other international human rights organizations, including Amnesty International.[36]

The ex-communists opposed this course of action, arguing that creating an official opposition would only lead to more repression. Others, such as the philosopher Ladislav Hejdánek, argued that it would be a profound error to change the original objectives of the charter, and that such work should be carried out independently or under a new organization. For Hejdánek, a former student of Jan Patočka, the charter was concerned not with politics but with the truth.[37]

# 11

## ATONEMENT

AFTER FIVE MONTHS AWAITING TRIAL, HAVEL WAS finally convicted in October 1977 along with Jiří Lederer, František Pavlíček,
and Ota Ornest of conspiring against the government. The charges
appeared to be related to smuggling the memoirs of Jiří Hájek to
émigrés who lived in the West, probably Pavel Tigrid in Paris.[1] Havel
and Pavlíček received suspended sentences, and the other individuals
were sentenced to more than three years in prison each.

Presumably, Havel's suspended sentence was meant to compromise him, to keep him running scared while also keeping him out
of prison, where he would become an international symbol. Instead
of making him cautious, however, the suspension irritated him. The
shame that Havel felt upon his release from detention in May had
been one of the most traumatic moments of his life. By the time of his
trial, Havel had decided that returning to prison was his only chance
to prove himself, which made his suspended sentence appear like a
cruel joke. Like Leopold Nettles in *Largo Desolato*, he longed for a
prison sentence.

Many of Havel's closest friends and associates from those years say
that it was common knowledge that the idea of redemption weighed

on his mind. Everyone, including Havel, seems to have seen his release from detention as a "momentary personal weakness." To individuals such as Miloš Rejchrt, an active member of Charter 77 and an evangelical priest, Havel longed for a chance not only to prove himself but to atone for his mistake.[2] Havel made a similar point in a later correspondence with Karel Hvížďala, when he spoke of being driven in those years by an "uptight" longing to "rehabilitate" himself from his public humiliation. After a few drinks one evening with Zdeněk Urbánek, Havel confided he was "going to get himself caught." This was the only way, Havel told Urbánek, for him to satisfy the doubts about his character.[3]

Meanwhile, beginning in the summer of 1978, the secret police had stepped up their surveillance of Havel's life by blocking off the one-and-a-half-lane road leading to Hrádeček. A pair of uniformed policemen kept watch in eight-hour shifts. Anyone who approached Havel's home was then warned by police that they should enter "at their own risk." Twice during that first month, Havel walked down to the police car for clarification. Was this merely an attempt to intimidate his friends, or would they face criminal charges if they visited? Those on duty told him they were "not authorized to specify the danger."[4]

During this period of intimidation, policemen also began following Havel whenever he left the house, including when he took his dogs for walks in the woods surrounding Hrádeček. If he and Olga drove into Trutnov for shopping, the police shadowed them around town, immediately checking the identity papers of anyone he met. If Havel made a telephone call from a booth or a store, a policeman would lean in closely enough to overhear the conversation.[5]

It was during this atmosphere of harassment that Czech dissidents began working with their Polish colleagues. The initial contact was apparently made by a young Slovak, Tomáš Petřivý, who traveled to Warsaw and arranged for two small groups to meet in the high mountains along the border in an area that could only be reached after a strenuous hike by both sides. The Czech side of the delegation included Marta Kubišová and Jiří Bednář, who traveled to the Giant

Mountains from Prague. Havel somehow managed to shake his tail and meet them on the hiking trail in the mountains. The Polish delegation included Adam Michnik, a dissident journalist and historian who would later play a decisive role in negotiating for democratic elections. After greeting each other, Havel pulled out a bottle of expensive vodka to help take the weariness out of the day, and the two sides shared ideas and plans and created a joint statement.[6]

Although the two dissident groups were only able to meet twice, their cooperation proved decisive in at least one way. One of the ideas that came out of their joint meeting was a samizdat collection to be published in Poland about the meaning of dissent, with Havel agreeing to write the lead essay, which he was to call "The Power of the Powerless." It was, perhaps, the most important work of Havel's entire career, and it was also probably the most influential dissident essay written by anyone in the Communist bloc. In Poland, the essay became essential reading, a blueprint for how to face the regime. Zbigniew Bujak, a union organizer in a large tractor factory, later said that "when we read Havel we knew what to do." He recalled the first time he read the essay, feeling as if he were "at the end of the road." He went on: "We had been speaking on the shop floor, talking to people, participating in public meetings, trying to speak the truth about the factory, the country, and politics. There came a moment when people thought we were crazy. Why were we doing this? Why were we taking such risks? Not seeing any immediate and tangible results, we began to doubt the purposefulness of what we were doing. . . . Then came the essay by Havel. Reading it gave us the theoretical underpinnings for our activity. It maintained our spirts."[7]

Havel wrote the one-hundred-page essay quickly at Hrádeček, working in his studio, with windows that overlooked the garden. Afraid that the new police surveillance meant that his house might be searched at any time, he took to hiding his thick manuscript at night in the crook of a tree outside his house. When he had finished the essay, in October 1978, he drove in to Prague, leaving it in his father's apartment to be read by Jan Lopatka. Havel waited in a restaurant on

Mikulandská Street, where Lopatka soon joined him to confirm that the essay was brilliant.[8]

Havel's essay, which was published in Edice Petlice, focused on what it meant to live as a "dissident."[9] Like many intellectuals, Havel disliked the term "dissident," feeling that it was an imposition, but it was also probably inevitable that Western journalists would need a simple term to describe the nonconformists who, like himself, had decided to live their own truth.

Dissent, as Havel explained it in the essay, was an "inevitable consequence" of a system that "for a thousand reasons, can no longer base itself on an unadulterated, brutal, arbitrary application of power." Instead, the regimes in Eastern Europe maintained control through fear and propaganda, as well as the willingness of citizens to pretend to support its policies. In short, the communist system had become what Havel called "post-totalitarian." It was not the most precise term, but it distinguished the communist system of Eastern Europe from classic dictatorships. "Post-totalitarian" systems were part of a huge machine overseen by the Soviet Union, and principles, ideologies, and slogans in the system were almost religious in nature. In many ways, those who wielded power were just as powerless as those they governed, having been swallowed up by the monster they had helped create, forced to live within an ideological framework that was increasingly divorced from the world of everyday experience. It was this alienation that concerned Havel most. He defined dissidence as the struggle against such alienation. A dissident was someone who took an "existential attitude," attempting not to serve an ideology but to serve "truth" and the "real aims of life."

Havel dedicated the essay to Jan Patočka, the philosopher who had helped lead Charter 77. No doubt Havel did so because the essay had been inspired by a number of Patočka's most important ideas, such as the sense that Western civilization had a tendency to create ideological systems and technological enterprises that endangered our ability to remain human. There may have been another reason. Patočka had once told Havel that "the real test of a man is not how well he plays the role he has invented for himself but how well he plays the role that destiny has assigned." Just as Patočka had been haunted by the sense of philosophers looking over his shoulder, judging his actions, Havel was becoming haunted by Patočka and his idea of self-sacrifice.[10]

As winter approached in 1978, the Havels returned to Prague to be in close contact with other members of Charter 77. On December 7 the police placed two uniformed men on the landing below their Prague apartment, allowing no one to visit. Two days later, they informed Havel that he was not allowed to leave the building, although they did allow Olga to go out for food and errands. Several of the police guarding the apartment were abusive, including one who would regularly ring the doorbell, then tell Havel, "Today, you son-of-a-bitch, we're going to beat the shit out of you."

Given the harassment, the Havels soon returned to Hrádeček, an action the police were only too happy to oblige. As soon as they returned to Hrádeček, the police erected a modular guardhouse directly across from the narrow road that led to their house. Once again, no one was allowed to visit, but both Havels were allowed to go shopping or to go on walks in the woods, as long as a few operatives could trail along behind them.[11]

During his trip to Prague, Havel had been able to get his hands on a short essay (known in Czech as a *fejeton*) written by his old friend Ludvík Vaculík.[12] Vaculík had written the piece, which he titled "On Heroism" upon receiving a letter from Jiří Müller, a political prisoner who was advising him "to act in an effective way and to avoid arrest."[13] The advice sobered Vaculík, perhaps because he had been so close to arrest many times in the past decade.

"I sometimes wonder if I'm mature enough to go to prison," Vaculík wrote in his essay. "It frightens me. We should all come to terms with this problem once we reach adulthood, and either behave in such a way as not to have to fear imprisonment or consider what is worth such a risk. It is hard to be locked up for something that will have ceased to excite anyone even before your sentence is up." Vaculík went on to suggest that it was impossible to say whether Charter 77 had improved the situation in the country or made it worse. Further, he said, reasonable people could hardly expect to support the charter if it continued to take confrontational stands, since most people refrain from actions whose consequences frighten them. The real struggle in the country belonged not to those few who wished to be heroes, perhaps ending up in prison, but to "everyone" who can "bravely adhere to the norm of good behavior at the price of acceptable sacrifice."[14] When writing those words, Vaculík was almost certainly thinking of Havel.

Vaculík's essay was probably passed along to Havel for the first time when he visited his father and brother at the family flat. By that time, Ivan Havel was himself connected to various underground activities, including a weekly lecture series that was attended by intellectuals and philosophers.[15] However the essay reached him, Vaculík's words disturbed him. At Hrádeček, he wrote a strongly worded reply, giving it to a friend to deliver to Prague, where it was retyped and sent through the underground circles.[16]

Havel's original letter appears to have been lost, but portions of it can be found in Vaculík's chronicle of that year, *The Czech Dream Book*. In Vaculík's account, Havel wrote that the overall impression given by the essay was that "heroes are dangerous" and "police informers are quite decent on the whole." Václav added that he had "nothing against a man if he moves into the background when he's tired or even if he emigrates." He did, however, have a quarrel to pick with anyone who failed to stand for the truth.[17]

Others took issue with Vaculík as well. Jiří Gruša, for instance, told Vaculík that he had "a Freudian bone" to pick with him when the two ran into each other near Old Town Square. It's hard to see what Freud had to do with Gruša's concerns, but Gruša suggested that Vaculík's words would be used to sway dissidents in interrogations. Vaculík held his ground, saying that as "free men" they shouldn't censor their thoughts just because "the secret police listened in on us." However, after his wife and son sided with Havel, Vaculík wrote and distributed a second essay, saying that even he agreed with the "logic" of the arguments against him. As he wrote in his fictionalized chronicles of those years, he had not meant to argue against heroism but rather to suggest that the silent and continuous humiliation of anonymous citizens was far more difficult to bear than the fate of well-known dissidents whose quarrels with the state allowed them to appear heroic.[18] Vaculík had risked as much as anyone, living on the edge of arrest for almost a decade. His short essay most likely represented the reservations of a deeply eccentric writer who reserved the right, as Ladislav Hejdánek once said of him, to be brilliant on one occasion and imbecilic on another.[19]

If Havel harbored secret "heroic aspirations," as some of his friends suspected, he also harbored a deep ambivalence. Despite his longing to get arrested, the new attention of the police troubled him. Staying at Hrádeček, under virtual house arrest, he began to suffer from insomnia, headaches, and stomach ailments. In his dreams, he was haunted by the faces of the operatives who followed him, often hearing their footsteps behind him, as if he was being tracked by some authority he couldn't shake. The old depression came back as well, and he found himself unable to concentrate on his writing. The symptoms were serious enough to prompt a visit to a doctor, who diagnosed a "neuro-vegetative" condition,[20] almost certainly a reference to the onset of a clinical depression that affected his judgment and ability to concentrate.

Havel's medical condition may have made it even more difficult to face a new harassment campaign that was apparently part of a larger strategy to get the most prominent dissidents to emigrate. Electricity to his flat was cut, sometimes for days at a time, and sugar was poured in the gas tank of his Mercedes, gumming up the gas line, the fuel pump, and the carburetor. On another occasion, he discovered the windshield of the Mercedes had been destroyed. After a long negotiation, the police allowed him to drive to Česká Skalice to replace the glass at a service station. After the service order was filled out, an embarrassed mechanic emerged to tell Havel that he couldn't finish the repair, explaining Havel should "realize where he's living." Havel then telephoned the manager of a service station in a nearby town in order to buy a windshield that he would replace himself. Before making the drive, Havel asked the manager of the station to give his "word of honor" that he would sell him the windshield if Havel drove there to pick it up.[21]

Such techniques were all too effective. Zdeněk Mlynář and Eugene Menert emigrated after similar harassment, as did Pavel Landovský, the actor who had been in the car with Havel when he was arrested with documents from Charter 77, and who had picked Havel up from prison. Landovský finally decided to leave the country after he was attacked one night in downtown Prague, leaving him with a broken leg. Havel also lost Pavel Kohout, his closest friend, who was allowed to visit Vienna in order to work with the Burgtheater, only to see his citizenship revoked after he left the country.

The exodus of dissidents led a reporter at the *New York Times* to declare that "[some] of the most vocal and effective critics who were living in the country at the start of 1977 now live in Tel Aviv, Paris, Vienna and New York."[22] The steady stream of emigration left a wake of loneliness for those who remained behind. In the late 1970s, there was a rumor that Havel planned to emigrate as well, a story that was no doubt planted by the secret police, who had told Havel that they could get him a passport within twenty-four hours if he would leave the country. Havel politely declined their offer.

After the many heated debates within Charter 77, two new spokespersons were added in late 1977, the philosopher Ladislav Hejdánek and the folk singer Marta Kubišová. The following year, Hájek was replaced by Jaroslav Šabata. A tradition was thus established that the organization would retain three spokespersons, each representing a different segment of the resistance. The spokespersons served short terms, usually no longer than a year, and were replaced by another member, establishing a continuity that was difficult for the state to combat. Despite harassment from every level of the state, the charter itself grew from a mere 242 signatories in January 1977 to more than a thousand a decade later.

In November 1978, however, the charter faced a crisis. After two of its spokespersons resigned, Havel stepped in while a new generation of leaders could be appointed.[23] That was the winter that Havel tried to spend in Prague, facing perpetual house arrest, before retreating to Hrádeček. In February he returned, when the city was buried under a large snowstorm. The official reason for Havel's visit was a summons by the secret police, who interrogated him in a room at Ruzyně prison. One of its officers had been preparing the prosecution of Jiří Gruša, an old literary friend whom Havel knew from the 1960s. Gruša had faced a number of legal problems since 1974, when he had been caught distributing nineteen copies of his own samizdat novel, *Dotazník*.[24]

That winter, Havel had unofficial business in Prague. Although a large contingent of secret police was assigned to watch him, including the operatives who were normally assigned to Petr Uhl, Havel managed to slip his tail in the metro and visit Václav Benda, one of the new spokespersons of Charter 77, in Benda's large, book-lined flat overlooking Charles Square. Havel had a good fifteen minutes with Václav Benda before the secret police caught up with him.[25]

One reason for visiting may have been congratulating Benda on the honor of being appointed spokesperson, but the two men had other affairs to discuss as well. Both of them were working on establishing a new, more aggressive organization, known as the Committee for the Defense of the Unjustly Prosecuted, which would document the treatment of political prisoners, an idea that may have come out of an experience the year before when about one hundred members of Charter 77 had attended a ball together in the Vinohrady district of Prague. They had bought the tickets legally, as something like an innocent prank, a chance to have some fun together, with Havel arriving in cuff links and a black tie. The police responded by arresting both Havel and Pavel Landovský, giving them both six weeks in jail before releasing them without charges or a trial.[26]

Often referred to by its Czech acronym, VONS worked to provide legal aid and publicize cases that involved the abuse of the law. In the next few months, Havel spent a great many hours in the Benda flat, often sitting in the overstuffed chair opposite of the room-length bookshelf, just a few feet away from listening devices that were later discovered by the Benda family.[27] Unlike Charter 77, VONS occupied in a gray zone. Not only did it look like an organization, with an outreach program for political prisoners, but it functioned as watchdog group, meaning that it probably required state approval in order to operate legally. As a result, VONS would soon become one of the most persecuted organizations in the country.

By his own admission, Havel was not in good mental health during the late 1970s. His fragile emotional state had been gradually worn down by constant activity and police harassment, and perhaps also by his own need for redemption. He appears to have found some solace in the arms of Anna Kohoutová, the ex-wife of his good friend Pavel Kohout. The affair was far more than a casual fling. Anna was a smart, intelligent, vibrant woman who provided a connection, in absentia, to his old friend, who was now living in Vienna. When the two wanted privacy, they retreated to Kohout's weekend house in Sázava, a good place to frolic and remember happier times.

Havel alluded to his trysts in a letter to Kohout, dated March 11, 1979. After discussing his many problems, including his inability to write and increased pressure from the secret police, he told Kohout that "I am always luckiest whenever I am unlucky. Just whenever I feel the worst, some precious creature appears who brings a little bit of light into my life." Havel didn't mention that the precious creature was Kohout's ex-wife, but Kohout had probably already heard about the affair through mutual friends. At any rate, it may not have been hard to guess what was happening, since Havel admitted to writing the letter from Kohout's former weekend home. "Thanks for lending me the sanctuary," Havel wrote, "even if you weren't aware of it."[28]

Two days after Havel wrote the letter, Kohout was called into the Czech embassy in Vienna, where he was told to stop allowing his house in Czechoslovakia to be used as "meeting places against the government." Kohout immediately sent a strongly worded letter to Havel, making it clear that he resented Havel using his house and that, because of his actions, the state might confiscate his property.[29] Havel was flustered by Kohout's letter, knowing he was on thin ice. He wrote back to his old friend that "I read the letter that was addressed to unknown perpetrators or offenders committing illegal activities inside your dwellings." Havel went on to say, feeling somewhat enraged, that he understood the letter was addressed to him. "I'm the only rotten one who has spent the night in the house at Sázava," he wrote, "and I was very, very saddened by your letter." Havel added that Kohout didn't have to change the locks on his weekend house because "I would not again climb into one of your dwellings, hoping that it wouldn't be used against you, that terrible stupidity I would never do again in my life."[30]

Two months later, the state decided to take action against the organization that Havel had started with Václav Benda, the Committee for the Unjustly Prosecuted, or VONS. At 5 a.m. on a Tuesday morning, the police arrived at the Benda apartment above Charles Square. When Václav Benda refused to unhook the latch, the police broke down the door. They searched the house and arrested Benda in his nightgown.[31]

Later that same morning, the police detained sixteen members of VONS. Havel, however, was not at Hrádeček when the police arrived to arrest him. Instead, they found him in the apartment of Anna Kohoutová, where he had prepared himself with his "prison kit," a large blue bag containing pajamas, slippers, underwear, four shirts, and a book to read, Ken Kesey's *One Flew over the Cuckoo's Nest*.[32]

Although Havel was arrested in May, the trial didn't begin until five months later. Part of the delay appears to have been a split between party leadership over the wisdom of sending Havel to prison.[33] When he and his codefendants were finally brought before a judge, security was tight. Although the court released no transcripts of the hearing, dissidents published a thirty-page samizdat report compiled from notes and memory by close relatives who were allowed to attend. According to those documents, the proceedings began with the chairman of the tribunal, Antonín Kašpar, reading the indictment, which accused the defendants "of hostility to the socialist state system of government in Czechoslovakia . . . with the purpose of aiding and abetting anti-community propaganda abroad, [and] evoking hostility among the population towards the socialist system." The defendants were also charged with establishing an illegal organization. Over the next two days, a handful of witnesses were called, none of them seeming to confirm the accusations in the indictment. Finally, the defendants were allowed to make statements. The first to speak was Havel, who told the tribunal that "in January 1977 I was arrested and, on the basis of untruthful testimony provided by the police, charged with attacking a public official. I spent six weeks in prison and a year later the charges were dropped. I was fortunate, for a large number of witnesses came forward to testify to what really happened, confirming my innocence. Thus I had directly experienced what it was like to be unjustly prosecuted. At the time of my arrest, a committee was formed to help obtain our release."

At this point, Havel was interrupted by the tribunal and asked to "please try to keep to the point." Havel responded, "I merely wanted to say that I have reasons to believe that the existence of that committee, the fact that my name was well-known abroad, and the pressure of world public opinion contributed greatly to my release and subsequent discharge."

The chairman of the tribunal gave Havel a fatherly smile. "There, you see, Mr. Havel? Justice was done after all," he said. Undaunted, Havel went on to attack the system. He pointed out that although the prosecutors had suggested that VONS had slandered the state, they had never provided any evidence of inaccuracy or distortion in the VONS reports. In short, the state hadn't even attempted to prove their case. At this point, the judge interrupted, again, asking Havel to be brief. Havel replied,

> I wanted to point out why I thought the powers-that-be decided to move against VONS. They made the *a priori* assumption that the state organs can never do anything unjust. Court decisions are considered infallible in principle. This assumption of infallibility is a very dangerous matter. . . .
>
> There exist a whole series of illegal procedures which are beyond public control. I have in mind the practical lack of public access

to trials, and the preventative arrest of persons who are merely assumed to be interested in attending given trials. All this runs counter to our constitution and the international pacts on human rights.[34]

After the defendants finished with their statements, the court found all five guilty of subversion. Havel was sentenced to four and a half years in prison. Peter Uhl was sentenced to five years, Václav Benda to four years, and Otta Bednářová and Jiří Dienstbier were sentenced to three years. Dana Němcová received a suspended sentence. Since her husband was already in jail, incarcerating her would have left no one to care for their seven children.

In the five months of pretrial detention, Havel faced two ordeals that tested his resolve, his feeling that he would feel "best of all, relatively speaking, in prison."[35] The first was the death of his father. Authorities had let him out of prison for the funeral, allowing him to change into a dark suit and tie, sitting in the front row next to Olga and his brother. Photographs of the day show him looking somber, his hair drifting over his ears, his sideburns crawling down the sides of his cheeks. The emotional difficulty for Havel, he later said, was not the funeral but returning to prison after the ceremony, knowing what the regime had taken from him and his family.[36]

Three months after his father's funeral, Havel was called into the warden's office at Ruzyně. Behind the scenes, his old friend Miloš Forman had been using his success as an Oscar-winning director to apply international pressure to have Havel released. He eventually convinced Joe Papp, the director of the Public Theater in New York, to contact the chargé d'affaires of the Czech embassy in Washington, D.C., offering to provide Havel a theater position for a year if the state would release Havel from prison. As Papp told the Czech officials, Havel's trial "would inevitably create a strong protest here." The letter was written in a friendly style in the spirit of solving a problem for all sides.[37] Papp's offer was not only accepted by the government but delivered to Havel by the minister of interior, who sat down over coffee in the warden's office to explain the advantages of leaving the country. Havel was even allowed to consult with Olga over the decision at her next visit, on September 5, 1979.

Olga was clearly ambivalent about the choice, probably because so much was left unclear. What kind of statement would Havel have to make in order to be freed? Would they be allowed to return to Czechoslovakia after spending a year in the United States? She told some friends she would never leave; to others, she said that she wouldn't mind emigrating. In the end, she deferred the entire decision to her husband, saying that only he could decide. He was the one in prison, after all, and no one, Olga explained, could know how they would face such a temptation until they actually experienced it.[38]

Havel took the offer to emigrate seriously and assumed it would be a permanent decision, since the government could be expected to revoke his citizenship as soon as he left the country. At night he was dreaming of his friends who had emigrated to the United States and Austria, and during the day he worried about how people like Joseph Papp would feel if he turned down their offer to help him. It was an impossible dilemma. On the one hand, he was unsure he could survive prison. On the other hand, prison would mean proving to himself that his fame had not protected him all along, that he had not benefited, as in his childhood, from one more undeserved privilege.[39] In addition to all of the personal considerations, to all of the hopes, fears, and neurotic rationalizations, there can be little doubt that Havel was also ruminating (in some sense) over the advice given to him by the philosopher Jan Patočka shortly before he died that "the real test of a man is not how well he plays the role that he has invented for himself, but how well he plays the role destiny assigned him."[40] Emigrating would provide him personal freedom, the chance to think and write without interference, perhaps even artistic and financial success. Havel's fate, however, seemed to suggest a different direction.[41]

**Father and son:** Václav M. Havel and Václav Havel, May 1938, sitting in the restaurant owned by the family in the Barrandov area. The Havel family had a restaurant, film studio, and housing estate in the hills on southwestern outskirts of Prague. Václav Havel Library.

**The family:** Božena Havlová and Václav M. Havel with their two children, Václav (*right*) and Ivan (*left*) at the family retreat, known as Havlov. In the background can be seen the vine-covered house (*to the left*) and the tennis courts (*to the right*). The photograph was taken during the summer of 1939. Václav Havel Library.

**Two brothers:** Miloš Havel (*sitting*) and Václav M. Havel (*standing*) pose during the filming of Rosina Sebranec in 1940. By this time, the German war machine had already effectively taken control of the film studio. Karl Ludwig, Archive B&M Chochola.

**The writer at work (*above*):** Havel in 1966, seated at the typewriter in his bedroom at the family apartment on the embankment to the Vltava River, where he wrote many of his early plays, often working all night with the help of pep pills. Václav Havel Library.

**After the fall (*opposite page, top*):** Miloš Havel smoking a cigarette in 1940, sometime after the establishment of the Czech and Moravian Protectorate. Karl Ludwig, Archive B&M Chochola.

**Night life (*opposite page, bottom*):** Havel and his future wife, Olga Šplíchalová, in the late 1950s at their usual hangout, the Slavia Café, across the street from the National Theater. Václav Havel Library.

**A playwright abroad:** April 1968, Havel strolls through Central Park on his trip to New York City to attend the English-language premiere of The Memorandum at the New York Shakespeare Festival. Jan Lukáš.

**With the exiles:** On his 1968 trip to New York City, Havel stayed briefly at the Jackson Heights home of Ferdinand Peroutka, a Czech émigré and one of the most talented journalists of the First Republic era. Jan Lukáš.

**Smoking break:** Havel shown after visiting with another Czech exile, the actor George (Jiří) Voskovec, on his trip to New York City, 1968. During the First Republic, Voskovec had been the partner of Jan Werich at the Liberated Theater, and it was Werich who gave Havel his first job as a stagehand. Jan Lukáš.

**The great philosopher and his wine** (*above*): Jan Patočka (*facing the camera on the left*) and Ivan Klíma (*on Patočka's right*) have a talk with the American playwright Arthur Miller on his visit to Prague in 1973. Oldřich Škácha, Václav Havel Library.

**Drinking party** (*opposite page, top*): Jan Tříska and his wife, Karla Chadimová, posing for the camera with the Havels after an evening of fun at Hrádeček, sometime in 1975. Jan, in particular, liked to come for long visits during the summer. Bohdan Holomíček.

**The little castle** (*opposite page, bottom*): Hrádeček as seen from the back in 1974, after most of the renovations were complete. The Krobs' cabin lies a few dozen yards uphill to the righthand side of the photograph. Bohdan Holomíček.

**Postperformance review (*above*):** Havel, Andrej Krob, and Pavel Landovský (*left to right*) at the restaurant U Medvídků after the performance of Beggar's Opera in November 1975. More than a few people had expected the secret police to bust in on the performance. Bohdan Holomíček.

**A hot afternoon at Hradeček (*opposite page, top*):** Havel and Ivan Klíma in the backyard of Hrádeček after a trip into Trutnov during the summer of 1975. The woman is unidentified. Bohdan Holomíček.

**Excursion (*opposite page, bottom*):** Havel, Karel Kosík, Ludvík Vaculík, Pavel Kohout, and Alexander Kliment (*left to right*) pose for a photograph before one of sojourns from Hrádeček, summer of 1975. Bohdan Holomíček.

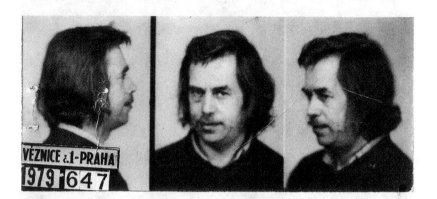

**Mug shot (*above*):** Havel's official prison photograph from Pankrác Prison, 1979. Václav Havel Library.

**Dissidents at work (*opposite page, top*):** Havel, Ludvík Vaculík, and Pavel Kohout (*left to right*) look over the draft of a document in a Prague apartment in 1977. Oldřich Skácha, Václav Havel Library.

**Charter 77 (*opposite page, bottom*):** Jiří Hajek, Ladislav Hejdánek, and Havel (*left to right*) discuss strategy while sitting in the flat of Kamila and Václav Benda on Charles Square. The Bendas later discovered a listening device in the room, in the wall near where Havel is sitting. Ondřej Němec, Václav Havel Library.

**At the White House** (*above*): On his trip to Washington, DC in 1990, Havel met with American president George Herbert Walker Bush, who promised aid to help rebuild the Czechoslovakian economy. The American ambassador to Czechoslovakia, Shirley Temple Black, can be seen just over President Bush's shoulder, and Jiří Dienstbier and Václav Klaus can be seen looking on from the Czech side of the delegation on the left side. Bohdan Holomíček.

**A day and night of music** (*opposite page, top*): Havel and Pavel Landovský sit in the audience during the Third Festival of Underground Culture, November 1977. Havel was awaiting prison sentencing at the time the festival took place, using makeshift stages in the back of Hrádeček and in Andrej Krob's barn, which is where Havel and Landovský appear to be sitting. Ondřej Němec, Václav Havel Library.

**Inside the Capitol** (*opposite page, bottom*): On February 21, 1990, less than two months after winning the presidency, Havel is given the rare honor of giving a speech to a joint session of the United States Congress. Bohdan Holomíček.

# PART THREE

## The Politics of Love

### August 1979–July 1990

Poison is in everything, and no thing
is without poison. The dosage makes
it either poison or a remedy.

—PARACELSUS

# 12

## IN THE DARK

SOME HAD BECOME COMMUNISTS TO BUILD A new kind of society. Others had lost faith in liberal democracy or been radicalized by world war. By the late 1970s, however, the true believers were gone. Privately, most citizens regarded the Communist Party with the contempt normally reserved for the town drunk. In this respect, a dark irony gradually worked its way into the life of the nation. Those wishing to avoid conflict voiced the slogans of the party, taking part in the rituals of allegiance while knowing they no longer carried meaning. The whole society floated in an ocean of slogans, half-truths, and ideology, a world of absurdity governed by the expediency of the moment.

Those who refused to play the game faced a series of escalating punishments, the endpoint of which was prison, where totalitarianism existed in its purist form, the warden possessing total control over every moment of an inmate's waking life. While awaiting trial, Havel strove to treat his future prison sentence lightly, speaking of it as another adventure, a challenge to be mastered, even a chance for self-improvement. In a letter written to his wife while in detention, he suggested that prison might be good for him. The stress of the past few years had worked him into a fever pitch. He hoped the new surroundings might have a "calming effect" on his nervous behavior. He mentioned that prison might also cure preoccupations with the "intimate" side of his life, an apparent reference to chasing women and the strain it had put on their marriage.[1]

The optimism of his pretrial detention letters may have been paper thin. Havel made lists of what he wanted to accomplish in prison. He expected to use his isolation to learn a foreign language, catch up on his reading, and write two new plays. He also planned to teach himself yoga. In short, Havel strove to see prison as a chance to find the peace and self-reflection that eluded him in the outside world. Behind the brave face lay profound self-doubts. While in prison, Havel kept a wary eye on his mental health, which he chronicled in detail to his wife. His prison depression in 1977 had led to a humiliating decision, and he vowed to himself that he wouldn't let his guard down again.

Havel first mentioned concerns over his "nervous disposition" some three months after entering detention, saying: "It's sad and oppressive here, and the people are cold, but don't worry, I'll survive unscathed." He added that

> after all of those earlier experiences, I can experience everything
> in a reflective manner and I keep a watchful eye on myself, so that
> I am in no danger, I think, of succumbing to the various forms of
> prison psychosis. I try to respond to the many subtle warning
> signs—which is why I am writing to you in my normal hand and not
> in that neat little chicken-scratch; even such details, it seems to me,
> are important; there is, in that tight, perfectly legible calligraphy
> something of an involuntary curtailment, something squelched
> that naturally influences the way I express myself and thus the way
> I think as well.[2]

Havel knew from experience what prison could do to a man. He knew he needed strength and courage, and he knew that his own disposition placed him in extreme danger. In March of the next year, in another letter to Olga, Havel reflected that "I've discovered that in lengthy prison terms, sensitive people are in danger of becoming em-

bittered, developing grudges against the world, growing dull, indifferent and selfish." He vowed "not to give an inch" to such impulses. He
wanted to "remain open to the world, not to shut myself against it,"
and this meant retaining his hope in people "and my love for them."
If he gave into hate, he wrote, then all would be lost.[3]

Prisons in Czechoslovakia suffered from the same malaise as the rest
of society. In many prisons, inmates were malnourished. Breakfast
typically consisted of dry bread and coffee. Those who met their work
quotas received a portion of meat and two hard-boiled eggs, but the
work quotas were often impossibly high for political prisoners. And
failure to meet the work quotas meant being placed on half rations.[4]
The human rights group Charter 77 documented many of the abuses
in prison and accused the communist regime of "an overall brutal-
ization of conditions."[5] Human Rights Watch agreed with the assessment. According to a 1989 report: "Prisons and jails are miserable
places, but those in Czechoslovakia seem exceptionally inhumane.
Inmates are often packed into overcrowded, stuffy, smelly, filthy dark
cells that are too hot or cold; guards brutally abuse them, physically
and verbally; medical aid is almost always grossly inadequate; food is
usually meager, tasteless, and poor in nutrition. Further, punishments
are unfair and harsh, prisoners are terrorized by fellow inmates, and
religious practices of any kind are prohibited."[6]

Criminals in Czechoslovakia were sorted into two kinds of facili-
ties, the pretrial detention centers and what were known as "corrective
educational institutions." Category III prisons, such as Heřmanice,
where Havel was first placed, were "corrective educational institutions" reserved for dissidents and dangerous criminals. At Heřmanice,
prisoners served hard labor and could be sent to solitary confinement
for such issues as referring to a fellow prisoner as "comrade" in an
ironic tone or not taking off a prison cap when talking to a guard.

Most category III prisons had their pecking order, with accomplished criminals at the top. Political prisoners, however, occupied
a separate but equal space. Despite the macho culture among hardened convicts, many prisoners respected the courage and conviction

of dissidents. Perhaps this was because, as Havel himself said, many criminals were intellectual and emotional cripples, and they watched dissidents with a sense of open-eyed awe. Havel, like many political prisoners, spent a great deal of time advising other inmates on legal matters and on disputes inside the prison. Havel also helped illiterate prisoners write letters home, and in one case he received a stint in solitary confinement for helping a fellow inmate, a Gypsy, write a love letter to his wife. With perhaps only a little hyperbole, Havel's Czech biographer Eda Kriseová said that Havel, like many of his fellow dissidents, acted "as parish priest, judge, counselor, and a psychologist to his fellow prisoners."[7] As a result, the "kings" (as the alpha males were called) largely avoided him, except when they needed a favor.[8]

Havel's ideas for self-improvement were dashed within the first few months. He dropped his project to improve his English after reading *To Kill a Mockingbird* and *The Pickwick Papers*, finding the vocabulary overwhelming. His yoga was blocked by physical ailments, including lumbago (or perhaps rheumatism), making it difficult for him to stand up or sit down. A week after his lumbago lightened, he was struck with an excruciating case of hemorrhoids, an ailment that often haunted him when he felt overwhelmed. The prison doctor ordered five days' rest in bed and warm water for his "backside."[9]

By the time of his sentencing hearing, Havel was also having digestive issues. He found it difficult to concentrate and impossible to write. For one thing, the other inmates prattled on about all manner of inanities, especially about their trouble with women, which Havel found unbearable. "Hell is other people," Havel wrote home. He could get along with anyone, he felt, but in prison the intimacy felt overbearing. There was no escape from the constant chatter. He complained to Olga that in prison he lived in more close contact with his cell mate than "a man lives with his wife."[10]

As far as writing went, Havel wrote Olga that although he had "plenty of ideas chasing around in my head," he now realized that finishing a play while in prison would be impossible. His life was "sad and oppressive, full of difficult, cold people," exactly the opposite of the calm atmosphere he needed to compose a play. Instead of writing his most important plays behind bars, he was slowly sinking into a morose, angry mood.[11]

Early in his prison sentence, Havel had a series of dreams about his old friend Miloš Forman, who was living in America. Havel saw the dreams as a kind of wish fulfillment, a sign that he regretted not emigrating to the United States and that he secretly resented Forman for having the Hollywood success that Havel desired. Havel also had a dream of Olga vacationing at a beautiful house in Italy. Although he refrained from analyzing his dream of Olga, she had always represented the undeveloped side of his personality, his longing to be close to the earth, to be a regular guy, close to regular working-class folks from whom he had been alienated in his childhood. It's hard not to suspect that the dreams of Olga and Forman referred to an internal movement he was experiencing, a deepening sense of sorrow and sadness that was at odds with the upward-bound success that had always been encouraged by his family. By his own admission, he became more paranoid in prison, more melancholic, more frightened of the state. He was also deepening his idealistic convictions, which were now colored by personal suffering.

The emphasis at Heřmanice prison was on discipline and order. Some eight hundred prisoners were overseen by three psychologists and two social workers whose primary goal was ensuring the cultural and educational conformity according to the collective ideals of society.[12] The prison warden was Comrade Košulič, a former Nazi sympathizer whom Havel called "a half-demented" and "genuinely dangerous person." Košulič, who had started his career overseeing a labor camp in the Stalinist era, possessed special dislike for political prisoners, and he appears to have singled out Havel for frequent threats. In Havel's account, Košulič told him upon their first meeting that "Hitler did things differently—he gassed vermin like you right away."[13]

A few days after Havel's arrival at Heřmanice, he was assigned a prison psychologist, who conducted a customary four-page profile. The report begins by describing prisoner 9658 as a well-mannered, "almost timid" middle-aged man who responded to questions "without latency." The psychologist noted that Havel admitted to using alcoholic beverages and smoking about a pack of cigarettes a day. Although Havel had never tried to commit suicide, he had once walked into a psychiatry unit for evaluation. The psychologist described Havel as a "liberal, free thinking, radical, . . . attention-seeking, ambitious, . . . prone to insecurity, excitable, sensitive to disapproval of others . . . dependent, nervously restless."[14]

After the psychological evaluation, Havel was forbidden from taking part in the self-governing activities of the prison and given a job as a spot welder. His inability to meet the work quotas for his welding job allowed the warden to find creative ways to punish him, including withholding food rations. Havel was allowed to write one four-page letter home each week. The letter had to be legible, no foreign phrases were allowed, and humor and graphics were forbidden. He could write nothing about politics or current affairs. Almost immediately, Havel turned to the idea of using the letters to reflect on grand themes (art, philosophy, theater, morality), each letter serving as an independent essay.[15]

If the letters to Olga were short on affection and personal feeling, it was partly because the Havels had never openly discussed personal emotions. In many ways, their relationship had always been more about partnership, originally revolving around the theater and later political dissidence. In the spirit of that partnership, Havel's letters home were not conventional love letters from a husband but rather epistles on the art of living in a totalitarian state. The letters were widely read by family, friends, colleagues, and fellow dissidents. While Havel originally spoke of his letters home as a way to keep his sanity, by May 1982 he was already thinking about how his letters might be published in the samizdat press. He had stumbled, almost by accident, into one of his most important works.[16]

While in prison, Havel was plagued by one health crisis after another, often precipitated by nerves, poor nutrition, and overwork. One of the first of these episodes occurred in the summer of 1981, when he fell seriously ill while serving fifteen days of solitary confinement for "disobeying an order." On return from solitary, he wrote a long meditation to Olga on the nature of suicide, a topic of lifelong interest, perhaps because it involved hope and despair, themes close to his heart.

It's unclear exactly what happened during solitary confinement, but Havel did become ill enough during his stay to scare authorities. His hemorrhoids swelled so much that he could hardly move, and he also suffered from fevers and trembling. On Monday, January 20, he was driven all night to the prison hospital in Prague, where he underwent a proctoscopy, a bowel X-ray, and ECG. Doctors discovered not only hemorrhoidal inflammation but also what Havel called "something else unwholesome inside" that was apparently a nonmalignant tumor. The result was a "strange and mostly wonderful" stay in the hospital, where he was able to lounge in bed in a room to himself for two weeks, the only unpleasant effect being he was denied cigarettes, which he had been smoking heavily for thirty years.[17]

Havel returned to the hospital again in September, this time unable to lie in bed without experiencing severe pain. In a dark and sorrowful mood, he wrote Olga a letter about what he called "the meaning of life and Being." Finding it "practically impossible" to think without a cigarette, he nevertheless summarized his ideas. Being, he wrote, was something like a tablet "on which everything is drawn on or written down" so that no personal event ever vanishes, giving our fleeting experience of daily life the feeling of permanence or stability needed for any meaningful or ethical action.[18] The notion of the memory of being, drawn from the phenomenological tradition of philosophy, was that due to the experience of consciousness it seems *as if* someone is watching our actions, allowing us to feel that everything has a purpose, a direction.

Havel continued the theme in his next letter, written a few days after his surgery. What he called "the memory of Being" was, he thought, the reason humans could commit a selfless act. As he wrote to Olga, the desire to do good was the result of the feeling that our actions are recorded on the tablet of Being. This is the reason, he wrote, that "when we are travelling alone (a single stop) in the second car of a conductor-less streetcar, so that obviously no one could catch us not paying, we still usually—though perhaps after an inner tussle—drop our fares in the box."[19]

The language was rather abstract and depersonalized, but Havel was trying to articulate his own personal experience, the feeling that he was being judged by himself, not least while he faced the challenges of prison. Havel's contact with what he called the "ground of Being" was, he reflected, "a supremely spiritual experience." He preferred not to speak of God, he wrote, since he thought of God as a personification of the deep mysteries of consciousness. But the concept of both God and Being gave every action a permanent meaning. He went on: "I think this experience, and this experience alone, is the 'suboceanic mountain range' that gives coherence and integrity to all those isolated 'islands of meaning' adrift on the ocean of Nothingness, the only effecting defense against that nothingness." Though it reveals nothing of the secret of Being, nor responds in any way to the question of meaning, it is still the most essential way of coexisting with it.[20]

Recuperating in the hospital, Havel ran a temperature and faced an obstructed bladder. The most serious sufferings, however, involved the spirit. After his fever topped 104 degrees Fahrenheit, he fell into a sense of despair.[21] A few days later, he wrote home once again about the many "intelligent and decent people" he had known who had become bitter and misanthropic. Havel knew only too well how easy it was to become embittered. "The temptation of Nothingness is enormous and omnipresent, and it has more and more to rest its case on, more to appeal. Against it, man stands alone, weak and poorly armed . . ."[22]

As Havel began to see it, surviving prison meant giving up a personal sense of self for something much larger, of seeing and experiencing himself not only from the point of view of Being—which he had roughly equated as the point of view of God—but identifying with other people. It was only by looking outward, by "throwing himself over and over again into the tumult of the world," that he could find a sense of harmony.[23]

After Havel was released by the prison hospital, he was returned not to Heřmanice, with its demented warden, but to the Bory prison in the town of Plzeň, where his Uncle Miloš had once served time for trying to emigrate illegally. Havel was delighted by the change. Bory was "infinitely better in every way" than the prison in Heřmanice, he wrote. The change in scenery put him "in a constant state of euphoria."[24] At Bory, he was assigned to work in the laundry room, which was less taxing than his previous jobs. He was also given access to the library and allowed to subscribe to magazines and journals, even to join a geography study group. Havel regarded all of this as a stroke of magnificent luck, but it may also have been a strategic decision on the part of authorities. Havel's health was shaky at best, and the state didn't want its most famous prisoner to die in their custody.

Shortly after entering Bory, Havel was also allowed to apply for parole, having completed one-half of his sentence. Although parole seemed unlikely, Havel nevertheless allowed himself to indulge in what he called "sweet fantasies." His favorite reverie, which he lingered over at length, involved his first day of freedom, which he fantasized would involve a trip to the sauna and swimming pool, followed by sunbathing and a nap, then putting on a stylish set of clothes and driving Olga to a fine restaurant. He went so far as to imagine each course of the meal and the taste of each portion.

And yet, as Havel reported later, even these fantasies, once he let them run their course, eventually left him feeling empty. As he played his life outside of prison through his mind, letting it run like a scene in a play, he always came to a moment where he asked, "Is that all? What's next?" Reflecting on the experience in a letter, he came to the conclusion that "[most] people's lives . . . are fragmented into individual pleasures . . . that give people the elementary and essentially spontaneous feeling that life has meaning."[25] He surmised that if the gaps between these pleasures are narrow enough, the question of meaning never comes up. Prison, however, had thrown him into an existential abyss. He realized, he wrote Olga, that the joyful activities of his life, from throwing dinner parties to creating theatrical plays, were little more than "islands of meaningfulness floating on ocean of nothingness." Havel suggested that the absence of simple pleasures had not only thrown him into despair but had led him to question his old life and all of its distractions—indeed, to see much of his life as a distraction. What was beyond and beneath these distractions and islands of pleasure? Was it possible to root oneself in another field of experience that had no beginning or end, located in the timelessness of Being? Such an experience was beyond his ability to imagine.[26]

Havel's parole hearing didn't occur until December 1981. The formality of the occasion cheered him immensely. Havel's brother, Ivan, was there, as was Olga and Zdeněk Urbánek and his wife, as well as Havel's lawyer. Naturally, Havel was denied parole but even that didn't diminish the joy he felt in the ceremonial aspect of the process, including the dignity he felt in being addressed, for the first time in years, as "Mr. Havel" during the hearing.[27]

The uplift in his mood was fleeting, however. By the time the Christmas holidays rolled around, Havel had another fit of bittersweet melancholy. While sitting alone in the prison courtyard, he watched a heavy, silent snow fall at sundown. As he wrote to Olga, "It struck me how odd it was that in other circumstances the sad and barren place can make me feel such joy at being alive." Although Havel claimed that his new melancholy had nothing to do with the holidays, the Christmas season had always been especially difficult for him, a matter of what he called survival. His first Christmas, he had spent much of the time in bed with hemorrhoids, although he had felt better enough by New Year's Eve to open a bottle of champagne and sing with his cellmate. The following holidays found him confessing to Olga that "the most important thing of all is not to lose hope and faith in life itself."[28]

In the fall of 1982, Havel received a surprise visit from two senior officials of the secret police, one of them, Major Říha, a man he knew from previous rounds of interrogation. After an exhausting three-hour interview, the men explained to Havel that the state would like to release him from prison, although only if Havel agreed to officially request a "reprieve" in writing. The catch, the two men told him, was that the request had to be written that afternoon, without consultation with friends, family, or fellow dissidents. If he didn't request the pardon that afternoon, he would have to serve out his entire sentence without leniency.[29]

When Havel refused to ask for leniency without first consulting fellow dissidents, the two members of the secret police compromised, allowing him to meet for seven minutes with three other prison inmates to discuss his situation. One of the prisoners told Havel to accept the offer; the other two quietly said that they would refuse if they were in his place. Havel himself was tortured by the choice. On the one hand, he fantasized that the state had decided, perhaps as the result of international pressure, to release him and only wished to extract a concession on his part so that he would "not look like too much of a winner." On the other hand, he feared making a mistake like the one he had made during his first prison term. He didn't know how it would appear to other dissidents if he asked for leniency, and he couldn't be sure the state wouldn't twist the words of his letter—or simply rewrite them to suit their own ends. He feared another controversial return from prison, once again discrediting himself, and he suspected that in asking for a pardon he would be admitting that he had actually committed a crime in the first place.[30]

Havel didn't turn down the offer outright. Instead, he told the agents that although he himself could not request a presidential pardon, he didn't object if his wife and brother did so on his behalf. Writing Olga later that week, he declared he was certain that he had acted correctly. Having declared his certainty, however, he begged Olga to not second-guess him, telling her his nerves had been worn thin. "Please don't write to tell me that I messed it all up," he begged her, explaining that he was terrified of being overwhelmed by regret. He felt close to a breakdown, he said, and above all else he didn't want to find himself sobbing in front of his fellow prisoners.[31]

Of course, this hadn't been the first time that Havel had faced ambivalence about his fate. His parents, after all, had dithered in 1948 rather than fleeing the state, and Havel himself had done the same in 1968. Then in 1979 he had refused to emigrate rather than face trial. The theme of his ironic fate came up often in his weekly letters to Olga. Havel wrote that "it seems increasingly clear that my

prison term is merely a necessary and inevitable phase of my life."
The only surprise, he suggested, was how long it had taken the regime
to put him behind bars. He went on to suggest that prison had been
a necessity, that his life "couldn't well have ended anywhere else."
Looking over his life, he wrote: "It even seems to me that after those
two unsuccessful runs at it, I subconsciously did everything I could
do to ensure that the inevitable would happen."[32]

If Havel didn't find the peace he hoped for in prison, he did perhaps
discover something else. He came to realize that prison was designed
to break the individual and then to reeducate the broken person who
was left.[33] It was in the broken places of himself that he found meaning.
Dragged down by what he referred to as the hopelessness of the world,
he fought to remain in contact with the beautiful and unattainable
absolute. As a result, he found himself caught between torment and
joy, nothingness and meaningfulness. Although he did not convert
to Christianity, he thought of his own torment as akin to a Christlike
state, nailed down to these two dimensions of the world, "the horizon-
tal of the world and the vertical of Being." Meditating on this theme in
one of his letters to Olga, Havel added a personal insight, suggesting
that, like Christ, we are all only victorious in our defeats, rediscovering responsibility through our personal sorrow, our time on the
cross. To that note, Havel added another thought: "The same thing
in fact applies—this must be added for the sake of completeness—to
these meditations of mine: they are a defeat because in them I have
neither discovered nor expressed anything that hasn't already been
discovered long before and expressed a hundred times better . . ." He
went on, "Yet they are, at the same time, a victory: if nothing else, I
have at least managed, through them . . . to pull myself together to the
point where I now feel better than when I began them. It's strange, but
I may well be happier now than at any time in recent years. In short,
I feel fine and I love you."[34]

# 13

## HOMECOMING

THE EVENTS LEADING TO HAVEL'S RELEASE FROM prison began
on a Sunday afternoon in January 1983, when he came down with
a dangerous case of influenza. By evening, he had the shakes and
fell into a fugue, unable to talk. That night, with his heart racing,
he quivered so violently that his bed shook. By dawn, the fever had
dropped slightly, although it was still a dangerously high 104 degrees
Fahrenheit when he was admitted to the clinic. Three days later,
X-rays revealed lung complications, probably pneumonia complicated
by pleurisy. Prison officials took him by ambulance back to the same
hospital in Prague where he had been operated on the previous year.[1]

On Havel's first full day in Pankrác hospital, he took advantage
of the relaxed censorship to write Olga a shaky note, describing his
symptoms and his fear that he might be dying.[2] As soon as they got
the note, Olga and Ivan Havel flew into action. They immediately
drove to the hospital, but the staff refused to let them enter or confirm
Havel's condition. Olga responded by telephoning Pavel Kohout, who
had been exiled to Vienna in 1976. Kohout loved a good drama, and
he told Olga that he would move heaven and Europe to set Havel

free. As a world-famous playwright, Kohout had connections within both the literary and political worlds, and he immediately began a telephone campaign, calling Czech exiles on two continents and, according to Havel's later account, "various Chancellors of Western European states."[3]

Kohout's campaign made an immediate impact. Havel's imprisonment had been a constant diplomatic problem, and the state had been under increasing pressure from the governments of Western Europe to release him from prison.[4] On the night of February 7, Havel's doctors told him that President Husák had indefinitely suspended his sentence for health reasons, and he was immediately transferred by ambulance to a nonprison hospital. Suddenly he found himself addressed as "Mr. Havel," which disoriented him almost as much as trying to figure out why there was no guard next to his gurney in the ambulance to keep him from escaping.

After Havel was admitted to the Pod Petřínem Hospital as a civilian, news of his release was broadcast on Voice of America (presumably Ivan had sent them a quick note). Havel remained in the hospital for almost a month, scores of visitors pouring into his room each day, bringing gifts, flowers, bottles of gin, samizdat texts, and messages from Charter 77. The world, Havel later said, showed him "its kindest face." For a brief period, he had a carefree existence with no responsibilities beyond entertaining his hospital guests, who treated him like a returning hero. The euphoria wouldn't last long, however.

Assessing another person's inner life, much less a major depression, is difficult at best. Some of Havel's melancholy, after leaving the hospital, may have been simply the shock of change, or a traumatic response to the previous three years. Those closest to him found his depression both profound and frightening. In the first few days, he had trouble dressing himself, or making simple everyday decisions that he had been shielded from in jail. He obsessed constantly about friends still in prison, such as Petr Uhl, who was serving time in solitary confinement. Doctors diagnosed post-prison depression, but the issue was also existential: within the terrible confines of prison, there was the strange comfort of being relieved of personal decisions; freedom was a double-edged sword.

After his release from the hospital, Prague life felt like a dizzying Ferris wheel. Havel told friends that he felt a longing to experience everything; he swept through as many theaters and concerts as he could pack into a week, meeting with everyone he knew, trying to accomplish everything, telling himself that he had an obligation to take advantage of every moment of his newfound freedom. As he told Pavel Kohout, he felt haunted by the sense that at any moment an alarm clock would ring and he would wake up in prison, telling his fellow inmates about a colorful, rich dream he had.[5]

Even in this initial whirlwind of activity, Havel had the sense that nothing he was experiencing was quite real—he felt, as he later recalled, that he wasn't quite participating in what was happening to him. His self-diagnosis was that he was undergoing the first phases of a typical "post-prison depression suffered by a returnee who is suddenly cast loose into the absurd terrain of freedom."[6]

Just a few days after his release from the hospital, he joined a group of literary friends for a short trip out to the country, where they planned to read and discuss one another's work. The train left at 9 a.m. from the Masaryk train station in downtown Prague. Eight of them squeezed into a cold train compartment, the small radiator under the train window delivering just enough heat to take the ice out of the morning air. According to Eda Kriseová, who was with the group, Havel carried his body like a dead weight, as if he struggled to move. It was clear that he was suffering from a deep case of melancholia that he was desperately trying to escape. He said that he wanted to start on a new play as something of a therapeutic cure, but he had no idea what to write. He asked everyone for suggestions. Finally, feeling too agitated to sit any longer, he and Eda Kriseová walked together up to the restaurant car, where they each took a shot of vodka. Havel told her about a dream in which an owl had landed on his shoulder. The owl whispered in his ear that it was a singer and then its face turned into a woman. Havel asked, somewhat helplessly, if he might not turn the dream into a play.[7]

There was another incident on the train, one that revealed his jitters. After returning from the restaurant car with Kriseová, several friends pulled out cigarettes, while Karel Pecka kept watch for the conductor through the half-open door. Havel appeared morose. If he lit up, he objected, he was sure to get caught. Pecka, having spent twelve years in a Stalinist concentration camp, laughed darkly, understanding what prison could do to a man. After Havel smoked half a cigarette, a train conductor did indeed arrive. Everyone denied they had been smoking, except Havel, whose face turned bright red while one of his eyes began twitching. After savoring his victory, the conductor, a large ogre of a man, leaned down and said, "I don't want a fine. Just promise me you'll never do it again."[8]

Havel's nerves didn't go away. If anything, they only got worse. On the one hand, he felt the inner necessity to rejoin his fellow dissidents, many of whom saw him as someone who could breathe new life into Charter 77. On the other hand, he had a deep, bodily fear of returning to prison. Havel's ambivalence came up in a meeting that spring with Kamila and Václav Benda in their book-lined apartment above Charles Square. Kamila encouraged Havel to return as spokesperson for Charter 77, much as her husband was planning to do. Havel was unnerved by the suggestion and refused to consider the matter further. "They hate me too much," he told her, referring to both the "state" and the secret police. "If I did that they would destroy me."[9]

As soon as Havel was healthy enough to travel, he and Olga retreated to Hrádeček, where Havel wrote a long account to his old friend, Pavel Kohout, who was living in Austria. Havel described his post-prison depression, which made it difficult to take on many basic daily tasks, such as dressing himself in the morning. Life outside of prison seemed to demand an unimaginable number of decisions, and Havel described himself as feeling paralyzed. Not least of his problems, he wrote, was that he was experiencing himself as two individuals, as if he were "split in two" between the physical man, the one who had just served a prison sentence, and the "imaginary floating legendary me, weighted down with endless Missions, Functions, Tasks, Jobs, and Expectations." He was caught in a crisis of freedom and identity, unsure of how to move forward, a feeling that had been magnified by a series of meetings that members of Charter 77 had held to see what new role he would play in the organization. As he told Kohout, the entire situation left him feeling trapped. He didn't know any way out of his dilemma except to show the world that he was just "an ordinary boy, full of whimsy, moodiness, uncertainty, hesitations, and eccentricities."[10] While he identified with the man who wanted to participate in Charter 77, feeling an inner necessity, he also wanted to quit being a dissident.

Although Havel was a prodigious writer of letters, he sometimes struggled to keep up with his correspondence, procrastinating for weeks or months before responding to a note. Now that he was free from prison, three years of belated thank-you notes weighed on his mind. To Miloš Forman, now an important film director in the United States, he sent a long apology for turning down the opportunity to emigrate that Forman and others had orchestrated behind the scenes. To Josef Škvorecký, he sent thanks for helping commute his prison sentence.

Havel also turned, almost frantically, toward writing, having convinced himself that finishing a play was the only activity that could help him escape depression. He felt the need to write another hit play, but working at the wooden desk at Hrádeček, staring for hours at the paintings and posters or out the garden window to the forest, all he could come up with were individual scenes, little snippets of conversation, many of them seemingly disconnected from each other. Whether because of what he called "the old psychological and nerve-wracking troubles," or because he felt too much pressure to sit down and "write an excellent, full-length play," the words just wouldn't come. In March he wrote to Kohout, telling him that he was working on an idea. He had "a very exact vision of how the play is going to look, the only thing I'm missing is a detail: I don't know at all what it's going to be about. I know the theme, but the storyline is missing."[11] By midsummer the situation worsened. Whatever self-confidence Havel had once possessed began to disappear.

There were other issues agitating Havel. Shortly after returning from prison, Olga informed him that she was having an affair with Jan Kašpar, a longtime friend and handyman at Hrádeček who provided Olga with safety and companionship while Havel was in prison. Kašpar hadn't replaced him, Olga said. In fact, Kašpar expected that he would return to his original role as handyman when Havel returned.

After describing the affair, Olga, with her characteristic bluntness, raised the question of what to do with their marriage, including the possibility that she and Havel should separate. She pointed out that such an arrangement would "suit the police quite well," damaging Havel's standing with dissidents (which may or may not have been true). After a long, emotional conversation, the two apparently reached a private agreement. They would continue to live together but each of them would lead their separate private lives, something akin to an open marriage.[12]

Havel brooded over the new arrangement. He'd had many affairs himself, but it was far more difficult for him to accept Olga's infidelities than his own, and he felt betrayed by the news of her affair. At the same time, however, what he called his tendency toward "Don Juanism" was in full force in the first few weeks after being released from prison, as if he needed to make up for all that time—or could only find happiness in the arms of another woman.

During this period of multiple infidelities, Havel became infatuated with Jitka Vodňanská, a blond-haired beauty of about forty with blue eyes and a devilish smile. Havel had always maintained that none of his affairs threatened his marriage. With Jitka, however, he was in real trouble. Their initial connection seems to have been that Havel was lost and that Jitka was a brilliant psychotherapist who helped people find their way home. Havel encouraged her to psychoanalyze his difficulties, which she often accomplished with brilliant insight.[13]

Jitka was an old friend of Havel's brother, Ivan, as well as the ex-wife of Jan Vodňanský, a somewhat eccentric poet and dissident who had been an early member of Charter 77. She had attended living room seminars in Ivan's apartment every two weeks in the 1970s and then organized her own seminars in her home in Zahradní Město, on the southeast side of Prague. She had also been a member of a group that met regularly at a restaurant on the quay, where they discussed cultural events and wrote letters to Havel in prison.[14]

Jitka had first met Havel during the Easter holidays of 1979. She then ran into Havel roughly a month later at a small restaurant in Prague, which she visited with a friend, Karl Trinkewitz (her husband having remained at home with their young son). Jitka described the occasion as a "classic Charter 77 soiree," which first closed down the restaurant and then retired to the apartment of Anna Kohoutová, Havel's mistress at the time. The two had flirted that evening, and the next morning several of those attending the party were arrested. Havel spent the next three and a half years in prison.[15]

By the time of Havel's homecoming party, held in Ivan's flat on the quay in early April 1983, Havel had been daydreaming about Jitka for years. Not only had Jitka been writing him letters in prison, but he had sent her little notes in his letters to Olga. At the party, the two connected immediately. A photo from the night shows Havel holding her hand, his brother sitting next to them. Another photo shows Havel staring deeply into her eyes, hands on both of her shoulders. According to Jitka's account, the picture was taken just as Havel asked her what would happen if they fell in love with each other that night.[16]

Jitka was deeply smitten with Havel from the beginning. Although he was married and had a number of girlfriends, she felt they possessed a secret bond. Havel must have felt the same way. Three days after the party, he asked her to join Olga, Anna Kohoutová, and himself, the four of them making a trip to a concert. Afterward, they all went to the Slavia Café. Havel was involved with all three women, he told them, and he expressed the desire that everyone accept the situation, even to get along together as one harmonious group. After that, Havel and Jitka began to see each other regularly, including at her apartment and at Havel's Prague flat when Olga was in Hrádeček, as well as at a variety of small, intimate bistros around town, including Paroplavba, which was located on a boat on the embankment.

According to Jitka, the early days of the affair were "a happy and painful time," complicated by Havel's marriage and by his role in society. In her own account of their years together, she suggested that she would never have pursued Havel on her own, regarding him as "too married." Although she sometimes regretted falling in love with him, she was immensely attracted to what she called Havel's "total presence," his truthfulness, charisma, and absurd sense of humor. Their relationship, she wrote, was a constant dance between hope and despair, and together they tried to make the best of a heavy experience.[17]

Two months after the affair began, Olga invited Jitka to Hrádeček for a talk so that the two women could develop a mutual understanding. The two women couldn't have been more different. Olga was a practical, down-to-earth woman who no longer wore makeup or colored her graying hair. She had a biting, sarcastic wit, and people in dissident circles were generally afraid of her, a sentiment that Olga encouraged. In contrast, Jitka was a free-spirited, lively woman with interests in Buddhism, meditation, and African rituals. Slowly, the two developed a deep kinship, and they were close enough that Jitka played a major role at Olga's funeral fifteen years later.

By summer, Jitka became a regular visitor at Hrádeček, where she was given a permanent upstairs bedroom. Meanwhile, Olga continued to see Jan Kašpar, the four of them sharing the house on weekends and holidays. All four made generous efforts to get along, but at times the tension was thick. Olga, for instance, could be territorial, especially in the kitchen, where she ruled over Jitka much as Havel's mother had ruled over Olga in the 1960s.

As Havel and Jitka's relationship developed, Jitka became even more important to him, and over the next few years they spoke on and off about marriage and creating a life for themselves. In many ways, Jitka was the love of his life, and of all Havel's girlfriends she was the woman who understood his complexities the most. She was chiefly responsible for the new burst of creativity in the 1980s, and for a round of introspection in which Havel began to take account of his own behavior. In all, Havel wrote more than 150 letters and notes to her, many of them full of plans for self-improvement (cutting back on pills and alcohol and working on his "inner fragmentation") but also about his constant worry of how to solve their romantic situation.

Havel refused to use the word "love," which seemed banal, but he found it hard to imagine life without her, just as he found it impossible to think of leaving Olga. Havel told Jitka that his relationship with his wife was strictly of a "utilitarian character." When she was jealous of Olga, he would tell her, "You're jealous of my right hand, my soap in the kitchen."[18]

Havel found the tension among all of these triangulated relationships almost unbearable. He was often remorseful during their first year together. In a letter from October 1983, for instance, Havel worried about how his relationship was affecting each of the three women in his life. He wondered whether his behavior was "moral," whether he wasn't being selfish and hurting everyone involved. In typical Havel fashion, he didn't try to resolve his own question, but simply noted how complicated everything felt to him. He didn't want to hurt either Olga or Anna Kohoutová, whom he was still close to, but he couldn't bear, he said, to give Jitka up. He asked her to think about his situation "from a psychological point of view" and give him advice.

In another letter, dated October 20, he wrote: "It seems to me . . . that [my behavior] is not right. But what should I do?" It disturbed him, he wrote, that he was being accused (he didn't say by who) of being a "whoremonger." He added, "Please, I would like you to think about it as a woman, as a friend, my closest person, and finally as a psychologist. . . . I need your help because I am helpless in this matter."[19]

Part, but not all, of Havel's desperation came from the fact that he was at that time in the deepest part of his post-prison depression. When he felt depressed, as he wrote to her on November 10, 1983, he thought of her and it eased his depression. Thinking of Jitka brought him temporary relief, and going to Prague to visit her took his depression away for days at a time, not least because they spent much of their time psychoanalyzing his problems, which Havel encouraged. One of Jitka's discoveries was that Havel gravitated toward strong, powerful women who exercised a power over him that he then felt compelled to rebel against. The pattern started with his own mother, an attractive, dynamic, and overbearing woman whom he both loved and rejected. Jitka told Havel that his marriage to Olga was based on the same unresolved feelings and his need to constantly live up to Olga's expectations while secretly wishing to fail.[20] Havel agreed with her insights, except, perhaps, as he said in a letter, "for some small details."

The unbearable heaviness of Havel's romantic life reached a climax the following spring, when Jitka announced she was pregnant. In April she wrote a letter to Olga about carrying Havel's child.[21] Olga suggested to Jitka that the three of them live together in a communal relationship in which they would raise the child together, a situation that may have intrigued Olga since she couldn't have children herself. Olga seemed to show interest in the situation, but Havel was horrified. In late April Jitka decided on her own to terminate the pregnancy in Prague, which required permission from a board of doctors. She informed Havel by letter. According to John Keane, she thought that Havel dreaded the possibility of fatherhood, especially fathering a child out of wedlock. Havel seemed uncomfortable around children, treating her own eight-year-old as if he needed a lecture in philosophy.[22]

Although Havel had been ambivalent about having a child, he seemed even more troubled by the turn of events. For one thing, he worried why he couldn't commit to Jitka and his seeming emotional paralysis when it came to leaving his wife. The entire situation, Havel told Jitka, seemed hopeless and unbearable. Havel was so bothered by his inability to act that he could sleep at night only by drinking and "taking pills." He worried his love life was aggravating what he considered his delicate emotional constitution, and in a letter dated May 13, 1984, he revealed that as a youth, a psychiatrist, trying to help keep him out of harm's way, had given Havel an evaluation that suggested he had a tendency toward depression with an unconscious wish for suicide.[23]

The crisis over the pregnancy may have actually strengthened the bond between Jitka and Havel. By this time, Jitka believed she was in love with him, and Havel flirted with making a new start with her. In the Christmas season of 1984, Havel gave her a pair of gold earrings that had once belonged to his mother, a choice that must have wounded Olga. Havel sent her constant presents with the Tuzex vouchers, treats that she couldn't afford, being quite poor and raising a child by herself. When Havel complained that their relationship was too chaotic, that he longed to find harmony in his daily routine, Jitka reminded him that anxiety was a part of life. Adrenaline, she told Havel, was the cheapest drug. She also seemed to realize, with the insight of a psychologist, that extramarital affairs were a natural reaction to living in a totalitarian society, providing a sense of belonging that was otherwise difficult to find. She accepted the necessity of such relationships.[24]

Whatever Jitka's attraction, Havel always came to the conclusion he couldn't leave Olga. As Havel put it, Olga was "the one certainty" in his life. He could imagine "a more ideal lifetime partner," but he couldn't imagine "living with anyone else," a fact, he said, that has "brought unhappiness to more than one rare creature."[25] Photographs from those years reveal a married couple who had become something like business partners, together overseeing a complex and vital group of enterprises that required their constant cooperation. One picture from 1983 shows a beer-soaked garden party held at Hrádeček that lasted most of the day and into the night. By Havel's count, sixty-five people showed up for the traditional midsummer celebration of Olga's birthday. Sometime during the evening, someone took a photograph of Havel and Olga dancing. Havel is wearing a T-shirt, a cigarette in his left hand, his eyes groggy and red. The two share a half smile as they embrace stiffly, two old friends hardened by battle.[26]

With Havel's home from prison, social life at Hrádeček returned like a spring rain. Once again, a steady torrent of visitors poured in from the city, many staying days or weeks, often showing up unannounced, which was a decidedly un-Czech thing to do. There was a sense that the normal rules of society did not apply at the Havel household, and many of those who arrived came not only for the glamour, the sense of feeling welcome at the house of a world-famous playwright, but also because Hrádeček, sitting in the foothills of the Giant Mountains, seemed to exist outside the rest of rule-bound society. The guests included not only fellow dissidents but friends, friends of friends, and loose acquaintances, including one of Havel's roommates from prison, who showed up unannounced along with his entire family. Havel was too courteous to turn anyone away, and he relied on Olga to chase them off after a few days, when they had outstayed their welcome.

Gone were the days when Hrádeček felt like an old farmhouse. Jan Tříska's old room, which once smelled of goats, was now a comfortable guest wing, and the entire house was modern, stylish, and comfortable, one of the few places where one could get a sense of worldliness, of the luxury of the First Republic.

In addition to unannounced guests, Havel returned to his habit of sponsoring all sorts of unofficial gatherings and conferences. In June 1984 he hosted Kampademie for four days, the famous underground seminar that had originally begun meeting on Kampa Island in Prague. The nine participants included Radim and Martin Palouš and Jitka Vodňanská, who had ended her pregnancy the previous month. Havel gave each resident a day-by-day itinerary and a color-coded menu for the week. Havel liked to set his formal table for meals, all of the spoons, forks, napkins, and plates in just the right order, set just so, and he was nervous when he cooked, often remarking that he was more concerned about how people enjoyed his food than how they enjoyed his plays. As soon as the food was served, he impatiently waited the critical judgment of his guests, asking them to elaborate on the experience. A menu Havel typed up from Easter Day in the mid-1980s, when Jitka and her son joined Havel and Olga, lists Nescafé with cream, baguettes, soft-boiled eggs, cheese, and jam for breakfast; gin and tonic, followed by smoked fish and English beefsteak for lunch; and a supper of goulash, followed by champagne.[27] As Jitka noted, Havel loved people, parties, and entertainment. He loved having a full house of friends around him, but he also resented the time this took from his work. He longed for companionship, and whenever he had companions he longed for solitude.

Since Havel couldn't find any promising material for a play, he soon set aside the idea and proposed editing a volume of philosophical essays designed for the general reader, a book that was meant to focus,

Havel said, on such fundamental questions as "life, the world, [and] existence." It was a book for people who had the sorts of questions that he struggled with in prison.[28] In an undated letter to Josef Škvorecký written in the fall of 1983, Havel explained that he wanted to ask twenty local and fifteen exile philosophers to write a short essay each on how they saw the world. Havel's role would be as a nonspecialist who would keep the philosophers focused on the bigger picture. He'd also write a short biographical sketch of each author.[29] Škvorecký loved the idea and agreed to publish it in Czech, marketing it mainly to émigrés living in North America and Europe.

In the meantime, Havel's samizdat organization, Edice Expedice, published his letters from prison, and 68 Publishers later published a Czech edition abroad.[30] The job of editing the collection fell to Jan Lopatka, an old literary friend, who started work on the project while Havel was still in prison, creating a second typewritten copy of each letter as insurance that the entire project wouldn't be confiscated by the secret police. Lopatka edited the manuscript, proofreading the letters against the originals, with Havel looking over the final manuscript to correct unclear passages. Originally, Havel had wanted only the philosophical portions of the letters, but Lopatka fought to include the comments on the daily experience of prison and personal messages to Olga, arguing that it was the details and context of prison life that made the book special.[31]

The resulting book, *Letters to Olga*, made an unusual and fascinating book, something unlike anything Havel had previously published. It was both a book-length essay and personal diary of a man struggling with imprisonment. Havel often claimed that he had written the letters for himself, as a way of coming to terms with prison, and for his wife, but he had also been aware, from the very beginning, that Olga was passing the letters to friends in the dissident community. Zdeněk Urbánek came to their flat in Prague almost every day that Olga was in town, meaning he was one of the first to read the letters, but she passed them along to almost everyone. And, when Olga was at Hrádeček, it was customary for her to open a window and shout "letter" whenever one arrived so that "everyone would immediately come running to listen."[32] Thus in many ways, the letters were not written to Olga as much as to the entire dissident community. Havel spoke to them and for them. His struggle was theirs—or rather, he articulated the struggle that everyone in his community felt, the struggle not only against injustice but the struggle to rise above it, to rediscover a code of civility and philosophical sense of life worthy of a human being.

When the letters were published in samizdat, they had a profound effect on the dissident community, especially on those who already regarded Havel as a sort of beacon of hope. The dissident novelist Eda Kriseová spoke for many when she wrote Havel a personal note, telling him how profoundly moved she was by the book. She said, in part, that "it has also occurred to me that my beloved philosophy has found a way to return to life. Almost no one reads philosophy anymore: people don't have time. But if meditations come with the exciting packaging of a famous writer in prison they read them, then maybe they understand what they would not have understood from Heidegger or Patočka. What may seem to you to be naïve and unoriginal philosophizing plays a part whose impact is, I hope, beyond our estimations."[33]

News of Havel's post-prison depression spread quickly, no doubt sped along by a wide circle of friends who were concerned about his well-being. By the end of summer, Havel's translator, Věra Blackwell, wrote to the British playwright Tom Stoppard about Havel's growing depression, which she feared would preclude the two authors from working together on a new play. She made a personal appeal for Stoppard to call Havel directly on the telephone, telling Stoppard that Havel "felt pretty cut off from the outside world." Stoppard tried and failed to reach him a number of times.[34]

The two playwrights admired each other deeply, and for his part Stoppard had identified with Havel's persecution, so much so that he had dreamed that he was joining Havel in prison.[35] In part, the identification may have had to do with the fact that Stoppard himself was Czech, his parents having fled to Singapore after the Germans invaded in 1938. Stoppard had maintained a lifelong connection to the country of his birth, and he had followed the creation of Charter 77 with great interest. Although he failed to reach Havel by telephone, he did send news through Věra Blackwell that he wanted to collaborate with Havel on a project. Havel eventually turned the offer down, feeling he had to prove he could still write a play on his own.[36]

Another friend who was worried about Havel's emotional health was Škvorecký, whose wife arranged for the University of Toronto to offer Havel a position as a visiting professor. In a letter sent by underground mail that Havel received around Christmas of 1983, Škvorecký told Havel the change in scenery would do him some good. In addition to getting him out of Czechoslovakia, the university would provide him with an office, a secretary, and $20,000 a year to live on, a substantial amount of money. "I don't have to say your stay here would make a lot of people happy," Škvorecký wrote. He added that he understood that Havel was reluctant to leave because the state might revoke his citizenship while he was gone, as it had done to Kohout. Nevertheless, he urged Havel to consider the peace he might find after emigrating and finally being rid of his government. "Personally, I think that you already did a lot for things [for your country], more than enough, and you have a right for a quieter lifestyle since you are not quite one-half through the creative course of your life." And, if Havel did hope to return to Czechoslovakia, Škvorecký wrote that he could "guarantee" that Havel wouldn't be required to make any political statements that might get him in trouble back home.

Havel wrote back immediately, saying that he found the invitation "fascinating." He assured Škvorecký that he "wouldn't hesitate for a second if there wasn't that damn-fool thing—losing the citizenship. I am considered the most dangerous dissident, and it seems for now that if I left for only one day, I would never be able to return." Havel added that he couldn't imagine such a fate: "It's not only a sense of responsibility to my mission or some other noble thing but also some kind of strange stay-at-home-ness: I am just a Czech package . . . and I can't possibly imagine that I would be capable at my age for such far-reaching change. I would probably just . . . embarrass everybody."

Škvorecký didn't give up on the idea. The two exchanged a number of letters on the subject, with Škvorecký countering Havel's minor objections, such as the language barrier, which Škvorecký thought would not be an issue, since no one would expect him "to sound like Lawrence Olivier." As for the possibility of losing his citizenship, Škvorecký stressed that in Canada Havel would finally have the freedom, for the first time in his life, to write without fear of censorship.[37]

Havel's final reply in late January provides one of the best illustrations of how he thought about emigration. He told Škvorecký that if he left, "I would disappoint a lot of people. . . . I am not overestimating myself and my meaning to others . . . [but] I see how many eyes are watching me carefully—some with fear and some with hope—and they are waiting to see if I am going to make this kind of step or not. Somebody else would ignore all of this, but I personally can't do it, almost as if I am 'falling into my responsibility.'"[38]

Once again, Havel decided to stay home. It was a bleak decision that gave him little satisfaction.

# 14

## JITKA

IN HIS FIRST YEAR OUT OF PRISON, Havel had read a mountain of eclectic material, partly because he felt the necessity of catching up with what had happened in the world. He began with a pile of books on alchemy and magic, borrowed from his friend Eda Kriseová, but he also read extensively in philosophy and literature, including the recently published blockbuster by Milan Kundera, who was then living in Paris.[1] Like many dissidents, Havel hated *The Unbearable Lightness of Being*, which included a character thought to be based on Havel. Olga was so disgusted with Kundera's portrayal of dissidents that she threw the book across the room.[2]

In January 1984, while Havel was in the midst of his reading schedule, the University of Toulouse announced it would award Havel an honorary doctorate at its graduation ceremonies in May. Unable to travel to France, Havel asked Tom Stoppard, the British playwright, to accept the award on his behalf. Radio Free Europe broadcast the ceremony back across the Czechoslovakian border, as well as a sit-down interview between Stoppard and Havel's translator, Věra Blackwell. Just as they were wrapping up the program, Blackwell turned to Stoppard with a last question. "This interview," she said, "will be broadcast to ČSSR—maybe by tomorrow. It will certainly be listened to by Havel. I'm sure he'd love to hear a few words from you—a few personal words—from this place, Toulouse, where he should be now, but cannot be."[3] Havel had indeed been listening on Radio Free Europe, and he immediately sent Stoppard a letter expressing how much his "personal message" had meant. Havel went on: "You can't imagine how moved I was by all of this. Indeed, you talked about me so nicely and cordially that I felt rather ashamed."

Part of the personal message, as repeated in Havel's letter, had to do with Stoppard wishing him "strength and better times." What he really needed, Havel said, was inspiration. "While I have already started work on my new play, the work proceeds slowly, mostly due to my lack of self-confidence, concentration, and internal composure. So please keep your fingers crossed for me in this respect."[4]

The "new play" that Havel had been working on was abandoned sometime before the end of summer, one more in a string of false starts.

Havel had never been one of those writers who simply plugged themselves in to the electrical socket, writing freely and easily. Like everything else in his life, his creative process was tortured. It often took him months or years to absorb a topic, as if he needed to either struggle with a topic or struggle with himself.

With Jitka, however, Havel was learning new habits, ones that would have a profound effect on his creative life. He was also trying to get healthy. The two talked of marriage, and Havel made repeated vows to exercise, cut down on his use of pills, and to reestablish his life. Gradually, during 1984, his post-prison depression began to lift, a fact he attributed to Jitka's influence. "You are the one who picked a motionless rock from the ground," he wrote her later. "You are the inspiration for a new life. You fell from the sky just for me. Don't ever leave me."[5]

There can be little doubt to the emotional importance Jitka played in his life, or her role as chief muse. The years they were together, 1983 through 1989, were the most productive of his life. During those years, Havel wrote a one one-act play as well as three of his best pieces of work, *Largo Desolato*, *Temptation*, and *Redevelopment*, and he completed the book-length series of interviews, *Disturbing the Peace*, that formed the core of his international reputation.

During these years, Havel struggled with his identity, with whether to continue his role as a dissident, and with opening up to his emotions. The wellsprings of his creative world responded in kind, and he emerged from this period with a new creative process in which he worked more like a shaman-seer than the tortured artist. The man who wrote as laboriously as a mule pulling a plow through a field, who spent years writing and rearranging his plays, began writing so quickly and with such fury that he described it as falling into a trance.

In August 1984 Havel barricaded himself at Hrádeček to begin an autobiographical play about a middle-aged dissident, Leopold, who suffered from many of the same torments as Havel. Leopold's wife had taken a lover, and Leopold himself was in love with a beautiful young woman but couldn't bring himself to commit to her completely; like Havel, he was also stuck between feeling compelled to lead the dissident movement and secretly wishing the dissidents would stop hounding him. Like Havel, Leopold was a nervous wreck, fresh out of prison, haunted by depression, and addicted to popping pills to keep his depression at bay.

Once Havel started writing the play, he found he couldn't stop. He had never written a full-length play in less than a year (*Mountain Hotel* had taken six years to write), but in a frenzy of exhaustion, vitamin F, and sleepless nights, Havel produced the new play, more or less finished, in four days, knowing that he was writing the best play that he had ever written, trying to capture what happens when a dissident such as himself reaches the end of his rope. After three nights of nonstop writing, Havel collapsed from mental exhaustion, feeling (as he wrote to a friend) that he had been tormented by demons.[6]

Both Olga and Jitka were at Hrádeček for the four days Havel unleashed his new play. As he wrote out the scenes, he gave passages for them to read, and on the fourth day, after he had finished, he read the entire play to both of them in the living room. Since the 1960s, Olga had always acted as Havel's first reader, and it was natural that Jitka now shared the role since she was spending long spells at Hrádeček as Havel's mistress. How the two women reacted to the autobiographical elements of the play isn't entirely clear, except for Havel's allusions that the play earned him both silent and vocal "rebukes" of those closest to him.[7]

But whatever their personal doubts about having their private life made public, Olga and Jitka both shared a commitment to art, especially to Havel's art, and it was the women who suggested the name of the play, *Largo Desolato*, which refers to a movement in a quartet by Alban Berg that they had been listening to on the stereo that week.[8] The play was clearly a breakthrough for Havel, something akin to clearing away the emotional blockage that Jitka believed was the true source of both his post-prison depression and his fear of making a long-term commitment to the love they felt for each other. To the outside world, Havel would later suggest that he had written the play quickly because he was worried the secret police might raid his house and confiscate the manuscript. In this public description of what had happened, he sought to diminish the extraordinary emotion around the creation of the play, as if he found his feverish state embarrassing, unfit for an intellectual. The truth is that the play was his own personal crucifixion, a deep encounter with his demons.

Like Havel, the protagonist, Leopold Nettles, is an intellectual who uses his head to distance himself from a frightening world. "I prefer to say less than I feel rather than to risk saying more," Nettles says in the play, explaining why he can't bear to tell Lucy (Jitka) how desperately he loves her. Nettles was prickly, cold, emotionally distant, afraid of looking like a fool. He couldn't bear the tawdriness of having a lover, and he needed to experience their relationship as pure and glorified rather than a quest for carnal desire. In short, Leopold Nettles, like Havel, was an emotionally blocked intellectual, trapped by his ambition and by an old, worn-out identity. As Leopold puts it, he's gone lame inside, acting the part of himself rather than actually living his life. As Lucy tells him (sounding suspiciously like Jitka), "You're afraid to give in to any emotion or experience—you're controlling, observing, watching yourself every minute." She promises to unblock him with "mad, passionate love—not the theoretical love, the one you write about." And it is her sexual passion that offers his only hope in the play, a salvation through love. As Havel later wrote in a letter to Pavel Kohout, the play was "a mythological exaggeration" of the "night-side" of himself, a fever dream of who Havel might become.

Havel was careful to guard against his high expectations of the play, however. When writing his translator, Věra Blackwell, about the play, he claimed that "I don't know whether it's any good. I have very little distance from it." He added, however, that he couldn't imagine any revisions. "I am quite capable of leaving it the way it is—or throwing it away!"⁹ The last little bit, about throwing it away, was a typical piece of Havel bravado. Far from throwing it away, he hid a copy of the manuscript in the woods behind Hrádeček so that the secret police wouldn't confiscate it in one of their raids.

The response from around the world came quickly. Josef Papp in New York City ordered a translation, saying he wanted to produce it as soon as possible. The Burgtheater in Vienna wanted to produce it as well, and Tom Stoppard, to whom the play had been dedicated, agreed to write an adaptation for the English stage.¹⁰ Just about everyone thought it was the best thing Havel had ever written.

Another burst of creative energy came in the fall of 1985, when Havel sat down at Hrádeček to write out a play on the theme of Faust, which had bedeviled him during his detention in 1977. Alone at Hrádeček, he quickly scribbled out the stage action for the play, sketching out scenes and a few charts for how long each scene would be and how long each character would have to speak. Falling into something like the trance in which he had written *Largo Desolato*, he then wrote one scene a night for ten nights, finishing the play in a state of exhaustion. He was so physically tired that he fell down the stairs at Hrádeček, which resulted in a nasty bump on his head. When he was finished, he went to bed with a fever and chills.[11] As Havel told Pavel Kohout: "Simply put, I was in some trance and I spit out the play during ten days and now it has its own life, and all that's left for me is to observe it with moon-eyed interest."[12] Just about everyone agreed that *Temptation* was even better than *Largo Desolato*, making it his best play yet. Havel had gone from a brooder, who suffered over his plays for years, to a writer who ejected his plays in short, ecstatic states.

The story of Faust first grabbed Havel while being held in detention for his role in founding Charter 77, and he had made at least two previous attempts to write the play, suffering from writer's block both times. While in detention in the 1970s, Havel had read both Goethe's Faust and Thomas Mann's retelling of the Faust story, and he had the palpable, physical sensation that he was being tempted by the devil, even that he was in the devil's "clutches." He was troubled by strange dreams and stranger ideas.[13]

By Havel's own admission, his possession by the story of Faust had been one of the blackest moments of his life, coinciding with his agreement to sign a statement that made it appear that he had renounced Charter 77 before being released from jail. He felt as if he had sold his soul, as if he had been tricked by some devilish turn of events. Afterward, as he put it, he spent years in "silent desperation, self-castigation, shame, inner humiliation, reproach and uncomprehending questioning" over what had happened to him.[14] The theme seemed ripe for a play, and in 1978 he completed about half of a play he couldn't finish, suffering from what he called "a blockage of ideas."[15] While in prison the second time, he returned to the Faust theme almost immediately, going so far as plotting out the action. In one version, he imagined transforming Faust into a Beckett-like comedy set in prison, something along the lines of *Waiting for Godot*, which would allow him to explore the themes of isolation, pseudo-hope, and what he called the discovery of "naked values."[16] Prison, however, proved to be no place to write about prison.

The reaction to the manuscript Havel wrote in 1985 was immediate and unremittingly positive. A copy made its way to London by way of Havel's literary agent. The Royal Shakespeare Company immediately ordered a literal translation of the play, which was followed by a treatment by Tom Stoppard. In New York, Havel's old pal Joseph Papp also produced the play, although with a translation by Marie Winn. In Vienna, the Burgtheater produced a version in German. With so many productions in so many foreign countries, Havel was once again an international star, earning money from foreign royalties that he couldn't have spent if he tried. Havel had little chance to influence the foreign productions, however, and the version put on at the Bergtheater in Vienna was a catastrophe. He got regular reports from his friend Pavel Landovský, but there was nothing he could do from afar except wait for opening night and a phone call from Pavel Kohout, who confirmed that the director didn't know what he was doing.

The Royal Shakespeare Company was more accommodating. Before rehearsals began, the director of the play visited Havel in Prague to discuss the production. Then, on opening night, timed to coincide with the curtain call in London, a dozen violets were delivered to Havel's apartment in Prague, all of which mirrored a scene in the play. Havel was even more ecstatic when Tom Stoppard arranged for the director and one of the actors to visit Prague with a video of the performances, giving Havel a sense for the first time in almost twenty years of what it felt like to see one of his plays in a theater.

By the time his guests arrived from Great Britain, Havel had prepared an itinerary, taking them around Prague for meetings with friends in the Prague theater. The main event, of course, was viewing the video his guests had brought from the Royal Shakespeare Company. Havel had organized fifteen or so colleagues to watch the play in his Prague apartment. Glasses of whiskey were passed around the room, the curtains were drawn, and Havel squatted down close to the screen, chortling and laughing at the possibility of finally watching his own play, enjoying himself like he hadn't in years.[17]

Havel was so delighted with the production that he took his two guests, Roger Michell and John Shrapnel, for a Czech-style celebration, an evening of drinking Czech beer and Moravian wine. At one point, someone mentioned the name of the American president, Ronald Reagan. "Ah, yes," Havel said, "my pupil." Reagan had apparently quoted Havel in a speech, and Havel had been jokingly referring to him as his "dear student." Later, driving his guests out to the airport, Havel was in "what seemed to be a very high state . . . like an excited kid." Speaking in English, which he rarely used, he muttered the same thing over and over again. "I can't believe it," he said.[18]

Havel now had two hit plays showing simultaneously on the international scene. At the Public Theater in New York City, *Largo Desolato* was being called a "harrowing portrait" of dissident life.[19] In London, *Temptation* was being hailed as a masterpiece. The *Daily Telegraph* called George Theiner's translation "a flashing and shimmering stream of wit." The *London Times* called the play an "exuberant" comedy of life behind the Iron Curtain.[20]

One of Jitka's complaints was that Havel withheld affection in public, as if he were embarrassed by their relationship.[21] She was used to living with eccentrics—her ex-husband, a dissident writer who had been known for such antics as cooling his socks in the refrigerator—but Havel's reticence couldn't have been easy, even less so for a curious, free spirit like Jitka.

The summer after writing *Largo Desolato*, however, Havel agreed to take Jitka around the country in his new Volkswagen Golf, introducing her to his dissident friends. According to Jitka, Havel referred to it as their "engagement trip," leading her to hope that she might one day have Havel to herself, free of Olga and the marriage.[22] Havel prepared for the trip by typing out multiple drafts of an itinerary, which he color-coded with markers, listing the friends they would visit, the meals they would have, and which films they would watch in the local theaters.

After picking up Jitka in Prague, Havel noticed he was being followed by a Tatra 613. He pulled over to the side of the road and asked the two gentlemen in the car behind him if they were with the secret police. Working under the theory that everyone would be better off if his tail wasn't anxious about losing him, he provided them with maps and addresses to all of his planned destinations and promised not to lose them.[23] The police let him go on his way but finally arrested Havel and Jitka when they stopped at the house of Ladislav Lis in North Bohemia. Everyone, including Jitka, Havel, and his hosts, were taken in for forty-eight hours of interrogation. After being released, Havel and Jitka returned to their journey, visiting Vlasta Chramostová in North Bohemia, Augustin Navrátil in Olomouc, and Eda Kriseová in the Moravian countryside, all under the watchful eyes of the agents following them. In Slovakia, they were arrested a second time while visiting Miroslav Kusý. The arrests were apparently stressful for Jitka, who, according to Eda Kriseová, "did not know how to behave or communicate in prison," the experience being rather new. Meeting her in the corridor between interrogations, Havel gave her a gesture to encourage patience.[24] When they were finally released, the police having confiscated cassette tapes of John Lennon and Pink Floyd, Jitka was escorted by train back to Prague without any luggage or personal items.

Police harassment was part of a larger attempt that year to shut down Charter 77. That fall, the police interrogated the current spokespersons of Charter 77, warning them against making their anniversary document public. The following winter, the police actively sought to keep the organization from issuing new documents or meeting with foreign journalists. Members of Charter 77 responded by holding a press conference in a restaurant. Everyone attending the press conference, including foreign journalists, were placed under surveillance and subjected to interrogation.[25]

Despite Havel's deep feelings for Jitka, he felt unable to leave his wife and unable to end the affair. He longed, he said, to live a peaceful life full of harmonious relationships, and yet he seemed unable to extricate himself from the triangle with Jitka and Olga that produced a great deal of anxiety. When Havel spent the night at Jitka's house in 1985, her ex-husband was there, as he visited sometimes to be with his son. They all had breakfast together, the four of them, trying to make the best of the situation.

For a time, Havel despaired of being able to make a decision. He often analyzed the situation in excruciating detail, as in a 1985 letter of some five thousand words, followed by a short note written the following day in which he raised the same issues again and then drew a cartoon figure of a man in a bar thinking about love, signing the note "Your infant-like immature 'guy'—V." He asked Jitka to please respond immediately with her own thoughts by telegraph.[26]

Sometime toward the end of 1985, Havel resolved to take action. In an undated letter, he told Jitka that he and Olga had finally sat down for a discussion about their future. Havel came clean with Olga, he said, regarding the depth of his feelings for Jitka, and they agreed that the best thing was to get a divorce. Although the conversation was difficult—Havel called it the hardest of his life—Havel felt a certain pride in his ability to make a decision, telling Jitka that he felt like a "man" who had "jumped out of his baby diapers."[27] For reasons that aren't immediately clear, Havel then had immediate misgivings. Rather than leave Olga, he sent Olga and Jitka to a bistro to talk over the entire situation again. It seemed clear to all of them that the situation had not, in fact, been resolved, and that Havel felt he could never leave Olga. The two women got drunk together and had a good cry, and the romantic situation returned to what it had been before. Havel remained with Olga and Jitka remained his lover.[28]

The relationship continued in this fashion for several more years. Eventually, Jitka began seeing other men, perhaps because Havel could not make a commitment to her, and Havel felt tortured by what he considered as her betrayals, much as he had felt intense jealousy when Olga had taken a lover. In a letter to Jitka in 1987, he admitted his jealousy didn't make sense. Nevertheless, he felt tortured, unable to "eat, write, or sleep," and he had taken to drinking and taking meprobamate, a minor but addictive tranquilizer, to help him through the situation. He understood the irony, that he wanted everything from her, loyalty, monogamy, and constant attention, while being unable to provide any of that in return. But that is what he wanted.[29]

By the summer of 1988, Olga began to assert herself. She had briefly toyed with the idea of leaving Havel, feeling that she could not continue to live with the constant chaos of their relationship. Rather than leaving, Olga demanded that Havel end the relationship with Jitka. She told him he could still see Jitka occasionally, as a sort of fling, but that if Jitka came to Hrádeček, Olga would seek a divorce. Havel informed Jitka by letter, telling Jitka that they would have to stop seeing each other, since a divorce would upset his tranquility. In the next month, he sent her at least four more letters on the same theme, something like a long goodbye. In the final letter in the series, he reported getting drunk with two friends and taking Rohypnol, a drug used to treat insomnia. As if saying goodbye, he told her how much she had meant to him, how much she had inspired him and "helped me to live."[30]

The two would continue to see each other from time to time, and after Havel became president, they would resume a passionate love affair. Even then, however, it was clear that Havel would never be able to give her what she wanted.

Around the time Havel received his honorary doctorate, he was approached by the young editor of a new underground journal, who asked Havel to reflect on the prospects of Czechoslovakian culture for the *Revolver Review*. Jáchym Topol was the son of one of Havel's closest friends, a frequent guest at Hrádeček, and Havel had all but adopted the young man, who, like many other dissidents, had been in and out of jail. Havel also admired the ambitious idea of creating a first-rate literary journal that would be typewritten in secret and then mimeographed on a machine that Topol himself had carried in a backpack over the Polish frontier. During those years, pamphlets, underground journals, and samizdat books were thriving more than ever, often lovingly retyped and passed along via underground distribution networks.[31]

Havel's essay in the *Revolver Review* was an attempt to understand what Havel and others called "parallel culture," meaning the part of the living culture that existed separate from state control. In the essay, Havel distinguished between the art of First Culture, which enforced official ideology, and the art of "parallel culture," which was defined by its hostility to dogma, uniformity, or political message. Unofficial culture didn't confront the regime with a different ideology, but, rather, Havel suggested it represented "a clash between the anonymous, soulless, immobile and paralyzing power" of the state and what Havel called "life, humanity, Being, and its mystery."[32]

Although the essay was relatively short, it distilled a number of important ideas that had been germinating in underground circles for the past decade, beginning with the very term and idea of "parallel polis," which had been first articulated by Václav Benda in a paper he delivered in a living room seminar in the 1970s, with Havel in attendance. In the 1980s Havel repeatedly returned to Patočka's ideas on the necessity of sacrifice and on what Patočka called "the solidarity of the shaken," by which he meant the silent communion of those who had been terrorized by the impersonal power of the state. Following Patočka, Havel had come to believe that what is good and valuable in a culture is often purchased with sorrow. "Might not sacrifice," he asked, "under some circumstances, be simply the consequence of a thought, its proof, or conversely, its moving force?"[33] Havel thought so, even if it was dangerous to think that way.

One of the biggest literary challenges of those years had to do with the difficulty of finding translators who could accurately and artistically render Havel's work into a foreign tongue. Until the early 1980s, Havel's only English translator had been Věra Blackwell, a Czech who had emigrated to London to marry an Englishman, later following him to New York. Throughout the late 1970s, however, Blackwell had gotten into a number of yelling matches with Klaus Juncker, Havel's agent, who felt like her translations were holding back his popularity.

Havel tried, in dozens of letters, to mediate the war going on between his two supporters. However much it pained him, he came to reluctantly agree with at least some aspects of Juncker's point of view, which is why he had personally asked Tom Stoppard to provide an adaptation of *Largo Desolato* and then of *Temptation*. Although Havel was in no position to judge the differences in translations, and, as he wrote her numerous times, he wanted to remain faithful to Blackwell, he couldn't bear the constant infighting between her and Juncker or her emotional letters, in which she painted his literary agent as an "evil spirit."[34] When he asked her to make a literal translation and then give the play to Tom Stoppard for revision, their relationship never recovered. However much these personality issues pained Havel, though, they were the problems of a man practicing his profession, a playwright dealing with the difficulties of producing his work abroad in a world of big egos and high stakes. He was a writer again. Something in him had been changed by writing *Largo Desolato* and *Temptation*.

He didn't understand what had happened, but he knew he had become a different man. In an interview shortly after the success of *Temptation*, he put it this way: "Perhaps I have found through this play a new starting point; perhaps I have rediscovered myself; perhaps it is really the beginning of a new stage in my writing."[35] Few had the chance to see the transformation as clearly as Joseph and Gail Papp, who came to visit Havel in September 1984, not long after Havel had finished writing *Largo Desolato*. They were met at the Prague airport by Havel's brother, Ivan. After giving them a tour of Prague, Ivan drove the Papps out of the city, following the zigzag country roads of North Bohemia to Hrádeček at the foot of the Giant Mountains.

In his travel diaries, Papp remembered Hrádeček as a "rustic, comfortable, spacious, and well appointed" cabin that was decorated "with rugs, ceiling mounted HiFi speakers, sofas, goosedown comforters, and many books, records, and cassettes." There was no sign of Jitka Vodňanská, probably because Havel would have thought it inappropriate for international guests to snatch such an intimate peek into his private affairs. Olga was there, however, holding court over the house, her youthful face framed by gray hair. Havel himself was "cheerful, despite his recent years of imprisonment." Dressed in a dark blue sweater and elegant trousers, he sat in the great room telling the Papps about his life in prison and about his exchange with the warden when news had come that Joe Papp had arranged for Havel to receive asylum in the United States. First, the warden offered Havel a cigarette. Then, when Havel finished the letter from Papp, one of the prison officials told him: "You can go."[36] Havel decided not to leave, of course, choosing life in a totalitarian prison over freedom in the United States. Sitting in the great room of Hrádeček, Havel tried to explain his decision, suggesting he couldn't bear to abandon all of his friends who would never get such an opportunity. As Papp noted in his travel diary, Havel was being careful with himself, knowing he could be called back to prison for the smallest infraction. Havel was also learning how to face the establishment.

# 15

## THE OPEN DOOR

WHEN MIKHAIL GORBACHEV TOOK OVER THE HELM of the
Soviet Union, many in the West hoped for a new era. Just after being
named general secretary of the Communist Party, in March 1985, a
West German newspaper compared him to Peter the Great, the czar
who opened the door to Europe. The British prime minister called
Gorbachev "a man we can do business with."[1] Dissidents in Czechoslovakia, however, were far more skeptical. Many believed the system
could never be changed from the inside.

One reason to be skeptical, from the dissident point of view,
was that Gorbachev, like Alexander Dubček, had been steeped in
the ideology of the Communist Party. He was a true believer who
sought to reform communism in order to save it, believing (probably
mistakenly) that the party was interested in progress. To dissidents,
Gorbachev's twin programs of *glasnost* (openness in government) and
*periostroika* (economic and political restructuring) sounded suspiciously similar to Dubček's idea of "socialism with a human face."
Havel himself believed that Gorbachev, like Dubček in the Prague
Spring, underestimated the ruthless nature of the system.

Havel's mistrust of the man he called "the Glasnost Czar" was probably visceral, a resistance to placing his trust in either the Russians or anyone who continued to work from inside "official culture." Gorbachev may have brought hope to ordinary citizens, who saw him as a potential savior, but the Czechoslovakian government used his visit in 1987 as an excuse to crack down on dissidents, searching houses, seizing books, and warning members of Charter 77 not to talk to the foreign press.[2] Despite Gorbachev's bold talk, his visit to Prague brought no changes in policy and leadership—quite the opposite. The Husák government made it clear that it would not be following the path of reform being followed by the Soviets, an irony that Havel bitterly resented, since the Soviets had forcibly installed the anti-reformists' regime in Czechoslovakia in the first place.

Havel had the chance to see Gorbachev in action on his visit to Prague. At the time—it was the summer of 1987—Havel and his wife had returned to live at the old family apartment on the embankment, a flat that they were sharing with Havel's brother. At half past nine in the evening, Havel took his dogs for a walk, wandering upriver. As he neared the National Theater he came across an impressively long bank of black limousines. Remembering that Gorbachev was in Prague for a visit, Havel followed a growing crowd that had lined up along National Street and along both sides of the embankment. A few minutes later, the state police snapped to attention. Gorbachev and his wife emerged from the theater, bodyguards swarming. The passersby who gathered on the streets burst into applause, transformed, Havel recalled, "as if by magic, into an enthusiastic frenetically cheering crowd."[3] Havel even waved back at the important man as he passed him along the street, but the entire scene irked him. As had happened so often in the past, his countrymen were placing blind hope in a savior, a lifelong communist from another nation, rather than sticking their own necks out for change.

Gorbachev may have charmed politicians in the United States and Great Britain, who had become "irrationally fascinated" by his sense of style, or by the fact that, like a Westerner, he "drinks whiskey or plays golf,"[4] but Havel felt this was merely one more cruel ruse, one more way in which the real issues were being hidden from view. Communism might be softened, even made more humane, but as Havel saw it the communist system (and Gorbachev as its chief spokesperson) existed in direct conflict with the intrinsic diversity and uniqueness of life. It was not in Gorbachev that he placed his hope.

By the mid-1980s, Havel was already something of a living legend. Even ordinary Czechs knew he was a convicted felon and a so-called enemy of the state. There were a few hundred active dissidents in country at the time, but none of them had Havel's sense of organization or style, and there were only a handful of people who had actively and steadily resisted the government in public over the decades. Havel's status as the preeminent dissident of his time led Karel Hvížďala, a former Czech who had emigrated to West Germany, to begin a book-length series of conversations with Havel in 1985 that were published in samizdat under the title *Dálkový výslech*, which means "Long-Distance Interrogation." The book, later published in English as *Disturbing the Peace*, was part autobiography, part philosophy, and part politics. The *New York Times*, reviewing it several years later, called it "unquestionably . . . the finest work this Czechoslovak artist has yet produced." The grace and courage threaded throughout the conversations left no doubt, it said, about Havel's "place in the moral pantheon of our century."[5]

One reason for the book's eventual popularity was its simple style. Havel discussed his plays, Czech history, and the erosion of spirit in the modern world, all in an erudite but down-home voice that was grounded in a deep moral vision. Havel also seemed to come alive in the conversations. He described himself as an uncompromising truth-teller, a Cassandra warning of the moral decay of society, and an intellectual whose job was to remind fellow citizens of what others were afraid to say. But although his tone was serious, Havel spoke of himself in the self-mocking terms he'd grown used to, going so far as to question his growing notoriety. He also discussed all of the absurdities and paradoxes of his life, his work, his time in prison, and his marriage to Olga. The result was something of a masterpiece, a book-length discussion that was not only deeply personal but also an exploration of his struggle to live a life of civic responsibility.

Hvížďala and Havel had known each other since the 1970s, when Hvížďala had asked the playwright to write a short history of the theater that was to be published as a version of a short encyclopedia, presumably to be written under a pseudonym. According to Hvížďala, traditional encyclopedias had been almost completely prohibited under communism, since it was difficult to provide such extensive information without running afoul of censors. To fill the gap in missing information, Hvížďala created a series of books on individual topics, such as *The History of Shoemaking*. In 1974, when he asked Havel to write a history of theaters, Havel turned down the project because he was busy with writing his open letter to Dr. Husák. After finishing a doctorate in architectural history, Hvížďala and his wife fled to West Germany, where he eventually began writing a series of book-length conversations with Czech intellectuals who were out of favor with the government.[6]

One of the chief difficulties in preparing the interview with Havel was how to avoid the attention of the secret police until after the book went public. To keep the project secret, Hvížďala sent his proposal for a long-distance interview by way of Vilém Prečan, an émigré historian who had long been smuggling books into Czechoslovakia, making use of international diplomats who handed off packages to Jiřina Šiklová, a Prague dissident who had once been imprisoned for distributing prohibited books. The first stage of the interview involved Havel sending Hvížďala written answers to about fifty questions. Neither man was satisfied with the results. In order to keep Havel from composing his answers like formal essays, Hvížďala sent him a Western-style tape recorder, asking him to record his answers orally. The two men had agreed that Havel would borrow a flat from a friend between Christmas and the New Year, dictating his answers in marathon sessions fueled by "Petra cigarettes and whiskey."[7]

After Havel returned the first round of tapes back to West Germany, Hvížďala transcribed the conversations by typewriter and then cut up the manuscript into discrete sections, trying to find a secret order in the rambling dialogue. He then sent a round of supplemental questions for what he called "drama." Finally, the whole manuscript was returned to Havel for revision. Havel added new material and sent the whole package to Zdeněk Urbánek, the Shakespearean translator, who added his own suggestions, and then the corrections were returned to Germany by underground mail.[8]

The book proved to be something of an international rarity: a small book published by an émigré press in England that got international attention despite being published in Czech. It also earned Hvížďala a place on the state enemies list, so much so that West German intelligence officers visited Hvížďala to tell him that they had intercepted coded messages from inside Czechoslovakia suggesting he might be in personal danger.[9] On the other side of the Iron Curtain, ten to fifteen typewritten samizdat books were published by Havel's own imprint, Edice Expedice. Passed along the underground network, the book was read, copied and retyped, and discussed in pubs until it took on a life of its own. Havel was once again becoming a sensation.

By the mid-1980s, Havel had somewhat become reconciled to his role as a symbol of resistance. When he had time to visit his beloved Hrádeček, guests were a constant presence. Oftentimes friends just showed up, staying for days or weeks until Olga put her foot down and sent them home. Havel craved the companionship and distraction, and, at the same time, he complained about being unable to get anything done.

When in Prague, Havel was constantly faced with meetings and unanswered letters, leading him to hire a personal secretary to organize his time. He fielded at least a dozen letters a day, usually from people he didn't know, many of them involving desperate requests for him to look into violations of civil liberties. Increasingly, he found himself recognized when he was walking around town. As Havel put it in an interview at the time, he would often, while paying bills or filling out paperwork, find the person reading his name with a sense of shock. They would inevitably ask if it was really him. "Well, yes it's me," Havel would respond. And they would say, "But are you *our*

Václav Havel?" They didn't necessarily know his plays, or his dissident essays, but they knew his name from Radio Free Europe. They knew he was in trouble with the regime, and they loved him for that.[10] Perhaps Havel found some of the attention satisfying, but he also felt burdened by the constant demands, the sense that he was being made to play the savior. When reading requests for intervention, he said, he often felt the desire to tell them to "risk something yourselves! I'm not your redeemer."[11]

A snapshot of those years can be found in a profile in the *New York Times* written by Marie Winn. Winn was a native Czech whose family had fled Czechoslovakia during her childhood. When she visited Prague in 1987 as an American citizen, she found almost no one willing to talk to her. She found the city oppressive.[12]

Havel was one of the few Czechs who was willing to meet her for an interview. He met Winn at the door of the family apartment dressed his traditional V-neck sweater pulled over an Oxford shirt. He immediately opened a bottle of Moravian wine, pouring two glasses to the rim before telling her what was happening in Czech society. When Winn asked Havel if their conversation was being bugged, Havel smiled. "Almost certainly, but it doesn't matter. I'm not going to change what I say because of it. A man would go crazy living like that." Winn was charmed by the response, especially given the reaction she had encountered all over Prague, which led her to a paradoxical truth. "In a totalitarian society," Winn observed, "only a dissident enjoys freedom."[13]

Havel was living in elegance at the time of the interview, a result of his recent royalties from *Largo Desolato*. The kitchen gleamed with new counters and shiny appliances. The spacious study where they talked provided a beautiful view of the Vltava River and, in the distance, Prague Castle. When she asked him about his comforts, Havel told her his opulent lifestyle could change at any time. He also spoke of the despair he felt as a writer, his battles with guilt, depression, and black moods. He lived a life of irony and paradox, he told her, not least of which was the knowledge that the suppression of his writing, which made his life difficult, was part of what led to his fame. "I'm certain the paradoxes will continue," he told her. He went on: "I'll keep struggling with my writing, I'll despair that I can't write, that the words won't come—and then, finally, I'll somehow manage to write a new play. I'll keep feeling wretchedly oppressed by all the expectations people heap on me—and then, finally, I'll always fulfill the tasks set before me. I suspect that somewhere in my deepest depths I'll always enjoy this paradoxical life. That's the most paradoxical paradox of all."

Havel added, "I know they can kick me out [of my apartment] any time they want. The reason I can be free is simply because I say the hell with it. Let them take my apartment. Let them not put on my plays. Let them throw me in prison. I'm not going to change what I say or how I live."[14]

Not long after the interview with Winn, Havel sat down in his Prague apartment to write his third play since leaving prison, this one a spoof on political reformers trying to redeem a system that they no longer believed in. Once again, the words poured out of him. He finished *Redevelopment* in five days and then revised the manuscript during a second five-day spree. Havel's new, spontaneous writing process meant that he was no longer a man tortured by words. After sending the play off to his agent in Germany, he heard back that Tom Stoppard, the British playwright, was interested in writing an English-language adaptation.[15] Stoppard never did finish his adaptation. In a stroke of irony, Marie Winn, his interviewer from the *New York Times*, wrote a literal translation that was then adapted by James Saunders. A premiere followed in Switzerland, trailed by an English-language premiere at the Orange Tree Theater in England.

The premieres coincided with the increasing respect Havel received in the late 1980s as a seasoned dissident. As far back as 1984, Havel's Canadian publisher, Josef Škvorecký, had been pushing Havel's nomination for the Nobel Peace Prize. Havel made the short list several times in the 1980s without ever receiving the award. To compensate for the perceived insult, the man who ran the Charter 77 Foundation from Sweden, František Janouch, worked behind the scenes for Havel to be awarded the Erasmus Prize in 1986, given for contributions to culture, society, or science. The award had previously been bestowed to the likes of Martin Buber, Karl Jaspers, and Claude Lévi-Strauss, and it was considered one of the most distinguished prizes in Europe.

At the time, the Erasmus Prize came with a medal and two hundred thousand Dutch guilders, an enormous sum of money for anyone living behind the Iron Curtain. Havel wanted to donate the money to support dissident activities, but accepting the award, even if the cash wasn't deposited in his personal bank account, would open him up to charges of criminal activity. From the state's point of view, any hard currency earned by Havel belonged mostly to the government. By law, the state had the right to seize the award, returning in Tuzex vouchers whatever portion Havel was owed after taxes for foreign writers, which for banned writers could be more than 90 percent.

The solution, devised by Havel, was to ask the Erasmus Foundation to officially offer the prize to Havel without financial compensation. Meanwhile, Erasmus made plans to secretly donate the same amount of money that would have ordinarily been given to Havel to the Charter 77 Foundation, which had been established in Sweden to financially support the families of Czech dissidents. Janouch controlled the foundation, and Havel gave Janouch detailed advice, through hundreds of letters, regarding how the money should be doled out.

Originally, Havel had planned the Erasmus Prize to be accepted by two old political friends: Pavel Kohout, the playwright who had emigrated to Vienna after losing his citizenship, and Zdeněk Mlynář, a former governmental official who had emigrated to Austria after falling out of favor with the regime. Once again, however, the deep divisions in Charter 77 erupted into the open. Anti-communist dissidents complained it was inappropriate for such an award to be accepted by former communists, as both men were. Eventually, Havel settled on a new choice in his old pal Jan Tříska, the legendary actor who had been vacationing with Havel in Liberec when the Soviets invaded in 1968. Tříska had long since emigrated to America, playing a variety of character roles in Hollywood, but he remained a beloved figure in Czechoslovakia, where his films were remembered with a fondness usually reserved for saints.

All in all, some fifteen people traveled to Rotterdam, all of them exiles, the Erasmus Foundation and Charter 77 Foundation footing the bill. The whole affair became quite complicated, with numerous individuals asking for financial help to attend, exasperating Havel. "I cannot imagine," he wrote Janouch in Sweden, "that if I were receiving an honorary doctorate from the University of Olomouc [in Czechoslovakia] and invited one hundred friends from Prague that it would ever occur to a single one to ask [anyone] to pay for the trip. The idea would be completely absurd. Some people would hitchhike, someone would borrow the money from someone in a pub, another from a rich friend, for whom he would perhaps carry twenty sacks of cement up to the fourth floor in return."[16]

Although Havel received news of the award in January 1986, the prize ceremony didn't take place until November, when Tříska flew to Sweden. At the award ceremony, in the presence of the Royal Family, the late afternoon sun flowing through the cathedral windows, perhaps the most emotionally alive actor in the history of Czech cinema gave Havel's acceptance speech with a quivering voice, one that conveyed all of the pathos of his tragic country. Tříska later remarked, in an interview, that Havel's speech, like his writing style, was "extremely rational, extremely dry I would say."[17] Tříska's genius was to deliver Havel's talk with unrestrained emotion, allowing himself, as an interpreter, to be carried by the spirit of the occasion. He spoke in an extremely rapid pace, his voice conveying the rarified emotion that lay underneath the dry facts of Havel's prose.

It may have been the most remarkable moment in the history of the Erasmus Prize. Radio Free Europe was there, broadcasting the event to Czechoslovakia. Back in his apartment in Prague, Havel listened to the entire ceremony by radio, hearing Tříska deliver his own words as only a Method actor could.

By the mid-1980s, Radio Free Europe was broadcasting to more than four million Czechoslovakians, more than a third of the population.

Many people tuned in every day, listening through the static created by government jamming devices.[18] The large audience of Radio Free Europe was part of a change in society, a blurring of the lines between dissidents and those who had relatively high posts in government but wanted to see change. Many of them, individuals in the so-called gray zone, began cooperating with dissidents in various small ways. Meanwhile, several new civics groups were formed, including the Independent Peace Initiative, the Democratic Initiative, and Czech Children. Protests, especially regarding environmental and religious freedoms, became much more normal.

Many of the new activists came from a younger generation. They had little sense of the charter's history and even less patience with its idealistic and philosophic positions. They listened to punk and New Wave music, not to the Velvet Underground, and they wanted direct action rather than intellectual debate.[19] The central difference between Charter 77 and the new groups was described by Petr Pithart, a Charter 77 member, as the difference between "the dissent of activity" and "the dissent of reflection."[20] In Pithart's distinction, the new protests and demonstrations were fundamentally different from the practice of writers, philosophers, and critics who were chiefly concerned with uncovering the truth of the situation, whether it involved historical facts or the existential situation of living in a totalitarian society.

Václav Havel was one of the few individuals who belonged to both groups, and he was the most prominent dissident in each arena. Other dissidents had Havel's courage or intellectual skills, but no one could combine that with Havel's gift for the dramatic, his ability to inspire and bring people together, and his ability to explain complicated ideas in captivating prose. As a result, Havel came to represent the opposition, and he was perhaps the only man in the country capable of bringing both camps together.

Although somewhat dismissed by some of the younger generation, Charter 77 remained extremely active. Its main role was still to document the state of society. Under the leadership of Miloš Hájek, Bohumír Janát, and Stanislav Devátý, in 1988 it produced some sixty official documents monitoring civil liberties. In March 1987, commemorating the tenth anniversary of the death of Jan Patočka, Havel and other members of Charter 77 met at Patočka's grave, where they laid a wreath and held a policy meeting for expanding their activities.[21] When charter spokesman Martin Palouš later held a press conference with foreign journalists in his apartment to talk about the event, the secret police went into action, arresting sixteen dissidents.[22]

There was also a growing demand on the part of Catholics for religious freedoms. The church had been the object of a systematic but unsuccessful repression since the late 1940s, when the first communist president, Klement Gottwald, resolved to break the institution. Although legal structures of the church had been dismantled and church leaders were either imprisoned or sent to labor camps,[23] the communists had been unable to destroy the church completely. Faith continued, often handed down in families or secret ceremonies. The rising tide of religious demands in the 1980s may also have been affected by what was happening with their northern neighbors in Poland, where Pope John Paul II had once served as archbishop before being elevated to the papacy in 1978. Returning to Poland for a nine-day trip in 1979, drawing crowds up to two million, he told a crowd in Krakow that "the future of Poland will depend on how many people are mature enough to be nonconformists."[24]

In Czechoslovakia, Catholics felt increasingly emboldened by the pope's anti-communism. The first petition on religious freedom in 1984 gathered a few thousand signatures. In 1987 a Moravian Catholic farmer named August Navrátil led a similar petition on religious freedom that was signed by six hundred thousand citizens. Among other things, the petition demanded that the state release its control of the church.

There were other events that seemed to suggest that change was in the air. In 1987 a group of dissidents led by Jiří Ruml, Jiří Dienstbier, and Ladislav Hejdánek began openly publishing a monthly samizdat newspaper under the name of *Lidové noviny* ("newspaper of the people"). The name came from a daily newspaper that had been founded in 1893 and then interrupted during World War II before being permanently closed by the communists. Citing precedents in the Soviet

Union, Ruml's group began negotiating in early 1988 to register it as an officially recognized publication.[25]

The mood in the country had changed so much by that time—and the communist hold on power had become so fragile—that the secret police watching Havel began showing him new sympathy. Once during the holidays in 1987, when Olga had family for a visit, Havel grabbed a pitcher to go fetch a few pints of beer from the pub around the corner. One of the agents who had been tasked with watching his front door politely took the pitcher from him and offered to come back with beer himself. By this time, even some of the secret police were turning against the regime.[26]

Husák's government did what it could to hold on to power. In 1987 the police had arrested four members of Charter 77. The next year, the police interrogated charter members 185 times, often as a way of keeping dissidents from attending meetings or rallies. Police were also used to break up two international symposiums, the first a forum on peace, the second a series of lectures on the twentieth anniversary of the Prague Spring.[27] Another tool to keep dissidents in line was old-fashioned intimidation. In 1988 the mayor of Prague sent the administrators of the public schools a typical notice listing which employees had attended events sponsored by Charter 77.[28] Tactics like that remained quite effective.

Throughout 1987 and 1988, Havel was involved in a dizzying number of activities. He kept up his samizdat publication, the logistics having been delegated to others, and was involved in constant communication with dozens of Czech exiles, including Vilém Prečan and František Janouch, who were raising a half million Czech crowns a year to support dissident families with members in prison. Havel personally oversaw the distribution of money, usually to well over one hundred families a year.[29]

Havel also helped oversee the Tom Stoppard Prize, which provided recognition (and cash) to struggling writers.[30] He also helped Olga start her own samizdat magazine, *O Divadle*, in 1988, which introduced the first serious theater criticism into the country since the late 1940s. *O Divadle* was Olga's creation, with Havel's neighbor at Hrádeček, Andrej Krob, serving as the managing editor. Each issue carried up to three hundred pages of reviews, becoming more closely read than the official publications on theater. Zdeněk Urbánek took charge of binding the journal, and a large carload was sent out after each issue, driving to each major city where an underground distribution point was located, often in a pub or in the basement of a dissident's house.[31]

The government was powerless to stop most of these activities, not least because some of them were technically legal. Further, Havel was increasingly treated by foreign states as something like a one-man shadow government who was seen to have more legitimacy than those in power. The American ambassador, William Luers, took to throwing lavish parties for Havel and other dissidents, often including guests from America, such as Kurt Vonnegut, William Styron, Phillip Roth, an Edward Albee. State officials were sometimes invited as well. At one party in 1985, the deputy foreign minister of Czechoslovakia showed up to an event celebrating American Independence Day. After catching sight of Havel, he stormed off the premises, along with the entire delegation from the foreign ministry.[32]

Increasingly, it became common for foreign dignitaries to meet with Havel when they came to Prague on state business. This sometimes led to a cat-and-mouse game with the secret police, who were tasked with making such meetings as difficult as possible. This trend culminated in December 1988, when the French president François Mitterrand insisted on meeting with Havel and seven other dissidents for breakfast in the French embassy. Mitterrand told a news conference later that day that economic ties between the two countries would be impossible unless Czechoslovakia improved its human rights record. Later that week, Havel helped organize a demonstration, the first state-approved protest since 1968, attended by about six thousand people. Holding a megaphone, Havel called for the release of all political prisoners. He told the cheering crowd that "we are living in a dynamic and promising period, and our society is recovering from a long slumber."[33]

Truthfully, Havel had never really chosen this role for himself, and many times in the past twenty years he had tried to resist it. By the second half of 1988, however, he was reconciled to the idea that this was his fate. Meanwhile, the number and size of the protests were growing. In August, on the twentieth anniversary of the Soviet invasion, Havel had helped lead a protest with ten thousand Czechs who gathered to sing the national anthem. On the seventieth anniversary of the independence of Czechoslovakia, two months later, he joined an even larger demonstration that was met by riot shields and dogs. Havel was arrested after each protest and then released after forty-eight hours of interrogation.

One illustration of the changing mood is Havel's reception at an open-air folk festival in Lipnice, which Havel attended that fall. The master of ceremonies, Jan Rejžek, had asked Havel if he would speak to the audience. It was a brave idea, not least because even the mention of Havel's name could bring down the full force of the state. Although Havel had been involved in demonstrations, he had not made an official public appearance in nineteen years.

Almost no one in the audience knew what Havel looked like, but they all knew his voice from foreign radio broadcasts. When they heard his characteristic mumble from the microphone, the crowd went wild. First, a few here and there and then the entire audience stood and gave an ovation. Havel kept his remarks short, speaking of a sense of community he felt with the audience, the sense of "conspiracy" he felt with everyone at the festival, the sense that through the music they were witnessing the birth of something new. The audience roared. After the show, Havel stood at the back of the auditorium for ninety minutes signing autographs.[34]

# 16

## THE MAGIC LANTERN

IF THE FALL OF 1988 SUGGESTED THAT communism was losing its hold on the country, the new year showed that the regime would fight to remain in power. The battle lines formed in early January, when several dissident groups, including Charter 77, applied for a permit to conduct a memorial service on Wenceslas Square for Jan Palach, the student who set fire to himself in January 1969 to protest the Soviet invasion of Czechoslovakia. Naturally, the regime denied a permit to lay a wreath in his honor, but the organizers of the demonstration decided to march anyway.

The tense run-up to the demonstration was complicated by an anonymous, one-paragraph suicide note that was sent by mail to Václav Havel in early January. The author of the anonymous note was a student who praised both Havel and referred to Charter 77 as "a light in these dark times." To support the dissidents, the note claimed that the author and a group of fellow students planned to light themselves on fire "at the top of Wenceslas Square" in order to "rouse all citizens to the kind of public expression of national identity that took place exactly twenty years ago."[1]

The letter was signed "Torch #1," who claimed to be a member of the "Organizational Council for the Return of Collective Suicide." Since Charter 77 had set January 15 as the date for the memorial service of Jan Palach, the note seemed to suggest that several students planned to use that occasion to commit public self-immolation.

An ethicist by temperament, Havel took the note seriously. Like most other members of Charter 77, he was repelled by the idea of expediency, of using the ends to justify the means, and he seems never to have entertained the idea that such a suicide might indeed help the dissident cause. Instead, Havel immediately contacted Dušan Macháček, the editor in chief of a television news station in Prague. Havel wanted to deliver an on-air appeal to the student group, asking them not to harm themselves. Macháček originally entertained the idea and then denied the request after being told by colleagues it would destroy his career. Havel then turned to Radio Free Europe, where he made an on-the-air appeal to the author of the letter, telling him that the nation needed young men like him to stay alive. He also invited the young man to join him on January 16 for a demonstration on Wenceslas Square.

On January 15, the evening before the anniversary of Jan Palach's death, a crowd of about five thousand gathered around the statue of St. Wenceslas. Havel may or may not have been there when about one thousand riot police rolled into the square, along with the People's Militia, the paramilitary arm of the Communist Party. At least ten firetrucks with water cannons tried to disperse the crowd. Demonstrators held their ground, singing the national anthem while riot police moved in, beating individuals with truncheons and arresting others.[2]

The next day, another demonstration took place in which Havel watched from the awning of a nearby shop while friends laid a wreath in memory of Jan Palach. After the crowd was ordered to disperse, Havel apparently retreated down a passageway in the direction of his apartment before being arrested by two agents of the secret police. He was charged with inciting participation in an unlawful demonstration (including inviting the young man who had threatened suicide) and, secondly, refusing to leave the square when ordered by police.[3]

While in pretrial custody, Havel missed a whole week of protests, the crowds becoming larger each day, even while the police tactics became more brutal. By the end of the week, the police threw up barricades and closed off the downtown metros, entirely closing down Wenceslas Square and arresting more than four hundred people who were holding a vigil at Jan Palach's grave in Všetaty, eighteen miles from Prague. Everyone who couldn't prove they lived inside the village was either detained or arrested.

The January demonstrations seemed to represent a shift in the country. For one thing, the protestors in the crowd began to include citizens who had previously avoided confrontation with the state, members of the so-called gray zone. Demonstrations took on the aura of normalcy, as did facing down water cannons. Michael Žantovský, who was there most of the week, later wrote that everyone panicked the first time they faced water cannons. The second time they faced water cannons, it only emboldened them.[4]

Havel's trial, held on February 21, 1989, took place at the same time that the Soviet Union was pressuring Czechoslovakia to ease up against dissidents, making the regime's position seem precarious. There were also reports in the international press that several members of the Central Committee thought it unwise to take a hard line against Havel.[5] Hundreds of individuals and human rights observers, including a group from the Canadian embassy, turned out for the proceedings but were locked out of the courtroom, where only one Western journalist was allowed entry. Nevertheless, the crowd of well-wishers packed the third-floor stairwell of the court house and chanted "long live Havel" and "freedom" when Havel was escorted through the hallway, his hands cuffed in front of him.[6]

After a short, one-day show trial, the judge sentenced Havel to nine months in a minimum-security prison, an unusually light sentence for challenging the state. Used to serving hard labor, Havel was given a cozy cell with a television and two cellmates who were serving time for embezzlement. A prison official dropped by each week to enquire about his condition, a sign that the warden had instructions to give Havel the velvet treatment.[7]

Shortly after Havel's sentencing, Anna Freimanová, his neighbor at Hrádeček, began a petition for his release.[8] The first step was collecting the names of twelve prominent supporters, which Freimanová arranged to have broadcast over Radio Free Europe, followed by private gatherings in homes and theaters to gather signatures. By April more than a thousand people had signed. About the same time, an editorial in the *New York Times* attacked Havel's imprisonment as "disgraceful."[9] Apparently taken aback by the international attention, the regime orchestrated an appeals court to reduce the sentence to eight months, dropping one of the charges. This, too, was reported by the international press, which noted that about 150 dissidents had shown up at the appeals hearing and vowed to go on a one-day hunger strike.[10]

A further turning point came when a screenwriter, Jiří Křižan, created his own independent campaign to collect signatures from professionals who still worked in the world of theater and film. Křižan gathered another three thousand signatures, almost all of them from people who rarely associated with dissidents. Anna Freimanová's little campaign had turned into the most important political event of the spring, setting the stage for a new era of opposition in which those living in the gray zone (*strukturáks*, or those who lived within the official structures of society) began to join hands with dissidents.[11]

As a result of the petition (and perhaps the editorial in the *Times*), Havel was released after less than three months, on May 17, based on the warden's recommendation that he be rewarded for good behavior. That afternoon, Havel emerged from the prison wearing a brown sweater and gray jeans, his hair cropped close to the skull. Olga met him at the gates with three read carnations and a small group of international journalists. When asked how it felt to be free, Havel replied: "It's a good feeling. I recommend you go to jail yourself to get that feeling."[12]

After returning home, to the old Art Deco building on the embankment of the Vltava River, Havel was visited by Alexander

Dubček, the former president who had been living in internal exile since the Prague Spring. For about three hours, the two men discussed the political situation in the country.[13]

On the following day, Havel spoke at a press conference organized by Charter 77, along with the dissident Jiří Wolf, who had been released from Valdice Prison on the same day. Dubček came to the press conference as well, embracing Havel in front of the foreign press, including reporters from the United States, France, and the Soviet Union. Afterward, there was a gathering at Havel's flat, where a steady, daylong stream of hundreds, if not thousands, of artists, writers, friends, dissidents, and other supporters came to congratulate him. A Polish dissident was there as well, sharing information about demonstrations in his own country and Hungary—and about the possibility of Solidarity gaining a foothold in the Polish parliament.[14]

The Havel apartment quickly became a central depot for opposition, the closest thing to a campaign headquarters. A few days after his release, a diplomat from the Canadian embassy arrived. He reported that Havel looked tired, thin, and in poor health but was also full of "energy, determination, and optimism." The amount of activity taking place in Havel's flat seemed to him nothing short of astonishing. The doorbells and telephone rang incessantly, and Havel spent the day talking to dozens of journalists from foreign countries. Between interviews, Havel joked that he was expected to be an expert on everything, from developments in the Soviet Union to dissidents in China.[15]

One condition of Havel's early release from prison was that he refrain from political activity for the remainder of his term. As a result, he tried to avoid needlessly provoking the regime, while behind the scenes he was working on a new petition, this one written with Alexander Vonda and Jiří Křižan, who had helped free Havel from prison.

Written in the dry, nonconfrontational language that Havel had perfected over the past twenty years, the petition opened by declaring that there was now a danger of an open crisis between the citizens of

Czechoslovakia and their government. In order to avoid the crisis, the petition asked for the government to make "systematic change" in seven areas, including the release of political prisoners and the establishment of a freedom of speech and religion.[16] Havel circulated the petition among dissidents, and Křižan focused on individuals living in the gray zone.

One of the most striking elements of the petition, known as "A Few Sentences," was the moderate language that would have seemed radical just a few years earlier. In stage one of gathering signatures, Křižan gathered the support of three hundred prominent individuals in the gray zone who had survived precisely because they never questioned authority, at least in public. By the time they went public, on June 28, reading the petition on Radio Free Europe, they had collected the signatures of eighteen hundred prominent leaders of official culture. Over the next three months, forty thousand citizens added their names.

The popularity of "A Few Sentences" revealed that the regime was losing its grip on power, and the Central Committee launched a counterattack, a communiqué that warned local and regional officials against signing the "anti-socialist" petition, which was characterized as a work of "enemy forces." In classic communist fashion, the communiqué ignored the actual wording of "A Few Sentences" and instead issued talking points. Officials were told, for instance, that it was untrue that "political prisoners" existed in Czechoslovakia, and that freedom of assembly was already fully guaranteed under the constitution (in a revealing few sentences, however, the communiqué suggested that the rights of the constitution could not be applied to "criminal elements," including individuals who had signed the petition). As for religious freedom, the communiqué claimed that this, too, was guaranteed under the constitution, while noting that for "the good of society" religious expression was "overseen" by the state.[17]

Given the success of the latest petition, some members of the Central Committee called for jailing Havel again on the grounds that he had violated the conditions of parole. However, the general secretary of the Communist Party, Miloš Jakeš, argued for taking a soft line toward Havel. In a closed-door meeting of the Central Committee, he suggested that the regime had erred in jailing Havel earlier that year, turning Havel into a martyr and creating an international uproar. Instead of focusing on Havel, Jakeš suggested jailing lesser-known figures who could be more easily intimidated.[18]

In the meantime, Prime Minister Ladislav Adamec agreed to meet with members of the opposition, including Charter 77, to discuss the complaints within the petition. He had two conditions: first, that Havel could not be present and, second, that all discussion of the petition be removed from the broadcasts of Radio Free Europe. These demands were little more than a rearguard action, an attempt by the regime to forestall what appeared to be a rapid collapse. In September the General Secretary, Jakeš, told the presidium (which functioned like the Soviet politburo) that "we are quite alone, solitary, without a word of support from below, from the population."[19] Without an intervention from the Soviet Union, which seemed unlikely, he suggested the regime might be unable to hold on to power.

In the Hungarian People's Republic, a neighboring communist state, the government had all but faltered. At the beginning of the summer, the regime had decided to remove the barbed wire fence separating Hungary and Austria, in effect punching a hole in the Iron Curtain. Hungarians were crossing the border into Western Europe, but so were thousands of citizens from the rest of Eastern Europe, since it was still relatively easy to get a visa to travel to Hungary.

Few people had more motivation to make this trek than East Germans, who received automatic citizenship in West Germany if they could make it across the Iron Curtain. As a result, up to fifty thousand East Germans (along with another one hundred thousand Poles) flooded across the northern border of Czechoslovakia on their way to the Austrian-Hungarian border. In the ensuing crisis, East Germany closed its embassies in Prague and Budapest, attempting to slow down the exodus. By early September the Czechoslovakian government attempted to lend a helping hand, locking down the entire border with East Germany, a long, wooded area, much of it full of hills and mountains.[20]

By that time, however, Czechoslovakia was flooded with refugees, many of them sleeping on the streets of Prague, all of them en route to Hungary and then Western Europe. The communist government in Poland had already collapsed under pressure from the Solidarity movement, which had organized protests throughout 1988, leading to elections in which Solidarity won a resounding victory. In Hungary, the government had agreed to what were known as Round Table Talks in June 1989, the result of which was the creation of a multiparty democracy. In addition, the East German regime looked shaky as well, as citizens began almost-weekly protests, the largest on October 23 reaching at least three hundred thousand demonstrators. In an attempt to prevent the unrest from spreading to Czechoslovakia, the regime announced in October that the Communist Party would defend its leading role "at any cost." The head of ideology, Jan Fojtík, declared that the military and police would be ordered to fire on crowds with live ammunition if there were any demonstrations in Prague.[21]

Such intimidation tactics were mostly successful. Throughout the summer and early fall, the demonstrations inside Czechoslovakia were tiny. A typical demonstration on August 21, commemorating the twenty-first anniversary of the invasion, attracted no more than five thousand to ten thousand protestors. Another protest, held on October 28, was of a similar size.

The dam finally broke on November 11, the fiftieth anniversary of the death of Jan Opletal, a Czech student who was killed while demonstrating against the Nazis in World War II. To commemorate Opletal, a group of several thousand students gathered at the Vyšehrad Cemetery, south of the center of Prague, and marched up the embankment of the Vltava River to the city. When they passed the Havel family apartment, many in the crowd called out "Long Live Havel."

By the time they reached Národní Street, near the National Theater, the crowd had grown to the thousands. There, they encountered riot police with white helmets and anti-terrorist squads with red berets. Refusing to turn back, the students approached the police lines, singing "We Shall Overcome" in Czech. The riot police then cut off routes of escape and descended upon the crowd with long, white truncheons, beating protesters unconscious as pools of blood formed on the cobblestone streets.[22] More than a thousand demonstrators were hospitalized.

The next morning, a clear, cold Saturday, a group of students and dissident leaders called for a national strike. Václav Havel wasn't in Prague at the time, having returned to Hrádeček for a quiet birthday celebration for Jitka Vodňanská, his former mistress.[23] Once he heard the news, however, he rushed back to Prague, knowing the revolution had finally begun.

By the time Havel arrived in Prague on Saturday afternoon, the revolution was well underway at the Realistic Theatre, where students discussed how to organize a national strike. The meeting continued early the next morning at Havel's apartment, where Havel and a handful of older dissidents, associated with Charter 77, agreed with students to create a new group (Havel and Jan Urban, a history teacher, suggested the name "Civic Forum") that would lead the demonstrations and attempt to begin negotiations with the state. Havel then announced the creation of Civic Forum that night (Sunday) at a small theater, the Činoherní Club. The next morning, Monday, he held a press conference for foreign reporters in the living room of his apartment. Wearing an open white shirt with rolled-up sleeves and looking as if he hadn't slept that night, Havel announced the creation of Civic Forum and released a short declaration demanding the resignation of President Husák and the release of all political prisoners.[24] Immediately afterward, Havel rushed to meetings and then to Wenceslas Square, where a surging crowd of more than 150,000 had been building all day. At the top of the square, near the National Museum, the statue of St.

Wenceslas was covered in Czech flags and banners calling for free elections. A series of speakers, including Havel, addressed the crowd from the street using portable speakers, but in the mass confusion and rustling of the crowd, almost nothing could be heard.

By the next day, things had become more organized. The socialist newspaper *Svobodné slovo* offered Civic Forum a second-floor balcony over the square, and sound engineers from local theaters set up a system of speakers capable of broadcasting to several hundred thousand people. The rally started promptly at 4 p.m., following a carefully scheduled program that Havel had orchestrated himself. In addition to Havel, the crowd of approximately four hundred thousand heard from Václav Malý, the popular underground priest, and Karel Kryl, a poet and singer-songwriter whose music had been banned in the country since 1969. The crowd also heard from Karel Gott, a recording artist who had previously been associated with the regime. Promptly at 5 p.m., the demonstration was closed with the singing of the national anthem, led by Marta Kubišová, a folk singer who had been a symbol of national resistance since the Soviet invasion. Everyone was asked to go home peacefully in order to prevent provocateurs from inventing an excuse for a military intervention.

Sometime during the first week of the revolution, Civic Forum set up shop at the Magic Lantern, a large theater complex known for its combination of drama, music, and performance. Central headquarters was located belowground, down a flight of stairs from the theater foyer. A few students served as security, regulating who could get in and out. The first meetings were held in a smoking room and then, as Civic Forum grew from dozens to hundreds, moved to the main auditorium, which also served as a briefing area for the international press. The real heart of the revolution, however, was down another flight of stairs, where Havel occupied dressing rooms number ten and eleven. It was there that he and his private secretary and a few lieutenants worked out the details of what had been decided at the daily meetings, as well as crafting press releases and developing negotiating positions with the government.[25]

The organizational structure of Civic Forum evolved day by day in the first week. Most of the leaders were longtime dissidents who had been making their living as coal stokers and window washers. Politically, they included both Marxists and right-wing anti-communists. They met at a daily plenum, where the details of the revolution were delegated to committees and teams. At one plenum, the novelist Ivan Klíma (Havel joked that Klíma would have to give up writing any new books) was nominated to the Conceptual Committee, which was responsible for working out the "political science" and for getting the entire nation behind the revolution. Generally speaking, Civic Forum tried to balance each committee with representatives from the major constituencies that were leading the revolution, including the students.[26]

Sometimes the revolution looked like little more than chaos, or anarchy, but a great deal of it was actually coordinated from the Magic Lantern. By the end of the first week, theaters all over town were opened for guest speakers. During the day, there were protests and marches all over town, usually with at least one large rally, along with the daily press conference and a Civic Forum plenum, as well as negotiations with the government and strike committees meeting in factories, schools, and universities.[27] The political terrain changed day by day, if not hour by hour.

By the beginning of the second week, Prime Minister Vladislav Adamec was having daily discussions with Civic Forum, the only condition being Havel was not allowed to attend. At one meeting, Adamec agreed to rule out declaring martial law, even though defense minister Milán Václavík had announced the army was "ready to defend socialism."[28]

To some, it seemed like the regime had lost its nerve, or that the national strike by workers, whom the Communist Party was supposed to represent, had taken them by surprise. The entire support structure of the Communist Party appeared to be in disarray, including the press, which now began commenting on unjustified police violence at the demonstrations. On top of that, the government and the Communist Party had become so unpopular that when Adamec was allowed to speak to a crowd during one of the early rallies, pleading for the national strike to end, he was booed off stage. Other communist leaders seemed equally unsure how to react, having been psychologically paralyzed by glasnost and perestroika, the reforms that were sweeping the Soviet Union.[29]

In negotiations on November 28, the eleventh day of the revolution, Prime Minister Adamec agreed to establish a new governing coalition by December 3 and release all political prisoners by December 10. By this time, Adamec had allowed Havel to join the negotiating team; Havel also orchestrated most of the statements of Civic Forum and personally organized the program for each day's demonstration, keeping careful control of the schedule in order to keep the events short and thus minimizing the chance of violence and unrest.

In addition to popular stars, the daily demonstrations often included former president Alexander Dubček, a white-haired, slightly stooped man who still sported the slightly stiff smile everyone remembered from the Prague Spring. Dubček was largely embraced but also treated as a piece of nostalgia rather than a key to the future.

The protestors on Wenceslas Square worked hard at keeping the demonstrations peaceful, constantly reminding one another to avoid any kind of provocation that might give the police an excuse to act. Many gave out flowers to policemen or chanted for the police to join them. Thousands of protestors made daily pilgrimages to the site of the student protest of the previous month, leaving candles at the site of the massacre. While that was going on, students held teach-ins on democracy, museums went on strike, and columns of youth marched through Old Town almost every day with onlookers cheering them on.[30]

Havel was seemingly everywhere in those days, sleeping only a few hours a night and taking big handfuls of vitamins to keep from getting ill.[31] He seemed to be the one individual who could speak for all of the opposition groups. One night early in the revolution, when Havel was speaking to a spellbound crowd in the Realistic Theater, Professor Milan Machovec was overheard in the wings saying that Havel had become "greater than God," a statement that Havel himself took jokingly as a reference not only to the adulation that was being heaped on his shoulders but also to the uncritical acceptance of his ideas, as if he could do no wrong. Later on, Havel would say he had to pay a high price for that "adulation." As he reflected some years later, "Uncritical respect is always punished," first by worship and later by hatred.

Paul Wilson, who was in town to talk about translating *Disturbing the Peace*, captured the spirit of those days by describing an attempt to track Havel down during the middle of the revolution. Wilson wrote that

> in the frantic swirl of revolutionary events, Havel seemed as elusive as the wind. He was everywhere, but always on his way to somewhere else. I caught glimpses of him—once in the Theatre on the Balustrade, another time being swept from one meeting to another by his suite of volunteer bodyguards and handlers. Everyone had stories of "sightings." One of my friends was on Wenceslas Square the day Alexander Dubček first appeared on the balcony with Havel. When the demonstration was over and the spotlights were turned off, she saw Havel and Dubček, backlit against the window of the Melantrich building, doing a little dance.

Wilson finally caught up to Havel at the family apartment. It was a cold, overcast Sunday, and Havel had demanded four hours of free time in order to take a walk with Olga. Over breakfast, Havel and Wilson talked about the translation of *Disturbing the Peace*, and about the political situation. "Revolution is chaos and confusion," Havel told him, "and I'm a lover of order. I've always been put off by revolutions. I thought of them as natural disasters, the kind of thing that probably has to occur once in a while in history, but it's not the kind of thing you plan for, or get ready for, or look forward to." Before Havel could finish his thought, the telephone rang. When Olga came into the room to tell him Dubček was on the line, Havel gave an exasperated look. "There goes another hour of my free time," he said. [32]

After one Civic Forum event, probably in late November, a journalist joked with Havel about whether he would ever have time to write a play again. With a characteristic sense of self-irony, Havel replied that he was negotiating "with the future Minister of Interior" so that he could spend four days a week writing, followed by three days in jail, "resting from the new freedom."[33]

The official position of Civic Forum was that it was trying to avoid a constitutional crisis. Havel himself said that he didn't want the government to collapse but to meet specific, concrete demands, such as the establishment of free elections. Up until December, almost none of the dissidents imagined that the government would be essentially turned over to them. Nor did their interests run in that direction, at least for the most part. When Havel coined the term "Velvet Revolution" to describe what they were trying to accomplish, in a conversation with Rita Klímová, he meant at least partly that Civic Forum wasn't really involved in a revolution at all. Of course, the term "Velvet Revolution" was also a nod to Lou Reed, whose band, the Velvet Underground, had been one of the gods of the Czech underground, along with Frank Zappa. Revolutions, as Havel told the historian Timothy Garten Ash, were far too dangerous and exhausting.[34] He preferred to think of the demonstrations as something like the creative energy that he found in Western rock music, with its dark and complicated beauty.

After the prime minister resigned on December 3, the situation changed dramatically. Almost immediately, a committee at Civic Forum began drafting its candidates not only for ministerial positions but for the presidency. Havel was the overwhelming favorite.[35] About the same time, Havel attended a backroom meeting held in an apartment where someone produced badges, made in Hungary, that said "Havel for President." Havel shyly asked if he might have one and slipped it into his pocket, perhaps as a joke, a token to show to friends.

The idea that Havel might be elevated to the presidency would have seemed absurd only weeks earlier, but many of Havel's friends had long suspected Havel of political ambition. Both Pavel Kohout and Pavel Tigrid had suggested the possibility years earlier. Olga must have suspected his political ambitions, but she was dead set against him accepting any political post, however minor. Havel himself seems to have been ambivalent, fascinated by the idea and resentful of the possibility.

Havel was not the only one mentioned as a presidential candidate. The short list included Zdeněk Mlynář, who had been a minister in the Prague Spring, and Alexander Dubček, the former president. Mlynář had worked behind the scenes to support Charter 77 before emigrating to Vienna in the 1970s, and in early December he made a number of inquiries in Prague and Moscow, exploring the possibility of running the country as a reform communist who would follow the general direction that Gorbachev had set in the Soviet Union. After a few days of weighing his prospects, he withdrew his name, apparently feeling he was the wrong man for the job.

Conversely, Alexander Dubček wanted the job badly, not least as personal vindication for the twenty years he had spent in internal exile. By mid-December, however, Havel had become convinced that only someone who had been a dissident, such as himself, would be accepted by the country. Having made up his mind, he immediately went to work to convince Dubček to step aside in his favor. The two men held at least five meetings on the topic, several of them contentious, resulting in an agreement that Dubček would support Havel for president in exchange for Havel stepping down at the next election in favor of Dubček. In addition, Havel promised to support Dubček as Speaker of parliament, a highly coveted position. Havel kept his end of the bargain with the speakership, which Dubček won, but not with the presidency. By the following year, communism had become so thoroughly discredited that Dubček was no longer considered a serious candidate.

Candidates for president were not elected by popular election but by parliament, which was still controlled by the Communist Party. Havel found an unlikely ally in Marián Čalfa, who had become prime minister after the resignation of Adamec. Although Čalfa had risen through the ranks of the Communist Party, he was also a pragmatist rather than an ideologue, part of a new generation who came of age in the shadow of Gorbachev's *perestroika*. Čalfa saw Civic Forum not as the enemy but as part of the new political reality, and he quickly aligned himself with supporting their demands, which included sharing power in the government.

Havel himself was relieved to find a working partner within the communist government, a result, perhaps, of his love of order. Just five days after Čalfa agreed to form a new government with Civic Forum, the two men came to a crucial agreement. Havel would continue to support Čalfa as prime minister, and Čalfa would support Havel for president under the rules of the existing constitution, an agreement that provided Havel with a sense of stability, since Čalfa not only knew how to run a government but who could be trusted to support reform.

The actual vote in the Federal Assembly on December 27 was anticlimactic. Čalfa told everyone in parliament how to vote, a common practice in the communist years, and every member of parliament obeyed. Three days later, Havel appeared before a jubilant nation to give one of the most curious speeches ever given by a head of state. "My Dear fellow citizens," Havel began, speaking before the nation on New Year's Day. "For forty years you heard from my predecessors on this day different variations of the same theme: how our country flourished, how many million tons of steel we produced, how happy we all were, how we trusted our government, and what bright perspectives were unfolding before us. I assume you did not propose me for this office so that I, too, would lie to you." After Havel spoke, it was as if a terrible spell had been lifted. Morning had come, finally, and with it the promise that order would be restored.

Havel's election as president was the end of one story, but it was just the beginning of another, one that was so colorful, absurd, and improbable that it grabbed the attention of the entire world. Just a few months out of jail, Havel suddenly became one of the best-known politicians in Europe. Next to Lech Wałęsa of Poland and Nelson Mandela of South Africa, he became a symbol of a new world order, one based on tolerance and respect for democratic principles. Unlike

Wałęsa and Mandela, however, Havel was a first-rate intellectual as well as an avant-garde artist, a deeply creative man who had not only been a dissident but also a poet, essayist, playwright, editor, publisher, and amateur philosopher. He began his adult life by imagining the theater as a place to change society. Now, at fifty-three-years old, he was on a larger stage. He wanted to change the way the entire nation, and perhaps the world, thought about themselves and the obligations each person owed to their conscience.

By his own admission, Havel had once suffered from a fragile constitution. For much of his life, he had been prone to melancholy and depression. Whatever magic had transformed the nation began to work its way on him as well. In his first six months in office, preparing for the first fully free elections, he delivered scores of speeches across Europe, the Middle East, and America. Many of the speeches were reprinted in literary journals across the world, including the *New York Review of Books*. During his lunch hour, he worked on rewriting the constitution, to which he eventually contributed the preamble and several important ideas. In his free time, while on summer holiday, he wrote a book-length essay to explain his vision for the country.

The challenges were enormous. Czechoslovakia hadn't had a market economy in forty years. The democratic traditions of the First Republic had been destroyed, and the population had become used to living in an authoritarian society. The country lived, as Havel put it, "in a contaminated moral environment" in which citizens had gotten used to "saying something different from what we thought." Everyone had "learned not to believe in anything, to ignore each other, to care only about ourselves." Concepts such as "love, friendship, compassion, humility, or forgiveness" had lost their meaning, becoming little more than historical peculiarities.[36] The order of business, from Havel's point of view, was to restore civil society, to return to the nation the spiritual and humanistic ideals that made democracy possible.

As a careful judge of history, Havel knew the task wouldn't be easy. He guarded himself, telling himself that the nation wouldn't change overnight. And he was under no illusion, he said, that people would suddenly begin acting "wisely, unselfishly, altruistically, ready to make sacrifices for a good cause."[37] After all, there had been little resistance to the communist takeover in 1948 and the Nazi occupation before that.

The first days of the presidency were a heady and chaotic time. The entire situation was unprecedented, one of the few moments in modern history when a state was being run by writers, playwrights, philosophers, and professors.

Each day was a leap into an unknown future.

# PART FOUR

## The Final Offering
### July 1990–December 2011

A worker may be the hammer's master,
but the hammer still prevails. A tool knows
exactly how it is meant to be handled,
while the user of the tool can only have
an approximate idea.

—MILAN KUNDERA

# 17

## THE CORRIDORS OF POWER

A LITTLE MORE THAN TWENTY YEARS AFTER the Velvet Revolution, I sent Václav Havel a series of letters by way of his personal secretary, Michael Žantovský. I also sent along a letter of introduction from the film director Robert Redford, whom I knew personally as the result of a series of coincidences. I was certain the letter of introduction would make an impression. Like many Czechs, Havel had a long fascination with American Westerns—and with Robert Redford in particular. During Havel's presidency, they spent a week together at Karlovy Vary Film Festival, the two men and their wives, the four of them exchanging the intimacy of the extremely famous. Havel was captivated by the star power of his new American friend, and Redford found Havel entertaining, fascinating, and extremely complicated. "I could sense that he was a very conflicted man," Redford said.

In July 2009, I had the chance to see Havel briefly while visiting the garden party he had been holding each summer at his house since his dissident days. In the space between Hrádeček and the cottage of Andrej Krob, someone had erected two homemade stages. Large crowds of friends, former dissidents, and their children milled about the yard, drinking beer and watching productions of several plays that were put on throughout the day. Havel spent much of the afternoon resting in his house, but I spotted him here and there, once walking slowly (and with great difficulty) through the crowd with a heavy jug of plum brandy, stopping here and there to offer a snort to old friends. Another time he ambled out of his house to see a homemade production of one of his plays, my brother-in-law graciously giving up his chair so that Mr. Havel could have a seat.

Havel's health had taken a turn for the worse that summer. He had been in and out of the hospital with bouts of pneumonia. Having been freed of the presidency in 2003, he had returned to writing, including finishing a play and a memoir. The play, known in English as *Leaving*, had been turned into a Czech film, directed by Havel himself. Finishing the film, it was said, nearly killed him. I elected not to push myself on Havel at that party, knowing that I had just sent a second request to sit down with him for an interview. I was playing the long game, or so I told myself. Through his secretary, Havel sent a note later that summer to let me know he would not be sitting down with me to talk about his life. He had already said so much about his life, his secretary explained, that he had nothing left to say. Four months later, he succumbed to his final illness. The long game, as it turned out, didn't work so well, not for me.

I heard about Havel's death by way of breaking news, while I was sitting at my desk at my house in Santa Fe. On my computer screen was a four-page letter I planned to mail during the holidays, explaining once again why I thought we should sit down for an interview. As I had written in my letter, there was still a great deal of his life I didn't understand. I wanted, for instance, to know more about the writer's block that haunted him for much of his life, and I wanted to know why he thought it vanished after his depression in the early 1980s while he was in the midst of his love affair with Jitka Vodňanská. I wanted to know just what Jitka had given him, and I wanted to know how a man who often spent years writing a play turned into the president who dashed off scores of the most interesting speeches in his era while being overwhelmed by the duties of the state. I wanted to know how a famously cerebral man, an analytical intellectual, known for his dry discourse, had taken to signing his name above a heart, often one he drew in red ink. What did it signify?

In retrospect, I doubt an interview would have provided any fresh insight. Havel was an enigma, and no matter how many times anyone covered the same ground with him, the enigma remained. Havel's gift, I realized, was that he had been taught by despair, heartache, loss, and the emptiness of the culture around him. Witnessing the twentieth century, he called the world absurd. His life was his response.

Havel's life didn't conclude with the Velvet Revolution. By some accounts, it had just begun. The long years of resistance gave way to something entirely new. As president, he was, as he himself said, "catapulted overnight into a world of fairy tales." The international fame, the press coverage, and the trappings of being head of state were all part of what he called "a diabolical trap set for me by destiny."[1] For Havel, being president felt absurd, and he worried about his need for power, about how much he enjoyed it. In a speech given in Jerusalem, he imagined that he would wake up in a prison cell and realize that the entire presidency had all been a fabulous dream.[2]

From another point of view, however, the presidency is a mere footnote to the larger story of his life. The real Havel, the heroic part of his life, came earlier. In many ways, the presidency was a matter of tidying up what he had been working on for more than twenty-five years, putting things in order, attempting to institute the ideas of the Velvet Revolution into the offices of the government. In this regard, he made some important accomplishments as president, but his life as president was, by its nature, more routine.

From time to time, however, Havel tried to rise above being a mere functionary of the office. In many of his most memorable speeches, he tried to offer a new vision for the world, which in many ways was also a very old vision. One of the themes he returned to over and over again was the importance of the individual who stands on his own two feet. In many ways, this was the theme of his first presidential trip to America, when he addressed the Joint Session of Congress. "If the hope in the world lies in human consciousness," he said, "then it is obvious that intellectuals cannot go on forever avoiding their share of responsibility for the world and hiding their disdain for politics under an alleged need to be independent."[3]

The trip to Washington had been put together in a fortnight at the suggestion of Madeleine Albright, then a professor at Georgetown University. To his amazement, Havel discovered himself being treated as an international hero. President Bush invited him to meet in the Oval Office and then personally gave him a tour of the White House and his personal quarters, as well as a promising aid from the United States. The speech at the Joint Session of Congress, which Havel had written himself in a single afternoon, was also a roaring success, punctuated by multiple standing ovations.[4] The *New York Times* covered his talk on the front page, reporting that the audience was in rapt attention, "with Czechs in the visitor's gallery occasionally wiping away tears and Mr. Havel's aides drinking in the scene with that mixture of pride and bemusement that has characterized their rapid journey from prison cell to presidential castle."[5]

After two days in Washington, Havel and his team took a trip to New York City to meet with investment bankers who might be able to help bring in the foreign money they needed to rebuild the country. In addition to a rush of meetings, Havel and his team attended a party at the Guggenheim Museum given by Salomon Brothers and a private dinner at the house of William Luers, former ambassador to Czechoslovakia. The guests included E. Gerald Corrigan, the president of the Federal Reserve Bank of New York, and some of the most influential financiers in the United States. At the end of the evening, Havel exchanged his coat and tie for a sweater and blue jeans and joined his old friend, Miloš Forman, for a walk around the city, revisiting old haunts in the East Village, which the two men had frequented in 1968, when Havel had last been in New York. The late-night ramble ended at 1:30 a.m., after they had walked from Sheridan Square to Bleecker Street, people in the street lighting up in recognition of the famous men.[6]

The next morning, a Thursday, Havel was up early for breakfast at Gracie Mansion with Kurt Vonnegut Jr., Arthur Miller, and Joseph Papp, who had directed so many of Havel's plays at the Public Theater.

Later that day, Havel visited the archbishop of New York, where he received an award, a luncheon with Cyrus Vance (a former secretary of state), and a press conference at the United Nations, followed by a trip to Columbia University, where he received an honorary degree.

Somewhere in the middle of this whirlwind, Havel made time to stop by the Fifth Avenue offices of Helsinki Watch, a largely volunteer organization that publicizes human rights abuses around the world. In a voice full of emotion, Havel told a small crowd gathered in the offices that he felt that he was "here as a friend among friends. I know very well what you did for us, and perhaps without you, our revolution would not be."[7]

Returning to Prague later that week, life didn't slow down. During the first months of his presidency, Havel was busy reorganizing the office of the presidency, which had previously been controlled by the Central Committee of the Communist Party, proposing changes to the constitution, taking large tours of the country, holding weekly radio addresses, and making regular visits to foreign countries, where he sought financial and political assistance for transforming the country.

The situation at the castle was chaotic in the early days. Havel's inner circle consisted almost entirely of individuals who did not consider themselves politicians, mostly intellectuals, writers, and philosophers. Their task was to help build a new society, which meant privatizing a communist economy, protecting free speech, and creating a new constitution, which Havel wanted in place by the end of 1991.

One thorny problem was what to do with the Communist Party. Havel discussed with his aides an idea of setting up a tribunal, or truth-telling commission, in order to review human rights abuses among those who had been in power.[8] In the end, he and his aides decided there was no appetite or energy for such work, either among themselves or the nation at large. Instead, the Communist Party was allowed to reform itself into a legitimate political party that would operate under the rules of democracy.

Since a considerable portion of the government remained intact, Havel spent much of his time meeting with communists who still held the levers of power in bureaucracies, in parliament, and among the ministries. Many of them resisted democratic reforms, preferring to turn back the clock to the Prague Spring or to follow the Soviet model of reform based on perestroika. Communists in the cabinet created their own inner circle, holding private strategy meetings on such issues as retaining the constitutional language that gave the Communist Party the leading role in running the government. A related problem involved writing the laws for the first free elections. Havel preferred an American-style electoral system in which members of parliament would be elected directly, while the inner circle of communists fought for a proportional system in which political parties received seats based on the vote and then doled those seats out to loyalists, which is the system that was put in place. One thing connecting all of these issues was the problem of reconciling the past. At one time or another, a large portion of the Czech and Slovak population had belonged to the Communist Party, many of them for cynical reasons. A large portion of the country had also collaborated with the secret police.

Not long after being elected president, the government handed over Havel his secret police file, including a list of individuals who had informed on him over the years. Havel looked over the list and then misplaced it the same day. A highly introspective man, Havel suspected that this Freudian slip was simply a convenient way of letting go of the past. As president, he couldn't afford to know who had betrayed him, not least because he now had to work with some of them in the government.

The issue, as Havel saw it, was that the nation had been governed by a poisonous system, and there was a need to extract the illness. At the same time, Havel was concerned that a reckoning with the past might let loose a torrent of revenge, much like what had occurred after the Allied victory in World War II, when more than two million German Czechs were expelled from the country.[9] Havel didn't want to open the door to lawlessness, and he was further concerned that virtually every industry and government post was run by someone who had been compromised by the communists. As he told Adam

Michnik, a Polish journalist, he wanted to find a compromise, a way of accounting for the past without being overwhelmed by it. For Havel, this meant "finding the appropriate balance." He felt it was important for the country to "know how to face our own past, how to name it, how to draw conclusions from it" but also to do so "honestly, in a measured way, with tact, generosity, and imagination."[10]

After considerable debate, parliament issued a series of bills in October 1991 that prohibited any individual formerly employed by the StB, or who served in the People's Militia or on the Communist Verification Committees, from holding political office or holding upper-level positions in the government, the army, or other areas of civil service. Havel reluctantly signed the bills into law, feeling it was unfair. He then proposed an amendment that would allow individuals to appeal their case to a court, which would be allowed to judge the circumstances of their specific case.[11] Parliament ignored Havel's request.

One of Havel's first acts as president, in January of 1990, was to use his presidential power to give amnesty to everyone in the nation's jails who was serving sentences of two years or less, excepting those serving sentences for terrorism, murder, robbery, rape, or other sexual abuse. Havel asked Czechoslovak citizens "not to be afraid of released prisoners, but to help them in a Christian spirit after their return among us, to find in themselves what our prisons could not instill: repentance and a desire to lead a good life."[12] Havel's reasoning was that the system of justice had been corrupt and that, in practice, it was impossible to distinguish political prisoners from other criminals. His ruling affected about two-thirds of those in the prison system, and it proved to be deeply unpopular.

The run-up to the first free elections, held six months after the Velvet Revolution, was even more chaotic than the initial transition. More than a hundred political parties had been formed, many of them extremely minor and unable to gather the ten thousand signatures that were required to get on the ballot. Civic Forum and its Slovak counterpart, Public against Violence, were still immensely popular, but it was impossible to know if they would be able to gain a clear majority of the country, especially with the field so cluttered. In addition, neither of the two organizations functioned as a modern political party. Civic Forum, in particular, had no real platform, except for an appeal to consensus and democratic reforms, serving as an umbrella for dissidents who had been both on the left and the right of the political spectrum. Going into the first elections, its slogan was "Parties are for party members. Civic Forum is for everyone."[13]

The appeal for unity worked, however. Together Civic Forum and Public against Violence won a slim majority of votes in both houses of federal parliament, winning 164 of 300 seats, with the Communist Party winning 40 seats, the Christian Democratic Union 17, and a variety of other parties picking up the scraps. With an overall majority, Civic Forum and Public against Violence chose to establish a wide coalition, seeking to run the government through consensus. Havel once again selected Čalfa to be prime minister, despite the fact that he had previously worked for the communists, and Václav Klaus was tapped as finance minister, with orders to move quickly to a market economy.[14] Then, at the beginning of July, parliament reelected Havel as president.

In the early 1990s, Havel was often portrayed in the foreign media as a reluctant president, a playwright who had sacrificed himself for his country, a free-spirited, postmodern bohemian who was forced to buckle down and run a country. Later, Havel was sometimes demythologized and seen as a man who used his reticence as a ruse, secretly positioning himself to be in power while simultaneously appearing to avoid it. The truth is that he was both individuals. While Havel believed in the virtue of politics, he was also suspicious of the ease with which he accepted the role of the presidency and suspicious of how long he stayed in power. He enjoyed the presidency, and he also resented its seductive hold. With his sense of absurdity, he had always understood that those in power are often the individuals with the least amount of freedom, forced (as he once said of Gorbachev) to live a life "of endless meetings, negotiation sessions, and speeches."[15] At times, he found his life unbearable.

In the early years of his presidency, Havel spoke about these ironies incessantly. Perhaps the most honest moment came the spring
after the Velvet Revolution, on a weekend trip to the presidential
retreat, the country estate at Lány that had originally been created
by Tomáš G. Masaryk. Havel had managed in his hectic schedule
to arrange time to visit with Jitka Vodňanská. Olga (perhaps feeling guilty for separating the two back in 1988) had graciously disappeared back to Prague so that the two old lovers could be alone
for a few hours. Havel explained to Jitka what he was learning about
the office of the presidency and showed her his new diplomatic
passport, which listed his profession as "president," a source of deep
amusement.

Later, while they were on a sofa, Havel put his head in her lap
and told her this was the first moment's relaxation he had had since
becoming president. He then cried softly, and she gently stroked his
hair. Havel told her, "What have you done to me. I feel responsible for
the whole world. This is worse than prison. There I was responsible
for myself only. Here, not only am I watched but I cannot make a
single mistake."[16]

Being a dissident presented very different problems from running
the government. For one thing, dissidence required no positive political agenda, while the presidency required Havel to form opinions
on hundreds of practical issues involving international relations,
constitutional reform, and running elections. To make matters more
complicated, Havel sometimes imagined himself as overseeing an
existential revolution. For most of his adult life, he had criticized
conventional politics as "a mere technology of vying for power."[17] As
a citizen and independent intellectual, he had the luxury of imagining a different kind of politics, one that would be rooted in practical
morality. He borrowed this idea that there exists two kinds of politics
from a number of dissident philosophers, including Havel's friend
Ladislav Hejdánek, who distinguished politics as the manipulation of
power from an older idea, a dialogue in which each side works toward
a common good.

As president, Havel championed the second style of action, referring to it as "antipolitical politics." By antipolitical politics, he meant a style of governance that focused on civility, decency, and human interaction, replacing tactical maneuvering with a sense of morality and personal responsibility.[18] Rather than focus on the end results, Havel's politics focused on the means of political discourse, or "living in truth," a phrase that his political enemies saw as romantic and starry-eyed. One aspect of antipolitical politics was Havel's refusal to support any political party, even though many of his closest allies were originally with Civic Forum and later with Civic Movement. Some of these friends naturally felt abandoned by Havel's neutral stance toward the political parties. Occasionally, Havel was even accused of being against political parties altogether, although that wasn't exactly true.[19] As Havel argued after his presidency, he saw political parties as a natural form of association, but he also believed that political parties encouraged a great deal of negative behavior, much of it in the form of partisan maneuvering, or what he called "the dictatorship of partisanship."[20]

Havel himself believed the presidency should rise above partisanship. Although he wasn't hesitant to occasionally propose specific policies, he focused on ideas rather than programs. Havel's great theme was the state of the world. Another theme was "the crises of civilization." Havel had experienced the crises firsthand, under communism, but he also understood that the crisis of communism had been part of a larger problem, the nihilism, alienation, and inauthenticity that had made totalitarianism possible. For Havel, the crises in meaning was a direct result of modernity. It was rooted in the Enlightenment and in the dislocation of humanity from the natural world. The idea came straight out of Heidegger and Jan Patočka, who argued that society suffered from the industrialization of the spirit.[21] As Havel put it in *Letters to Olga*, humans had turned milk cows into milk output machines.[22]

As president, Havel claimed to consider himself a citizen first and a politician second. The idea was controversial. Many saw Havel's position as naive, or as misunderstanding the different roles played by intellectuals and politicians. Kieran Williams has argued, for instance, that Havel suffered from the basic mistake of confusing the role of critic and leader—that is, of trying to have it both ways.[23] This particular line of disapproval was forcibly argued by Timothy Garten Ash, the Oxford scholar who had befriended Havel during the Velvet Revolution. Ash pointed out that the job of the intellectual is to speak the truth, making them the natural adversary of politicians, who, Ash suggested, are required by their profession to "work in half-truths." Out of necessity, he said, the position of any politician is one-sided, designed to win votes or sell the public on a plan of action. Political parties, Ash suggested, are obviously reluctant to offer the sort of frank, critical analysis that involves weighing both sides of an argument. Ash thought that Havel had given up his independence when he became president, without quite understanding the nature of his new job. As Ash put it, "No politician worthy of the name," he said, "will seriously maintain in private that what he said in a public, party-political speech is the whole truth on a particular issue. It may possibly have been the truth; it might even have been nothing but the truth; but it is most unlikely to have been the whole truth—or he will not be a very effective party politician."[24] From this point of view, it had been a mistake for Havel to become president.

Not surpassingly, Havel took a different position from his old friend. For one thing, Havel refused to accept the distinction between the independent intellectual and the politician, such a distinction being alien to his temperament. Havel believed the world needs more intellectuals in public life, just as it needs public officials who are willing to speak the truth without regard to expediency. For Havel, such a politics is an honest attempt to face the complexity of the world. He had seen firsthand, in the dissident community, that it was possible for sensitive, highly ethical individuals to confront the power of the state, and he believed the same individuals could bring sensitivity and openness to government. As a dissident, Havel once suggested that antipolitical politics was a "politics of man, not of the apparatus . . . a politics from the heart, not from a thesis." As president, he took a similar tact, arguing that truth could never be achieved through deceit. He argued that the purpose of politics was to cultivate a climate of "tolerance, openness, broadmindedness, and a kind of elementary companionship and mutual trust."[25]

A charitable reading of Havel's idealism would be that culture, especially in Eastern Europe, requires involvement of those who have spent their lives thinking about society. Although Havel knew that intellectuals could be blinded by a grand ideal, he nevertheless believed they also had a special contribution to make to public life, not least because they had been trained to think about ideals and principles.

After the honeymoon of the first year in office, a new era began, one that was far less happy. Havel himself reflected on the change, suggesting the initial period of his presidency had been colored by the peculiarity of the times. During the first phase, during the Velvet Revolution and its aftermath, Havel had received uncritical adulteration that could scarcely last forever. Such uncritical worship, he wrote, is always punished, although as a rule it is "the object of that respect who is punished, not those who confer it."[26] The initial phase, characterized by "enthusiasm, unity, mutual understanding and dedication to a common cause" was over. Not only had the times changed, but "clarity and harmony" had disappeared. Clouds filled the skies, and it was clear to him that the country was "heading into a period of not inconsiderable difficulties."[27] In short, revolution had given way to the contentious realities of running a democracy.

Making things more difficult, the old constitution, which had been inherited from the communists, was dangerously inadequate, requiring parliament to amend it almost a dozen times in the first year after the Velvet Revolution. The result was a great deal of confusion about the relationship between the two parts of the federation, the Slovak and Czech Republics. Havel took it upon himself, with the help of Pavel Rychetský, to propose creating an entirely new constitution, one more appropriate for a democracy. Rychetský was a longtime lawyer—Havel knew him from his dissident days—and the two spent three weekends drawing up a draft document that Havel then presented on a televised news conference before handing it over to the Federal Assembly, which ignored it completely. The lack of consideration was probably related to the fact that Alexander Dubček, who was head of the Federal Assembly, was skeptical that he could find enough votes to pass it.[28]

Under the system inherited from the old regime, each republic was governed by their own parliament as well as by a bicameral Federal Assembly. While the House of People was representative of the population, consisting of ninety-five Czech seats and fifty-one Slovak seats, the House of Nations consisted of an equal number of representatives from Czech and Slovakia, a compromise that allowed members of parliament from Slovakia to effectively block any legislation. The head of state under the old constitution was the president, directly voted by parliament, but the government and ministries were run by the prime minister, who was appointed by the president.

One unusual aspect of the constitution was its emphasis on political parties. On election day, for instance, voters were given a ballot of the political party of their choice rather than a list of candidates; the voter could then choose up to four individuals they wished to support. Any party gathering more than 5 percent of the vote received proportional seats in parliament. Many observers called this system a "disastrous mistake."[29] In the 1990 elections, it hadn't mattered much, as there was still a sense of national solidarity, but in the following elections it became problematic. For one thing, members of parliament often had more allegiance to their party than to voters. The system also created a fragmented parliament, making it difficult for one group to win a clear victory. In the 1992 elections, for instance, voters had forty serious political parties to choose from, many with them with extremely narrow interests (parties for ethnic minorities, for cheap beer, for the environment, etc.).

By 1992, the far right of the country was dominated by the Civic Democratic Party (ODS), led by Václav Klaus, an overbearing and arrogant man who as minister of finance had been in charge of privatizing the economy. Klaus was essentially a Thatcherite who believed in low taxes, free markets, and cutting the social support system, sometimes rather ruthlessly. ODS was aligned with the Christian

Democratic Party, led by Havel's old dissident friend Václav Benda. The largest centrist group was Civic Movement, the political party that evolved out of Civic Forum. Consisting of most of the dissidents and members of Charter 77, the party was in favor of market reforms but wanted a strong safety net to protect workers. By the spring of 1992, in the run-up to the elections, Klaus had bitterly attacked Civic Movement, accurately seeing that his own party could only seize electoral power by tearing down the inheritors of the Velvet Revolution. It helped that Klaus had a visceral dislike of the artists and intellectuals who formed Civic Movement.

ODS was clearly the most organized political party in the second round of elections in 1992, having offices in the major cities, along with billboards that showed a portrait of Klaus under the slogan "Don't Betray Your Future."[30] Klaus himself was not a charismatic man, but he exuded confidence. As the minister in charge of reforming the economy, he also had the natural support of businessmen and entrepreneurs who shared his dream of turning Czechoslovakia into a prosperous European nation.

Much of the disquieting tone of the election had to do with regional differences in the country. The western half of the federation—roughly equivalent to the Czech Republic—had survived the first shock of market reforms with relative ease, while Slovakia faced financial calamity from the closing of large factories. Klaus himself threatened to split the nation in two if Slovakia would not agree to continued market reforms. At the same time, a regional party in Slovakia, the Movement for a Democratic Slovakia (HZDS), began demanding independence from the rest of the country.

HZDS had been formed by Vladimír Mečiar, a demagogue and former communist who was said to have ties to the Slovak mafia. In other regions of the country, Mečiar was regarded as something of a joke. Few took his political movement seriously until shortly before the election. In Slovakia, however, his calls for independence struck gold. Just before the elections, polls showed that 40 percent of Slovaks were against the economic reforms being pushed by the federal government.[31]

The election itself was a mass of confusion. For one thing, it was difficult for voters to get clear information about the subtle differences between the forty parties on the ballot. Complicating matters further was an electoral law from the previous January that was interpreted to mean that radio and television could not broadcast programs or speeches of individual candidates, presumably in order to be fair to everyone involved. The exception were small public service slots that were equally allotted. As a result, there was almost no broadcast news about the election and no televised debates.

The results on election day were shocking. Civic Movement failed spectacularly, not getting enough votes to get past the threshold of representation, removing almost all of the former dissidents from office, and leaving Havel with few allies. Within the Czech Republic, ODS received about 35 percent of the vote, and within Slovakia HZDS came in with about the same amount, with the communist and socialist parties having the next highest votes. The leaders of the two leading parties—Klaus and Mečiar—immediately began negotiations on forming a government but quickly switched to discussing how to dismantle the federation.

The situation was distressing to many Czechs and Slovaks, as neither of the parties had won a majority of the vote, nor was any referendum planned or offered. In the end, the momentum proved to be too much. A few weeks later, an agreement was made to peacefully break up the country. Havel was helpless to stop the dissolution, and on July 17, 1992, a few hours after the Slovak parliament voted on a declaration of sovereignty, he resigned from the presidency.

The Velvet Revolution had come to a bitter end.

After resigning from the presidency, Havel retreated to the old family building on the embankment. Officially he had no legitimate source of power, but aides and friends provided him with administrative support as he watched the slow dissolution of the country. After several months of silence, he returned to the public scene in October 1992, when he launched a new collection of essays ("Dear Citizens") and publicly called for the constitution of the new nation, eventually to be called the Czech Republic, to have direct elections of the president. Parliament ignored his advice. Then on November 16, Havel announced his candidacy for the new country. By that time, he had the support ODS, not least because Klaus craved the legitimacy that Havel would bring to the government. In the meantime, the new constitution, which was largely influenced by ODS, handed over most of the former power of the presidency to the prime minister, the exception being foreign affairs.

It's not clear why Havel was interested in returning to the presidency. Many of Havel's closest advisors thought it was a mistake, not least because his influence was on the decline. Further, Klaus clearly wanted to keep him under his thumb.[32] One theory for why Havel returned to office is that he had gotten a taste of power. An alternative theory, offered by his aide Michael Žantovský, is that he did so out of a sense of guilt for having failed to prevent the breakup of Czechoslovakia, feeling that he deserved to be punished by serving again as president.[33]

Havel himself seemed to dread returning to the day-to-day duties. He certainly dreaded having to work directly with Klaus, whom he disliked. As prime minister from 1992 to 1997, Klaus was by far the most important politician in the country, controlling much of the government and federal assembly. His dislike of Havel was legendary, based in part on their rivalry but also on a visceral reaction to Havel's orientation. "He is the most elitist person I have ever seen in my life," Klaus once said of Havel. "I am a normal person. He is not." Klaus did little to hide his contempt for many of Havel's ideas, including Havel's devotion to civil society. In a *New York Times* interview, Klaus called those around Havel a "moralizing elite with perfectionist ambitions."[34]

Underneath the differences of the two men lay two competing visions for society. Klaus was a right-wing politician who sought to privatize the Czech economy as quickly as possible, despite knowing the process would throw thousands out of work. For Klaus, the economy was primary, whereas Havel's top priority was the reestablishment of civil society. Havel was appalled by the unfairness involved in privatizing the economy, which led many insiders to become overnight millionaires while ordinary Czechs suffered.

Havel not only disliked Klaus, but he dreaded their meetings together, not least because Klaus was a master at delivering little discourtesies that Havel did his best to ignore. According to Havel, Klaus "used all kinds of techniques" to undermine him in meetings. Klaus also imposed conditions on the president that Havel regarded as "polite blackmail." Despite their mutual dislike, Klaus insisted on meeting Havel every Wednesday for one hour, which Klaus often used to berate Havel over statements from the previous week.[35] Painfully courteous, Havel's approach was to try to defend his positions, while Klaus apparently used the time to gain the upper hand in their relationship. In hindsight, many of the complaints that Klaus brought to Havel were petty, such as Klaus's objection that Havel had issued a statement on the death of Frank Zappa, which Klaus thought was beneath the dignity of the presidency. In the end, Havel finally refused to continue their meetings, but not until several years into his presidency.[36]

The workaday drudgery at the castle became quite intense after his 1992 election. Havel gave twenty to thirty major speeches a year. He almost always wrote the early drafts of the speeches himself, sending them out for review by the staff, who often provided endless suggestions and revisions. In a typical memo from 1995, Havel complained that he had already "suffered over the writing of a speech" for three days and would have to spend another ten days on it if he was going to comply with all of the suggested edits.[37]

In addition to the speeches, Havel faced a daunting number of briefings, staff meetings, state visits, and official memos, often involving him in hundreds of mundane affairs, such as the arrangement of flowers at the castle or the protocol for foreign visitors. Although Havel had little executive authority, he was also determined to use his position to set themes for the country, which he emphasized in his speeches and regular radio broadcasts, chiefly the importance of clean energy, of decentralizing the Czech government, rebuilding a civic society, entering the North Atlantic Treaty Organization (NATO), thus becoming part of Western Europe.

Despite his best intentions, the presidency, as Havel later reflected, swallowed him "up whole." His previous pleasures, interests, and pursuits had to be cut back or eliminated. The job, he said, "consumed me entirely and made it almost impossible for me to pay attention to anything else."[38] Ironically, however, his marriage had never been better. Seeing the stress he was under, Olga gave him her full sympathy. She even ignored his many dalliances and didn't object to the rekindling of his romance with Jitka, the one woman whom she regarded as a true threat to their marriage.

Havel made a habit of slipping out of Prague Castle to visit Jitka whenever he could get an evening free, attended by his bodyguards, who waited outside the apartment steps until morning. The nighttime visits were an open secret around Prague. On an official presidential visit to Jitka's hospital in 1990, Jitka remembers a bodyguard giving her a knowing wink, telling her the president was going to make a surprise visit to her later that night. Jitka went home and made pork ribs, and when Havel arrived, he told her about what was happening in the castle, with an eye toward the absurd little details of life as president. It was clear to her that living as president was not only difficult but left him feeling awkward with his old friends.

For his part, Havel often tried to find humor to make light of the situation. Over breakfast on the mornings after a visit, he would tell Jitka, in his ironic voice, "Jitka, I have this kind of little office to run. I have to go to work."[39] Somehow it eased the situation to laugh about the absurdity of it all.

# 18

## A HEAVY STONE

THE SECOND HALF OF HAVEL'S PRESIDENTIAL TERM was difficult and exhausting. Having once been revered as a national hero and martyr, Havel was now referred to in much of the media as a president who had made mistakes. Politicians on the right accused him of being soft on former communists. Politicians on the left accused him of being right-wing.

Havel's health also took an ominous turn. The strain of the office began taking a physical toll on Havel by the mid-1990s, while Havel continued to smoke one to two packs of cigarettes a day and consume generous portions of alcohol, along with a laundry list of pills, uppers to get him working and downers to get him to sleep. He began alternating between several weeks of near-constant work, going late into the night, followed by a "partial collapse" that usually included difficulty breathing.[1]

Havel remained a world-class speech writer, sought after on four continents, but there were increasing objections that his speeches were peppered with references to unconventional ideas, such as the Gaia hypothesis, which suggests the world is alive, or the anthropic cosmological principle, which posits the reality of God. Both ideas were floated at a speech in Philadelphia, which earned praise in the *New York Times* as a remarkable example of a politician speaking of transcendent ideas while winning condemnation at home.[2] In Prague, politicians often rolled their eyes when Havel began one of his philosophical talks, seeing him as a "mad hippie" or a "crazed theologian."[3] More than a few resented his discussions of morality and responsibility.

And President Havel continued to push big ideas. Having helped negotiate the end of the Warsaw Pact, he called for the expansion of NATO into Eastern Europe—a controversial idea, especially within the foreign policy establishment in the United States, which worried about antagonizing Russia—and championed the integration of Europe and creating a common market. Havel argued, almost nonstop, that the Czech Republic should play a crucial role as the crossroads of Europe, bridging East and West, a gambit that was at least partly about what he saw as the importance of his country being engaged with the international community rather than becoming mired in its own narrow national interests.

In the process of his near-constant international travel, Havel often forged unconventional relationships with a number of other world leaders, many of whom saw him as a great man. The American president Bill Clinton publicly talked about Havel's influence, which preceded his first visit to the White House in 1993 for the opening of the National Holocaust Memorial Museum. At that meeting, Havel and Polish president Lech Wałęsa cornered Clinton on the White House porch and urged him not only to enlarge NATO but to create a peace-keeping operation in the former Yugoslavia, two issues that Clinton eventually supported.[4]

The friendship with Clinton was strengthened in 1994 when the American president visited Prague with Madeleine Albright, the secretary of state, to announce his support of the expansion of NATO. Havel gave Clinton a private tour of the castle and took him to a pub in Old Town and then to the Reduta Jazz Club to listen to music. After a set, Havel presented the American president with a Czech-made saxophone and invited Clinton to join the band to play a rendition of "My Funny Valentine."[5] The two men established an intimate enough bond that they met years later in New York City, at the Clintons' house, after both men had left office, for an afternoon that combined chitchat and serious discussions about world affairs and whether Hillary Clinton should run for president.[6]

In addition to being ill and exhausted, Havel was described by aides as spending most of his first five-year term as president of the Czech Republic "in an almost permanent sub-depression" that affected his mood and political outlook.[7] He grew so tired of his criticisms in the press that he sent one television newscaster a business card that said "Václav Havel, Author of Many Mistakes" to protest the way she referred to him on air.[8] He came to believe that much of the press coverage was an "inevitable hangover" from having once been revered as a national hero.[9]

Bedeviled by melancholy, weighed down by the heaviness of the tasks before him, Havel continued in the role of antiheroic politician. Whereas his communist predecessors were largely arrogant, headstrong men who were certain of the righteousness of their cause, Havel was often full of doubt, reticence, and hesitation. He spoke of his Kafkaesque feelings of inadequacy, the feeling that others saw him as a fool. As he put it in a speech he gave in Israel during his first presidential term, the lower his station the more proper his place seemed to him. And the higher his position, the stronger his suspicion "that there has been some mistake."[10] Authority, even his own, seemed to oppress him.

The comfort Havel found in his presidential years often came from sneaking out of the presidential castle. Havel kept a number of girlfriends in those years. He continued to see Jitka Vodňanská throughout the late 1990s, and he also had a serious affair with Dagmar Veškrnová, an actress whom he would later marry just one year after Olga died of cancer, in January 1996. There were other women as well, many of them. Havel reportedly bragged to aides about some of his conquests, remarking that power was an aphrodisiac.

For the balance of his time in office, Havel remained unpopular at home and in poor health. A typical opinion poll from the year 2000 showed that 53 percent of the respondents thought he should resign.[11]

As a result, two very different accounts emerged of his presidency, one from intellectuals around the globe who saw him as one of the great heroes of the twentieth century and another from his critics, mostly within the Czech Republic, who saw him as a busybody and ineffective bumbler.

In the negative assessment, Havel was an intellectual who didn't understand the nature of politics. As a result, he was outmaneuvered by Klaus and ODS, becoming irrelevant to the nuts and bolts of the parliamentary process. This view of Havel was most famously articulated by John Keane, who saw Havel's life as essentially tragic, with the presidency being an enormous mistake. Keane suggested that Havel's great misfortune was that his dream came true. In Keane's view, the presidency meant personal anguish and the loss of freedom, not to mention the temptations of fame and power. As Havel's health and influence diminished, Keane saw him as a humbled man, unpopular at home and unable to wield effective power.[12]

The other view was that Havel was instrumental in one of the few peaceful revolutions of the modern world and the transformation of Czechoslovakia from a totalitarian regime to a democracy. In this view, Havel's achievements were miraculous but hardly straightforward. After fifty years of totalitarian rule, Havel believed the nation needed a more limited government, and he was often more concerned with vesting power and responsibility in the people than in the state. As some have argued, part of Havel's remarkable achievement was not the power he wielded but the power that he relinquished, delegating politics to parliament.[13] As head of state, he oversaw the introduction of a free press, free elections, and a free market; played a central role in removing Soviet and Warsaw troops from his nation; and helped lead the Czech Republic into NATO and the European Union. He put his young nation on the map and created the template by which all subsequent Czech presidents would be judged. Many of those achievements were by no means inevitable, and some of them, such as the enlargement of NATO, were deeply controversial.

For Havel, the expansion of NATO was a matter of principle, one based on aligning the Czech Republic with other liberal democracies.

Although Havel has been thought of as a peacenik, his sense of moral purpose also made him, ironically, a forceful ally of a number of political figures on the political right. A month after joining NATO, for instance, Havel encouraged President Clinton's bombing campaign to stop ethnic cleansing in Kosovo, arguing that evil had to be confronted. On similar grounds, he supported George W. Bush's strategy to forcibly remove Saddam Hussein from power in Iraq. In these and other cases, Havel argued that NATO had a humanitarian duty to stand up to repressive regimes.

Some individuals, such as the political scholar Kieran Williams, have argued that Havel's most important legacy was his moral idealism.[14] In this view, Havel's chief accomplishment was not wielding power or pushing through legislation in parliament but giving voice to what it meant to be a democratic republic.[15] Aviezer Tucker, for instance, suggested that Havel essentially represented something new in politics, an existential revolution that tried to see liberal democracy in a new light. Havel's existential revolution was partly about rising above partisanship and demagoguery, and was based in politics as the art of telling the truth, essentially resisting the universal tendency among politicians to shade facts in order to make an ideological point. Such a politics was indeed quite radical, and the authenticity it preached was in many ways Patočka's "care of the soul," the attempt to search for a truth that reached beyond the concerns of any one ideology or party.[16]

Olga had been diagnosed with brain cancer sometime in late 1994. She viewed her condition as a private matter, and the couple kept her illness a secret for as long as possible, until she could no longer appear in public. There is little record of her illness, or how she experienced it in her own words, perhaps because Olga disliked speaking about herself. Havel later reported that "she bore her lot bravely" and with considerable stoicism, apparently finding consolation in the thought that "each of us has our own allotted time." In her final months, she was unable to leave their house in the Ořechovka neighborhood, which they had bought during the presidency to be near Prague Castle. According to Havel, Olga "never complained and never cried" about her illness and hated talking about her approaching death. Whenever Havel tried to say something "sweet" or consoling, she told him to save his breath.[17] They had never been in the habit of saying sweet nothings, and she wasn't about to start, perhaps because she felt it devalued what they had lived.

After what Havel described as a great deal of suffering, both from the illness and chemotherapy, Olga died in January 1996.[18] Havel was devastated by her death. He was also relieved when, on her deathbed, she told him that he had never "betrayed" her. As Havel put it, she was referring to the deep bond they shared that went beyond, he said, his "relaxed morals," which "had naturally bothered her."[19]

After Olga's public funeral, Havel sent a letter to staff, including the Castle Guard, thanking them for their help and for "being with me in spirit and for coming to pay their respect to her memory in such large numbers and with such obvious sincerity."[20] The condolence letters overwhelmed him, somewhat to his surprise, and he asked his staff to send out a form letter by way of reply, explaining that he found it impossible, in his emotional state, to reply himself.

By most accounts, the marriage had been strengthened by their years in the castle, perhaps because they both experienced their new roles as a sacrifice, a shared attempt to put the country on democratic footing. Olga had thrown herself into the role of First Lady and had become something of a beloved figure, more popular by far than her husband. She spent much of her time pioneering the idea of charitable activities, which had few historical roots in Czechoslovakia, founding the Committee of Good Will in 1990 and then, in 1992, the Olga Havel Foundation, which raised money for people with disabilities. Partly as a result of these activities, she was nominated as European Woman of the Year from the Czech Republic in the mid-1990s.

In an obituary for Olga, Timothy Garten Ash wrote that "she was in many ways the perfect complement to her husband." While Havel was "ever polite, the bourgeois-bohemian intellectual agonizing over every phrase and decision," she had been "not an intellectual but full of forthright, even earthy common sense." She was, Ash said, admired as a "shrewd, intuitive judge of people" and for the "natural dignity which served her magnificently in the wholly unexpected—and un-wanted—role of president's wife."[21]

The couple had spent the last few years moving around to different households, an annoying side effect of life in the castle. They had spent a few months living in the apartment behind the president's office, which had been created for President Masaryk. They had also tried living in the small villa on the castle grounds that had been used by presidents of the communist era, finding the spaces unlivable be-fore finally settling on a compound in the nearby Ořechovka district, a short walk from the castle.[22]

In the meantime, Havel sold his share of the family apartment on the embankment to Ivan. Presidential life made it inconvenient to share a flat with Ivan and his second wife, Dáša, but another factor may have been a growing rift in the family, one caused by the return of the property that had been taken by the communists, including the legendary Lucerna Palace on Wenceslas Square, where Louis Arm-strong and Josephine Baker once played, and where the communists had held party conventions.

Neither brother had the time and interest to manage the building, or its many businesses. Ivan turned over his shares to his wife. She and Havel bickered over business decisions. After trying mediation, Havel asked a third party to get rid of his shares on the open market, and they were eventually sold to the Chemapol Group, a rather murky enterprise connected to Russian oligarchs. The brothers were left barely speaking, at least for a time.[23]

After Olga's death, Havel faced ever-growing health issues him-self. He had trouble breathing, and he had several serious falls, one of which caused him to dislocate his jaw and splatter blood about the room. With Olga gone, he thought about his own death a great deal, and put his affairs in order. His mistress at the time, Dagmar Veškrnová, was worried about him enough that she tried not to leave him "home alone in the evenings." About this period, Havel later said that he couldn't "rule out the fact that shortly after Olga's death I might have subconsciously wanted to follow her."[24]

Then in November of that year, in the middle of crucial international negotiations for the Czech Republic entering NATO, Havel fell seriously ill with a case of pneumonia that wouldn't respond to treatment. On November 18, after Havel developed double vision, his girlfriend, Dagmar, stepped in to remove his doctor, getting a second opinion from an elite specialist who discovered a spot on his right lung. Havel was suffering from both a pulmonary crisis and a half-inch tumor. A surgical team removed half the lung in a four-hour operation, after which a new pneumonia was discovered in the left lung, requiring the doctors to perform a tracheotomy, opening a hole in Havel's throat for a ventilator that would keep him from suffocating to death.[25] After a long and complicated convalescence of six weeks in which he was thought to be on the verge of death multiple times, he recovered and was sent home on December 27.

In Havel's mind, Dagmar had saved his life. Eight days later, he announced that the two planned to marry.

Havel's marriage to Dagmar proved widely unpopular. For one thing, many felt it was too soon after Olga's death for Havel to marry, and this feeling was probably exacerbated by the understanding that Dagmar had been a mistress long before Olga's death. Both the media and the public seemed to feel the marriage was in poor taste, and Dagmar soon became the butt of insults and vulgar jokes, as well as the target of hostile commentators on television. Many of the aides in the castle found Dagmar abrasive and presumptuous.

Havel addressed the situation in a series of memos to his staff. In May he wrote that staff at the castle seemed "incapable, in any reasonable way, of responding to the fact that the president of the republic has gotten married."[26] Although Dagmar had given up her career to serve as First Lady, Havel fumed that she had not been given an office, a secretary, or administrative help, all despite the fact that she had to deal with mountains of letters, invitations, and requests on a daily basis.

Six months later, the problem had hardly gotten better. Havel wrote to the castle staff that "whether anyone likes it or not a married couple is once again installed in Prague Castle, and has been for over a year now. That is to say one state official elected by parliament, and one wife, whom he himself has elected (and naturally she him). This wife has fought for a year for her place in the sun and today she feels she is worse off than she was a year ago."[27] Another year later, Havel was still complaining. Although his wife had been given a small staff, he felt she was not receiving advise befitting a president's wife.

Generally speaking, Havel had an extraordinarily close relationship with his personal staff at the castle. Many were extremely loyal, falling just short of worship. Dagmar tested those relationships, and over the next few years Havel grew more temperamental over the control of his private life. It didn't help that, like Olga, Dagmar was a tough, blunt woman with a tendency to speak her mind, or that she was protective of her new husband and often attacked those who worked for Havel when she felt he wasn't being served. As a result, many of Havel's advisors felt that she "was an interloper," as Havel admitted, an outsider who "had leap-frogged over them and suddenly had more influence than they did."[28] It didn't help matters that she had been a popular actress, nor that Havel was the first president in the country's history who had married while in office, nor that there was no clear definition of the role of First Lady.

The marriage with Dagmar precipitated a number of changes. First, Havel was quite naturally eager to find more balance in his work, with the result that he soon began cutting down on his workload. According to one of his closest aides, Michael Žantovský, Havel now "refused to spend as much time in the office as he used to, and insisted that all but the most important meetings and events be removed from his diary." Žantovský found all of this "perfectly understandable." Havel enjoyed spending time with his new wife, far more than his endless meetings in the castle. Furthermore, "he was sixty-one years old and he had achieved more than most people manage in a thousand lives."[29]

Another change involved Havel's relationship with Jitka Vodňanská. Jitka first discovered that Havel was having an affair with Dagmar during the summer after Olga died. Havel invited her to the villa that he and Olga had bought after he became president; two days later, she visited again to give Havel a deep tissue massage known as Rolfing. While she was there, Dagmar called and Havel explained over the telephone that Jitka was there. After Havel put down the phone, he smiled shyly and said that she couldn't stay. According to Jitka, Havel then turned to her and said, "I'm sorry but you should leave. She's rather hysterical. She could come over [and] make a scene."[30] Jitka's recollection of this event might well be colored by the bitterness of the rivalry between the two women, but there can be little doubt that, like Olga, Dagmar had a hold on Havel that Jitka never did. Later that fall, when Havel was in the hospital, Dagmar refused to allow Jitka to visit his room, a galling injustice. In January 1997, when Havel called Jitka to tell her that he was marrying again, Jitka responded with silence, refusing to bless the marriage.

Václav Klaus remained a popular and vibrant politician until the fall of 1997, when he was linked to a financial scandal involving a political slush fund, kept hidden in Swiss bank accounts, that appeared to involve money donated to ODS in exchange for insider deals.[31] The scandal reached its peak while Klaus was visiting Sarajevo for a political summit. Havel was recuperating at Lány from another bout of pneumonia that had led him to cancel a visit to Britain and lunch with Queen Elizabeth.[32] While recuperating, Havel received a telephone call from Jan Ruml, the interior minister, who announced that he and the minister of finance, Ivan Pilip, were resigning from the cabinet.[33]

Havel lacked constitutional authority to dismiss the government, but he gave a televised speech in which he argued that "the only fully sensible resolution would be for the Government as a whole, with its chairman in the lead, to hand in its resignation as soon as possible."[34] The government collapsed in the next few days, with the Christian Democrats and the Civic Democratic Alliance withdrawing the support needed to give ODS control of parliament. Havel then appointed Josef Tošovský to lead a caretaker government until elections could be scheduled.

When elections were held in the spring of 1998, the Social Democratic Party won a plurality but not a majority of the seats in parliament. As a result, Havel asked the parties to form a coalition government, with the leader of the Social Democratic Party, Miloš Zeman, becoming prime minister. Zeman was a populist, a former communist, and something of a demagogue who went on to have a long and successful career, becoming president in 2013. He immediately stirred up controversy by appointing an all-male cabinet. Two years later, when he replaced five ministers with another set of men, he explained that "male candidates appear to be better experts than women."[35]

Havel regarded Zeman as a court jester, someone who was "capable of being very tough, stubborn, and loudmouthed," as well as a politician who often made public statements that were "banal, superficial, or even untrue."[36] Nevertheless, the two men were able to work together closely. For the most part, Zeman was on his best behavior when it came to Havel, perhaps because Havel had refused to condemn Zeman for his demagoguery, believing he should stay above the fray of daily politics.

At the beginning of 1998, Havel's five-year term as president expired. Although he longed to return to private life, he was persuaded by aides and other politicians who urged him to run again, arguing that without the stability he provided, the country might lurch toward a postcommunist demagogue or toward the far-right nationalists. Jan Ruml, the former dissident who had resigned as interior minister in the Klaus administration, was one of several politicians who traveled to Lány during this time, advising Havel that the Czech Republic would never gain admittance to NATO without Havel at the helm and thus "forever remain in a sphere of dubious quasi-democracies, teeming with populists and nationalists."[37] In the end, Havel relented and was elected in parliament by a single vote. He was sworn in as president on January 3 and then immediately returned to a health clinic where doctors and nurses supervised his recovery from his latest bout of pneumonia. According to a Western diplomat, Havel's lungs were "shot to pieces" and his heart was in bad shape.[38]

Whether Havel should have accepted a final term as president remained an open question in his mind. He sometimes wondered if it wasn't somehow a terrible mistake. At times, he wondered if his entire experience in the presidency, at least after his first term at the end of the Velvet Revolution, had been "a single, extended blunder."[39]

Not only did he worry he was no longer up to the job, but he also had little desire to postpone his freedom for another five years, including his chance to rest, travel, think, and "sleep in the morning until I was good and ready to get up."[40] Among other things, he missed the normalcy of life and the loss of contact with friends, former dissidents, and the wide circle of literary colleagues with whom he no longer got to see, either because he was too busy or because when he had time off from the presidency he now needed to rest.

Havel's ambivalence toward the presidency continued with the start of his new term. Some of his dissident friends joked that they should kidnap Havel from the castle and set him free. Others seemed to resent the fact that Havel was too busy to see them anymore. At its extreme, the criticism was that Havel had grown too self-important to see his old friends, a reproach that particularly irked Havel since it was leveled by some of those who had argued, back in the Velvet Revolution, that he had a responsibility to run for president.

Havel's irritation at his situation boiled over in June 1998, when, appearing ill and short of breath, he was recorded by a journalist on television as saying that he was fed up with his job, his staff, and the political situation in the country. When asked if he was considering resigning, he answered that he didn't think he would resign because he was "fed up," but that his ill health was a serious concern. "I can imagine that I would abdicate if my struggles against death, illnesses and operations went on indefinitely," he said. Havel then continued to explain the source of his personal frustration: "During the whole of my life, I've not been interested in my body. I took it for granted that it was something like a natural carrier of my personality and spirit. It was in prison, when suffering from chronic pneumonia, that I noticed for the first time that I had a body. I was half dead and because of that they released me early. Since 1996, I've again had to realize that I have a body, and that I have to look after it."[41]

The interview was considered scandalous, and Havel immediately apologized to his staff in a memo, saying he "very much regretted what had happened." Havel added that he believed the televisions had been turned off when he made those comments. By way of explanation, he conceded to his staff that his moods were "caused by a confluence of many circumstances, including my annoying and chronic health problems and the fact that I can't smoke." He acknowledged that he had become increasingly upset by minor incidents and suggested that if his aides found him speaking "in an irritated or exaggerated way," they should simply ignore his mood.[42]

Havel often spoke about his depressions in those years, going so far as to apologize in staff memos "if I spoiled anyone's mood."[43] Increasingly, those moods and fits of depression took him over. A year after going off the rails on television, he wrote his staff that "the cup hath spilled over. There is something rotten either in me, or in society. Whatever it is, I can't take it any longer." He added that he was "in a state of revolt," and that he wanted enough peace to live his life.[44]

Havel never resigned, however. Instead, perhaps by way of compromise, he and Dagmar bought a villa in Portugal, where they increasingly retreated. Havel now spent about half of his time convalescing at Lány, Hrádeček, and the new house near the Portuguese beach. Understanding that he was limited by his ill health, he now conserved his strength, focusing on fewer projects. Naturally, his convalesces became controversial, not least because they raised questions about his performance.

The situation spilled over in 2002, during the devastating Prague floods. Havel was in Portugal at the time, once again recuperating from a bout of ill health, and decided not to immediately return to the castle (the prime minister appears to have told him there was no reason for his presence). After Havel was attacked in the press for being absent, he fumed at his staff for its mishandling of public relations, writing to them that "at the conclusion of a lifelong public career," he had been branded as someone who preferred to sunbathe on the beach than serve his country.[45]

One of the issues that infuriated Havel during the flood crisis was that castle staff had released a statement, attributed to the president, as to why he was remaining in Portugal. Not only had Havel not approved the statement, but he found the wording callow, making him appear as if he wasn't concerned about the suffering of those affected by the rising waters of the Vltava River. In his memo to his staff, he demanded that in the future "every statement that concerns my intentions or my state of mind must be run by me." He went on: "I alone wish to bear responsibility for my acts, but I will not go on bearing responsibility for the ill-considered acts of others."[46]

After thirteen years in office, many of them in ill health, Havel's final term came to an end in February 2003. He had been president of the Czech Republic for ten years, and president of Czechoslovakia for almost three years before that. For most of that time, he had been the symbol of democratic possibility. He had been the only democratically elected president in the new nation's history.

The last few weeks in office were full of goodbye parties, including an "underground" farewell party given by former dissidents in which everyone got drunk. A few nights later, at the National Theater, a black-tie gala was held in his honor. Ivan Král sang a ballad by the Plastic People of the Universe, the underground music group that had been so close to Havel in the 1970s. Shortly afterward, an actor read an article from the 1970s. Printed in a communist party newspaper, it predicted that Havel and Charter 77 would "end up in the dustbin of history."[47]

From Havel's point of view, his final prison sentence had come to an end. In an interview in his last few days in office, he discussed his proudest accomplishments but also lamented what the presidency had cost him personally. "I find myself in the world of privileges, exceptions, perks, the world of V.I.P.s who gradually lose track of how much a streetcar ticket or butter costs, how to make a cup of coffee, how to drive a car, and how to place a telephone call," he said.[48] He was looking forward to returning to real life.

Havel gave his farewell address on television on the first Sunday in February 2003. It was a short speech, no longer than the Gettysburg Address. It couldn't have taken more than five minutes to deliver. "To all of you whom I have disappointed in any way," Havel said, "who have not agreed with my actions or who have simply found me hateful, I sincerely apologize and trust you will forgive me."[49]

And then he was free, once again a private citizen.

# 19

## THE FINAL YEARS

THE DAY AFTER LEAVING OFFICE, HAVEL TOOK a five-week vacation with his wife. By this time, he was coughing all the time, and he breathed with considerable difficulty. He returned to smoking, even with the loss of one lung. Despite his poor health, he was determined to return to his roots as a writer. He was also unbelievably busy in the way of ex-presidents. After a brief hiatus to catch his breath, he faced an endless series of meetings with human rights groups, international figures, and journalists, as well as uncountable invitations to write and speak. He had a hand in countless projects, including establishing an American-style presidential library.

In interviews, however, he spoke about wanting to write an "absurdist play" or working on a book-length conversation with Timothy Garton Ash and Adam Michnik. Although he hadn't kept a diary while in office, he also spoke about writing an offbeat memoir of his presidential years, a writing project that would be "somewhere between Henry Kissinger and Charles Bukowski."[1] As much as anything, this was meant to be an accounting of his time in office to fellow citizens, a way of opening up the ledger books. He was also thinking a good deal about death. He felt something akin to a compulsion to organize his affairs. As he told Karel Hvížďala a few years later, he was preparing for the end of life "in a slightly bureaucratic way." He wanted to leave "order" in his wake, and that meant finishing his unfinished projects and putting out a collected edition of all his writings, as if, he reflected, like a playwright he wanted "to have complete control of what remained after me."[2]

Havel also made time to catch up with old friends, to read, and to attend the theater. After thirteen years as president, he was left with what he called a permanent gap in knowledge of current trends in art and society, and he did his best to catch up.[3] The distractions of being an ex-president, however, made it impossible to concentrate for any length of time on his writing.

By most accounts, Havel's health started to rebound in the first year after leaving office. Rest and relaxation played a part, but Havel also had a new medicinal routine by the end of 2003. He drank one beer in the morning for his stomach and had another one at night to help him sleep. During the day, he drank wine, especially with meals,[4] and he cut down on the pills he had used to keep him going.

With a bit of distance behind him, he found himself reminiscing over the presidency, trying to find out what it had meant and whether his years in office had made any sense. A part of these reflections, which he returned to again and again, had to do with a sense of accounting for what he had and had not accomplished. In the spirit of a retiree, he began asking himself: "Did I win in life or did I blow it?"

In a conversation with Adam Michnik, which took place ten months after he left office, Havel admitted that it sometimes seemed to him that he had been given "everything" he had "ever yearned for, or competed for, or considered constructive." At other times, however, it seemed to him that "life stuck out its tongue" at him, making it clear that he was "an utter clown."[5] In the end, he seems to have concluded that neither impression was completely true. He was simply a man full of contradictions. In reviewing his life, he was pleased with some things and displeased with others.

His evaluation of the Velvet Revolution was likewise mixed. In many ways, the sudden and total collapse of communism exceeded his wildest expectations. Nor could he have foreseen that his nation would become a stable democracy with himself as president. And yet the fall of communism seemed to him to open up new worries, worries that were somehow deeper, involving the alienation of citizens, even under democracy, in all of the Western countries, coupled with the erosion of the social and natural world. His own struggle, as he understood it, was but part of a much larger story, the crises of civilization. In the larger story, one with global implications, he believed he had not done enough and perhaps had even failed at the primary mission, not having adequately communicated to the West the lessons he had learned from living under totalitarianism. It seemed to him that the Western democracies were preparing to make the same mistakes they had made before World War II, appeasing dictators and ignoring the growing democratic problems in their own country. In its essence, he thought, the new crisis in the West was chiefly a crisis of meaning. As he told Michnik, the modern state, with its "formalistic, scientist and technocratic character," had forgotten its purpose, even as people had forgotten how to live—and forgotten the simple truth that "the state is the work of people, while the person is the work of God."[6]

By the time Havel reached the one-year mark of his retirement, it must have been clear to him that he wouldn't be able to get any serious writing done without leaving the country. His old writing demons returned, and he found it difficult, if not impossible, to set aside time for either his memoirs or a new play. In part, this may have had to do with his living situation, as the villa that he had bought with Olga was occupied not only by himself and Dagmar but with Dagmar's aging mother, and her daughter and granddaughter. Havel referred to it as a "house of horrors" and longed for more peace and quiet.[7] Parliament had provided him a lifelong office, along with a small staff and security detail, but Havel found his official office an even more difficult place to concentrate than his home, since he was constantly barraged with demands for his time and energy.[8]

In the old days, Havel had always turned to Hrádeček when he wanted to write, since it was the one place he could find seclusion. There had always been an irony involved, however. As much as Havel craved seclusion, in order to reflect and write, he also dreaded it. He had a lifelong need to gather people around him, and he disliked going to Hrádeček alone. Dagmar herself disliked long trips there, perhaps because of its strong associations with Olga and Jitka, or because she didn't feel welcomed by the neighbors, the Krobs. Perhaps more importantly, Hrádeček was too far from her beloved Prague. As an aging film star, she thrived on the celebrity lifestyle, attending theater, social events, film festivals, and the glittering parties of high society.[9]

In order to escape all of this, in 2004 Havel accepted a fellowship as a writer in residence at the Library of Congress in Washington, D.C. A series of illnesses forced him to put off the trip until the spring of 2005, when he and Dagmar (along with their two boxer dogs) rented a house in Georgetown around the corner from Madeleine Albright, who served as their guide to the elite social scene of the American capital.

The fellowship at the United Nations had been a standing invitation, presumably issued when Havel received the Presidential Medal of Freedom by George W. Bush in 2003. Havel was given a small office in the Kluge Center, which was on the first floor, through the main entrance, past the great hall, with its elaborate neoclassical interior, and to the left. His chief purpose for the trip was to write his presidential memoirs, and he arrived at his small, no-nonsense office each weekday morning, spending the time dutifully at his desk untangling memos, letters, and recollections, impressing the staff at the Library of Congress as a disciplined scholar who found it difficult "to do his work when everyone wanted and actually needed him to be an emblem for their democratic aspirations for freedom."[10] For once, Havel was able to zealously guard his time, keeping visits and interviews to an absolute minimum and giving only one talk at the library during his visit. Most days, he worked in blue jeans and a sweater. On days when he had evening engagements, he arrived in the morning in a suit so that he wouldn't have to return home to change.

The book was odd by political standards, resembling one of his absurdist plays more than a memoir. Perhaps this was something of an inner compromise between the promise he had made to give an accounting of his years in office and the demands he was feeling to get back to his artistic craft. The result was either a work of genius or a head-scratcher, depending on the point of view. It consisted of three alternating kinds of material. The first consisted of a series of "long-distance" interviews between Havel and Karel Hvížďala, picking up the conversation they had together in *Disturbing the Peace*. Interspersed between batches of questions and answers, Havel included contemporary sketches and diary entries from Washington, D.C. These were often followed by excerpts from memorandums he had written the castle staff, which he had been in the habit of composing regularly, often in extraordinary length and detail.

Havel's style of presidential memo was almost always in the form of lists, and the items on any given day included everything from philosophical ideas to issues of protocol, including how to set cutlery at a state dinner. Item ten from December 17, 1995, involved his deep unhappiness with how Prague Castle was illuminated at night, amateurish to his eye. In item six from August 21, 1999, Havel reported on finding a bat in the closet near his office, the light bulb having been unscrewed to leave the bat undisturbed.[11]

In many ways, Havel's memoirs were like a collage, with a writing style that reached back to his early years as a poet. Running through the entirety of the book were a number of themes, including Havel's unique concern with the crises of civilization.

Although the memoirs were intended as an accounting of his presidency, written for fellow citizens, they were immediately translated into a number of foreign languages. The job of translating the book into English for Knopf publishers fell to Paul Wilson, who had been translating most of Havel's work since the early 1980s. Havel wanted to keep the Czech title of the book, which translated as "Please Be Brief," and Wilson mounted a campaign to change the name, which referred to a Czech television announcer who would invite guests onto his show to ask them a complicated question then requesting that they be as brief as possible. Havel didn't see the point of asking guests "to shut up" before they had a chance to speak their piece, and his title was a way of poking fun at the television show and what it represented.[12] Wilson's campaign to change the title in the English translation turned out to be an enormous task. Although successful in the end, after enlisting the help of Havel's publisher, it gave him insight, he said, to the stubbornness in Havel "that must have driven the communists nuts because once he decides on something it's almost impossible to get him to change his mind."[13]

Havel returned to the Library of Congress the following year, in 2006, for another writing fellowship, this time to work on a new play, the idea of which had been ruminating in his head for just under twenty years. The original draft of the manuscript had been written sometime before the Velvet Revolution, in the late 1980s, and involved the theme of what a sudden loss of power could mean to an individual. In Havel's later recollections, the original theme had occurred to him after reading an essay about Shakespeare's *King Lear*, but he also appears to have been thinking about some of the individuals surrounding Charter 77, who had once held high government positions during the Prague Spring and then suddenly lost power.[14] Havel seems to have lost interest in the play—and, in any event, the Velvet Revolution interrupted his career as a playwright.

It's not clear exactly when he rediscovered the manuscript and dusted off his old notes, but the theme now had a personal element, since during the intervening twenty years he himself had been through a similar experience as the main character (originally named Lír). He rewrote the entire manuscript during his months at the second residency at the Library of Congress, changed the names of many of the characters, and added additional elements from Chekhov's *The Cherry Orchard*. The center of the play, however, remained what reviewers later called a *King Lear*–like mediation "on the seductiveness of power."[15]

After finishing his second residency at the Library of Congress, Havel traveled down the road to Columbia University, in New York

City, for a seven-week fellowship, giving a number of lectures and participating in a two-month "Havel Festival" that included productions of sixteen of his plays. There was time for attending Broadway theater and cocktail parties, time to visit old haunts and make new plans for the future. There were other plays he wanted to write, plans for new projects and new adventures.

There in New York City, Havel still had six good years left, six years of adventure. He had time to write and reflect in one of the great cities of the world, the city he had fallen in love with during the Prague Spring, a city he found alive, vibrant, full of endless possibility.

One of the central ironies of Havel's life was that he was always more popular in Western democracies than he was at home. After he left the presidency, he was replaced by his archrival, Václav Klaus, Havel's opposite. At the end of Klaus's term, in 2013, he was replaced by Miloš Zeman, a right-wing nationalist. Most of what Havel preached from the presidency was thoroughly rejected by his nation, and by most estimations (even that of Havel) his attempt to bring a moral consciousness to politics was largely a failure. During the last years of his life, he sometimes despaired over the situation in the Western democracies, which he saw as becoming ever more prone to demagogues and charlatans. The times, he liked to say, were favoring what is mean.

In the last few years, as Havel's health faded, there was time for a few more adventures. This became something of a running joke among his closest friends, because after every last adventure, another lurked on the horizon. In 2009 Havel got to witness the premiere of his play *Leaving* at the Archa Theatre, with Jan Tříska playing the lead. The event was unprecedented, Havel having been silent as a working playwright for more than twenty years, much of that time serving as the head of state.

Although Havel had told friends that he planned to retire after the premiere, he hit upon the idea of turning the plan into a film.[16] The ambition dated to his attempts to enter the film academy—and perhaps, on some level, to the secret affinity he had felt with his Uncle Miloš, the renegade film magnate. The entire effort, from adapting the script to shooting the picture as director, took him eighteen months, a total emersion in which he became so obsessed with the demands of making a feature-length film that he talked of little else, much to the annoyance of some of his friends. On the set, he was tan and frail and absolutely devoted to seeing every detail of the project through to completion, jealously guarding the script and daily film footage from outsiders and leaks.[17]

Shot in Česká Skalice, a short distance from Hrádeček, the film was greeted with disappointment after its premiere in March 2011. The problem may have been partly a matter of timing, the film reaching audiences just a few years after the twentieth anniversary of the Velvet Revolution. The public wanted heroic stories about the resurrection of democracy, and Havel gave them a film of the absurd.[18] No one could make out what the film had to say about his presidency, if anything, and the audience naturally wanted to know whether the character in the play known as Vlastík Klein was a stand-in for Václav Klaus. Meanwhile, Havel's play was closer to being an homage to themes in Shakespeare and Chekhov than having anything at all to do with his presidential years. In short, he had attempted, one last time, to produce a work of art, and his audiences had been hoping to see him settle old scores.

As Havel slowly slipped from the political stage, the world seemed to miss him more and more. In December 2011, when news spread across the nation that he had died at Hrádeček, crowds began to gather all across the nation, tens of thousands of individuals coming together in parks and squares to light candles, seeming to need companionship or to in some way come to grips with what had transpired and knowing, intuitively, that with his passing an entire era of history had passed from the earth. In death, Havel was suddenly more popular than he had been at any time since the Velvet Revolution.

Three years later, far from Prague, the Library of Congress organized a special tribute on the twenty-fifth anniversary of the Velvet Revolution to honor the life and legacy of Havel and to unveil a bust of the man that would be placed inside the U.S. capitol. Among those who spoke to the crowd was the Dalai Lama. "I think," the Dalai Lama said, "that the whole world, the entire planet, needs such a person from time to time."

Later, John McCain, the conservative senator, called Havel a great man, saying he "epitomized the cutting edge of what led to the end of the Soviet empire." McCain had been in Prague during the Velvet Revolution, inside the Magic Lantern, singing "We Shall Overcome" on the day that Havel announced the demand for free and open elections, a moment McCain said left him feeling "fortunate to be alive." Madeleine Albright had been there, too, making a state visit with McCain. Speaking on stage with McCain, she remembered the event and called Havel one of the great heroes of the twentieth century. "In the New Testament," she noted, "it says that a prophet is often not respected in his own country. We all respect Václav Havel here in this room, and are celebrating him, and I wish the people of the Czech Republic understood what an incredible legacy he leaves for them today."[19]

# ACKNOWLEDGMENTS

GEORGE ORWELL SAID, "WRITING A BOOK IS a horrible, exhausting struggle, like a long bout with some painful illness." Thankfully, I had a great number of people to help me along the way. It's a pleasure to thank those who read early versions of the manuscript and provided much-needed advice: Brad Wexler, Juan Palomo, Jeff Barton, Ric Williams, and Jan Tříska, the late Czech actor. My daughter, Kate Barton, a graduate student in journalism at New York University, provided editing of several chapters just before I sent it in to the publishing house, and my wife, Jolana Janišová, read the entire book many times, offering hundreds of suggestions, both large and small. She also served as a companion on many trips to archives and as one of several translators on hundreds of letters that form the basis of this book.

With the aid of a research grant from Northern New Mexico College, I had help from three research assistants: Gabriella Romanová provided help translating letters from Václav Havel from the 1950s and 1960s and guided me through a mountain of confusing material. Also in Prague, Jana Kotrlová provided research into the life of Václav M. Havel, the father of Václav Havel. Her ideas and insights proved invaluable. In New Mexico, a former student, Carlos Martin, helped track down material that provided color and detail to Havel's later life as a dissident and president. Other research help came from Petr Jandáček, who helped me translate and make sense of scholarly work on Havel.

I am also indebted to the staffs of archives at Columbia University, the New York City Library, the Hoover Institute, the University of Texas at Austin, the Ford Foundation Archives, and the Václav Havel Library in Prague, all of whom provided indispensable aid. Blanka Chocholová, Helen Lukas Martemucci, Bohdan and Eva Holomíček, and Tomki Němec all provided photographs of considerable historical interest.

My family and I are also indebted to Pavel and Eva Urbanovi, who agreed to a summer exchange of homes, allowing me to spend the second of two summers in Prague, and to Jiří and Božena Janišovi for inviting us into their home too many times to count and for providing the perfect example of Czech hospitality. To Jirka Janiš and his wife, Eva, I offer thanks for agreeing to join me on a trip to Hrádeček and for many evenings of good food and drink.

In the Czech Republic, I had the good fortune to meet many people from the dissident community who provided me with invaluable help in understanding what it was like to live under the totalitarian regime. Of all of those whom I met, special thanks goes to Ivan Havel, Kamila Bendová, Eda Kriseová, František Stárek, Miroslav Pohlreich, Petr Stránský, Miloš Rejchrt, Jan Sokol, Ladislav Hejdánek, Karel Hvížďala, Jiřina Šiklová, and Jan Tříska. The first conception of this book, which proved to be too ambitious for my own talents, involved a joint biography that would interweave the stories of Václav Havel, Jan Patočka, and Jiří Hájek. For providing the deep background on Patočka and Hájek, I am deeply thankful for the help of Jan Hájek and Ivan Chvatík. And thanks goes also to Barbara Day, for giving me a historian's perspective on the intellectual activity of dissidents in the 1970s.

In addition, I want to thank the actor Robert Redford and his wife, Bylle, for sending a letter of introduction to Václav Havel, and for their friendship and kindness. I would also like to thank Markéta Balajková for sending much-needed books from the Czech Republic, and to Monika Moores for bringing back material and connections from Liberec, the town where Havel found himself during the 1968 invasion.

My wife and I are grateful for the presence of a lively community of Czech ex-patriots who make their home in Santa Fe, many of whom have remained close friends and companions through good times and bad. Other friends who provided hospitality and other kinds of support, great and small, are: Greggory Leon Baird, Marci and Steve

Schwartz, Jerome Bernstein, Heather Winterer, James McGrath, Helga Williams, Carolyn Burns, David Cloutier, Ann Yeomans, Michael Benanav, Carol Anthony, Abigail Ryan, Marilyn Fitzgerald, and Pam Piccolo in New Mexico; and in the Czech Republic, Petr Filák, Jana Taperr, Petr Urban, Martin and Hana Otevřelovi, Robert and Jára Černí, and Vojta and Helena Zbrankovi, who in the old days gathered each Friday night under the trees at Pod Lipou. We think of you often. To Kuba Barton, I offer thanks for many nights of exquisite musical escape.

Finally, I want to thank the staff at the University of Pittsburgh Press for giving this book a home. To Peter Kracht, who provided excellent insight into the book, Nicole Wayland, for her diligent and thorough copyediting, and Amy Sherman, who helped oversee the manuscript editing, I owe an immense debt of gratitude that I may never be able to repay.

# CHRONOLOGY

1936   Havel is born October 5 in a Prague hospital.

1938   October 11: Havel's brother, Ivan, is born.

October 21: The Nazi occupation of Czechoslovakia begins with the annexation of the northern and western border regions under the Munich Agreement.

1939   German troops invade the remaining regions of Czechoslovakia on March 15. Hitler proclaims Bohemia and Moravia as a protectorate of Nazi Germany.

1945   The war in Europe officially ends on May 8, three days after the Prague uprising.

1947   Miloš Havel is exonerated of charges that he collaborated with the Nazis during World War II.

1948   The Communist Party of Czechoslovakia seizes control of the country. Free elections are abolished and family businesses are seized.

1949   Miloš Havel begins a two-year prison sentence for attempting to flee the country.

1951   Václav Havel is denied access to secondary school and forced to find work.

1955   Václav Havel meets Olga Šplíchalová in the Slavia Café.

1957   Václav and Ivan Havel enter military service.

1959   Returning from military service, Václav Havel finds work as a stagehand at the ABC Theater.

1960   Havel moves to the Theater on the Balustrade, one of the small theaters that emerged in the late 1950s.

1961   Jan Grossman joins the Theater on the Balustrade as creative director. He promotes Havel to assistant dramaturge.

1963   The Theater on the Balustrade premieres Havel's first full-length play, *The Garden Party*, on December 3.

1964   July 9: Havel marries Olga Šplíchalová in a private ceremony at the Prague Town Hall.

November: Klaus Juncker, a literary agent from Germany, arrives in Prague to scout *The Garden Party*.

1965 Havel joins the editorial board of *Tvář*. Havel's play *The Memorandum* premieres at the Theater on the Balustrade on July 26.

1966 Havel completes a correspondence course at DAMU, receiving a baccalaureate in the arts and fulfilling a wish from his mother that he be an educated man.

1967 Havel gives an address at the Fourth Congress of the Writer's Union. Officials respond by having him removed from the union elections.

1968 April 11: The Theater on the Balustrade premieres Havel's play *The Increased Difficulty of Concentration*. About the same time, Havel publishes an essay calling for free multiparty elections. August 20: Czechoslovakia is invaded by four Warsaw Pact countries in order to shut down democratic reforms.

1969 Olga and Václav Havel's passports are confiscated in August, preventing them from leaving for the United States.

1970 Havel wins an Obie Award for the English-language version of his play *The Increased Difficulty of Thinking*, which is performed at the Public Theater in New York City.

1971 Havel's work is effectively banned from schools and libraries.

1974 Havel works at the Trutnov Brewery.

1975 April 6: Havel writes an open letter to Dr. Gustáv Husák, general secretary of the Communist Party of Czechoslovakia. November 1: Havel's play *Beggar's Opera* is performed in the back room of a pub on the outskirts of Prague.

1976 Havel begins a campaign to defend the psychedelic rock band Plastic People of the Universe, whose band members are on trial for disturbing the peace.

1977 Charter 77 is founded in early January, with Havel serving as one of three spokespersons.

1978 Havel cofounds the Committee for the Defense of the Unjustly Persecuted, known in Czech by the acronym VONS. In October he writes his essay "The Power of the Powerless."

1979 The state agrees to free Havel if he will leave the country. Havel refuses and is sentenced to four and a half years in prison.

1980 Havel is transferred to Heřmanice prison in Ostrava.

1981    After an illness, Havel is taken by ambulance to the prison hospital in Prague. He is later moved to Bory prison in Plzeň.

1982    Havel refuses a request in December that he officially ask for a pardon in exchange for being released from prison.

1983    Havel is released from prison for health reasons.

1984    Havel writes *Largo Desolato*, which has its premier a year later at the Burgtheater in Vienna.

1985    Havel conducts the long-distance interviews whose transcripts will be published in English as *Disturbing the Peace*. He also completes *Temptation*, a play about Faust that he first attempted to write in the late 1970s.

1986    Havel is awarded the Erasmus Prize but is unable to attend the ceremony in Rotterdam.

1988    Gorbachev launches radical reforms meant to reduce the control of the Communist Party inside the Soviet Union. In Czechoslovakia, government leaders try to prevent reforms from inside the Soviet Union from spreading to their own country.

1989    January: Havel is arrested for participating in a mass demonstration and sentenced to nine months in prison.

        May: Havel is released early from prison.

        November: After a student demonstration is met with police violence, mass demonstrations sweep the country.

        December: After the collapse of the communist government, parliament elects Havel as president.

1990    Havel gives an address to the Joint Session of the United States Congress.

1992    Havel resigns as president on July 20, saying he refused to preside over the breakup of Czechoslovakia.

1993    After the breakup of Czechoslovakia, Havel is elected by parliament as president of the Czech Republic.

1996    January: Olga Havlová dies of cancer.

        December: Havel is hospitalized for pneumonia, and doctors remove part of a cancerous right lung.

1997    Havel marries Dagmar Veškrnová.

1998    Parliament reelects Havel as president of the Czech Republic.

2003   Havel steps down as president. In the United States, he is awarded the Presidential Medal of Freedom.

2005   Havel becomes a resident scholar at the Library of Congress. He later returns to the Library of Congress as a resident scholar in December 2006 to work on his memoir, *To the Castle and Back.*

2007   Havel publishes a memoir of his presidency, *To the Castle and Back.*

2008   Havel's first play in two decades, *Leaving,* premieres in Prague.

2010   Havel begins work as a film director on an adaptation of his celebrated play *Leaving.* The film is released in March 2011 by Bonton Films.

2011   Havel dies at his country home in Hrádeček on December 18.

# NOTES

## List of Abbreviations Used throughout the Notes
### Newspapers and Periodicals
NYT. *New York Times*

NYRB. *New York Review of Books*

RPR. *Rudé Právo*

### Libraries and Archives
FFA. Ford Foundation Archives, New York City

HRW. Human Rights Watch/Helsinki Watch, Rare Books and Manuscript Library, Columbia University

JPC. Joseph Papp/New York Shakespeare Collection, New York City Library for the Performing Arts

JSC. Josef Škvorecký Collection, Hoover Institution Archives, Stanford University

JWC. John Wheatcroft Collection, Library of Congress, Washington, DC.

PZC. Pavel Žáček Collection, Hoover Institute, Stanford University

RFE. Radio Free Europe Corporate Records Collection, Hoover Institute, Stanford University

TNA. Central Foreign Policy Files, The National Archive, Washington, DC.

TSC. Tom Stoppard Collection, Harry Ransom Center, University of Texas

VBC. Věra Blackwell Collection, Rare Books and Manuscript Library, Columbia University

VHL. Václav Havel Library, Prague

## Prologue
1. Mary Heimann, in *Czechoslovakia: The State That Failed* (New Haven, CT: Yale University Press, 2009), makes a convincing case that the reputation of the First Republic is overblown, and that there were serious issues in the nation regarding the rights of ethnic minorities. Even so, the First Republic was far ahead of its time when it came to maintaining civil rights in a complicated, multiethnic democracy.

2. Timothy Garton Ash, "Prague—A Poem Not Disappearing," in *Václav Havel: Living in Truth*, ed. Jan Vladislav (London: Faber and Faber, 1987), 213–21. For a more complete account of the protests of the Velvet Revolution, see Timothy Garton Ash's account in *The Magic Lantern: The Revolution of '89 Witnessed in Warsaw, Budapest, Berlin, and Prague* (New York: Vintage, 1999), 78–130.

3. NYT, November 22, 1989; Ash, *Magic Lantern*, 83–84.

4. Václav Havel, "The Power and the Powerless," in *Open Letters: Selected Writings 1965–1990*, trans. Paul Wilson (New York: Vintage, 1992), 207, and "Politics and Conscience," 259–60.

5. See David Remnick, "Exit Havel," *New Yorker*, February 17 and 24, 2003, 90–101.

## Chapter 1. Growing Up and Growing Down

1. King Wenceslas served as duke of the Bohemian Lands from 921 to his murder in 935. He became a saint shortly after his death and was posthumously given an honorary title of king by Holy Roman Emperor Otto I. During the middle ages, his story deeply influenced the idea of the *rex justus*, or the righteous king. Although this may have some technical differences from Plato's idea of the philosopher-king, the concepts are similar, involving a wise ruler who understands the nature of his duty. To this day, King Wenceslas occupies a large place in the Czech imagination. It is probably no coincidence that the first president of Czechoslovakia, T. G. Masaryk, and Václav Havel were both interpreted through this tradition.

2. Technically speaking, Czechoslovakia in the period between 1948 and 1989 is considered a socialist state, communism being the next historical stage that was expected to evolve out of the socialist state. In practice, however, the state was ruled by the Communist Party of Czechoslovakia. Both everyday citizens and most dissidents usually referred to *komunismus* when referring to the system they were overturning. And they had no doubt they were "living under communism."

3. NYT, December 23, 2011.

4. From a talk given at Hebrew University on April 26, 1990. For the full speech, see Havel, *The Art of the Impossible: Politics as Morality in Practice* (New York: Fromm International, 1997), 29–31.

5. Reed's visit to the White House was highly problematic, as President Bill Clinton was amid the Monica Lewinsky scandal. Havel insisted that Reed be allowed to perform. See "Lou Reed and Václav Havel: From Velvet Underground to Velvet Revolution," *Economist*, October 30, 2013.

6. John Keane, *Václav Havel: A Political Tragedy in Six Acts* (London: Bloomsbury, 1999), 20.

7. *Disturbing the Peace* is a book-length series of interviews with Havel, conducted by Karel Hvížďala, a Czech journalist who immigrated to West Germany. The interviews took place through the dissident mail. In the first section of the book, titled "Growing Up 'Outside,'" Havel discusses his sense of exclusion. See Havel, *Disturbing the Peace: A Conversation with Karel Hvížďala*, trans. Paul Wilson (New York: Vintage Books, 1991), 3–8.

8. Havel's self-reflections on his childhood, originally referred to in a 1987 BBC documentary (*Václav Havel: A Czech Drama*), can also be found in Keane, *Václav Havel*, 20.

9. A description of the flat is provided by Havel's father, Václav M. Havel, in his autobiography. See Václav M. Havel, *Mé vzpomínky* (Prague: Nakladatelství Lidové noviny, 1993), 27–28. As for the grandfather, he constructed seventeen tenement houses and the Lucerna Palace. After World War I, he sold everything except the family house and Lucerna, which was kept as the family business. Upon his death, these were taken over by Miloš and Václav M. Havel. The street name of the embankment on which the Havel home is located changed a number of times throughout the years. During the communist era, the street was renamed Engelsovo, after Frederick Engles, a colleague of Karl Marx. For the history of Havel's father and grandfather, see Havel, *Mé vzpomínky*, 18–24, and Havel, *Disturbing the Peace*, 3–5.

10. Krystyna Wanatowiczová, *Miloš Havel: Český filmový magnát* (Prague: Václav Havel Library, 2013), 23.

11. The phrase "grand-bourgeois" comes from Havel's interview with Karel Hvížďala. Havel discussed the family history at length, saying: "Yes, I do come from a bourgeois family, you might even say from a grand-bourgeois family." See Havel, *Disturbing the Peace*, 3.

12. The insights into the family spirit come from Ivan Havel, personal interview, August 4, 2009, and from letters Václav Havel sent to his brother, Ivan, from prison in 1979. In *Disturbing the Peace*, Havel discusses his father's ethos in this way: "You can feel in almost every sentence [of his autobiography] that what drove my father (as it had my grandfather) was not the notorious capitalistic longing for profit and surplus value, but enterprise, pure and simple—the will to create something. . . . There's something almost touching about the way he apologizes at great length to the world for the fact that during the era of private enterprise there was nothing else he could do but carry on his enterprise privately" (4–5).

13. In April 1940 the debt of both brothers was 31.6 million crowns, equal to more than half the capital at Agrární Banka Československá, a midsize bank. The family survived mainly because of their extraordinary contacts. See Wanatowiczová, *Miloš Havel*, 125.

14. For a fuller account of these activities, see Havel, *Mé vzpomínky*, 297–412.

15. The Munich Agreement (known in Czech as the Munich Diktát, or sometimes as the Munich Betrayal) was a settlement among the major powers of Europe allowing Nazi Germany to annex the portion of Czechoslovakia inhabited by as many as three million German speakers. After the annexation, the nation lacked a defensible border, leading Germany in the following year to invade the rest of the country. Given its strategically hopeless position, the Czech army was ordered not to fight.

16. An excellent analysis of Czech life during World War II can be found in Andrea Orzoff, *Battle for the Castle: The Myth of Czechoslovakia in Europe, 1914–1948* (Oxford: Oxford University Press, 2009), 204–6. Orzoff points out that only 2,000 Nazis oversaw a protectorate bureaucracy of 250,000, and that Czech resistance (at least inside the country) was quite limited.

17. The name of the village is Žďárec, and the school was apparently attended by about fifty students. The estate was purchased near the turn of the century by Václav Havel's grandfather, Vácslav (this being an older Czech spelling of the same name). Up until World War II, the family used the retreat for holidays and during hunting season.

18. In 1927, when the mother lodge of Václav M. Havel (the father) had too many members, he helped found the lodge Bernard Balzano. In the period before World War II, he held the position of the seat master of the lodge. Like all Masonic lodges, it was closed in 1948 by the communist government. Whether Havel's uncle was a Freemason is hotly disputed. While in prison in the 1950s, he told authorities that he had never been a member of a Freemason lodge, but he bragged to a cellmate that his masonic connections in the United States had been indispensable in forming his film empire (Wanatowiczová, *Miloš Havel*, 24, 189–90).

19. Havel, *Disturbing the Peace*, 5–6.

20. Ivan Havel, personal interview, August 5, 2011.

21. Havel, *Letters to Olga*, 179–81.

22. Josef Šafařík is often considered the chief twentieth-century philosopher of Moravia, just as Jan Patočka is considered the chief philosopher of the region of Bohemia.

His only book of philosophy is *Seven Letters to Melin,* which was published just after the end of World War II. The book influenced not only Havel but many other Czechs of his generation. An overview of Czech philosophy, including Šafařík, can be found in *Czech Philosophy in the XXth Century,* ed. Lubomír Nový, Jiří Gabriel, and Jaroslav Hroch (Prague: Paideia Press, 1994), 144. For an overview of Czech philosophy that affected Havel, see Tucker, *Philosophy and Politics of Czech Dissidence from Patočka to Havel.*

23. Ivan Havel, personal interview, August 5, 2011.

24. From a letter written by Havel to his wife, Olga, from prison, May 22, 1982 (Václav Havel, *Letters to Olga,* trans. Paul Wilson [New York: Henry Holt, 1989], 319).

25. This letter does not appear in VHL, but a translated excerpt can be found in Keane, *Václav Havel,* 63.

26. The Czech army was ordered to stand down at three pivotal moments in history: in 1938, after the Munich Agreement handed over the western portion of the country (the Sudetenland) to Germany; a year later, during the Nazi invasion; and in 1968, in the face of the Soviet invasion. Havel reflected on the implications of this on the Czech psyche in a speech he gave during his presidency in Spain on May 11, 1995. For the full text, see Havel, *Art of the Impossible,* 210–15.

27. Ironically, the American Third Army, led by General Patton, was only ninety kilometers away in Plzeň at the beginning of the Prague uprising. General Patton had asked for permission to aid in the uprising in Prague but was forbidden from doing so by the American high command. Since 1943 the Allied powers had agreed that Soviet troops would be responsible for liberating Prague, and military leaders feared that moving American forces farther east would increase postwar tension between the Soviet Union and the United States. As a result, 1,700 Czechs were killed trying to liberate the city without military support. The communists used this incident to their advantage, spreading the story that the West was indifferent to the suffering of Czechs.

28. Miloš Havel managed to keep some shares of the AB Company in Czech hands. In September 1940 he made a deal with the protectorate government, a compromise that compensated him with eight million crowns for his loss of the majority shares. For more on the AB Company and Barrandov during the war, see Wanatowiczová, *Miloš Havel,* 80, 151.

29. Miloš Havel's suggestion that his work in the film studios was a form of "resistance" is best seen as a smoke screen for the guilt he felt for not standing up to the Nazis. As the war drew on, the Germans became less tolerant of his production of Czech films. One film prohibited by the Nazis was *Babička,* which weaves together a remembrance of agrarian life and folk customs with the love stories of several women. That film is now one of the most beloved in the country.

30. The memory comes from Dušan Hubáček, quoted in Wanatowiczová, *Miloš Havel,* 27.

31. In contrast, Božena Havlová didn't mind another partner, František Čáp. As a promising film director, she evidently considered him the right kind of material. Wanatowiczová, *Miloš Havel,* 95.

32. Because of their social connections, the family could still borrow money. In 1940, for instance, they had mortgaged the family jewel, the Lucerna Palace, in order to consolidate their growing debts. After the communist coup, the Lucerna was stripped from the family and given to the state. In the process, the debt was erased. Wanatowiczová, *Miloš Havel,* 126.

33. The school was in a small town in the former palace of George of Poděbrady, the king of Bohemia during the fifteenth century.

34. Eda Kriseová, *Václav Havel: The Authorized Biography* (New York: St. Martin's Press, 1993), 68–70.

35. Forman's family was not Jewish. The concentration camps were used to imprison all types of "undesirables," including those who were anti-Nazi. Forman told the anecdote about the bicycle on a number of occasions. The earliest version appears to be found in Kriseová, *Václav Havel*, 70. A collection of stories about the Academy of King George can also be found in Forman's memoir, *Turnaround: A Memoir* (New York: Villard Books, 1994), 40–65. It should also be pointed out that Havel's nickname, Chrobák, has a double meaning in Czech. It can refer to a beetle or to someone who is sickly.

36. For a full account of the communist coup, see Heimann, *Czechoslovakia*, esp. chapter six. A highly readable account can also be found in Albright, *Prague Winter*, 376–84. The communists received 38 percent of the vote in the 1946 election but were losing popularity, having alienated whole blocks of voters. By 1948 Stalin had given up on the idea of an electoral victory in Czechoslovakia, ordering the Communist Party to seize power by other means, leading the Communist Party to activate its worker's militia. Fearing a civil war and the possibility of Soviet intervention, President Beneš appointed a new cabinet, one handpicked by Gottwald, that was dominated by communists and fellow travelers.

37. Forman, *Turnaround*, 63.

38. Forman, *Turnaround*, 63.

39. Havel, *Letters to Olga*, 177. This was written in March 1981, while in prison, but Havel is discussing his characteristic way of seeing the world.

40. Havel, *Disturbing the Peace*, 194. Relatively little has been made of Havel's interest in language and the way in which cliché and logic can be used to obscure reality, but in this insight lies a serious critique of the twentieth century.

41. In Eastern Europe, communism worked as a self-enclosed "science" that lacked any outside point of reference from which to critique itself. As a "science," it is based on the "indisputable" laws of dialectical materialism. Many of these laws (such as the law of interrelation, which holds that the individual exists only as part of a collective) seem absurd from the rational point of view, but the expression of the law carried quasi-religious feelings for those inside the communist movement. For a classical understanding of the totalitarian impulse, see Erich Fromm, *Escape from Freedom* (New York: Henry Holt, 1965), and Hannah Arendt, *The Origins of Totalitarianism* (New York: Schocken, 2004).

## Chapter 2. Under a Cruel Star

1. Czechs have a long history of assassinating political opponents by throwing them to their deaths. The word "defenestration," which means "to throw someone out a window," was coined from the Latin *finestra* (window) to describe two famous incidents in Czech history, known as the "defenestrations of Prague." The first, in 1419, occurred when seven town officials from Prague were thrown to their deaths from town hall for plotting the Hussite Wars. The second case was in 1618, when two imperial governors were thrown from Prague Castle, igniting the Thirty Years' War. Defenestration is a deeply symbolic act, one that represents the removal and fall of political adversaries, which is no doubt why Masaryk's opponents chose this form of assassination. Few people believed the official

reports that declared his death an accident or suicide. The Czech joke, repeated on the streets, was that Masaryk was such a polite man he closed the window behind himself after he jumped. In 1990—after the Velvet Revolution—a national investigation concluded Masaryk had been murdered.

2. Václav M. Havel, *Mé vzpomínky* (Nakladatelství Lidové noviny, 1993), 70–71.

3. Krystyna Wanatowiczová, *Miloš Havel: Český filmový magnát* (Prague: Václav Havel Library, 2013), 26.

4. According to Havel's father, Miloš was deeply offended by the suggestion that his presence was no longer welcome (Havel, *Mé vzpomínky*, 71–72). However, it also appears that Havel's father tried to intercede on Miloš's behalf, going so far as to gather petitions for his release from prison. A side note: While in prison, a desperate Miloš appears to have temporarily cooperated with the state security forces (StB). When he refused to inform on anyone, however, the StB broke off contact.

5. The conversation was reported by František Novák. See Keane, *Václav Havel: A Political Tragedy in Six Acts* (London: Bloomsbury, 1999), 72. Whether Božena Havlová ever said those words—and there is some trouble with the timeline provided by Keane—this clearly represented her feelings.

6. Keane, *Václav Havel*, 72.

7. Ivan Havel, personal interview, August 4, 2009.

8. Eda Kriseová, *Václav Havel: The Authorized Biography* (New York: St. Martin's Press, 1993), 81.

9. Ivan Havel, personal interview, August 4, 2009.

10. Václav Havel, *Disturbing the Peace: A Conversation with Karel Hvížďala*, trans. Paul Wilson (New York: Vintage Books, 1991), 22.

11. In an interview with his uncle's biographer, Havel said that "I know that my mom used to strongly disapprove of his homosexuality. She belonged to the bourgeoisie class, which used to be full of strange prejudices" (Wanatowiczová, *Miloš Havel*, 95). Among those who have said that Božena regretted her behavior toward Miloš Havel was Jiří Kuběna, who knew her well over many years. Kuběna himself was a gay man. The fact that Božena befriended him might suggest an attempt to atone for the intolerance she had shown her brother-in-law.

12. The assessment of character comes from Jiři Kuběna, quoted in Wanatowiczová, *Miloš Havel*, 387.

13. Ivan Havel, personal interview, August 4, 2009. Václav Havel referred in passing to his youthful rebellion on a number of occasions. See, for instance, his interview with Jiří Lederer, "It Always Makes Sense to Tell the Truth," in Václav Havel, *Open Letters: Selected Writings 1965-1990* (New York: Vintage, 1992), 98.

14. Havel's maternal grandfather, Hugo Vavrečka, had worked for Tomáš Baťa in Zlín. Havel's imaginary business empire seems to resemble the Baťa empire. The word "Dobrovka" is a Havelism, a play on words. *Dobro* means "good," and the ending ("-ovka") suggests a place, making it similar to English suffixes such as "-berg," "-shire," and "-ville." Thus it could be translated as "Goodtown." For more on Dobrovka, see Michael Žantovský, *Havel: A Life* (New York: Grove Press), 27.

15. Václav Havel, letters to Jaroslav Seifert, March 14, 1954, and May 15, 1954, VHL.

16. Miloš, *Turnaround*, 56.

17. Václav Havel, letter to Vladimír Holan, April 9, 1955, VHL.

18. Havel, *Disturbing the Peace*, 26.

19. Havel, *Disturbing the Peace*, 27.

20. Havel, *Disturbing the Peace*, 27.

21. Václav Havel, letter to Jindřich Chalupecký, January 8, 1956, VHL.

22. Václav Havel, *Letters to Olga*, trans. Paul Wilson (New York: Henry Holt, 1989), 252.

23. Havel, *Letters to Olga*, 126.

24. Taken from a talk given by Václav Havel in Jerusalem on April 26, 1990. See Václav Havel, *The Art of the Impossible: Politics as Morality in Practice* (New York: Fromm International, 1997), 29.

25. Radim Kopecký, letter to Václav Havel, September 25, 1952, VHL.

26. Radim Kopecký, letter to Václav Havel, December 7, 1952, VHL.

27. Radim Kopecký, letter to Václav Havel, December 7, 1952, VHL.

28. Václav Havel, letter to Jiří Paukert, November 22, 1953, VHL.

29. Petr Stránský, personal interview, July 7, 2011.

30. Petr Stransky, personal interview, July 7, 2011, and correspondence with the author.

31. There are a number of sources regarding Mrs. Havel's dislike of Fischerová, including Keane, *Václav Havel*, 111–12.

32. Žantovský, *Havel*, 40.

33. Václav Havel, letter to Jiří Paukert, September 5, 1954, VHL.

34. Václav Havel, letter to Jiří Paukert, March 8, 1953, VHL.

35. Jiří Paukert, letter to Václav Havel, July 11, 1953, VHL.

36. Václav Havel, letter to Jiří Paukert, September 17, 1953, VHL. The capitalization of "INNER LIFE" is Havel's emphasis.

37. Václav Havel, letter to Jiří Paukert, July 11, 1953, VHL.

38. Taken from two separate letters to Jiří Paukert: March 8, 1953, and August [?] 1953. VHL.

39. Václav Havel, letters to Jiří Paukert, October 22, 1955, November 1, 1955, and November 18, 1955, VHL.

40. Havel, *Disturbing the Peace*, 31. One of the writers who was critical of the communist regime was Jaroslav Seifert, the great national poet whom Havel had visited in the early 1950s. The two men continued a correspondence until Seifert's death in 1986.

41. Václav Havel, "Second Wind," in *Open Letters*, 4–5.

42. Havel, *Letters to Olga*, 365.

43. Havel's understanding of faith and optimism are most clearly expressed in his prison letters. In particular, he argues that genuine faith and optimism are profound experiences of mystery. In contrast, ideologies leave people full of overblown enthusiasm that, when things don't turn out well, flip into the opposite point of view. See Havel, *Letters to Olga*, 150–51, as well as his discussion on fanaticism in an August 1982 letter (360–65). Although the prison letters were written in a much latter period of his life, they seem to articulate ideas that he first began exploring as a youth.

## Chapter 3. Smokey Roads and Muddy Paths

1. The account of Havel's dress comes from Andrej Krob, who first met Havel on a train to military camp in České Budějovice, reported in Eda Kriseová, *Václav Havel: The*

*Authorized Biography* (New York: St. Martin's Press, 1993), 21. Havel's brother, Ivan, went into the army at the same time but was stationed in a separate location.

2. See Václav Havel, *Disturbing the Peace: A Conversation with Karel Hvížďala*, trans. Paul Wilson (New York: Vintage Books, 1991), 38.

3. Václav Havel, letter to Jiří Paukert, December 21, 1957, VHL.

4. Václav Havel, letter to Jiří Paukert, September 25, 1957, VHL. I have used Michael Žantovský's translation from *Havel: A Life* (New York: Grove Press, 2014), 45.

5. Petr Stránský, personal interview, July 7, 2011.

6. Havel, *Disturbing the Peace*, 38–39.

7. Havel and Brynda also wrote a draft of a screenplay together, *Oh, the Army*, about a conscript and his troubles with love. It's unclear whether the screenplay was intended to be entered into some kind of competition or as part of an entrance application to the Film Academy.

8. The speculation that Havel's father approached Werich comes from Ivan Havel, personal interview, August 5, 2011.

9. Ivan Havel, personal interview, August 5, 2011.

10. Václav Havel, *Letters to Olga*, trans. Paul Wilson (New York: Henry Holt, 1989), 121. The Prague Free Theater (Osvobozené Divadlo) was in operation from 1926 to 1938, although there was a brief period in the 1930s when it operated under a different name. Today, the theater is considered an important cultural influence in the First Republic. Although Werich returned after World War II, his partner, Jiří Voskovec, remained in the United States, acting in more than sixty films, including *12 Angry Men*. For a longer discussion of Werich, see Carol Rocamora, *Acts of Courage: Václav Havel's Life in the Theater* (Hanover, NH: Smith and Kraus, 2004), 25–29.

11. Havel, *Disturbing the Peace*, 39–41.

12. Havel, *Disturbing the Peace*, 39–41. See also Havel, *Letters to Olga*, 121, 248. When Werich died, while Havel was in prison, Havel wrote Olga that his death signified the "end of an era in Czech intellectual history."

13. Havel, *Disturbing the Peace*, 40–41.

14. See Václav Havel, *Open Letters: Selected Writings 1965–1990*, trans. Paul Wilson (New York: Vintage, 1992), 4. "Second Wind" was originally written as an author's note to be included in a collection of plays published by Josef Škvorecký, who ran an exile press in Canada known as 68 Publishers.

15. This is a theme that Havel returned to again and again, most clearly in his letters from prison, which often served as meditations on the nature of theater. In a prison letter to his wife from November 1951, he distilled a number of his lifelong thoughts about theater: "Theater of this type faithfully describes life, yet in a certain sense, precisely because of its fidelity, it more or less lies about it: an artful rendition of the surface (not leaving a single crack for mystery to show through) essentially obscures any view beneath it" (Havel, *Letters to Olga*, 252).

16. For more on Czech theater in this period, see chapter four of Jorka Burian, *Modern Czech Theater: Reflector and Conscience of a Nation* (Iowa City: University Iowa Press, 2000).

17. In Havel, *Disturbing the Peace*, 43, Havel writes that "an inseparable part of the kind of theatre I've been drawn to all my life is a touch of obscurity, of decay or degeneration,

of frivolity, I don't know quite what to call it; I think theatre should always be somewhat suspect." Descriptions of the early days of the Balustrade vary. Here I've relied on those in Rocamora, *Acts of Courage*, 31, and Havel, *Disturbing the Peace*, 43, as well as my own observations of what the theater looks like today.

18. Rocamora, *Acts of Courage*, 33–34.

19. Albert Camus, *The Myth of Sisyphus*, quoted in Martin Esslin, *The Theater of the Absurd* (New York: Vintage Books, 1961), 23.

20. Havel, *Disturbing the Peace*, 53.

21. Esslin, *Theater of the Absurd*, 399–402.

22. Havel, *Open Letters*, 5.

23. References to vitamin F show up in a number of Havel letters, including one to Jan Grossman (undated but written sometime in the early 1960s) and one to Pavel Kohout (March 3, 1974), VHL.

24. Petr Stránský, personal interview, July 7, 2011.

25. The poem first appeared in *Revue K*, a journal in which Havel also published literary essays, such as a piece in 1956 titled "On the Prose of Bohumil Hrabal" (see Kriseová, *Václav Havel*, 11). In 1981 a journal by the same name was founded in Paris by Havel's friend Jiří Kolář; the journal focused on Czech artists and writers and the large community of Czech exiles who moved to France after 1968.

26. The witnesses to the wedding were Jan Grossman, who was then creative director of the theater, and Libor Fára, a set designer. See Pavel Kosatík, *Člověk má dělat to, nač má sílu* (Prague: Mladá Fronta, 2008), 94–95.

27. Václav Havel, letter to Václav M. Havel, July 14, 1964, reprinted in Anna Friemanová, *Síla věcnosti Olgy Havlové* (Prague: Knihovna Václava Havla, 2013), 12.

28. The poem is from the late 1950s and appears in John Keane, *Václav Havel: A Political Tragedy in Six Acts* (London: Bloomsbury, 1999), 142.

29. Kosatík, *Člověk má dělat to, nač má sílu*, 29. Although Olga fought with her mother, that was apparently just part of the Žižkov way. Olga was also proud of her family and her background. After Havel was elected president in 1989, she openly spoke of her sister as a cook, and she often invited her working-class family to Prague Castle for events.

30. Václav Havel, letter to Olga Havlová, April 4, 1981, in Havel, *Letters to Olga*, 181–82.

31. The phrase comes from a letter written on November 17, 1979. Speaking of what it would be like to enter prison, he writes Olga that "in recent years I have been living a strange, unnatural, exclusive and somewhat 'greenhouse' existence. Now this will change. I will be one of many tiny, helpless ants. I'll be thrown into the world much as I was when I was a lab assistant, a stagehand, a soldier, and a student" (Havel, *Letters to Olga*, 50).

32. The memory is from Marie Málková, an actress who eventually became Grossman's wife (Rocamora, *Acts of Courage*, 37).

33. Havel considered Vyskočil the godfather of the little theater movement. However, Vyskočil was also a chaotic and eccentric character, and many people found it impossible to work with him. For Havel's reflections on Vyskočil, see Havel, *Disturbing the Peace*, 46–47.

34. Rocamora, *Acts of Courage*, 37–38.

35. Barbara Day, personal interview, July 20, 2011.

36. Havel alludes to this idea in letters and writings from the 1960s but expanded the idea more clearly in a letter to Olga from December 5, 1981 (see Havel, *Letters to Olga*,

255–56). Havel's long-standing interest in human identity probably began with this basic theatrical experience, the question of the stage and actor as being both real and not real. Many of his plays from this era dealt with a similar theme: the loss of identity or what it meant to have an identity.

37. See Havel, *Letters to Olga*, 271–77, for this in relation to theater. The idea that our actions effect the order of Being became a major theme at a later date, providing a philosophical framework for dissident activity. The idea was parallel to Patočka's notion of undertaking certain matters for the "care of the soul." In both Havel's formulation and the formulation of Patočka, certain sacrifices may be worthwhile even if they have little chance for immediate success in the outer world.

38. Havel's account of this event can be found in Havel, *Disturbing the Peace*, 60–61; Vyskočil's account can be found in Rocamora, *Acts of Courage*, 38. The latter does sound both more like the final play and more like an idea that could have come from Vyskočil's mouth.

39. The discussion on *The Garden Party* is indebted to Paul I. Trenský, "Havel's *The Garden Party* Revisited," in *Critical Essays on Václav Havel*, ed. Marketa Goetz-Stankiewicz and Phyllis Carey (New York: G. K. Hall and Co., 1999), 159–71. A similar point has been made by many others, including Jan Grossman in the preface to the second Czech edition of Havel's plays. The main character in Havel's early plays is the cliché, which serves as a mechanism of totalitarian control. Grossman writes, "It is conceived as a variation on the observation that a man never makes his clothes but rather the clothes make the man: that is, a person does not use clichés; instead the cliché uses him" (also quoted in Kriseová, *Václav Havel*, 52).

40. The statement comes from Andrej Krob, quoted in Kriseová, *Václav Havel*, 42. Krob made similar (although less dramatic) comments in a personal interview with the author, August 2011.

41. Jan Sokol, personal interview, July 28, 2011. The play appears to have gotten by the censors because the attack on the Communist Party was in the form of hidden metaphors that never directly discussed ideology.

42. The saying (which appears in Albright, *Prague Winter: A Personal Story of Remembrance and War, 1937–1948* [New York: Harper, 2012], 32) is typical of Czech humor, which can be exceedingly dark.

43. The information comes from Klaus Juncker, letter to Václav Havel [undated but probably 1965], VHL.

44. See Esslin, *Theater of the Absurd*, 324–26.

45. Pavel Žáček, "Státní Bezpečnost Kontra Václav Havel," 1994, 1–19, PZC.

46. Pavel Žáček, "Státní Bezpečnost Kontra Václav Havel," 1994, 1–19, PZC.

## Chapter 4. The August Surprise

1. Michael Justin Kilburn, "The Merry Ghetto: The Czech Underground in the Time of Normalization," diss., Emory University, 1998. The estimate of those who listened to "underground" music, including Radio Free Europe, comes from a memorandum titled "Czechoslovak Service Program Review," December 1, 1986, RFE. Rock 'n' roll was first played live in alternative clubs in Prague, such as the Reduta Jazz Club, in 1959. Rock 'n' roll was seen as antiestablishment and therefore anti-communist.

2. The New Wave film movement in Czechoslovakia was distinct from the French New Wave. Both movements shared a youthful iconoclasm, but Czech New Wave filmmakers had come out of film school. As they entered into the nationalized film industry, they had greater access to studios and funding. The themes were typically about taboo subjects that had previously been rejected by censors. By the late 1960s, however, liberalization allowed them more freedom to explore contemporary culture.

3. Information from Havel's StB file is from Pavel Žáček, "Státni Bezpečnost Kontra Václav Havel," 1994, PZC, 1–19.

4. PEN International is an organization devoted to promoting literature and the freedom of expression. Details of the interrogation come from Věra Blackwell in a letter sent to Joseph Papp that appears in Helen Epstein, *Joe Papp: An American Life* (New York: Da Capo Press, 1996), 224–25, and from Žáček. As Havel's English-language translator, Blackwell had regular contact with Havel.

5. NYT, June 9, 1966.

6. The incident occurred in May 1967. For Havel's reaction, see his letter to Jiří Kuběna, May 8, 1967, VHL. Havel was never charged with a crime in 1967, so it is unclear what the police might have been investigating. Presumably, he was still being watched for his attempt the previous year to give a lecture in the United States that was critical of the regime.

7. The description of the play belongs to Zdeněk Hořínek, who wrote that Havel's play depicts the dehumanizing effects of modern life. His review (from *Divadlo*, October 1968) appears in part in Carol Rocamora, *Acts of Courage: Václav Havel's Life in the Theater* (Hanover, NH: Smith and Kraus, 2004), 77.

8. Václav Havel, letter to Věra Blackwell, September 30, 1970, VBC.

9. Pavel Kosatík, *Člověk má dělat to, nač má sílu* (Prague: Mladá Fronta, 2008), 99.

10. Kosatík, *Člověk má dělat to, nač má sílu*, 99–102, and personal interview with Andrej Krob, July 28, 2011. The chateau was Březnice u Příbrami, not too far from Prague. Andrej Krob was serving as groundskeeper of the chateau, which made it easy to arrange a stay for Havel.

11. Rocamora, *Acts of Courage*, 74; Alena Stránská, *Svobodné slovo*, April 17, 1968. Czech language newspaper.

12. Czechs differentiate between types of cabins. A *chata* is a small, modern garden house that is usually located in a development of weekend huts, each with enough land for a small garden. *Chatas* are the Czech equivalent of Russian *dachas*. The size of the building was severely limited during the communist era. A *chalupa* refers to an old cottage or farmhouse built in the traditional folk style of the nineteenth century.

13. Jiří Sotona, "Třískárna, Neckář a Havlová Loktovka," *Dnes Víkend*, December 23, 2011, 10. Czech language newspaper.

14. Kosatík, *Člověk má dělat to, nač má sílu*, 102; John Keane, *Václav Havel: A Political Tragedy in Six Acts* (London: Bloomsbury, 1999), 189. Pavel Landovský liked to say that Havel's recipes were only edible if you pulled them out of the oven "two acts" ahead of schedule. In general, Havel's adventures as a cook were a source of constant amusement among his friends and even became a running gag in Pavel Kohout's one-act play, *Six and Sex*.

15. Kenneth Tynan, "The Theatre Abroad: Prague," *New Yorker*, April 1, 1967, 99–123.

16. For a detailed account Havel's role in the writer's union, see Václav Havel, *Dis-*

*turbing the Peace: A Conversation with Karel Hvížďala*, trans. Paul Wilson (New York: Vintage Books, 1991), 75–92.

17. Tim West, "Destiny as Alibi: Milan Kundera, Václav Havel and the Czech Question after 1968," *Slavonic and East European Review* 87, no. 3 (2009): 408–9; Michael Simmons, *The Reluctant President: A Political Life of Václav Havel* (London: Methuen, 1991), 74–78; Havel, *Disturbing the Peace*, 85. For a news account of the congress, see NYT, July 6, 1967.

18. NYT, July 6, 1967.

19. William Shawcross, *Dubček* (New York: Simon and Schuster, 1990), 85–86, 96; Galia Golan, *The Czechoslovak Reform Movement* (London: Cambridge University Press, 1971), 315.

20. Joseph Wechsberg, "Letter from Prague," *New Yorker*, April 27, 1968, 97.

21. Wechsberg "Letter from Prague," 97, 134–36.

22. Wechsberg "Letter from Prague," 97, 134–36; Václav Havel, reminiscences electronically recorded at salon of Kamila Bendová, [2003?]; Jan Tříska, personal interview, July 13, 2009.

23. Václav Havel, "On the Theme of an Opposition," in *Open Letters: Selected Writings 1965–1990*, trans. Paul Wilson (New York, Vintage, 1992), 26.

24. Havel, *Disturbing the Peace*, 99–100; Ludvík Vaculík, *Český Snář* (Praha: Atlantis, 1990), 43.

25. Václav Havel, *To the Castle and Back*, trans. Paul Wilson (New York: Knopf, 2007), 6–7.

26. Havel, *To the Castle and Back*, 7.

27. Internal memorandum from Radio Free Europe, author unknown, May 7, 1968, RFE; Havel, *Disturbing the Peace*, 19.

28. Internal memorandum from Radio Free Europe, author unknown, May 8, 10, and 13, 1968, RFE.

29. Keane, *Václav Havel*, 188.

30. Havel, *Disturbing the Peace*, 95.

31. Havel, *Disturbing the Peace*, 96.

32. Jan Tříska, untitled essay, in *Milý Václave . . . Tvůj: Přemýšleni o Václavu Havlovi* (Praha: Divadelní Ústav, 1997), 67–72. Czech language.

33. Václav Havel, electronic recording of reminiscences given at the home of Kamila Bendová (unknown date).

34. Jan Tříska, personal interview, July 14, 2009; Hana Seifertová, correspondence with the author, June 14, 2010; Václav Havel, letter to Měda S. Mládek, October 1968, FFA.

35. Czechoslovakia was not in a military position to effectively resist the invasion. For context on this decision, see Alexander Dubček, *Hope Dies Last: The Autobiography of Alexander Dubček* (New York: Kadansha America, 1993), 183.

36. Keane, *Václav Havel*, 212–13; Jan Tříska, personal interview, July 14, 2009. The Czechs connected to Jezerka Tower, which was the main TV and radio transmitter in the region.

37. Havel, *Disturbing the Peace*, 108–9; Václav Havel, letter to Měda Mládek, October 1968, FFA. Czechoslovakia was invaded by Nazi Germany in 1938.

38. Havel, *Disturbing the Peace*, 106–8.

39. Václav Havel, letter to Měda Mládek, October 1968, FFA.

40. NYT, September 4, 1968.

41. Shawcross, *Dubček*, 161–62.

42. Václav Havel, reminiscences given at the home of Kamila Bendová, electronic recording (date unknown).

43. Kosatík, *Člověk má dělat to, nač má sílu*, 106–9; Jan Tříska, personal interview, July 14, 2009.

44. Kusin, *From Dubček to Charter 77: A Study in "Normalization" in Czechoslovakia 1968–1978* (New York: St. Martin's Press, 1978), 48.

45. Havel's original letter to Mládek has been lost, but it is referred to in a number of places in their correspondence. See Václav Havel, letter to Měda Mládek, October 1968, FFA.

## Chapter 5. A Curtain of Iron

1. Weather records from 1775 to 2011 taken by Prague Klementinum, available online at www.climatestations.com.

2. Personal interview with Jan Tříska, July 13, 2009. Tříska and Havel wrote dozens of letters that fall, all of which have been lost. Tříska destroyed his letters in order to protect himself, and the letters in Havel's possession were either destroyed or confiscated by the secret police.

3. *Trud (Moscow)*, June 21, 1968, first quoted in John Keane, *Václav Havel: A Political Tragedy in Six Acts* (London: Bloomsbury, 1999), 172.

4. Krystyna Wanatowiczová, *Miloš Havel: Český filmový magnát* (Prague: Václav Havel Library, 2013), 430 and 475–81. Miloš Havel managed to start a small film company and a restaurant while living in West Germany, but neither venture found much economic success. And although he escaped Czechoslovakia with his boyfriend, Dušan Hubáček, the two had a falling out sometime before 1960. In an interview for Wanatowiczová, *Miloš Havel: Český filmový magnát*, Havel recalled opening a private safe of Miloš's after his funeral. He reported that "there were many people there and all of them had hoped that they would find some valuable jewelry or billions in the safe and that me and my father would give these away. They were disappointed, because we didn't find a single cuff link there. This story illustrates his fate—in the end, he was left with absolutely nothing."

5. From *Kveten* magazine, date unknown, quoted in Michael Simmons, *The Reluctant President: A Political Life of Václav Havel* (London: Methuen, 1991), 55.

6. On the occasion of his fiftieth birthday, Karel Hvížďala asked Havel to evaluate himself "as a person." This is part of a long string of paradoxes that Havel saw in his own character. See Václav Havel, *Disturbing the Peace: A Conversation with Karel Hvížďala*, trans. Paul Wilson (New York: Vintage Books, 1991), 202–6.

7. Lowry was vice president of the Ford Foundation and something of a visionary in the arts. He had begun making inquiries into bringing Czech artists to the United States as far back as January, at the very dawn of Prague Spring, and had asked Měda and Jan Mládek to serve as intermediaries with Czech artists. The project to get Czech artists out of the country was fast-tracked after the invasion, for obvious reasons.

8. Wolfgang Kraus, letter to Howard Swearer, September 18, 1968, FFA; Jan Mládek, letter to McNeil Lowry, October 14, 1968, FFA.

9. Václav Havel, letter to Měda Mládek, October 1968, FFA.

10. Václav Havel, letter to Měda Mládek, October 1968, FFA.

11. McNeil Lowry, letter to Václav Havel, November 14, 1968, FFA; author unknown, internal memorandum regarding "Travel and Study Award Budget Estimate Mr. and Mrs. Václav Havel," November 1968, FFA.

12. Václav Havel, letter to McNeil Lowry, date unknown but likely December 1968, FFA.

13. Power of Attorney document, November 14, 1968, Bakhmeteff Archive, Columbia University. The document is written in English, perhaps so that Blackwell could show it to her English contacts.

14. Kundera also used his position to support Havel's application to film school, which was denied in the mid-1950s. After Havel became a successful playwright in the 1960s, Havel was allowed to complete a correspondence course in the theater arts.

15. Havel, *Disturbing the Peace*, 172–78; Jan Čulík, "Man, a Wide Garden: Milan Kundera as a Young Poet" (unpublished, 2007).

16. Michelle Woods, *Translating Milan Kundera* (Buffalo, NY: Multilingual Matters, 2006), 92–93; see also Milan Kundera, *Testaments Betrayed*, trans. Linda Asher (London: Faber and Faber, 1996), especially 157–78.

17. Milan Kundera, "Český úděl," *Listy*, December 19, 1968. Czech language.

18. Havel discusses his rare "black rages" in his essay "Article 202," which can be found in *Open Letters: Selected Writings 1965–1990*, trans. Paul Wilson (New York: Vintage, 1992), 109–16. He writes that "I rarely have the kind of tantrums in which the world goes dark before my eyes and I'm capable of doing things I would never normally do; if they happen at all, then at the most only once every seven to ten years. When they do occur, such tantrums are never provoked by something important, like being arrested, or insulted, or having my flat confiscated; the cause is always something petty." The first of these rages probably occurred during his tour in the army, and the second might be the episode with Kundera.

19. Havel, *Disturbing the Peace*, 110.

20. Václav Havel, "Česky úděl?" *Tvař*, no. 2 (1969): 33. Czech language.

21. Kundera's reply to Havel, "Radikalizmus a expozice," was originally published in *Host do domu* 15, no. 15 (1969). Czech language.

22. Alain Finkielkraut, "Milan Kundera Interview," *Cross Currents: A Yearbook of Central European Culture* 1 (1982): 15–29.

23. H. Gordon Skilling, "Czechoslovakia," in *Communist States in Disarray, 1965–1971*, ed. Adam Bromke (Oxford: Oxford University Press, 1972), 59. A number of the hard-line communists, including Vasil Biľak and Alois Indra, had been in contact with Moscow, and they went so far as to send a formal letter requesting that the Soviet Union invade in order to save the communist system. Although the two men planned on taking control of the government after the invasion, they lost their nerve after seeing the level of resistance to the occupation.

24. Skilling, "Czechoslovakia," 63.

25. Data on the weather is taken from monthly charts recorded by Prague Klementinum. Records from 1775 to 2011 are available online at climatestations.com.

26. Josef Škvorecký, "I Saw Václav Havel for the Last Time," in *Living in Truth* (London: Faber and Faber, 1986), 274–77.

27. Václav Havel, letter to McNeil Lowry, January 14, 1969, FFA. Václav Havel, letter to McNeil Lowry March 20, 1969; letter to Judith Symington, March 20, 1969; letter to Judith Symington, June 1969, FFA.

28. NYT, January 11, 1969.

29. NYT, June 1, 1969. Among the first individuals to be kicked out of the Communist Party were Ota Šik, who had designed the economic reforms of the Prague Spring, and Jiří Hájek, the foreign minister. Eventually, Dubček would be purged from the Communist Party as well.

30. Vladimir V. Kusin, *From Dubček to Charter 77: A Study in "Normalization" in Czechoslovakia 1968–1978* (New York: St. Martin's Press, 1978), 145.

31. Václav Havel, open letter to Alexander Dubček, August 9, 1969, Havel, *Letters to Olga*, trans. Paul Wilson (New York: Henry Holt, 1989), 36–49. Dubček did refuse to condemn his own reforms. After being removed as general secretary of the Communist Party, he served briefly as an ambassador to Turkey before he was purged from the Communist Party in 1970.

32. Kusin, *From Dubček to Charter 77*, 148–50. In brief, the Ten Points Petition rejected Soviet intervention, the purges from the Communist Party that began in April, and the renewal of censorship. In addition, it called for market-based reform and the elimination of the central role of the Communist Party. It also affirmed the right of all citizens to disagree with their government.

33. Václav Havel, telegram to McNeil Lowry, date approximately August 25, 1969 (?), FFA. The extra "M" in "COMME" is in the original telegraph. Havel's use of the English language had always been shaky and a source of embarrassment, since he had years of lessons, starting in his teenage years.

34. Václav Havel, letter to McNeil Lowry, August 23, 1969 (?), FFA.

35. Věra Blackwell, letter to Václav Havel, October 11, 1969; Václav Havel, letter to Věra Blackwell, November 21, 1969, VBC.

36. Kusin, *From Dubček to Charter 77*, 148–50; Daniel Kaiser, *Disident: Václav Havel 1936–1989* (Prague: Paseka, 2009), 82; Eda Kriseová, *Václav Havel: The Authorized Biography* (New York: St. Martin's Press, 1993), 78.

37. Yorick Blumenfeld, Ford Foundation memorandum, July 16, 1970, FFA.

38. Václav Havel, letter to Věra Blackwell, November 21, 1969, VBC.

## Chapter 6. Into the Woods

1. Věra Blackwell, letter to Václav Havel, October 11, 1969, VBC.

2. Věra Blackwell, letter to Václav Havel, February 22, 1970; Věra Blackwell, letter to Václav Havel, March 19, 1970, VBC.

3. What Havel called "political apartheid" became even more pronounced a few years later, after he became more active (and well known) as a dissident. Others referred to this same phenomenon as the "dissident ghetto." After the government crackdowns that culminated in 1971, those who were in trouble with the government became isolated from former friends. It was not uncommon for former colleagues to cross streets in order to avoid running into dissidents, since any greeting or sign of friendliness could be recorded by the secret police. See Václav Havel, "It Always Makes Sense to Tell the Truth," in *Open Letters: Selected Writings 1965–1990*, trans. Paul Wilson (New York: Vintage, 1992), 89.

4. Václav Havel, letter to Věra Blackwell, November 21, 1969, VBC.

5. Věra Blackwell, letter to Václav Havel, October 23, 1969; Věra Blackwell, letter to Václav Havel, April 17, 1970, VBC. In just the English-speaking world, Grover Press published a book of plays, two literary agents in New York were trying to sell his work to Broadway, and BBC radio performed *Guardian Angel*. *Guardian Angel* was originally written in 1968 for Czech radio. It is a short play, not usually included in publications of his full-length works. Havel considered it a minor play that he had written in his spare time, and he was not keen on having it produced abroad.

6. Václav Havel, *Disturbing the Peace: A Conversation with Karel Hvížďala*, trans. Paul Wilson (New York: Vintage Books, 1991). 192–93.

7. Václav Havel, *Komentář* ke hře Spiklenci, unpublished manuscript, 9, JSC.

8. Václav Havel, "Jak Píšete," unpublished and undated manuscript, JSC.

9. Havel, *Komentář* ke hře Spiklenci, 9–10. A translated version ("Notes on the Conspirators") dated December 14, 1971, can be found in Tom Stoppard's papers, TSC.

10. Věra Blackwell, letter to Václav Havel, March 4, 1970, VBC.

11. Havel, "Second Wind," in *Open Letters*, 208–10; Carol Rocamora, *Acts of Courage: Václav Havel's Life in the Theater* (Hanover, NH: Smith and Kraus, 2004), 111–13; Václav Havel, letter to Josef Škvorecký, June 7, 1983, JSC.

12. Yorick Blumenfeld, memo to McNeal Lowry, July 16, 1970, FFA.

13. Rocamora, *Acts of Courage*, 119.

14. Václav Havel, letter to Věra Blackwell, June 12, 1970, VBC. Havel had already sold all the world rights for *The Conspirators* to Juncker in order to cover just this sort of situation; he had also given his power of attorney to Blackwell, but it's unclear whether this could be used to circumvent the new law. DILIA did successfully block *The Garden Party* from being produced at a Spanish theater in 1971–1972.

15. Václav Havel, letter to Věra Blackwell, May 19, 1970, VBC.

16. Václav Havel, letter to Věra Blackwell, June 12, 1970, VBC.

17. Václav Havel, letter to Věra Blackwell, July 15, 1970, VBC.

18. Václav Havel, letter to Věra Blackwell, July 15, 1970, VBC.

19. Václav Havel, letter to Věra Blackwell, September 30, 1970, VBC.

20. Paulina Bren, "Tuzex and the Hustler," in *Communism Unwrapped: Consumption in Cold War Eastern Europe*, ed. Paulina Bren and Mary Neuburger (Oxford: Oxford University Press), 29–30.

21. Bren, "Tuzex and the Hustler," 27–28.

22. After finishing *The Conspirators*, Havel began working on *Mountain Hotel*, which he would not finish until 1975. Pavel Kosatík, *Člověk má dělat to, nač má sílu* (Prague: Mladá Fronta, 2008), 112.

23. Václav Havel, letter to Václav Maria Havel, July 14, 1964, quoted in Anna Friemanová, *Síla věcnosti Olgy Havlové* (Prague: Knihovna Václava Havla, 2013), 12. Little is known about Havel's early affairs. During the 1970s and 1980s, however, he had a number of mistresses who became important in his life and work.

24. Havel refers to this in Havel, *Disturbing the Peace*, 156.

25. Kosatík, *Člověk má dělat to, nač má sílu*, 130–33.

26. Havel, *Disturbing the Peace*, 156.

27. Havel discussed his fate in a letter to Věra Blackwell in the summer of 1970. He

wrote that while his future was uncertain, "I have chosen my fate myself, at least in its basic features." Václav Havel, letter to Věra Blackwell, June 12, 1970, VBC.

## Chapter Seven: "VZDOR"

1. Carol Rocamora, *Acts of Courage: Václav Havel's Life in the Theater* (Hanover, NH: Smith and Kraus, 2004), 119–21. The authors present at the early meetings included Havel, Ludvík Vaculík, Alexandr Kliment, Pavel Kohout, and Eda Kriseová (who became Havel's authorized biographer). For Klíma's description of the events, see Ivan Klíma, *My Crazy Century: A Memoir*, trans. Craig Cravens (New York: Grove Press, 2013), 126–27. Havel discusses the same meetings in Václav Havel, *Disturbing the Peace: A Conversation with Karel Hvížďala*, trans. Paul Wilson (New York: Vintage Books, 1991), 121. Klíma and his wife, Helena, lived on Nad lesem, a second-floor flat in a villa some fifty meters from the forest. The house had been built in the 1920s and they renovated it shortly after taking over the apartment in the 1950s, turning a former maid's room into a kitchen and turning the kitchen into a dining room.

2. Ivan Klíma, letter to John Wheatcroft, June 19, 1973, Library of Congress archives. Klíma actually left the United States in 1970, after holding a position at the University of Michigan. The letter to Wheatcroft was in response to returning to the United States to teach at Bucknell.

3. Klíma, *My Crazy Century*, 1. Klíma remained a communist for almost exactly forty years. In his memoirs, he explains the appeal of communism among his fellow youth during the 1940s in this way: it gave "a faith in a cause and gave simple, understandable answers to the injustices of the world." It is also true that during the 1950s and early 1960s, communism served Klíma as an excellent career path, first in journalism and then as a published writer supported by the Writer's Union. Before he became a banned writer in the late 1960s, he published at least ten books, including novels and collections of short stories and essays.

4. For an insightful discussion on this theme of how state censors worked, see Paul Wilson, "Notes on the Underground," NYRB, January 9, 2014, which provides details on the process of censorship. In his memoir, Klíma discusses his interactions with censors in a number of places. See especially Klíma, *My Crazy Century*, 201–3.

5. This is from an essay on "The Party" that appears in Klíma, *My Crazy Century*, 438–44. Although Klíma is talking, generically, about the "faithful who joined the party," he is also clearly talking about his own experience. Among those who criticized the state at the writer's union were Milan Kundera, Pavel Kohout, and Ludvík Vaculík.

6. Klíma, *My Crazy Century*, 218.

7. Klíma, *My Crazy Century*, 287.

8. The word was "thunderstorm." Sidon was spared in the first round of blacklisting authors, most likely because he was largely apolitical. Later on, however, the head of the ideological department came to the Rubín Theater to see his play *The Latrines*, which fairly dripped with disdain for authority. Sidon was immediately made an outcast and had to find work at a kiosk, selling periodicals. He was working at the kiosk when the magazine *Ahoj*, under pressure from the secret police, published intimate pictures of Ludvík Vaculík and his lover. In an act of civil disobedience, Sidon cut out the offending pictures from each issue of the magazine. He was later fired from his job and forced to emigrate.

9. Havel, *Disturbing the Peace*, 121.

10. See Jonathan Bolton, *Worlds of Dissent: Charter 77, the Plastic People of the Universe, and Czech Culture under Communism* (Cambridge, MA: Harvard University Press, 2012), 72–74, for a history of the use of the term "normalization." Bolton argues that the word began "as a dishonest euphemism" used both by those against the Soviet invasion and by hard-liners who supported the Soviet invasion. It was thus originally used as a matter of duplicity, since "normalizing" the situation in the country could mean whatever one wanted to hear. By the end of 1971, however, the word took on a new connotation: the return to complete totalitarian control by the Communist Party.

11. The questionnaires consisted of fifty-two questions and three sections: personal information, career development, and political development. The section on political development asked about such issues as personal goals related to the building of a communist state. Another question asked whether one had come into contact with a foreigner or whether one had a relative living abroad. The answers were sometimes checked for accuracy by a member of the District Committee of the Communist Party. See Jiřina Šiklová, "Biographies and Resumes as Part of Life under Communist Rule in the Czech Republic," in *Legal Institutions and Collective Memories*, ed. Susanne Karstedt (Portland, OR: Hart Publishing, 2009), 317–28.

12. Havel began using the term "crisis of human identity" shortly after the Soviet invasion, and the idea figures prominently in the play he wrote after the invasion, *The Conspirators*. The quoted material, however, comes from his open letter to the head of the Communist Party, which wasn't written until a few years later, in 1975. See "Dear Dr. Husák," in *Open Letters: Selected Writings 1965–1990*, trans. Paul Wilson (New York: Vintage, 1992), 50–83.

13. Václav Havel, letter to Věra Blackwell, October 18, 1972, VBC.

14. Ivan Havel, personal interview, August 4, 2009.

15. One of the issues of continuing to work at the Institute of Information Theory and Automation was that they housed computers for the Department of Interior, including records for the secret police. After being forced out of the Academy of Sciences, Ivan Havel was able to find refuge in computer programing. Ivan Havel, personal interview, August 4, 2009. Additional information is available in an interview in Michael Long, ed., *Making History* (New York: Rowman and Littlefield, 2005), 23–36.

16. Eda Kriseová, *Václav Havel: The Authorized Biography* (New York: St. Martin's Press, 1993), 125–27, and Daniel Kaiser, *Disident: Václav Havel 1936–1989* (Prague: Paseka, 2009), 96–97. Jan Saudek is a Czech artist known for erotic and surrealistic photography. Havel's analysis of the erosion of the individual can be found most clearly in his "Letter to Dr. Husák."

17. Václav Havel, letter to Věra Blackwell, May 20, 1973, VBC.

18. See Ivan and Karel Kyncl, *After the Spring Came Winter* (Stockholm: Charta 77 Foundation, 1985), 54–55.

19. The incident of Landovský stealing Havel's car as a prank appears in Michael Žantovský, *Havel: A Life* (New York: Grove Press, 2014), 130.

20. Václav Havel, letter to Věra Blackwell, May 20, 1973, VBC.

21. The petition requested amnesty or, at the very least, allowing the prisoners to spend the Christmas holidays at home. The final draft of the petition read, in part: "Al-

though the views of the undersigned differ widely on various fundamental questions, we agree that magnanimity regarding political prisoners cannot in any way threaten the authority and capacity of the state's power; quite the opposite, will testify to its humanism."

22. Vladimir V. Kusin, *From Dubček to Charter 77: A Study in "Normalization" in Czechoslovakia 1968–1978* (New York: St. Martin's Press, 1978), 148–50; see also Jiří Pachman, *Socialist Opposition in Eastern Europe: The Czechoslovak Example* (London: Macmillan, 1976), 117–224. Pachman was eventually released early in order to allow him to emigrate to a foreign country. Uhl was sentenced to more than four years in prison. Later, after his release, he became a member of Charter 77, the human rights organization cofounded by Václav Havel.

23. The quote is Havel's remembrance of how those who refused to sign the petition felt, from Havel, *Disturbing the Peace*, 174. Klíma's memories, which are quite similar, can be found in Klíma, *My Crazy Century*, 297.

24. International PEN (known as PEN International since 2010) was founded in London in 1921 to promote cooperation of writers across the world. The acronym originally stood for Poets, Essayists, Novelists, although the group officially changed over the years to include other professions, such as playwrights and editors.

25. A lengthy recollection of the interrogation can be found in Klíma, *My Crazy Century*, 296–304.

26. Milan Kundera, *The Unbearable Lightness of Being* (New York: Harper and Row, 1985), 212–20.

27. Havel, *Disturbing the Peace*, 176–77.

28. Havel, *Disturbing the Peace*, 121; Rocamora, *Acts of Courage*, 120; Maya Jaggi, "Building Bridges," *Guardian*, April 30, 2004, 30.

29. Bolton, *Worlds of Dissent*, 98–113.

30. Bolton, *Worlds of Dissent*, 98–113.

31. An excellent and thoroughly researched profile of Vaculík and his "underground press" can be found in Bolton, *Worlds of Dissent*, 239–65. It's worth noting that Vaculík was not easily intimidated, and he knew which lines not to cross. He carefully avoided any activity that could allow him to be charged under paragraph 102 or 112 of the penal code, which made it illegal to defame the state or damage its reputation with false reports. When meeting with foreign reporters, Vaculík avoided anything that could be interpreted as an opinion (and thus defamation). Rather than speak about specific instances of state repression, he stuck to philosophical issues, such as the rule of law. In an interview with a Swiss journalist, later published in the *Nation*, he said that as a result of the state of repression "people do covertly things that they could, in all legality, do openly." He was no doubt thinking about his own Padlock Press, which was perfectly legal but operated as if it wasn't.

32. H. Gordon Skilling, *The Education of a Canadian: My Life as a Scholar and Activist* (London: McGill-Queen's University Press, 2000), 288.

33. Bolton, *Worlds of Dissent*, 101.

34. See Václav Havel, letter to Věra Blackwell, October [?], 1973.

35. Havel's assessment of Tynan's reaction appears to have come partly from intuition and partly from information passed on from Věra Blackwell, which he articulated in a

letter to Josef Šafařík on October 3, 1973 (quoted in Žantovský, *Havel*, 135), in which he said Tynan and those he was consulting with were "somewhat confused about the play, they don't know what to think about it and they don't seem to particularly like it."

36. The two men exchanged half a dozen letters about the play, many of them regarding Havel's frustration over repeatedly missing deadlines for providing a final draft, a fact that Havel said "worries me more than you can guess." Václav Havel, letters to Kenneth Tynan, March 15, 1971, and July 1, 1971, TSC.

37. Some scholars, such as Michelle Woods, have argued that British audiences wanted dissident writers from Eastern Europe to fit within their Cold War framework.

38. Václav Havel, letter to Věra Blackwell, January 2, 1971, VBC.

39. The phrase comes from a letter to Alfréd Radok, December 27, 1973, VHL. Havel told Radock that he was exploring questions of identity, including "how much we—as people—really exist."

40. Václav Havel, letter to Olga Havlová, January 27, 1980, in Václav Havel, *Letters to Olga*, trans. Paul Wilson (New York: Henry Holt, 1989), 85. Havel talks about the play in a number of other letters as well.

41. In a letter to director Alfréd Radok, December 27, 1973, VHL, Havel referred to the play as both a work of "Dada" and worried whether he could successfully write it. Havel referred to *Mountain Hotel* as his weakest play in letters to Josef Škvorecký on August 5 and December 22, 1976, JSC. Although he was pleased that *Mountain Hotel* was included in a collection of his plays, he was adamant that Škvorecký not include a commentary on *Mountain Hotel*. Havel thought it would be strange to have a commentary about "the weakest play" in the book.

42. Václav Havel, letter to Věra Blackwell, November 1, 1971, VBC. One finds this sentiment, perhaps borne out of frustration, in several letters to Věra Blackwell.

43. Václav Havel, letter to Věra Blackwell, undated but probably April 1972, VBC.

## Chapter 8. An Open Letter

1. NYT, October 5, 1981. After the Velvet Revolution, the Lenin metro station was renamed Dejvická. Discussion about creating an underground metro system in Prague began in the 1920s but was delayed by the Great Depression and then by World War II. Construction on the system by Soviet engineers began in the late 1960s but was delayed for many years.

2. Barbara Day, *The Velvet Philosophers* (London: Claridge, 1999), 10; Jiřina Šiklová, personal interview, July 2011. The term "underground university" was used by Czechs themselves to describe living room seminars that were conducted in secrecy and silence. It largely refers to the groups that were started in the late 1970s. In the early 1970s, the groups were typically less organized.

3. Václav Havel, *Disturbing the Peace: A Conversation with Karel Hvížďala*, trans. Paul Wilson (New York: Vintage Books, 1991), 120–21; Pavel Kosatík, *Člověk má dělat to, nač má sílu* (Prague: Mladá Fronta, 2008), 122–23.

4. For a detailed analysis of Kosík, see Peter Hrubý, *Fools and Heroes: The Changing Role of Communist Intellectuals in Czechoslovakia* (Oxford: Pergamon, 1980), 188–95. Born in 1926, Kosík had originally been a propagandist who quoted liberally from Stalin and Marx. Later, he became a Marxist philosopher. His Ph.D. thesis, titled "People's Democ-

racy as a Form of the Dictatorship of the Proletariat," gives a taste for the direction of his thinking. He became a so-called reform communist after the death of Stalin.

5. The second group also included Alexander Kliment, who became a character in Kohout's play *Six & Sex*, which fictionalized the group as partisans who had decided to blow up a train.

6. Ludvík Vaculík, "How a Writer Lives in Prague," *Nation*, May 21, 1973, 657.

7. The best analysis of the selective treatment of dissidents can be found in Jonathan Bolton, *Worlds of Dissent: Charter 77, the Plastic People of the Universe, and Czech Culture under Communism* (Cambridge, MA: Harvard University Press, 2012), esp. chapter 3. For information on Klíma, see 86–87.

8. The material on Kohout is taken from Hrubý, *Fools and Heroes*, 9–25, and from Pavel Kohout, *From a Diary of a Counter Revolutionary*, trans. George Steiner (New York: McGraw-Hill, 1969), 76–89.

9. For a short interview with Kohout on this theme, see Daniel Levinson, "Drama," *New Yorker*, December 15, 1980, 31–32.

10. Carol Rocamora, *Acts of Courage: Václav Havel's Life in the Theater* (Hanover, NH: Smith and Kraus, 2004), 121.

11. The Vaněk character was originally created in the play *Audience*, written for the amusement of Havel's friends and read at Hrádeček. Havel gave permission to Kohout to borrow the character, which led to two Kohout plays, *Permit* and *Morass*. After he emigrated to Austria, Pavel Landovský wrote a play based on the same character, titled *Arrest*. Finally, Jiří Dienstbier wrote a play using the same character.

12. Kohout, *From a Diary of a Counter Revolutionary*, 89.

13. Pavel Kohout, "The Chaste Centaur," in *Living in Truth*, ed. Jan Vladislav (London: Faber and Faber, 1989), 246.

14. Pavel Kohout, *Šest & Sex: Sedm jednoaktových her* (Praha: Mladá fronta, 1998). Czech language. In English, the name of the play is *Six and Sex*.

15. Kohout, *Šest & Sex*.

16. In an early portion of the play, Havel mentions that Olga is off in Slovakia. Later, when Havel mentions he needs to run to Hrádeček to make sure Olga isn't afraid, someone reminds him that she's traveling in Slovakia. "Oh, yes, that's right," Havel says. "So maybe someone else is there who will be afraid." Havel's attempt to hide his sexual affairs is a constant theme in the play. Havel was linked to a number of women in those years, including Ella Horáková, a beauty who worked with him on his samizdat press. The two had an intimate relationship that ended much later, after she married in 1979. For more on Horáková, see Vaculík's classic *roman a clef* about life in communist Czechoslovakia, *Český Snář* (Prague: Atlantis, 1990), 105.

17. In a letter to Pavel Kohout, undated, but the context places the letter as early 1974, Havel mentions a meeting at a café in which they talked about a "bag of garlic," which was obviously either samizdat material or a petition of some sort. In a January 14, 1974, letter to Kohout, Havel signed his name Drašar D. after inviting him to come visit (both letters at VHL).

18. Václav Havel, letter to Pavel Kohout, November 6, 1973; Pavel Kohout, letter to Václav Havel, November 19, 1973, VHL.

19. Pavel Kohout, letter to Václav Havel, October 31, 1973, VHL.

20. The arson at the weekend house of Pavel and Anna Kohout has been discussed in many places. Kohout himself first mentions it in a letter to Václav Havel that was written the day the house was burned down. See the letter to Havel, October 8, 1973, VCL.

21. Confidential Electronic Cable from the American Embassy in Prague, November 18, 1976, TNA.

22. Zdeněk Mlynář, *Nightfrost in Prague: The End of Humane Socialism* (New York: Karz Press, 1980), 13, 258–59.

23. Květa Jechová, *Lidé Charty 77* (Prague: Ústav pro Soudobé Dějiny, 2003). For a more detailed examination of Hájek's life after the Prague Spring, see Jiří Hájek, *Paměti* (Praha: Ústav mezinárodních vztahů, 1997), particularly chapter 11. Information about espionage activities provided by Miroslav Pohlreich, personal interview, July 27, 2011.

24. Václav Havel, letter to Pavel Kohout, March 3, 1974, VHL.

25. Václav Havel, undated letter to Věra Blackwell, [1974?], VHL.

26. Václav Havel, "'It Always Makes Sense to Tell the Truth': An Interview with Jiří Lederer," in *Open Letters: Selected Writings 1965–1990*, trans. Paul Wilson (New York: Vintage, 1992), 90.

27. Romany, or gypsy people (known in Czech as *Cigán*), faced extreme discrimination in communist Czechoslovakia. I have used the politically incorrect term "Gypsy" here since it more closely suggests the dispossession of *Romany* people under the communist system.

28. Václav Havel, letter to Pavel Kohout, March 3, 1974, VHL.

29. Václav Havel, letter to Alfréd Radok, February 1972, VHL.

30. Václav Havel, letter to Alfréd Radok, December 27, 1973, VHL. The 1972 letter to Radok was written before accepting the job at the brewery and the 1973 letter after taking the job.

31. Havel, *Disturbing the Peace*, 120.

32. Václav Havel, letter to Pavel Kohout, April 17, 1974, VHL.

33. Havel talked most openly about his experience at the brewery in the interview with Lederer. He wrote a one-act play based on the experience, known in English as *Audience*. Václav Havel, *The Garden Party and Other Plays* (New York: Grove Press, 1993), 185–211.

34. Under Czech law, all bands were required to have a professional permit allowing them to charge fees for their services, giving the government control over the nation's music. Without a permit, a band could no longer play in public in any venue in which money was exchanged. The loss of licenses also meant the loss of access to state-owned rehearsal space and state-owned musical instruments.

35. Bolton, *Worlds of Dissent*, 119–20. One of Jirous's many nicknames was Warhol—or in Czech, Vorholec, meaning "little Warhol" or "the Warhol man." The suffix "ec" is found in words like *umělec* (artist), which comes from the word *umění* (art). Similarly, *vlasy* means hair, but *vlasatec* is someone who wears long hair—a hippie.

36. This is a common theme of Jirous's work throughout the 1970s. It is most clearly articulated in his "Report on the Third Czech Musical Revival," later published in *Primary Documents: A Sourcebook for Eastern and Central European Art since the 1950s*, ed. Laura Hoptman and Tomáš Pospiszyl (Boston: MIT Press, 2002), 56–65.

37. Michael Kilburn, "The Merry Ghetto: The Czech Underground in the Time of Normalization," diss., Emory University, 2001, 72–73.

38. Bolton, *Worlds of Dissent*, 122 and 129.

39. Havel, *Disturbing the Peace*, 126. Havel refers to his visitor only as "snowman." At the time, hiding the person's identity was probably necessary to keep Havel's friend from receiving unwanted attention from authorities. More details are provided by Havel in reminiscences given at the home of Kamila Bendová, electronic recording, date unknown [2007?].

40. Havel, *Disturbing the Peace*, 125–27; Ivan Jirous, *Magorův zápisník* (Praha: Torst, 1997), 344–46, Czech language. Havel and Jirous remember the meeting differently. Havel clearly downplayed the reservations that Jirous and the underground musicians had about him.

41. Havel, *Disturbing the Peace*, 125–27.

42. Alexander Dubček, open letter to the federal parliament and the Slovak National-al Council, October 28, 1974, reprinted in *Since the Prague Spring: Charter 77 and the Struggle for Human Rights in Czechoslovakia*, ed. Hans-Peter Riese (New York: Random House, 1979), 64–85.

43. All of these letters can be found in Riese, ed., *Since the Prague Spring*. In addition to the letters mentioned earlier, a second campaign was begun by former members of the Dubček government. Zdeněk Mlynář, Jiří Hájek, and František Kriegel all criticized the government for police abuse, but this may have been a mere coincidence related to the Helsinki Accords that would be signed later that summer.

44. Kamila Bendová, personal interview, August 2009. Quotes are from Havel, *Disturbing the Peace*, 123.

45. Rocamora, *Acts of Courage*, 147; Eda Kriseová, *Václav Havel: The Authorized Biography* (New York: St. Martin's Press, 1993), 88.

46. According to multiple sources, the police raided 135 homes in Prague in the aftermath of Havel's letter.

47. Havel discusses his quarantine in a letter to Věra Blackwell, August 27, 1975, VBC.

48. Havel, *Open Letters*, 51.

49. Different drafts of this letter have appeared in print, a not uncommon problem in Havel's life, given the difficulties in writing, preserving, and sending his work while under surveillance of the secret police. This version is reprinted in Riese, ed., *Since the Prague Spring*, 23–39.

50. In Poland, Havel's "Letter to Gustáv Husák" was translated and published in *Krytyka*, a samizdat publication. It was followed by a postscript by Adam Michnik, who described Polish reactions to Havel's arrest, calling Havel "a symbol of the unity of our common ideals and aims." Havel's letter was also widely published in Western Europe. Like many of his friends, Havel was never fully comfortable with the term "dissident," feeling it isolated himself and others from their larger communities. Havel also felt that the term "dissident" oversimplified matters. Many of the dissidents lacked any shared political agenda and didn't consider themselves an opposition to any particular point of view. What they did share was a desire to live their lives without interference from the Communist Party. Complicating matters, "dissident" was a term originating with foreign journalists rather than with dissidents themselves. See Havel, *Open Letters*, 50–83.

51. Havel, *Open Letters*, 84–101.

52. The interview with Lederer has a number of other historically interesting aspects

that give us some clues into how Havel was imagining the future struggle. Lederer's final question, for instance, was whether Havel ever expected to be able to see a premiere of one of his plays in a Prague theater again. Havel replied, "That depends on how long I live. If I die tomorrow, or next year, then I won't. But if I'm here until I'm sixty, let's say, then I will certainly live to see it." As it turns out, by the time Havel was sixty, he had already been president of Czechoslovakia. See Havel, *Open Letters*, 84–101.

53. Václav Havel, letter to Věra Blackwell, August 27, 1975, VBC.

54. Václav Havel, postcard to Věra Blackwell, June 28, 1975, VBC. The postcard, written in a variety of colors, consists of well wishes to Blackwell from those attending the underground writing conference.

55. As Czech readers recognize easily, the name Vaněk is a play on Havel's own nickname, Vašek, which is a diminutive for Václav.

56. I have borrowed here from Pavel Kohout's observations of "The Chaste Centaur," in *Living in Truth*, ed. Jan Vladislav (London: Faber and Faber, 1986). Kohout writes insightfully that in *Audience*, "omnipotent authority is faced with a shy, polite, even obliging intellectual of a visibly non-athletic cast, the like of which it has come to deal with expeditiously, if he be furnished with the soul of an ordinary man—commonly a mixture of cowardice and cynicism—and therefore amenable to bargain. But when authority enters, this man does not rant and rave; he neither quarrels nor exchanges blows; he doesn't even lie. At the most, he is silent, as if the truth might hurt someone other than himself. When authority displays its candies of all flavors and whips of all sizes, it at first misses his quiet 'No' and when it finally hears it, it does not believe."

57. Andrej Krob, personal interview, August 2011. Portions of the letter can be found in Rocamora, *Acts of Courage*, 125–30. I have used Rocamora's translation.

58. For a more complete analysis of this element of the play, see Peter Steiner, introduction, *The Beggar's Opera*, Václav Havel, trans. Paul Wilson (Ithaca, NY: Cornell University Press, 2001), ix–xxi.

59. Andrej Krob, interview on Czech television by Miroslav Masák, "Krásný ztráty," April 26, 2010.

60. A collection of photographs of the troupe can be found in *Divadlo na tahu: 1975–1995* (Prague: Originální Videojournal, 1995).

61. Eda Kriseová, personal interview, July 10, 2009.

62. Ivan and Karel Kyncl, *After the Spring Came Winter* (Stockholm: Charta 77 Foundation, 1985), 62–66.

63. Jan Tříska, personal interview, July 13, 2009.

64. Jan Tříska, personal interview, July 13, 2009.

## Chapter 9. The Solidarity of the Shaken

1. Václav Havel, *Disturbing the Peace: A Conversation with Karel Hvížďala*, trans. Paul Wilson (New York: Vintage Books, 1991), 127.

2. Eda Kriseová, *Václav Havel: The Authorized Biography* (New York: St. Martin's Press, 1993), 100.

3. Ivan Havel, letter to Josef Škvorecký, July 9, 1976, JSC.

4. See Ivan Havel, letter to Josef Škvorecký, July 9, 1976, JSC, and Josef Škvorecký, letter to Ivan Havel, July 16, 1976, JSC.

5. "A Writer on the Cultural Situation," memorandum, July 1964, RFE.

6. Josef Škvorecký, letter to Malte Hartman, October 10, 1976, JSC.

7. Václav Havel, letter to Josef Škvorecký, August 5, 1976, JSC.

8. Václav Havel, postcard to Josef Škvorecký, undated but sometime in late December 1976, JSC.

9. Michel Justin Kilburn, "The Merry Ghetto: The Czech Underground in the Time of Normalization," diss., Emory University, 2001, 293–94. Jirous was the manager of the Plastic People of the Universe; Soukup and Karásek did not play with the band but were well known in the music underground. The vulgar language in the songs included words like *hovno* and *prdel* ("shit" and "ass").

10. Havel, *Disturbing the Peace*, 128.

11. Havel's statements about the trial have received a lot of scrutiny, given that he avoided mentioning that the music was partly political. Some authors speculate that Havel found it more strategic to paint them as innocents, but a more likely possibility is that the very nature of the music underground made it easy for them to be seen in this light, both by Havel and by others who signed petitions. Bolton, for instance, argues that the term "underground" had become an "empty signifier," a sort of blank slate that allowed everyone to see what they wanted to see, and Havel saw them as essentially nonpolitical (Jonathan Bolton, *Worlds of Dissent: Charter 77, the Plastic People of the Universe, and Czech Culture under Communism* [Cambridge, MA: Harvard University Press, 2012], 141).

12. Jaroslav Seifert et al., "Letter to Heinrich Böll, August 16, 1976," reprinted in *Charter 77 and Human Rights in Czechoslovakia*, ed. H. Gordon Skilling (London: George Allen and Unwin, 1981), 199–200.

13. Michael Simmons, *The Reluctant President: A Political Life of Václav Havel* (London: Methuen, 1991), 117; Václav Havel, reminiscences given at the home of Kamila Bendová, electronic recording, date unknown [2007?].

14. Kilburn, "Merry Ghetto," 175, 300. The four musicians on trial were Ivan Jirous, who served as manager for the Plastic People of the Universe; Pavel Zajíček, who sang for DG 307; Vratislav Brabenec, who played saxophone for the Plastic People of the Universe; and Milan Hlavsa, who played for both bands.

15. Václav Havel, "The Trial," in *Open Letters: Selected Writings 1965–1990*, trans. Paul Wilson (New York: Vintage, 1992), 102–8; Kilburn, "Merry Ghetto," 301.

16. Havel, "The Trial," in *Open Letters*, 107.

17. Havel, "The Trial," in *Open Letters*, 108.

18. Havel, "The Trial," in *Open Letters*, 106–7. The reference to "emergency exits" appears to be Havel's self-understanding that his literary fame gave him a trump card that he could use in a pinch to get out of the country. He struggled with those feelings as far back as 1968, when he asked Měda Mládek to help get him out of the country, and he would continue to struggle with that possibility later, in 1978, when he was offered a chance to leave the country rather than serve a jail sentence.

19. Miloš Rejchrt, personal interview, August 3, 2011.

20. Ludvík Vaculík, "Mortal Illness," in Skilling, *Charter 77 and Human Rights in Czechoslovakia*, 238–40, and Václav Havel, "Last Conversation," in Skilling, *Charter 77 and Human Rights in Czechoslovakia*, 242–44.

21. For more on Husserl, see Edward F. Findlay, *Caring for the Soul in a Postmodern Age* (Albany: State University of New York Press, 2002), 16–22. I am indebted to Findlay's insight into Husserl and his influence on Jan Patočka.

22. Jan Sokol, personal interview, July 28, 2011; Ivan Chvatík, personal interview, August 13, 2011.

23. Ivan Chvatík, personal interview, August 13, 2011.

24. Jan Sokol, personal interview, July 28, 2011.

25. Erazin Kohák, *Jan Patočka: Philosophy and Selected Writings* (Chicago: University of Chicago Press, 1989), 3.

26. Hájek had been involved in meetings with a number of reform communists, including Zdeněk Mlynář, who had along with Hájek been a member of the inner circle of government during the Prague Spring. And it was in those meetings that he heard about the creation of Charter 77, which he was told was trying to refresh or keep alive the spirit of 1968. From Hájek's point of view, Charter 77 was built as a sort of response to the Helsinki Accords. Hájek had also been impressed with the pluralism and commitment of the group behind Charter 77 and the first document they created, which reminded him of the Magna Carta.

27. Havel, *Disturbing the Peace*, 134.

28. Havel, *Disturbing the Peace*, 135.

29. Jan Sokol, personal interview, July 28, 2011.

## Chapter 10. Death of a Philosopher

1. The Czech minister of interior, Jaromír Obzina, later said he had been getting reports of the activities of the future Charter 77 since September 1976 (see H. Gordon Skilling, *Charter 77 and Human Rights in Czechoslovakia* [London: George Allen and Unwin, 1981], 128). There is some evidence supporting his claim that the government knew of these activities. For instance, the secret police was clearly concerned that Seifert, considered the most important national poet, was attending meetings with Havel. In addition, we know that the secret police heard something about the creation of a document through their listening devices in the apartment of Pavel Kohout (see Jonathan Bolton, *Worlds of Dissent: Charter 77, the Plastic People of the Universe, and Czech Culture under Communism* [Cambridge, MA: Harvard University Press, 2012], 148). The interesting question is why the state did nothing to prevent the creation of Charter 77. One possible answer is that the very public nature of the activities meant that they did not raise an alarm. Others have speculated that the state allowed Charter 77 to proceed because it would give the state an excuse to crack down on civil liberties.

2. Tom Stoppard, "Prague: The Story of the Chartists," NYRB, August 4, 1977. Eda Kriseová reports it was the brake lines of the car that had been cut. Others have suggested the hydraulic lines of the clutch had been tampered with. The discrepancy probably relates to differing memories over the years.

3. Zdeněk Urbánek was one of Havel's most enduring friends and one of his most trusted confidantes. Havel often relied on him for such issues as providing English translations. Urbánek not only had a great deal of good sense but also unquestioned courage. During World War II, Urbánek's house had been used to hide Jews from the Nazis.

4. Vaculík later maintained he had forgotten that this was the day for launching the char-

ter, which may or may not have been true. Vaculík was a colorful eccentric, one of the most important dissidents in the country, and his forgetfulness was legendary. Conversely, he had been in charge earlier that week of preparing 242 copies of the charter, so it's probable that he came by the apartment out of a sense of adventure.

5. In reconstructing the events of January 6–7, 1977, I have relied on accounts of Kriseová and Stoppard, both of whom interviewed everyone involved. Others, such as Jonathan Bolton, have pointed out how the retelling of those days eventually turned into legend, with the details becoming embellished (see Bolton, *Worlds of Dissent*, 148–51).

6. From Pavel Landovský's interview with Karel Hvížd'ala, in *Soukromá vzpoura* (Prague: Mladá fronta, 1990), also quoted by Bolton, *Worlds of Dissent*, 149–50. I have used Bolton's translation of Landovský. Other accounts of the chase can be found in Eda Kriseová, *Václav Havel: The Authorized Biography* (New York: St. Martin's Press, 1993), 115–20, and Carol Rocamora, *Acts of Courage: Václav Havel's Life in the Theater* (Hanover, NH: Smith and Kraus, 2004), 168–69, which differ slightly.

7. Skilling, *Charter 77 and Human Rights in Czechoslovakia*, 3; Kriseová, *Václav Havel*, 169.

8. As the power of the state became more subtle and sophisticated, the ways of dealing with dissidents became more limited. Gone were the days of hanging those who disagreed with the regime. Unlike the Soviet Union, relatively few dissidents were imprisoned in mental hospitals. The initial prosecution of the dissidents involved with Charter 77 was detailed under paragraphs 98 and 112 of the criminal code, and dealt with sedition and subversion of the republic. See Skilling, *Charter 77 and Human Rights in Czechoslovakia*, 137.

9. Stoppard, "Prague: The Story of the Chartists."

10. RPR, January 12, 1977, also quoted in Kriseová, *Václav Havel*, 122.

11. Skilling, *Charter 77 and Human Rights in Czechoslovakia*, 130.

12. The story was told to Eda Kriseová in an interview and appears in Kriseová, *Václav Havel*, 120. Landovský had a penchant for tall tales, but this one seems close to other accounts.

13. The first questions in an interrogation, Klíma had once said, "are always supposed to appear innocent so that refusing them would seem to be ridiculous or even indecent." Ivan Klíma, *My Crazy Century: A Memoir*, trans. Craig Cravens (New York: Grove Press, 2013), 298. See also Skilling, *Charter 77 and Human Rights in Czechoslovakia*, 136.

14. The human rights portion of the Helsinki Accords made it inconvenient to charge Havel and Kohout with subversion of the state, as that would have made them political prisoners. The state preferred lesser charges that could be used for purposes of harassment.

15. NYT, January 11, 1977.

16. Czech copies of Charter 77 official documents can be found in many places, including online. An English translation of charter documents 9, 12, 13, 15, 18, and 21 can be found in Skilling, *Charter 77 and Human Rights in Czechoslovakia*.

17. Bolton, *Worlds of Dissent*, 156.

18. From "What the Charter Is and What It Is Not." A full text and translation of Patočka's essay can be found in Skilling, *Charter 77 and Human Rights in Czechoslovakia*, 217–19.

19. Bolton, *Worlds of Dissent*, 155.

20. Havel, *Disturbing the Peace: A Conversation with Karel Hvížd'ala*, trans. Paul Wilson

(New York: Vintage Books, 1991), 141; Michael Simmons, *The Reluctant President: A Political Life of Václav Havel* (London: Methuen, 1991), 125.

21. Ludvík Vaculík, *A Cup of Coffee with My Interrogator,* trans. George Theiner (London: Readers International, 1987), 36–39.

22. Václav Havel, "Last Conversation," in Skilling, *Charter 77 and Human Rights in Czechoslovakia,* 242–44.

23. The essay ("What We Can Expect from Charter 77") can be found in Skilling, *Charter 77 and Human Rights in Czechoslovakia,* 220–23.

24. There is a great deal of discrepancy over the actual causes of Patočka's death, sometimes listed as a heart attack and sometimes listed as a brain hemorrhage. This account is taken from Bolton, *Worlds of Dissent,* 158, and Erazim Kohák, *Jan Patočka: Philosophy and Selected Writings* (Chicago: University of Chicago Press, 1989), 3. Havel's account of his last conversation with Patočka can be found in Skilling, *Charter 77 and Human Rights in Czechoslovakia,* 242–44.

25. See Václav Havel, "Last Conversation," in Skilling, *Charter 77 and Human Rights in Czechoslovakia,* 242–44.

26. Havel, *Disturbing the Peace,* 66–67. It's not clear what books Havel meant to order when he mistakenly received the books on Faust.

27. Václav Havel, "The Power of the Powerless," in *Open Letters: Selected Writings 1965–1990,* trans. Paul Wilson (New York: Vintage, 1992), 143.

28. Havel, *Disturbing the Peace,* 66–67; Václav Havel, *Letters to Olga,* trans. Paul Wilson (New York: Henry Holt, 1989), 347–55. Havel's statement was published in *Rudé Právo,* May 21, 1977, and is also quoted in Skilling, *Charter 77 and Human Rights in Czechoslovakia,* 25.

29. Havel, *Open Letters,* 348.

30. Taken from a later account given by Landovský. See Kriseová, *Václav Havel,* 135.

31. Jan Hájek, personal interview, July 12, 2011.

32. Miloš Rejchrt, personal interview, August 3, 2011.

33. Paul Vincent, "Interview with Charter 77 Supporter Hájek," Paris Domestic Service, February 8, 1977. A similar interview was conducted with the *New York Times* on the same day.

34. One of Hájek's fiercest critics was Jan Tesař, who wrote an open letter to Hájek dated February 20, 1978. Another document, "What Next with the Charter," described Hájek as a "retarding element" in the organization. JSC.

35. Skilling, *Charter 77 and Human Rights in Czechoslovakia,* 63.

36. Skilling, *Charter 77 and Human Rights in Czechoslovakia,* 69–70; Petr Uhl, personal interview, July 25, 2011.

37. Ladislav Hejdánek, personal interview, July 13, 2011. Hejdánek distinguished between two kinds of politics. The first, "politics" (with a lowercase "p") refers to the common way politics is understood: the manipulation of power for ideological or partisan gain. The second form, "Politics" (with an uppercase "p") corresponds more or less to Patočka's idea of "care of the soul," or politics as the search for "truth" in the philosophical sense. This second sense of politics was quite influential in dissident circles. Havel's "anti-political politics" refers to the same basic idea.

## Chapter 11. Atonement

1. NYT, October 16, 1977, and October 17, 1977.

2. Miloš Rejchrt, personal interview, August 3, 2011.

3. Eda Kriseová, *Václav Havel: The Authorized Biography* (New York: St. Martin's Press, 1993), 137, and Václav Havel, *Disturbing the Peace: A Conversation with Karel Hvížďala*, trans. Paul Wilson (New York: Vintage Books, 1991), 143.

4. Václav Havel, "Reports on My House Arrest," in *Open Letters: Selected Writings 1965–1990*, trans. Paul Wilson (New York: Vintage, 1992), 216.

5. Havel, "Reports on My House Arrest," in *Open Letters*, 216.

6. Elzbieta Matynia, introduction, *An Uncanny Era: Conversations between Vaclav Havel and Adam Michnik* (New Haven, CT: Yale University Press, 2014), 9–11.

7. Matynia, *An Uncanny Era*, 11–12.

8. Kriseová, *Václav Havel*, 162.

9. Havel, "The Power of the Powerless," in *Open Letters*, 127.

10. Perhaps it would be possible to overstate Patočka's influence. Some philosophers have warned that Havel and Patočka were never close friends, and that Havel himself was not a serious philosopher. There can be little doubt, however, that Patočka's work had penetrated Havel to the core, helping to supply logical undergirding for how he saw his role as a "dissident." Patočka's words come from the last conversation between the two men, recorded in Václav Havel, "Daleko od divadla" *Spisy 4* (Prague: Torst, 2001), 636. Czech language.

11. See Havel, "Reports on My House Arrest," in *Open Letters*, 215–29.

12. An English translation can be found in Vaculík's book *A Cup of Coffee with My Interrogators* (London: Readers International, 1987), 47–51.

13. Vaculík, *Cup of Coffee with My Interrogators*, 47.

14. Vaculík, *Cup of Coffee with My Interrogators*, 50–51. It should be noted that many people, such as Ivan Klíma, did not sign Charter 77 for similar reasons. Klíma's refusal to sign created a serious issue when this was discovered by the secret police, who tried to trap him into supporting the regime. The trap was laid by planting a story in *Rudé Právo* that the police had confiscated a letter telling foreigners who wished to contact Charter 77 to do so through Ivan Klíma. The secret police apparently hoped that Klíma would complain about the news story, asking for a retraction, which would give the regime a way to ingratiate themselves. About the same time, Klíma received notice that his daughter had been accepted into college, all this despite the fact that only months earlier he had been told that it would be impossible for her to attend. In February 1977 Klíma was called in for an interrogation. He was offered a passport to travel abroad in order to see one of his plays being performed in Switzerland if he was willing "to show a little good will." Goodwill was usually code for signing a statement against Charter 77. Klíma declined the offer, saying he preferred to wait until all of his friends could get passports as well. See Ivan Klíma, *My Crazy Century: A Memoir*, trans. Craig Cravens (New York: Grove Press, 2013), 345–47.

15. Ivan Havel, personal interview, August 4, 2009.

16. The messenger, Otta Bednářová, apparently delivered a number of "underground" letters from Hrádeček. It's unclear how Havel got letters out of his house, although pre-

sumably they were given to Olga, who handed the letters off when she went into town to buy groceries.

17. Ludvík Vaculík, *Český Snář* (Prague: Atlantis, 1990), 12–17. An English-language excerpt can be found in *Cardozo Studies in Law and Literature* 2, no. 1 (Spring 1990): 25–36.

18. Vaculík, *Český Snář*, 12–17.

19. Vaculík, *Cup of Coffee with My Interrogators*, 50; Ladislav Hejdánek, personal interview, July 13, 2011.

20. Havel, "Reports on my House Arrest," in *Open Letters*, 228. Havel had a lifelong susceptibility to mood swings, which he often discussed in reflections and letters, and which were serious enough that he worried about his mental fragility. Neuro-vegetative symptoms, such as fatigue and difficulty concentrating, are common in clinical depression.

21. Havel, "Reports on my House Arrest," in *Open Letters*, 221–29.

22. NYT, October 23, 1977. Kohout was stripped of his citizenship in October 1979. The event was covered extensively by the *New York Times* on October 9, which provided an excellent analysis of his case.

23. Šabata was an ex-communist who had been a prominent supporter of the Prague Spring. He was unable to continue as spokesperson after his arrest in the fall of 1978. Kubišová asked to be relieved of her duties after discovering she was pregnant. In February 1979 Václav Benda, Jiří Dienstbier, and Zdena Tominová were "elected" spokespersons. Benda represented the anti-communists, Dienstbier was a socialist, and Tominová was a Czech novelist. Since formal elections were impossible, given the difficulty of members of the charter gathering in one place, spokespersons were appointed in informal gatherings of a few prominent members and then announced through a variety of underground communications.

24. The title of the novel is usually translated in English as *The Questionnaire*. *Dotazník* was his first novel, published in samizdat form. Part of the case against Gruša was that he had voiced a desire to have the novel published abroad, in Switzerland. This was not against the law—and, in fact, others, such as Havel, were publishing abroad as well, but Gruša was not protected by international celebrity. Later, in 1981, his citizenship would be revoked, and he would be forced to immigrate to West Germany.

25. Kamila Bendová, personal interview, July 28, 2009; Havel, "Reports on my House Arrest," in *Open Letters*, 226.

26. According to Daniel Kaiser in *Disident: Václav Havel 1936–1989* (Prague: Paseka, 2009), Havel was acquitted (142). However, it appears there may not have been a trial. See Michael Žantovský, *Havel: A Life* (New York: Grove Press, 2014), 197. Rudolf Battek, who had spent a year in jail as a result of signing the Ten Points Petition with Havel in 1968, had secured more than one hundred tickets to the ball with the idea that it would be good fun for him and his fellow dissidents to gather for a night of dancing and drinking. Havel and Landovský were apparently held on charges of disturbing the peace.

27. Kamila Bendová, personal interview, July 28, 2009.

28. Václav Havel, letter to Pavel Kohout, March 11, 1979, VHL.

29. Pavel Kohout, letter to Václav Havel, March 1979, VHL.

30. Václav Havel, letter to Pavel Kohout, March 30, 1979, VHL.

31. Kamila Bendová, personal interview, August 2009. Although police arrested ten

members of VONS, the outrage caused by those arrests resulted in twelve new members joining the organization. Such was the predicament faced by the state when deciding how best to deal with dissidents.

32. Details regarding Havel's travel bag are from Žantovský, *Havel*, 213, possibly obtained from interviews.

33. NYT, February 7, 1977: "Local informants said that the hardline members of the party's Central Committee were pressing for another crackdown—and possibly more arrests—to discourage more endorsements of Charter 77, a manifesto demanding more civil and political freedoms." At the same time, Foreign Minister Bohuslav Chňoupek was advocating for a more moderate course of action that would defuse the situation as part of his campaign to improve relations with the West.

34. The original report of the Prague trial, collected by members of VONS, runs to about three pages. The translation relies on the version published by Palach Press in London in *Freedom Appeals Newsletter*, January–February 1980, VBC.

35. Václav Havel, letter to Olga Havlová, July 25, 1982, in Václav Havel, *Letters to Olga*, trans. Paul Wilson (New York: Henry Holt, 1989), 348.

36. Kriseová, *Václav Havel*, 96; Ivan Havel, personal interview, August 4, 2009.

37. Joseph Papp, letter to Edward Kukan, charge d'affaires of the Czech embassy, August 14, 1979, JPC.

38. See Kaiser, *Disident*, 167, and Pavel Kosatík, *Člověk má dělat to, nač má sílu* (Prague: Mladá Fronta, 2008), 147. To Eva Kantůrková, Olga said that she wouldn't advise anyone in such a similar situation. She didn't know how she herself would react. See Eva Kantůrková, "Je něco Jistě?" in *Index Koln* (Prague: BDR, 1980), 5–7. Czech language.

39. The idea that "undeserved privilege" played a role in Havel's thinking comes from Michael Žantovský, who came to know Havel well in the 1980s and during his presidency. See Žantovský, *Havel*, 214.

40. Havel, "Daleko od divadla," 636.

41. As Havel told Olga, he had his unresolved ambivalences. Perhaps he had a choice to leave—but it was never clear what that would involve or in what ways asking to leave prison might be used against him. Havel resolved, therefore, to remain in the country, saying, "I am a country bumpkin and I will stay one" (letter to Olga Havlová, January 12, 1980, in Havel, *Letters to Olga*, 68).

## Chapter 12. In the Dark

1. Václav Havel, unpublished letter to Olga Havlová, June 19, 1979, VHL. The full text of this letter is not available in *Letters to Olga*, as some of the more personal remarks are left out.

2. Václav Havel, letter to Olga Havlová, August 11, 1979, reprinted in Václav Havel, *Letters to Olga*, trans. Paul Wilson (New York: Henry Holt, 1989), 31–32. He mentions his "mental fitness" in at least three other letters: February 3, 1980, March 8, 1980, and May 30, 1981.

3. Václav Havel, letter to Olga Havlová, March 8, 1980, reprinted in Havel, *Letters to Olga*, 76–77.

4. *Prison Conditions in Czechoslovakia: A Helsinki Watch Report* (New York: Human Rights Watch, 1989), 19.

5. Charter 77, document #16.

6. *Prison Conditions in Czechoslovakia*, 1.

7. Eda Kriseová, *Václav Havel: The Authorized Biography* (New York: St. Martin's Press, 1993), 193. This was presumably based on interviews with Havel undertaken while he was still president. Havel himself broached this subject in three of the letters he wrote Olga from prison: April 13, 1980 (Havel, *Letters to Olga*, 81–83), September 21, 1980 (110–12), and March 14, 1981 (173–76).

8. Václav Havel, letter to Olga Havlová, September 21, 1980, in Havel, *Letters to Olga*, 110–12.

9. Václav Havel, letter to Olga Havlová, September 8, 1979, in Havel, *Letters to Olga*, 36. The state of Havel's hemorrhoids was a common theme in his letters from prison. Eventually, he would need surgery for the condition.

10. Havel seemed to enjoy the roommate assigned to him in pretrial detention, at least in the first weeks. He disliked the cellmate he received after moving to prison in Ostrava. None of the names of his cellmates are provided in his letters.

11. Václav Havel, letter to Olga Havlová, August 11, 1979, in Havel, *Letters to Olga*, 32–33.

12. Věra Vojtová, Ph.D., *Problematika uplatňování programu*, Diplomová práce, Masarykova univerzita, Brno 2006. Czech language dissertation.

13. Havel, *Disturbing the Peace: A Conversation with Karel Hvížďala*, trans. Paul Wilson (New York: Vintage Books, 1991), 148–49.

14. Prison report of Václav Havel, January 22, 1980, VHL. The report includes some information that seems to have been added later, perhaps in September 1981 in Plzeň, but most of the report was clearly created in Heřmanice. The psychological profile is signed by Lt. Bohumil Dytko and Lt. Jana Čapčová and dated January 15, 1980. The profile contains an interesting fact, which is that Havel apparently visited a psychiatric ward for diagnosis as a youth, although he was not admitted as a patient. It is unclear what episode in his life Havel was referring to. This might, perhaps, have occurred while he was in the army, either as part of a required examination or as a result of an incident. Otherwise, it would likely have been known to family and friends.

15. Pavel Kosatík, *Člověk má dělat to, nač má sílu* (Prague: Mladá Fronta, 2008), 154–58.

16. A collection of Havel's letters from prison first appeared shortly after his release as a typewritten edition of about a dozen samizdat copies that were circulated among dissidents. Within five years, *Letters to Olga* (as the book became known) was translated and published in English.

17. Václav Havel, letter to Olga Havlová, July 26, 1981, in Havel, *Letters to Olga*, 208–10. It should be noted that this was at least his second period of solitary confinement while in prison. Havel rarely spoke openly about the effects of being locked in isolation. The psychological effects on some prisoners were excruciating, since one result of solitary confinement is to deny the normal sensory input needed for peace of mind.

18. Václav Havel, letter to Olga Havlová, September 19, 1981, in Havel, *Letters to Olga*, 229–31.

19. Václav Havel, letter to Olga Havlová, September 26, 1981, in Havel, *Letters to Olga*, 232–34.

20. Václav Havel, letter to Olga Havlová, September 26, 1981, in Havel, *Letters to Olga*, 232–34.

21. Václav Havel, letter to Olga Havlová, September 26, 1981, in Havel, *Letters to Olga*, 232–34.

22. Václav Havel, letter to Olga Havlová, October 3, 1981, in Havel, *Letters to Olga*, 235–38.

23. Václav Havel, letter to Olga Havlová, October 3, 1981, in Havel, *Letters to Olga*, 235–38.

24. Václav Havel, letter to Olga Havlová, August 1, 1981, in Havel, *Letters to Olga*, 213–17.

25. Václav Havel, letter to Olga Havlová, August 15, 1981, in Havel, *Letters to Olga*, 214–18.

26. Václav Havel, letter to Olga Havlová, August 15, 1981, in Havel, *Letters to Olga*, 214–18. "I would even venture to say," he wrote Olga, "that the more 'serious' and time consuming the actuality that lends meaning to life, the more terrifying the emptiness that follows it."

27. Ivan Havel, personal interview, August 5, 2011; Václav Havel, letter to Olga Havlová, December 12, 1981, in Havel, *Letters to Olga*, 256–59.

28. Václav Havel, letters to Olga Havlová, December 31, 1979 (in Havel, *Letters to Olga*, 59–64), and December 21, 1980 (137–42).

29. Václav Havel, unpublished letter to Olga Havlová, November 13, 1982, VHL. In the letter, Havel specifically asked Olga to keep the letter private. Nor was it published with his other prison letters. Presumably, Havel was still extremely sensitive to any suggestion that he might "make a deal" with the state in order to seek leniency or have his sentence commuted.

30. Václav Havel, unpublished letter to Olga Havlová, November 13, 1982, VHL. Havel also discusses this incident in Havel, *Disturbing the Peace*, 158–59.

31. Václav Havel, unpublished letter to Olga Havlová, November 13, 1982, VHL.

32. Václav Havel, letter to Olga Havlová, March 20, 1982, in Havel, *Letters to Olga*, 300–303.

33. See Václav Havel, "I Take the Side of Truth: An Interview with Antoine Spire," in *Open Letters: Selected Writings 1965–1990*, trans. Paul Wilson (New York: Vintage, 1992), 240. Shortly after being released from prison in 1983, Havel said that the aim of prison was not just "to deprive a man of a few years of his life" but "to mark him for life, destroy his personality, score his heart in such a way that it would never heal completely."

34. Václav Havel, letter to Olga Havlová, September 4, 1982, in Havel, *Letters to Olga*, 372–76.

## Chapter 13. Homecoming

1. An account of Havel's final illness in prison can be found in Václav Havel, *Disturbing the Peace: A Conversation with Karel Hvížďala*, trans. Paul Wilson (New York: Vintage Books, 1991). 159–61. I have hewn closely to Havel's account since there are few records of the event. Among other things, Havel had health issues with his lungs, perhaps as the result of his addiction to cigarettes.

2. Havel sent at least two letters to Olga while in the hospital, on January 30 and February 5, 1982. The first letter described his alarming symptoms, including a very high temperature. By February 5, however, his condition began to improve due to large doses of antibiotics. The second letter, when he was recovering, contains a short description of an erotic dream he had of Anna Kohoutová, the woman he was with when arrested and sent to prison. Copies of the unpublished letters can be found at VHL.

3. Havel, *Disturbing the Peace*, 160.

4. One of many examples was a literary festival in Avignon, France, on July 21 1982, celebrating Havel's work. The program was attended by both Samuel Beckett and Arthur Miller. Before and after the performance, postcards were given to members of the audience that could be sent to authorities in Czechoslovakia demanding Havel's release. There were several such campaigns in Great Britain, the United States, and Canada in the 1980s.

5. Havel discussed these experiences thoroughly in a letter to Pavel Kohout, March 7, 1987, VHL.

6. Havel, *Disturbing the Peace*, 162.

7. Eda Kriseová, personal interview, July 10, 2009.

8. Eda Kriseová, personal interview, July 10, 2009.

9. Kamila Bendová, personal interview, August 2009. This was no idle suggestion by the Bendas. In fact, Václav Benda followed his own advice, serving as spokesman himself after getting out of prison, which certainly required a great deal of courage.

10. Václav Havel, letter to Pavel Kohout, March 7, 1987, VHL. It's probably accurate to say that this split was also felt internally. Although Havel identified with the man who no longer wanted to participate in Charter 77, he also clearly felt an inner moral demand to rejoin the group, which he experienced as the judgmental eyes of his friends.

11. Václav Havel, letter to Pavel Kohout, March 7, 1983. Havel did write a short, one-act play titled *Mistake* that he dedicated to Samuel Beckett. Beckett had dedicated a play to Havel the previous year, which was written as part of a festival in Avignon, France, and was put on in support of Havel. Havel's one-act play *Mistake* was written for an event at the Charter 77 Foundation in Stockholm, probably to raise money for Czech dissidents.

12. Pavel Kosatík, *Člověk má dělat to, nač má sílu* (Prague: Mladá Fronta, 2008), 244. The "new situation" between the Havels has been reported in a number of places, but many of the accounts are based on secondhand descriptions from friends.

13. For an example of her psychological interpretations of Havel's life, see Václav Havel, letter to Jitka Vodňanská, November 17, 1983, VHL.

14. Jitka Vodňanská, *Voda, která hoří* (Prague: Torst, 2018), 159.

15. Vodňanská, *Voda, která hoří*, 159–65.

16. Vodňanská, *Voda, která hoří*, 148, 165.

17. Vodňanská, *Voda, která hoří*, 166.

18. Vodňanská, *Voda, která hoří*, 285.

19. Václav Havel, letter to Jitka Vodňanská, October 20, 1983, quoted in Vodňanská, *Voda, která hoří*, 172.

20. Vodňanská, *Voda, která hoří*, 311–12.

21. Vodňanská, *Voda, která hoří*, 189.

22. John Keane, *Václav Havel: A Political Tragedy in Six Acts* (London: Bloomsbury,

1999), 313. It's unclear if Keane saw this letter. Jitka Vodňanská has not released this and many other letters to any archive, citing their personal nature.

23. Vodňanská, *Voda, která hoří*, 193.

24. Jitka Vodňanská, "Velká láska Václava Havla: Psychoterapeutka Jitka Vodňanská," IDNES, February 18, 2013. Czech language.

25. Havel, *Disturbing the Peace*, 155–56.

26. The photograph is dated July 8, 1983. A note by Havel at the bottom reads (in Czech), "As you can see, I'm quite drunk." JSC.

27. Vodňanská, *Voda, která hoří*, 179.

28. Václav Havel, letter to potential contributors, January 28, 1984, JSC.

29. Václav Havel, letter to Josef Škvorecký, undated but probably December 1983, JSC. After given the go-ahead, Havel wrote a letter to potential contributors on January 28, 1984, in which he explained the project further: "When I was in prison, radically cut off from all of the values, happiness and distractions of life, without friends, books, music, art, discussion, pubs, surrounded with only ugly walls, I was basically forced, like most of my friends who were in similar situations, to think more and focus more on things of a higher nature, about whether my dark stay in prison had any meaning, and about the basic questions of existence. In short, I started to philosophize." He wrote that after he was released from prison, he began surveying the field of Czech philosophy, whereupon he developed the impression that if there was one book missing, it was a survey of current philosophy for the general reader. Havel decided to organize the book himself.

30. The book was published in a variety of languages and first appeared in English, under the title *Letters to Olga*, in 1988.

31. Lopatka has spoken about the process of editing *Letters to Olga* in a number of places but perhaps nowhere as clear as in the interview that is reported in Eda Kriseová, *Václav Havel: The Authorized Biography* (New York: St. Martin's Press, 1993), 195–97.

32. This memory is by way of a neighbor, Andulka Freimanová-Krobová, wife of Andrej Krob, quoted in Kriseová, *Václav Havel*, 190.

33. Kriseová's letter does not appear to be preserved in the archives. It is reprinted in full, however, in Kriseová, *Václav Havel*, 197–201. The reference to Patočka and Heidegger is an obvious admission that in almost all of Havel's books is a reflection of the phenomenological ideas that Patočka introduced to intellectual life in Czechoslovakia. It was partly through the efforts of Patočka that Czech intellectuals began reading Heidegger.

34. Věra Blackwell, letter to Tom Stoppard, September 28, 1983, TSC.

35. Tom Stoppard mentions the dream in a letter to Václav Havel, May 29, 1985, TSC.

36. Havel discusses the idea of writing a play with Tom Stoppard in a letter to Josef Škvorecký, December 1983, JSC.

37. Josef Škvorecký, letter to Václav Havel, January 28, 1984, JSC.

38. Václav Havel, letter to Josef Škvorecký, January 6, 1984. Škvorecký brought up the issue again in letters of February 24 and May 25, 1984, JSC.

## Chapter 14. Jitka

1. Eda Kriseová, personal interview, July 10, 2009.

2. Václav Havel, correspondence with Josef Škvorecký, undated but perhaps De-

cember 1983. Havel also mentions that he hadn't liked the previous book he'd read by Kundera, but it's not clear which novel he was referring to.

3. "Tom Stoppard—Interview," typed notes/questions of Věra Blackwell in preparation of the radio interview with Tom Stoppard, undated, VBC. It's unclear what Blackwell meant by the poetic phrase "the moon has been messed up by men," but it seems to allude to the idea that humanity has disordered the natural arrangement of things—an idea Havel certainly shared.

4. Václav Havel, letter to Tom Stoppard, May 29, 1984, TSC. The letter is typewritten in English. Havel probably wrote the letter in Czech and had it translated by Zdeněk Urbánek or another friend. Although Stoppard was born in Czechoslovakia, he apparently does not speak Czech. All of the written correspondence between Stoppard and Havel is in English.

5. Jitka Vodňanská, *Voda, která hoří* (Prague: Torst, 2018) 150. Czech language.

6. Václav Havel, letter to Pavel Landovský, March 16, 1986, VHL.

7. See Václav Havel, *Disturbing the Peace: A Conversation with Karel Hvížďala*, trans. Paul Wilson (New York: Vintage Books, 1991), 64. Jitka briefly wrote about the moment she and Olga first heard the play, but her emotional reactions are unusually opaque. See Jitka Vodňanská, *Voda, která hoří*, 205.

8. Jitka Vodňanská, "Velká láska Václava Havla: Psychoterapeutka Jitka Vodňanská," IDNES, February 18, 2013. Carol Rocamora in *Acts of Courage: Václav Havel's Life in the Theater* (Hanover, NH: Smith and Kraus, 2004), 229, suggests that Havel wrote *Largo Desolato* in Prague, which is almost certainly wrong. Not only does it contradict the memories of Vodňanská, but she almost never stayed over with the Havels in the Prague apartment because there was little extra room. In Havel, *Disturbing the Peace*, 64, Havel does not mention where the play was written, but he tended to write in Hrádeček and not in Prague, where he was faced with continuous distractions.

9. Václav Havel, letter to Věra Blackwell, [date uncertain], VBC.

10. Stoppard started working on an adaptation in November 1984, just after receiving a Czech script, either sent directly from Havel, or, more probably, a manuscript from Havel's literary agent, Klaus Juncker. With Stoppard's encouragement, the National Theater funded what was called a "literal translation," which was sent directly to Stoppard, who promised to write a "performance text," although this was strictly on a contingency basis. As Stoppard wrote to Kenneth Tynan in a letter dated December 13, 1984 (TSC): "I have not been commissioned by anybody to do a text but I am quite happy to do it anyway. It will be a faithful translation and will not take long." However, the project proved to be a great deal of work, since he didn't speak Czech. On February 25 Stoppard wrote Tynan that the play was at a typist for a second time, and that he had "changed my mind in about 200 places" as a result of having to consider two or three alternatives for the translation of each line. In March he met with Karel Hubka, a Czech scholar working at an English university, to go over Stoppard's adaptation and compare it to Havel's original to see what nuances he might have missed. The entire process wasn't completed until June, when a press conference was held to announce the premiere of *Largo Desolato* in London.

11. Eda Kriseová, *Václav Havel: The Authorized Biography* (New York: St. Martin's Press, 1993), 216.

12. Václav Havel, correspondence with Pavel Kohout, April 11, 1986, VHL.

13. Havel, *Disturbing the Peace*, 67. Havel appears to have tried to write a play on the Faust theme once in 1978 and perhaps again after leaving prison. However, he also spent considerable time during his prison term fiddling with the play before deciding there were too many distractions in his cell to write.

14. Havel discussed his shame, and the way he fell into a Faustian bargain in two letters from prison. See his letters to Olga Havlová, July 25, 1982 (from which the quote is taken), and July 31, 1982, in Havel, *Letters to Olga*, trans. Paul Wilson (New York: Henry Holt, 1989), 347–56.

15. Václav Havel, correspondence with Ivan Havel, June 4, 1979, VHL.

16. There are a number of letters written by Havel while in prison that deal with the theme of writing a Faust play. In reconstructing these passages, I have relied on letters to Olga Havlová of June 4, July 8, July 21, and September 22, 1979, VHL.

17. The director of *Temptation* was Roger Michell, who visited Prague with actor John Shrapnel. Information about the visit was taken, among other sources, from a detailed account provided by Shrapnel in a letter sent to Tom Stoppard, November 11, 1987, TSC.

18. John Shrapnel, "Iron Curtain Up," unpublished manuscript, date unknown but probably 1987, VBC.

19. *Christian Science Monitor*, May 31, 1987.

20. *Daily Telegraph*, May 2, 1987; *London Times*, May 31, 1987.

21. Jitka Vodňanská, "Velká láska Václava Havla: Psychoterapeutka Jitka Vodňanská," IDNES, February 18, 2013.

22. Vodňanská, "Velká láska Václava Havla."

23. Kriseová, *Václav Havel*, 209. Havel almost always responded to the secret police with an extra dose of gentlemanly courtesy. Once on a cold winter morning at Hrádeček, for instance, he had taken two cups of cocoa to the agents outside his house, who had been ordered to watch his every activity.

24. Kriseová, *Václav Havel*, 213. Michael Žantovský, who interviewed Jitka Vodňanská, reports that about three hundred police officers had been involved in the operation of following Havel around the country.

25. Jeri Laber, notes, January 16, 1986, HRW.

26. Václav Havel, letters to Jitka Vodňanská, August 28, 1985, and August 29, 1985, Jitka Vodňanská, *Voda, která hoří*, 270.

27. Václav Havel, letter to Jitka Vodňanská, undated, Jitka Vodňanská, *Voda, která hoří*, 326.

28. Jitka Vodňanská, *Voda, která hoří*, 285.

29. Václav Havel, letters to Jitka Vodňanská, August 28, 1985, and August 29, 1985, Jitka Vodňanská, *Voda, která hoří*, 270.

30. Jitka Vodňanská, *Voda, která hoří*, 351.

31. *Revolver Review* was hardly alone. A young rock musician named František Stárek was jailed in 1979 for publishing *Vokno*, an information bulletin for those sympathetic to Charter 77. After being released, Stárek immediately conspired to steal a mimeograph machine. A friend at a state repair store brought him the entire machine, smuggling it out one small piece at a time and then helping Stárek reassemble it in his basement over two days (Frantisek Stárek, personal interview, July 12, 2009).

32. Václav Havel, "Six Asides about Culture," in *Open Letters: Selected Writings 1965–1990*, trans. Paul Wilson (New York: Vintage, 1992), 282.

33. Havel, "Six Asides about Culture," in *Open Letters*, 276.

34. Václav Havel, letter to Věra Blackwell, August 10, 1984, VBC.

35. Interviewed during the success of *Temptation*, Havel put it this way: "Perhaps I have found through this play a new starting point."

36. Travel diary of Josef Papp, Joseph Papp Collection, New York Public Library. On Sunday, after driving to Hrádeček, Ivan drove the Papps back to Prague by car for a meeting with Zdeněk Urbánek and a late dinner with the American ambassador.

## Chapter 15. The Open Door

1. John Kohan, "Soviets: Ending an Era of Drift," *Time*, March 25, 1985. Yuri Andropov died in 1984 while still general secretary of the Communist Party. He wanted to be succeeded by Gorbachev but instead the Politburo gave the job to Konstantin Chernenko, even though he was terminally ill at the time. *Perestroika* referred to restructuring Soviet society, including economic and political reforms. *Glosnost*, which means "openness," was the new policy of allowing political and social issues to be discussed.

2. NYT, November 23, 1987.

3. Gorbachev visited Czechoslovakia in 1987. Despite the fact that Gorbachev had been promoting his reforms, known under the terms of *perestroika* and *glasnost*, he gave his full endorsement to the regime in Czechoslovakia, one of the most repressive in Eastern Europe. Havel discusses seeing Gorbachev in his short essay "Meeting Gorbachev," which first appeared in English in *Granta* (Spring 1988). The essay can also be found in Václav Havel, *Open Letters: Selected Writings 1965–1990*, trans. Paul Wilson (New York: Vintage, 1992), 351–54.

4. Havel, "Anatomy of Reticence," in *Open Letters*, 300.

5. NYT, June 19, 1990.

6. Karel Hvížďala, personal interview, June 13, 2011.

7. Paul Wilson, "preface" to Václav Havel, *Disturbing the Peace: A Conversation with Karel Hvížďala*, trans. Paul Wilson (New York: Vintage Books, 1991), vii–ix. The reference to cigarettes and whiskey comes from the personal interview with Hvížďala.

8. In Czech, the book had been published under the title *Dálkový výslech*, which could be translated as "Long Distance Interrogation." This was a play on the fact that Hvížďala and Havel were conversing across the Iron Curtain, as well as on the ironic sense of the conversation being one more door of interrogation, this time by a journalist rather than a member of the secret police. When it was published in English, the editors at Knopf wanted a sexier title, settling on *Disturbing the Peace*, which seemed to capture the nature of what Havel had been doing all those years as a dissident.

9. Karel Hvížďala, personal interview, June 13, 2011. In England, the book was published by Rozmluvy, a Czech émigré publishing venture.

10. The anecdote regarding strangers comes from Marie Winn, "The Czechs' Defiant Playwright," *New York Times Magazine*, October 25, 1987. I've tried to capture the mood in something close to Havel's own words, which Winn reports as this: "Sometimes I'll go somewhere, say to an office to pay a bill and someone will read the name written there and exclaim, 'Is that really you?' And I'll say 'Well, yes, it's me,' and he'll say, 'But are

you our Václav Havel?' And then he'll clasp my hand or embrace me. It's not that these people are necessarily familiar with my writings—they just know about me from the Voice of America or BBC, they know that I'm in trouble with the regime, and they like me for that.'" Other dissidents, such as Kamila Bendová, have reported similar kindnesses from the public, such as bureaucrats and clerks who provided special favors with a wink.

11. Winn, "Czechs' Defiant Playwright."

12. Winn, "Czechs' Defiant Playwright"; Marie Winn, personal correspondence with the author, June 3, 2009.

13. Winn, "Czechs' Defiant Playwright."

14. Winn, "Czechs' Defiant Playwright."

15. Malte Hartmann of Rowahlt Verlag, correspondence with Tom Stoppard, July 27, 1988, TSC. Stoppard later backed out of doing an adaptation for *Redevelopment* for reasons that aren't clear. The world premiere took place in Zurich, presumably in a German translation. The first English-language premiere of *Redevelopment* took place at the Orange Tree Theater in England in 1990, some months after the Velvet Revolution.

16. Václav Havel, correspondence with František Janouch, September 6, 1986.

17. Jan Tříska, personal interview, July 13, 2009.

18. Office of the President of Radio Free Europe, memorandum, December 1, 1986, RFE. Havel religiously listened to Radio Free Europe. A number of his friends who had emigrated, such as Josef Škvorecký, could regularly be heard on the radio. In 1988, as part of reforms, the government stopped jamming foreign radio broadcasts.

19. Jonathan Bolton, *Worlds of Dissent: Charter 77, the Plastic People of the Universe, and Czech Culture under Communism* (Cambridge, MA: Harvard University Press, 2012), 266–67.

20. Petr Pithart, *Devětaosmdesátý* (Prague: Academia, 2009), 20–34, quoted in Bolton, *Worlds of Dissent*, 273.

21. NYT, March 14, 1987.

22. Notes of Jeri Laber from January 15, 1987, HRW.

23. George Weigel, *The Final Revolution: The Resistance Church and the Collapse of Communism* (Oxford: Oxford University Press, 1992), 169–70.

24. Tina Rosenberg, *The Haunted Land: Facing Europe's Ghosts after Communism* (New York: Random House, 1995), 160.

25. NYT, February 23, 1988. Talks were between the nine-member editorial board and the government. Government lawyers said a major obstacle was a legal requirement that only organizations belonging to the National Front—the Communist-dominated political alliance—may publish newspapers.

26. The anecdote comes from Karel Schwarzenberg, whom Havel called in Vienna to tell the story. It is reported in Michael Žantovský, *Havel: A Life* (New York: Grove Press, 2014), 275, and seems to accurately capture the change in mood in Eastern Europe just before the collapse of communism across all of Eastern Europe.

27. *Human Rights in Czechoslovakia* (New York: Human Rights Watch, 1989), 3.

28. Notes of Jeri Laber, undated, along with a translation of the letter from the mayor of Prague, Zdeněk Hořčík, Jeri Laber files, HRW.

29. Vilém Přečan was a historian collecting and promoting all of the various exile and samizdat literature being produced by exiles in a half-dozen countries, the most

important being Josef Škvorecký's 68 Publishers in Toronto, Pavel Tigrid's Svědectví in Paris, Jiří Pelikan's Listy in Rome, and Jan Kavan's Palach Press in London. Along with the underground presses inside Czechoslovakia, these were a formidable opposition to the communist regime.

30. The Tom Stoppard Prize was established in 1984, and Stoppard reluctantly allowed his name to be attached to the cash reward he provided, six hundred British pounds per year. The prize committee originally consisted of Havel and four others. In 1985 they awarded the prize to Eva Kantůrková for her book *My Friends in the House of Sorrow* and to Zdeněk Urbánek for his *Big Heart*.

31. Eda Kriseová, *Václav Havel: The Authorized Biography* (New York: St. Martin's Press, 1993), 220–25.

32. Žantovský, *Havel*, 251. The deputy foreign minister was Jaromír Johanes.

33. NYT, December 10, 1988; NYT, December 11, 1988. Although the state allowed Havel to visit with the French president, the press reported that Alexander Dubček had been placed under house arrest in order to prevent him from attending.

34. Václav Havel, *To the Castle and Back*, trans. Paul Wilson (New York: Knopf, 2007), 37; Michael Simmons, *The Reluctant President: A Political Life of Václav Havel* (London: Methuen, 1991), 170; Žantovský, *Havel*, 278.

## Chapter 16. The Magic Lantern

1. Quoted in Eda Kriseová, *Václav Havel: The Authorized Biography* (New York: St. Martin's Press, 1993), 233. The anonymous author of the suicide note has to my knowledge never been identified.

2. The account is from an eyewitness, Rob McRae, who worked in the Canadian embassy. See his book *Resistance and Revolution: Václav Havel's Czechoslovakia* (Ottawa: Carleton University Press, 1997), 22. McRae was a friend of Havel's brother, Ivan, and a close ally of a number of dissidents.

3. Accounts of the event differ slightly. I have relied here on Michael Žantovský, *Havel: A Life* (New York: Grove Press, 2014), 235, and Kriseová, *Václav Havel*, 234, both of whom appear to have discussed this event directly with Havel. McRae has Havel with his friends laying the wreaths for Havel; this is also the account from international newspapers (see NYT, January 22, 1989), which reported that Havel and twelve other dissidents were arrested after trying to lay flowers in memory of Palach, but accounts from both Havel and his brother, Ivan, make it clear that Havel either couldn't reach that part of the square, because of the police or the crowd, or had decided it was not worth the risk.

4. Žantovský, *Havel*, 284. Michael Žantovský, who was in most of the demonstrations in January, later wrote that the psychology of the crowds began to shift after the first few events. According to Žantovský, "the number of protesters who risked being hit over their heads or splashed down the pavement by water cannons" grew to a stable five thousand to ten thousand people whose courage seemed to grow after each event.

5. NYT, February 26, 1989. Earlier that month, Olga herself said that her husband's situation was much improved. "The situation this year has been different from the 1970s because in Russia there is Gorbachev" (NYT, February 5, 1979).

6. McRae, *Resistance and Revolution*, 29. McRae was prevented from attending the

trial as an international observer. At the time, the Canadian embassy was pressuring the Czechoslovakian government to honor the rights guaranteed to all citizens under new additions to the Helsinki Accords.

7. Kriseová, *Václav Havel*, 239.

8. Freimanová was the wife of Andrej Krob, who had worked with Havel at the Theater on the Balustrade, and, moreover, had directed the underground production of *Beggar's Opera*. Freimanová originally brought up the idea of starting a signature campaign to free Havel from prison with Sergej and Drahuna Machonín, Zdeněk Urbánek, and Karel Kraus.

9. NYT, February 23, 1989.

10. NYT, March 22, 1989.

11. Kriseová, *Václav Havel*, 238–39. Křižan would later play a role in the subsequent campaign around a text known as "A Few Sentences." His family had a tragic history, his father having been executed for treason during the show trials of 1951. During the Velvet Revolution of 1989, Křižan helped found Civic Forum and later became an advisor to President Havel. The word *"strukturáks"* comes from Kriseová.

12. NYT, May 18, 1989.

13. McRae, *Resistance and Revolution*, 42. McRae was in a position to know of Dubček's visit since he saw Havel a few days after this event.

14. Jiří Wolf and Stuart Rawlings, *Good Soldier Wolf: One Man's Struggle for Freedom in Czechoslovakia* (New York: University Press of America, 1994), 87–88. Wolf suggested that "there must have been a thousand people" in Havel's apartment during the party. Eda Kriseová, who was surely at the party, also reported more than a thousand guests. This may be an exaggeration, given the size of the apartment and building. The statements by the Polish dissident come from NYT, May 23, 1989.

15. McRae, *Resistance and Revolution*, 42.

16. Václav Havel, Jiří Křižan, and Alexander Vondra, "A Few Sentences," VHL. Here are the seven demands of the petition: (1) immediate release of all political prisoners, (2) that freedom of assembly ceases to be limited, (3) that various independent initiatives cease to be criminalized, (4) that the media and all forms of cultural activity be relieved of political manipulation, (5) that the justified demands of all religious citizens be respected, (6) that all planned projects be immediately presented for evaluation by experts and the public, and (7) that free discussion be established about mistakes made during the 1950s, the Prague Spring, and the subsequent normalization.

17. See Kriseová, *Václav Havel*, 241–43. A number of sources, including documents in the Radio Free Europe archive, refer to the teletype sent to communist officials, but it's unclear if the original still exists.

18. NYT, October 23, 1989. Havel was apparently picked up at least once for interrogation during the late summer of 1989 and warned that he would be returned to prison if he didn't cease his political activities. The threat may have made him more cautious, but it didn't stop his work in the petition campaign.

19. McRae, *Resistance and Revolution*, 72. The comment was tape recorded by a sympathetic member of the communist press and replayed on Radio Free Europe, making him look clownish. In the past, Jakeš had been considered a pragmatist. He had been promoted in his position in 1987 in response to the changing times. However, he also played an important role in helping crush the reforms of the Prague Spring.

20. NYT, September 2, 1989. Formally known as the German Democratic Republic, East Germany was a fellow member of the Eastern Bloc with a repressive system of communism similar to Czechoslovakia. For a thorough analysis of the crisis, see McRae, *Resistance and Revolution*, 63–70. The historian Timothy Garton Ash, in *The Magic Lantern: The Revolution of '89 Witnessed in Warsaw, Budapest, Berlin and Prague* (New York: Random House, 1990), provides an excellent analysis of the crises in Hungary (47–60) as well as an account of the fall of the Berlin Wall in East Germany (61–77).

21. McRae, *Resistance and Revolution*, 47.

22. The *New Yorker*, known for its exquisite fact-checking, reported that some five hundred students were making their way down Národní Třída when they were attacked. Eyewitness such as McRae put the number at fifteen thousand. Kriseová, who participated in part of the march doesn't give the number in attendance, but accounts from individuals like Ivan Havel, who participated in the walk and was arrested, indicate it was an extremely large crowd. Thus it would appear that the *New Yorker* report on the size of the crowd referred to the time the march came through downtown Prague, after which it grew dramatically larger. The confusion over the reporting represents the nature of the revolutionary times, making hard information extremely difficult to come by. The students began their walk at Charles University, before going to Vyšehrad Cemetery. There is some debate over whether they had originally planned to march to Wenceslas Square.

23. This comes from Žantovský, *Havel*, 296–97, who got the information from an interview with Ms. Vodňanská.

24. From an interview with Ivan Havel in Michael Long, *Making History: Czech Voices of Dissent and the Revolution of 1989* (Oxford: Rowman and Littlefield, 2005), 29–30. I've supplemented the information with information from Ivan Havel, personal interview, August 5, 2011, as well as McRae, who was also an eyewitness. Ivan and Václav Havel were still living together at this time, and Ivan became heavily involved in the Civic Forum movement, more as a witness than a political participant. Also attending the news conference were Rita Klímová, who served as interpreter, Ivan Havel, and Michael Žantovský.

25. Ash, *Magic Lantern*, 85.

26. Ash, *Magic Lantern*, 86–88. As far as the nondemocratic nature of Civic Forum, Ivan Havel told Long that "it was a very revolutionary situation, where decisions were more or less made in a nondemocratic way. Somebody had an idea and immediately realized it without discussing it with others. And then sometimes we spent hours and hours with discussion of some issue and we lost time. It was almost a unanimous consent, that we cannot make democratic, I mean, on a micro level; micro-decisions cannot be made by some group of people discussing" (31). The point was that Civic Forum did not have the time or structure to make every decision on a democratic basis.

27. Ash, *Magic Lantern*, 90.

28. Amos Elon, "Prague Autumn," *New Yorker*, January 22, 1990, 125. There were constant rumors of troops marching toward Prague in the first week of the revolution, and it was known that some party leaders were in favor of unleashing the People's Militia, the private army of the Communist Party.

29. The idea is borrowed from Elon, who suggests that communist leaders were in a

situation akin to an ultraconservative cardinal being told that the pope had converted to Judaism ("Prague Autumn," 130).

30. Elon, "Prague Autumn," 126.

31. Petr Stránský, personal interview, July 7, 2011. The information comes from telephone conversations that Stránský had with Olga. The vitamins were sent by émigrés who now lived in Western Europe.

32. Paul Wilson, "Introduction," in Havel, *Disturbing the Peace: A Conversation with Karel Hvížďala*, trans. Paul Wilson (New York: Vintage Books, 1991).

33. Elon, "Prague Autumn," 131.

34. Ash, *Magic Lantern*, 78. As for coining the term "Velvet Revolution," this is sometimes misattributed to Rita Klímová, who served as the translator for Civic Forum. Klímová, however, pointed out that she heard the term first from Havel. See Jeri Labor Files, typed notes on Rita Klímová, HRW.

35. Žantovský, *Havel*, 312.

36. See Havel, "New Year's Address," in *Open Letters: Selected Writings 1965–1990*, trans. Paul Wilson (New York: Vintage, 1992), 390–96.

37. Havel, *To the Castle and Back*, trans. Paul Wilson (New York: Knopf, 2007), 58–59.

### Chapter 17. The Corridors of Power

1. Václav Havel, "A Farewell to Politics," address at the Graduate Center of City University, New York City, September 19, 2002, reprinted in NYRB, October 24, 2002.

2. Václav Havel, address at Hebrew University, April 26, 1990, reprinted in *The Art of the Impossible: Politics as Morality in Practice* (New York: Fromm International, 1997), 29–31.

3. Address to the Joint Session of US Congress, Washington DC, February 21, 1990, reprinted in Havel, *Art of the Impossible*, 10–20.

4. Václav Havel, *To the Castle and Back*, trans. Paul Wilson (New York: Knopf, 2007), 142–43.

5. NYT, February 22, 1990.

6. NYT, February 23, 1990.

7. NYT, February 23, 1990.

8. Havel, *To the Castle and Back*, 62.

9. On his first visit to West Germany, Havel issued an apology for the expulsion of ethnic Germans in 1945, which created an intense controversy in Czechoslovakia. See Judith Renner, "Czech Republic-Germany: A Pioneer Apology," in *Apology and Reconciliation in International Relations*, ed. Christopher Daase, Stefen Engart, Michele-Andre Horalt, Judith Renner, and Renate Strassner (London: Routledge, 2016).

10. Elzbieta Matynia, ed., *The Uncanny Era: Conversations between Václav Havel and Adam Michnik* (New Haven, CT: Yale University Press, 2014), 34.

11. Matynia, ed., *Uncanny Era*, 35.

12. NYT, January 2, 1990.

13. Rob McRae, *Resistance and Revolution: Václav Havel's Czechoslovakia* (Ottawa: Carleton University Press, 1997), 261.

14. McRae, *Resistance and Revolution*, 267–72.

15. Václav Havel, "Meeting Gorbachev," in *Open Letters: Selected Writings 1965–1990*, trans. Paul Wilson (New York: Vintage, 1992), 353.

16. Jitka Vodňanská, *Voda, která hoří* (Prague: Torst, 2018), 369. Czech language.

17. Havel clearly defined "non-political politics in a speech to New York University in October 1991. For the text of the speech, see the *International Herald Tribune*, October 29, 1991.

18. Aviezer Tucker, *The Philosophy and Politics of Czech Dissidence from Patočka to Havel* (Pittsburgh: University Pittsburgh Press, 2000), 185.

19. This is the position championed by Tucker, who takes the position that Havel had originally been against democratic parties and only later saw their necessity. This ignores the fact that in the 1960s Havel had argued for the creation of a multiparty system in the country. It is much more likely that Havel's ideas on political parties were nuanced and not completely captured by his few references on the subject before becoming president. See Tucker, *Philosophy and Politics of Czech Dissidence*, 191–92.

20. Václav Havel, *Summer Meditations*, trans. Paul Wilson (New York: Knopf, 1992), 53.

21. Tucker, *Philosophy and Politics of Czech Dissidence*, 175.

22. Václav Havel, *Letters to Olga*, trans. Paul Wilson (New York: Henry Holt, 1989), 293.

23. Kieran Williams, *Václav Havel* (London: Reaktion Books, 2016), 184.

24. Ash's full statement: "There should be . . . a necessarily adversarial (but not necessarily hostile) relationship between the independent intellectual and the professional politician. The intellectual's job is to seek the truth, and then to present it as fully and clearly and interestingly as possible. The politician's job is to work in half-truth. The very word *party* implies partial, one-sided. (The Czech word for party, *strana*, meaning literally 'side,' says it even more clearly.) Of course, the opposition parties then present the other side, the other half of the truth. But this is one of those strange cases where two halves don't make a whole."

25. The passage from Havel's dissident years comes from his essay "Politics and Conscience," which was written in 1984 to be delivered at the University of Toulouse in France upon receiving an honorary doctorate (*Open Letters*, 269). The passage from his presidency is from Havel, *Summer Meditations*, 9.

26. Havel, *To the Castle and Back*, 60.

27. Havel, *Summer Meditations*, xvii–xviii.

28. Jiří Hochman, "Editor's Afterward," *Hope Dies Last: The Autobiography of the Leader of the Prague Spring* (New York: Kadansha, 1993), 273–75.

29. Paul Wilson, "The End of the Velvet Revolution," NYRB, August 13, 1992.

30. Wilson, "End of the Velvet Revolution."

31. Wilson, "End of the Velvet Revolution."

32. Paul Wilson, "Czechoslovakia: The Pain of Divorce," NYRB, December 17, 1992.

33. Michael Žantovský, *Havel: A Life* (New York: Grove Press, 2014), 427–28.

34. Remnick, "Havel Takes a Bow," *New Yorker*, February 23, 2003.

35. Havel, *To the Castle and Back*, 204–5.

36. Havel, *To the Castle and Back*, 203–5.

37. Havel, *To the Castle and Back*, 41.

38. Havel, *To the Castle and Back*, 77, 89.

39. Vodňanská, *Voda, která hoří*, 370–72. Czech language.

## Chapter 18. A Heavy Stone

1. Michael Žantovský, *Havel: A Life* (New York: Grove Press, 2014), 460. Žantovský worked closely with Havel during those years and observed his health personally. The prescription drugs that Havel was on regularly included Silnox, Paralen, Alnago, and Oikamid.

2. NYT, September 3, 1994.

3. Paul Berman, "The Philosopher-King Is Mortal," *New York Times Magazine*, May 11, 1997. The ideas mentioned were presented in a speech in Philadelphia on July 4, 1994. Although controversial, both the Gaia hypothesis and the anthropic cosmological principle are discussed by serious academic philosophers. Berman reported that these ideas were often ridiculed by some members of parliament.

4. There are differing opinions as to why Clinton supported the expansion of NATO into Eastern Europe. Following the arguments of Albright and Havel, Clinton publicly said that the NATO expansion would "lock in" the democratic and free market reforms in Eastern Europe. See NYT, July 13, 1997. Some have argued, however, that Clinton saw a partisan political advantage to NATO expansion.

5. NYT, January 12, 1994.

6. Havel, *To the Castle and Back*, trans. Paul Wilson (New York: Knopf, 2007), 161.

7. Žantovský, *Havel*, 459.

8. Havel, *To the Castle and Back*, 274.

9. Havel, *To the Castle and Back*, 274.

10. Václav Havel, address in Jerusalem, April 26, 1990, reprinted in Havel, *The Art of the Impossible: Politics as Morality in Practice* (New York: Fromm International, 1997), 29–31.

11. Žantovský, *Havel*, 487.

12. John Keane, *Václav Havel: A Political Tragedy in Six Acts* (London: Bloomsbury, 1999), 11.

13. James F. Pontuso, *Václav Havel: Civic Responsibility in the Postmodern Age* (New York: Rowman and Littlefield, 2004).

14. Kieran Williams, *Václav Havel* (London: Reaktion Books), 167. Kieran sees the four presidencies of Havel as distinct stages—the restoration of democracy and truth, the development of a positive vision of democracy, the creation of international security guarantees for the nation, and, finally, the breakup of centralized power, both to local governments and to the European Union.

15. Edward Findlay, *Caring for the Soul in a Postmodern Age: Politics and Philosophy in the Thought of Jan Patočka* (Albany: State University of New York Press), 124. However, it should be pointed out that Havel was neither an official student of philosophy nor someone who cared about the academic pursuit of philosophical thinking. As Havel admitted himself, he was decidedly an amateur philosopher, and his gift was in making philosophical ideas understandable to the broader public.

16. Tucker, *The Philosophy and Politics of Czech Dissidence from Patočka to Havel* (Pittsburgh: University Pittsburgh Press, 2000), 174–75.

17. Havel, *To the Castle and Back*, 235–36.

18. Havel, *To the Castle and Back*, 235.

19. Havel, *To the Castle and Back*, 236.

20. Václav Havel, presidential memos, February 4, 1996, and February 25, 1996, reprinted in Havel, *To the Castle and Back*, 240–41.

21. Timothy Garton Ash, *On Olga Havel (1933–1996)*, NYRB, March 21, 1996.

22. Žantovský, *Havel*, 465.

23. Berman reports that Chemapol appeared never to have engaged in illegal activity. Nevertheless, the company held a monopoly of importing Russian oil and had ties to former members of the KGB, making it a symbol of the sort of financial dealings that Havel had opposed. Havel himself appears not to have known who was buying the property, as he had turned over the matter to a third party.

24. Havel, *To the Castle and Back*, 236.

25. Berman, "Philosopher-King Is Mortal."

26. Václav Havel, presidential memo, May 18, 1997, in Havel, *To the Castle and Back*, 279–80.

27. Václav Havel, presidential memo, February 8, 1998, in Havel, *To the Castle and Back*, 280.

28. Havel, *To the Castle and Back*, 254.

29. Žantovský, *Havel*, 473.

30. Jitka Vodňanská, *Voda, která hoří* (Prague: Torst, 2018), 338. Czech language.

31. NYT, November 30, 1997. No one was ever indicted for the campaign slush funds.

32. NYT, December 1, 1997.

33. Havel, *To the Castle and Back*, 209.

34. NYT, November 30, 1997.

35. NYT, February 7, 2000.

36. Havel, *To the Castle and Back*, 219.

37. Havel, *To the Castle and Back*, 224–25.

38. NYT, January 3, 1998.

39. Havel, *To the Castle and Back*, 169.

40. Havel, *To the Castle and Back*, 226.

41. Television interview with Václav Havel by Bohumil Klepetko and Jolana Voldánová, ČTV 2, June 13, 1998, quoted in Keane, *Václav Havel*, 497. The translation is from Keane.

42. Václav Havel, undated memo, in Havel, *To the Castle and Back*, 109–11.

43. Václav Havel, presidential memo, March 2, 1998, in Havel, *To the Castle and Back*, 109–11.

44. Václav Havel, presidential memo, September 23, 1999. The memo is also quoted in Žantovský, *Havel*, 486, whose translation I have used.

45. Václav Havel, presidential memo, August 18, 2002.

46. Václav Havel, presidential memo, August 18, 2002.

47. David Remnick, "Havel Takes a Bow," *New Yorker*, February 9, 2003.

48. Remnick, "Havel Takes a Bow," *New Yorker*, February 9, 2003.

49. Václav Havel, Farewell Address to Czech Citizens, February 2, 2003, VHL.

## Chapter 19. The Final Years

1. David Remnick, "Havel Takes a Bow," *New Yorker*, February 9, 2003.

2. Havel, *To the Castle and Back*, trans. Paul Wilson (New York: Knopf, 2007), 236.

3. NYT, December 13, 2006. In an interview after leaving office, Havel said that "unfortunately I have to acknowledge that there's a sort of delay, a big retardation in my development in recent years and one which I will never be able to catch up with because of those 13 years as president."

4. Elzbieta Matynia, ed. and trans., *An Uncanny Era: Conversations between Václav Havel and Adam Michnik* (New Haven, CT: Yale University Press, 2014), 121.

5. Matnynia, ed., *An Uncanny Era*, 127.

6. Matnynia, ed., *An Uncanny Era*, 127.

7. Michael Žantovský, *Havel: A Life* (New York: Grove Press, 2014), 502.

8. During the time after his presidency, Havel was involved in a dizzying number of activities. With the help of American ambassador Craig Stapleton, he had imagined a presidential library along the American model, which took an enormous amount of work and fund-raising. He was deeply involved with projects he started during his presidential years—the VIZE 97 Foundation, Forum 2000, and Prague Crossroads—and he continued to speak regularly at events inside and outside the country.

9. Žantovský, *Havel*, 503.

10. Carolyn Brown, introductory remarks, "Paul Wilson Discusses His Translation of Václav Havel's Book 'To the Castle and Back,'" May 17, 2017, Washington, DC.

11. Havel, *To the Castle and Back*, 49, 137.

12. Paul Wilson, "Paul Wilson Discusses His Translation of Václav Havel's Book 'To the Castle and Back,'" May 17, 2017, Washington, DC.

13. Wilson, "Paul Wilson Discusses His Translation of Václav Havel's Book 'To the Castle and Back.'"

14. Matynia, ed., *An Uncanny Era*, 160–62.

15. NYT, July 26, 2008.

16. Michael Žantovský, "Tanned and Rested: Václav Havel Marks His Return with 'Leaving,'" *World Affairs*, January/February 2011.

17. Žantovský, "Tanned and Rested."

18. Kieran Williams, *Václav Havel* (London: Reaktion Books, 2016), 196.

19. "Václav Havel's Legacy Today," panel discussion, April 19, 2014, Washington, DC.

# SELECTED BIBLIOGRAPHY

The following works are cited frequently in the text.

Albright, Madeleine. *Prague Winter: A Personal Story of Remembrance and War, 1937–1948.* New York: HarperCollins, 2012.

Ash, Timothy Garton. *The Magic Lantern: The Revolution of '89 Witnessed in Warsaw, Budapest, Berlin and Prague.* New York: Random House, 1990.

Bolton, Jonathan. *Worlds of Dissent: Charter 77, the Plastic People of the Universe, and Czech Culture under Communism.* Cambridge, MA: Harvard University Press, 2012.

Day, Barbara. *The Velvet Philosophers.* London: Claridge, 1999.

Dubček, Alexander. *Hope Dies Last: The Autobiography of Alexander Dubcek.* New York: Kadansha America, 1993.

Esslin, Martin. *The Theater of the Absurd.* New York: Vintage Books, 1961.

Findlay, Edward. *Caring for the Soul in a Postmodern Age: Politics and Philosophy in the Thought of Jan Patočka.* Albany: State University of New York Press.

Forman, Miloš. *Turnaround: A Memoir.* New York: Villard Books, 1994.

Hájek, Jiří. *Paměti.* Prague: Ústav mezinárodních vztahů, 1997. Czech language.

Havel, Václav. *The Art of the Impossible: Politics as Morality in Practice.* New York: Fromm International, 1997.

Havel, Václav. *To the Castle and Back.* Translated by Paul Wilson. New York: Knopf, 2007.

Havel, Václav. *Disturbing the Peace: A Conversation with Karel Hvížďala.* Translated by Paul Wilson. New York: Vintage Books, 1991.

Havel, Václav. *The Garden Party and Other Plays.* New York: Grove Press, 1993.

Havel, Václav. *Letters to Olga.* Translated by Paul Wilson. New York: Henry Holt, 1989.

Havel, Václav. *Open Letters: Selected Writings 1965–1990.* Translated by Paul Wilson. New York: Vintage, 1992.

Havel, Václav. *Summer Meditations.* Translated by Paul Wilson. New York: Knopf, 1992.

Havel, Václav M. (father). *Mé vzpomínky.* Prague: Nakladatelství Lidové noviny, 1993. Czech language.

Heimann, Mary. *Czechoslovakia: The State That Failed.* New Haven, CT: Yale University Press, 2009.

Hrubý, Peter. *Fools and Heroes: The Changing Role of Communist Intellectuals in Czechoslovakia.* Oxford: Pergamon, 1980.

Kaiser, Daniel. *Disident: Václav Havel 1936–1989.* Prague: Paseka, 2009. Czech language.

Keane, John. *Václav Havel: A Political Tragedy in Six Acts.* London: Bloomsbury, 1999.

Klíma, Ivan. *My Crazy Century: A Memoir.* Translated by Craig Cravens. New York: Grove Press, 2013.

Kohák, Erazin. *Jan Patočka: Philosophy and Selected Writings.* Chicago: University of Chicago Press, 1989.

Kosatík, Pavel. Člověk má dělat to, nač má sílu. Prague: Mladá Fronta, 2008. Czech language.

Kriseová, Eda. *Václav Havel: The Authorized Biography*. New York: St. Martin's Press, 1993.

Kusin, Vladimír V. *From Dubček to Charter 77: A Study in "Normalization" in Czechoslovakia 1968–1978*. New York: St. Martin's Press, 1978.

Long, Michael. *Making History: Czech Voices of Dissent and the Revolution of 1989*. Oxford: Rowman and Littlefield, 2005.

McRae, Rob. *Resistance and Revolution: Václav Havel's Czechoslovakia*. Ottawa: Carleton University Press, 1997.

Mlynář, Zdeněk. *Nightfrost in Prague: The End of Humane Socialism*. New York: Karz Press, 1980.

Pontuso, James F. *Václav Havel: Civic Responsibility in the Postmodern Age*. New York: Rowman and Littlefield, 2004.

Rocamora, Carol. *Acts of Courage: Václav Havel's Life in the Theater*. Hanover, NH: Smith and Kraus, 2004.

Rosenberg, Tina. *The Haunted Land: Facing Europe's Ghosts after Communism*. New York: Random House, 1995.

Shawcross, William. *Dubček*. New York: Simon and Schuster, 1990.

Simmons, Michael. *The Reluctant President: A Political Life of Václav Havel*. London: Methuen, 1991.

Skilling, H. Gordon, ed. *Charter 77 and Human Rights in Czechoslovakia*. London: George Allen and Unwin, 1981.

Skilling, H. Gordon. "Czechoslovakia." In *Communist States in Disarray, 1965–1971*, ed. Adam Bromke, 43–72. Oxford: Oxford University Press, 1972.

Tucker, Aviezer. *The Philosophy and Politics of Czech Dissidence from Patočka to Havel*. Pittsburgh: University Pittsburgh Press, 2000.

Vaculík, Ludvík. Český Snář. Prague: Atlantis, 1990. Czech language.

Vodňanská, Jitka. *Voda, která hoří*. Prague: Torst, 2018. Czech language.

Wanatowiczová, Krystyna. *Miloš Havel: Český filmový magnát*. Prague: Václav Havel Library, 2013. Czech language.

Williams, Kieran. *Václav Havel*. London: Reaktion Books, 2016.

Woods, Michelle. *Translating Milan Kundera*. Buffalo, NY: Multilingual Matters, 2006.

Žantovský, Michael. *Havel: A Life*. New York: Grove Press, 2014.

# INDEX